ESSENTIAL HISTORY

Northwestern University
Studies in Phenomenology
and
Existential Philosophy

Founding Editor †James M. Edie

General Editor Anthony J. Steinbock

Associate Editor John McCumber

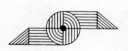

ESSENTIAL HISTORY

Jacques Derrida and the Development of Deconstruction

Joshua Kates

Northwestern University Press
Evanston, Illinois

Northwestern University Press
Evanston, Illinois 60208-4170

Copyright © 2005 by Northwestern University Press.
Published 2005. All rights reserved.

Printed in the United States of America

10   9   8   7   6   5   4   3   2   1

ISBN 0-8101-2326-6 (cloth)
ISBN 0-8101-2327-4 (paper)

Library of Congress Cataloging-in-Publication Data

Kates, Joshua
    Essential history : Jacques Derrida and the development of deconstruction /
Joshua Kates.
        p. cm. — (Northwestern University studies in phenomenology and
existential philosophy)
    Includes bibliographical references (p.   ) and index.
    ISBN 0-8101-2327-4 (pbk. : alk. paper) — ISBN 0-8101-2326-6 (cloth : alk.
paper)
    1. Derrida, Jacques. 2. Deconstruction. I. Title. II. Northwestern University
studies in phenomenology & existential philosophy.
B2430.D484K38 2005
194—dc22

                                                                    2005013748

⊗ The paper used in this publication meets the minimum requirements of the
American National Standard for Information Sciences—Permanence of Paper
for Printed Library Materials, ANSI Z39.48-1992.

For Hannah Kates, Laura Kates, David Kates,
and (in memoriam) Joseph L. Kates

Contents

Acknowledgments

I would like to acknowledge and thank the following institutions and persons: the University at Buffalo and the many fine faculty there with whom I studied—among them, Rodolphe Gasché for his pioneering work and intellectual example, Neil Schmitz, and above all Henry Sussman for his vivacious support, inspiration, and friendship in all phases of the present work and throughout my career; the Camargo Foundation in Cassis, France, where much of a first draft of this book was written; Tom Wortham and UCLA, where, as a part-time visiting associate professor, most of the final draft was finally done—and among the many colleagues who warmly received me there, especially Helen Deutsch, Eric Jager, Mark McGurl, and above all Kenneth Reinhard; St. John's College in Santa Fe, New Mexico, and its erstwhile dean, James Carey, who made it possible for me to take such a long leave and who has supported my endeavors and stimulated my thinking throughout all the years that we have known one another; readers and discussants of various chapters and drafts at my home institution and elsewhere, especially Jay Lampert, Thomas Scally, Frank Hunt, Mark Cooper, Dilip Yogasundram, and Bernard Rhie; Jacques Derrida, who, characteristically, generously helped this work get an initial hearing; John McCumber, who oversaw it coming to this series, and both of the remarkably receptive readers of it for Northwestern University Press; and, nonpareil, she whose contributions to this and so much else are far too great to detail, my be-all, Jennifer Fleissner.

Abbreviations of Works by Jacques Derrida

In the text and notes of this book, parenthetical citations of the same passage in the French or German original and an English translation are separated by a slash; when the foreign-language original is cited first, this usually indicates that the English translation has been altered. In the case of *Le problème*, because of the date at which the English translation appeared, all translations are the author's own.

"AA"   "Antwort an Apel." *Zeitmitschrift: Journal für Ästhetik,* Summer, 1987.

"AED"   "Afterword: Toward an Ethic of Discussion." In *Limited, Inc,* trans. Samuel Weber. Evanston, Ill.: Northwestern University Press, 1988.

"CHM"   "Cogito and the History of Madness." In *Writing and Difference,* 31–64.

DG   *De la grammatologie.* Paris: Éditions de Minuit, 1967.

DN   *Deconstruction in a Nutshell: A Conversation with Jacques Derrida.* Ed. John Caputo. New York: Fordham University Press, 1997.

G   *Of Grammatology.* Trans. Gayatri Spivak. Baltimore: Johns Hopkins University Press, 1974.

"GS"   "'Genesis and Structure' and Phenomenology." In *Writing and Difference,* 154–68.

IOG   *Edmund Husserl's "Origin of Geometry": An Introduction.* Trans. John Leavey Jr. Stony Brook, N.Y.: Nicholas Hays, 1978.

LOG   Introduction to *L'origine de la géométrie,* by Edmund Husserl, French translation by Jacques Derrida. Paris: Presses Universitaires de France, 1962.

LPG   *Le problème de la genèse dans la philosophie de Husserl.* Paris: Presses Universitaires de France, 1990.

P   *Positions.* Trans. Alan Bass. Chicago: University of Chicago Press, 1981.

PG   *The Problem of Genesis in Husserl's Philosophy.* Trans. Marian Hobson. Chicago: University of Chicago Press, 2003.

"PTT"   "Ponctuations: Le temps de la thèse." In *Du droit à la philosophie.* Paris: Galilée, 1990.

SP   *Speech and Phenomena and Other Essays on Husserl's Theory of Signs.* Trans. David B. Allison. Evanston, Ill.: Northwestern University Press, 1973.

"TT"   "The Time of a Thesis: Punctuations." In *Philosophy in France Today.* Ed. Alan Montefiore. Cambridge: Cambridge University Press, 1983.

"VEM"   "Violence et métaphysique: Essai sur la pensée d'Emmanuel Levinas." In *L'écriture et la différence.* Paris: Éditions du Seuil, 1967, 117–228.

"VM"   "Violence and Metaphysics: An Essay on the Thought of Emmanuel Levinas." In *Writing and Difference,* 79–154.

VP   *La voix et le phénomène: Introduction au problème du signe dans la phénoménologie de Husserl.* Paris: Presses Universitaires de France, 1967.

WD   *Writing and Difference.* Trans. Alan Bass. Chicago: University of Chicago Press, 1978.

Introduction

A radical reappraisal of Jacques Derrida's work is necessary, this book contends, if Derrida studies are to remain a viable field of scholarly inquiry in the future and if the humanities, more generally, are to have access to a replenishing source of living theoretical concerns. Valuable alternatives to the largely historicist practices regnant today in the humanities have been missed due to the inability to arrive at truly global interpretations of Derrida's thought, as well as that of other "foundational" French thinkers.

After all, even today, it can be argued, the most basic questions concerning Derrida's work remain unanswered. Is Derrida a friend of reason, of philosophy, or rather the most radical of skeptics? Are language-related themes—writing, semiosis—Derrida's central concern, or does he really write about something else, at best catachrestically related to these? Does Derrida's thought find its own locus in untold "systems" and "logics," or does it primarily consist of commentaries on individual texts?

No settled answers to these questions exist in the literature. Nor, more crucially, do viable accounts exist of how these competing alternatives relate, or of how they might *both* be true—for each doubtless gets something right. Instead, two different strands of Derrida interpretation have largely been pursued from the onset of deconstruction's reception, without ever finding a way to combine in a single, comprehensive outcome.[1] One version takes its focus to be language, and sees it as arriving at what is essentially a new, more radical form of skepticism. The editors of the 2001 *Norton Anthology of Literary Theory and Criticism*, to take one recent significant example, hold this view of deconstruction, emphasizing language's importance above all else to Derrida's project in the headnote to their section on Derrida.[2] Clearly, this version of deconstruction has been the one most influential on literary studies. With its doubts about the validity of theoretical knowledge, and a standpoint bordering on linguistic determinism, it is the direct precursor of much current historical and cultural work in this field, even though many today take "deconstruction" and "historicism" (or "cultural studies") to be opposed.[3]

Another school of thought has long insisted that Derrida's work would be ill defined by any sort of skepticism; it deems language at best

#1 – radical skepticism ∧ the importance of language

#2 -
more in
line w/
Traditional
philosophy
∧
the limits
of
philosophy

an ancillary concern of Derrida's, and it views deconstruction overall in much greater proximity to traditional philosophy. For Rodolphe Gasché (the first major proponent of this view) and those who follow his lead, deconstruction sets out conditions of possibility and impossibility of philosophy.[4] Here, though deconstruction does finally articulate what brings philosophical thought into doubt through its talk of *impossibility* (part of which indeed pertains to language and inscription), nevertheless, philosophy's traditional claim to authority over all other knowledges is said to be maintained by deconstruction, and Derrida's own themes can come into view only after the discourse of philosophy has been traversed.

The present book aims to address this rift, first and foremost by returning to the ground of Derrida's project in phenomenology. A deep acquaintance with the phenomenological projects of both Husserl and Heidegger is required, I will show, in order to mount new, more inclusive interpretations of Derrida that are able to take both sets of reference points into account. In particular, I emphasize Husserlian phenomenology throughout, this being the philosophical milieu in which deconstruction was first forged. This milieu remains largely foreign to many readers of Derrida, however. In particular, the complex and distinctive stances Husserl took toward questions of meaning, language, and truth remain absent from the majority of discussions of Derrida's work to date, including those of his early writings.[5] It was thanks to these positions, however, that Derrida was led to believe, even as he broke with phenomenology, that he could navigate between the outcomes thought to be implied by those who see his work on language as central (truth's outright denial, radical skepticism) and what is required by those who stress Derrida's philosophical and transcendental concerns (truth's affirmation, the truth of philosophy in particular).

Derrida ultimately managed this complex navigation, still to be successfully grasped in full, thanks to the resources provided him by Husserl's thought. Hence *Essential History* turns first to the factual ground of Derrida's project, his early, pre-deconstructive writings, in order to establish a broader working context than has hitherto been available in which to view Derrida's best-known 1967 project and texts. For the first fifteen years of his life as a scholar, we now know, Derrida devoted himself exclusively to work on Husserl, and not only does phenomenology turn out to be the smithy in which deconstruction's tools were forged, but in it, as I make plain, Derrida initially discovered the *motive* for this entirely singular enterprise, for fashioning this wholly unique way of working that he would soon bring to light under the heading of deconstruction.[6]

Essential History thus begins by setting out a previously unnoticed *developmental* movement—hence its subtitle—a new diachrony, from which

Derrida's first major works can be shown to result. The present work is thus committed to approaching Derrida's thought historically, yet to a historical approach differing from many current ones, bordering finally on what Deleuze and Foucault (following Nietzsche) sometimes called genealogy. By approaching Derrida's work through its development, this book attempts to break through the current reification of Derrida's project and the present immobilization of his thought, at least as concerns this still decisive, early stage of his thinking. *A genealogical approach*

Such reification is not only a matter of the sometimes inadequate, though now often canonical, interpretations of such works as *Of Grammatology* or *Speech and Phenomena,* but concerns the current view of Derrida's early corpus as such. After all, almost everywhere, even at present, Derrida's many works are taken to comprise an essentially homogeneous whole, a single continuous canon. The chronology of Derrida's writings is almost always ignored by commentators, and positions taken by Derrida some ten or twenty years apart are routinely viewed together, without further comment. No significant changes in Derrida's own positions, no important shifts in the interpretation of those he reads, take place, it has thus been assumed, sometimes even between 1954 (when Derrida completed *Le problème de la genèse dans la philosophie de Husserl*) and his most recent writings.[7]

Essential History thus more generally intends to revolatilize Derrida's corpus, putting back into motion these texts, along with the issues that first moved Derrida himself. In ascertaining the concrete twists and turns by which Derrida arrived at the triple publications of 1967, and by disclosing the actual problems that led Derrida to the singular way of working now known as deconstruction, this book returns Derrida's thought to its own becoming. Further, by approaching Derrida's thought through its development, the present work is able to mount new readings of Derrida's foundational texts capable of addressing the deepest impasses in the literature and Derrida's own thought.

After all, it must be recognized that another deep split has accompanied Derrida's work nearly from its reception: namely, a controversy concerning the *value* of this work, the legitimacy of Derrida's thought, and how much of importance for serious thought and scholarship it really provides. This dispute, whose very existence at this late date is itself an embarrassment, ultimately pertains to the status of Derrida's *commentary,* I will argue; it hinges ultimately on Derrida's own reading, on whether Derrida's interpretations do justice to his authors (most notably and most recently, as I show, Husserl).

While remaining deeply sympathetic to Derrida, *Essential History* aims to address this problem head-on. The historical treatment, the developmental approach that this project sets out, itself makes possible a richer model for the "hermeneutics of deconstruction," one that lets the genuinely deepest points of contact, as well as deviation, between Derrida and the tradition be discerned. For not only is there no consensus about the validity of Derrida's interpretations, but perhaps more gravely, no *model*, no *paradigm* for interpreting Derrida's own thought is at present available that has even the potential to someday resolve this controversy. At present, that is, no schema of interpretation exists whereby the rights of Derrida, as well as those of the authors he reads, may be respected together. *Essential History* thus offers new principles for reading Derrida which permit the radical singularity of Derrida's own thought to be given its due, without neglecting the often very different aims of those he reads.[8]

This work does not take for granted the validity of Derrida's interpretations. Rather, I return to those texts central to early deconstruction (those of Saussure, Husserl, and also Heidegger) and offer independent interpretations of these works, concretely broaching the question in each case of whether Derrida's discussion of them is finally persuasive. *Essential History* puts Derrida's thought back into contact with those on whom he comments—not to write off Derrida's project, not to reduce it, but indeed to capture this thought in its own specificity, as well as to sharpen the stakes of the problems that underlie it. Sometimes disagreeing with Derrida, my aim is to make clear that the interpretive decisions that Derrida has made are by no means always self-evident, that these take shape within a wider range of alternatives—with the aim, again, of ultimately revitalizing Derrida's thought and the sort of philosophical or theoretical discussion in which it participates more generally.

After all, the arguably salutary upheaval, the roiling of the disciplines accomplished by Derrida's work, as well as by a few select others, in the 1970s and 1980s has now essentially subsided.[9] Without the ability to raise questions anew, to discover new approaches, new modes of inquiry for philosophy and "theory," as it was once called, work in the humanities threatens to succumb entirely to an ever more efficient empiricism or pragmatism, which, though capable of bringing important findings of all sorts to light, is arguably quick to submit to the dispersal of the functions of knowledge, and the concomitant increasing professionalization, even corporatization, today overtaking the university. Access to new themes and concerns of the magnitude that occupied Derrida and his peers, however, itself appears beyond our reach at present, and seems unlikely to become available anytime soon. One starting point for the revitalization of this sort of discussion—though doubtless there are others—can be gained by following the path that I have here tried to tread: by finding a new type of access to the work of this earlier generation, by coming to grips with the

deepest problems that first goaded these thinkers themselves—even as
these are taken up from new standpoints, with different questions, and
perhaps even finally with a different orientation and aims than their own.
Along with the novel historical treatment of Derrida's thought this work
provides, along with its focus on a phase of Husserl's thought which, as we
shall see, provides something like a history of essences, the examination
of the development of Derridean deconstruction in this way, too, may well
prove to be essential history.[10]

* * *

In part due to the enormous amount of attention already received by
the texts upon which I finally comment, I begin *Essential History* not only
from Derrida's own writings—*Of Grammatology,* in particular—but with
this work as seen through the lens of a still important debate between
Richard Rorty and Derrida's quasi-transcendental interpreters (specifically Rodolphe Gasché and Geoff Bennington). I use this debate, and the
framing of *Of Grammatology* that it permits, in order to show how the split
in Derrida studies to which I have just alluded arguably stems from a problem in Derrida's own thought. This opening question concerning the
"success of deconstruction," as I call it (which itself undergoes transformation as I continue and which finally proves not open to an unequivocal
response), is the cornerstone of bringing forward a new way of discussing
these works; and just as with the more specific questions I raise pertaining
to Derrida's different interpretations, this opening question is by no
means intended to foster a dismissal of Derrida's thought, but instead to
help bring more definitively to light what is still urgent about it and to in-
vite us to grasp Derrida's project anew.

Thus, in my first chapter, "The Success of Deconstruction: Derrida,
Rorty, Gasché, Bennington, and the Quasi-Transcendental," I begin by
showing, first, that the schemas of reversal and reinscription, and the related one of quasi-transcendentality—both long taken as authoritative
descriptions of deconstruction's operation and still not concretely superseded today—do indeed apply to the first half of *Of Grammatology.* A gesture crucial for this entire work follows from this demonstration, for it allows Richard Rorty's criticisms to be translated back on to Derrida's own
thought. Rorty's ultimate target is Derrida's own work, I argue, and
Rorty's criticism of Derrida—which has not received sufficient notice in
most quarters—at least as applied in this single case, is substantially correct. The operation of deconstruction, as seen through the lens of reversal and reinscription, or conditions of impossibility and possibility, fails to
be wholly convincing. More specifically, reversal implies, as Rorty indicates, an extraordinarily wide-ranging semantic thesis that concerns all

terms in language, that sees them all as swept up in binary oppositions; and whatever else one may wish to say about this claim, it makes any authoritative recourse to the discourse of philosophy impossible—recourse that the second phase, of reinscription, demands. Deconstruction in the 1967 works thus cuts off the branch on which it needs to stand before arriving at it; it deprives itself of the transcendental aperture it requires before passing through it—at least in this single text for which Derrida perhaps remains best known.

The split within Derrida studies concerning deconstruction's aims, as well as the controversy in the humanities as to the ultimate value of Derrida's thought mentioned above, arguably stems from this—from the awkward relation between these two phases of Derrida's argument or interpretation. This issue, in turn, opens the door to a reevaluation of Derrida's project and a new engagement with these texts—not their delegitimation, I again wish to emphasize. Indeed, Derrida himself was doubtless aware of this difficulty in some form; and deconstruction arose in a context and in the course of a history in which its operation as a whole may have appeared well motivated.

Thus in the second half of my first chapter, through an engagement with both Gasché's and Geoff Bennington's accounts of deconstruction, I argue that it is indeed possible and necessary to return to Derrida's prior engagement with philosophy in order to seek a new context in which to view the 1967 works. Such a return must be made to Derrida's actual philosophical milieu, to Husserlian phenomenology, however; it cannot take the form of an ideal reconstruction centered on systematic concerns (and this is one place Bennington proves handy, making plain the limits of Gasché's project). Rather, it must be an inquiry into the actual history of Derrida's thought—with one foot in the real, and open to chance encounters, possible shifts in Derrida's standpoint, and changes in his interpretation of Husserl. Derrida's path to deconstruction is to be explored, in particular, with an eye toward discovering some single problem or occasion that motivated the invention of deconstruction as a whole, and this demand leads us back to Derrida's fifteen-year-long engagement with phenomenology: the actual philosophical medium in which Derrida's thought first found its footing.

Having established the importance of Derrida's engagement with Husserl, in my second chapter, "'A Consistent Problematic of Writing and the Trace': The Debate in Derrida/Husserl Studies and the Problem of Derrida's Development," I turn to the current state of Husserl/Derrida studies to sort out Derrida's relation to Husserl. Derrida/Husserl studies turn out to be held in the grip of a nearly irresoluble impasse, however, and this impasse, again, was a proximal cause for the composition of the present work. Indeed, when it comes to Derrida's interpretations of Husserl, with some notable exceptions, a polarization has taken hold between those well versed in Husserl's thought, but not in Derrida's, and those whose situation is more or less the reverse. These two camps find themselves at loggerheads, in particular, concerning Derrida's key 1967 work on Husserl, *Speech and Phenomena* (hereafter *Speech*). And this impasse in the literature demands, I argue, first, a reflection on "the hermeneutics of deconstruction": an examination of the singular role of interpretation in Derrida's own thought (and what this implies for subsequent interpretations aiming to do justice to both Derrida and the thinker upon whom he comments, in this case Husserl). Second, this impasse allows us to get the first real glimpse of development within Derrida's early writings. Many of the criticisms commentators have made of Derrida's Husserl reading could be answered were the assumption not in place that all of Derrida's works on Husserl form a single consistent whole—if shifts in Derrida's positions were recognized, as well as the possibility of significant sedimentation across Derrida's fifteen years of work on Husserl (i.e., Derrida taking for granted in later writings arguments he made in earlier texts). As a result, *Speech and Phenomena* would be seen as the culmination of a fifteen-year encounter with Husserl on Derrida's part, and with this in view, critics treating *Speech* would have to grant roughly equivalent stature to both authors, to both Derrida and Husserl, while also not taking for granted the wholesale correctness of Derrida's Husserl readings.

Whether such a view of his early works, in which significant differences emerge, is endorsed by Derrida himself turns out to be unclear, however, when Derrida's own occasional pronouncements on his corpus are examined. In the second half of this chapter I take up the 1967 interview in which Derrida first publicly commented on the organization of his corpus (reprinted in *Positions*), as well as his 1982 "Punctuations: The Time of a Thesis," a more extended, though less well known, account of his thought. In both works, particularly the 1967 interview, Derrida has been taken to deny any major development in his thought—especially between the 1962 "Introduction" to Husserl's *Origin of Geometry* (hereafter the "Introduction") and the 1967 writings. Yet Derrida's statements, I argue, when more carefully examined turn out to be deeply ambiguous. In the end, it proves impossible to tell whether Derrida is intending to say something about the actual history of his own thought in these pieces, or is simply summarizing his early work in respect to the contribution it made to his better-known writings—offering a retrospective teleology of his early works only possible on the basis of his mature thinking. Whether in "Time of a Thesis" or in *Positions*, Derrida is ultimately denying, affirming, or simply keeping silent about his own thought's development is thus finally obscure. Derrida's second, more extended discussion in "Time of a Thesis," however, does provide a criterion by which we can decide this for ourselves: namely, whether a "consistent problematic of writing and the trace" is already visible in Derrida's "Introduction" to Husserl's *Origin of Geometry*. Derrida specifies that a genuinely "consistent problematic of writing," a treatment going beyond Husserl's own breakthrough in respect to writing, would require thinking "the unthought axiomatic of Husserl's thought"; and this establishes a criterion for Derrida's development: namely, whether Derrida did think such an unthought and fashion a truly consistent problematic of writing in the "Introduction," there mounting a break with Husserl of this order.

Chapter 3, "Derrida's 1962 Interpretation of Writing and Truth: Writing in the 'Introduction' to Husserl's *Origin of Geometry*," which is devoted to Derrida's "Introduction," is organized by the attempt to answer this question: to arrive at a definitive resolution of the issue of development in Derrida's early thought. In this chapter I focus on the first text in all of Derrida's published corpus in which writing is made a theme: section 7 of Derrida's "Introduction" to Husserl's *Origin of Geometry*. I first take into account the broader context of Derrida's discussion of writing in section 7, however: the argument of the "Introduction" as a whole in respect to Husserl's late work on history. Husserl's very difficult late thought on history plays a far greater role in Derrida's thought than has been realized, both at this moment and afterward; and with an understanding of it in place, I turn to the "Introduction's" section 7 in order to show that Derrida by no means mounts a decisive break with Husserl at this moment, or fashions what he would later call a consistent problematic of writing. In section 7 Derrida puts forward a theory of the *book* (taken from his 1957 thesis proposal on the literary work of art); he depends on Husserl's own notion of the sign (just that definition in Husserl's *Logical Investigations* from which Derrida starts in *Speech and Phenomena*); and most decisively of all, whenever writing's transcendental function is in question, when it is a matter of writing's possible contribution to the constitution of truth, writing is understood exclusively from Husserl's transcendental phenomenological perspective. Writing is seen everywhere in section 7 through a set of stipulations drawn from Husserl: writing and language are said to be *pure,* as well as transcendental, possibilities, "intelligible for a transcendental subject in general," and their status is that of "spiritual corporealities," with their *Körper,* the worldly conventional body of the sign, taken to count for naught (*LOG* 85/*IOG* 88).

Chapter 3 demonstrates definitively that writing as it appears in the "Introduction" cannot be identified with writing in the 1967 works and that Derrida's thought does indeed develop. This does not mean, however, that Derrida in 1962 had not already begun to test the limits of Husserl's thought or had not somehow started to glimpse a writing passing beyond them. Derrida explores the hypothesis of a disappearance of truth at writing's hands in the last fifteen pages of the "Introduction's" section 7—a development that is initially thought to lead to outcomes, empiricism, and nonphilosophy, explicitly opposed to Husserl's own philosophical commitments. Derrida is never able to affirm such a disappearance, however; I show that he is continually led back within the parameters of Husserl's thought. Yet just this, I conclude by arguing—both this attempt and its *limits*—crucially provide the motivation for Derrida's 1967 work. Derrida invents deconstruction, beginning from the conviction that a previously unrecognized teleology (phonocentrism and logocentrism) has hold of every concept pertaining to writing, language, and signification, due to the experience of just those limits that Derrida ran up against in his treatment of Husserl's writing in the "Introduction." Deconstruction's invention is owed to the fact that it proved impossible in the "Introduction," through any sort of direct thematization, through any previously existing means of argument, to bring writing as it functions in Husserl into contact with worldly, factical, conventional writing, and thus to arrive at a global thought of writing at once transcendental and not, both the authentic possibility of truth and its genuine disappearance. Derrida adopts his deconstructive standpoint in the face of this generative problem, and this is the motivation for deconstruction that we were seeking all along, offering a new frame in which to view the 1967 works.

At the conclusion of chapter 3 of *Essential History*, the need to think a new, unprecedented functioning of writing and language, and the impossibility of doing so within existing means, both come forward. This dual recognition, I contend, most concretely occasioned the need for the invention of deconstruction. Yet while these themes, writing and language, are new, the strategy Derrida employs for this invention, as well as many of its other orienting concerns, does turn out to be continuous with Derrida's first, earliest engagement with Husserl's phenomenology. Thus, in chapter 4, "The Development of Deconstruction as a Whole and the Role of *Le problème de la genèse dans la philosophie de Husserl*," I explore the development of deconstruction from the standpoint of the continuity of Derrida's early thought as well as its discontinuity. In *Le problème de la genèse dans la philosophie de Husserl* (hereafter *Le problème*), Derrida had already envisioned a stance toward Husserl and toward thought generally that to some extent remains his; and for this reason, because key aspects of Derrida's mature standpoint are already visible in his earliest writings (as well as because of the confusion surrounding Derrida's occasional remarks), development has been denied to Derrida's thought altogether. In fact, the themes through which Derrida articulates his singular perspective in *Le problème,* "genesis" and the "real," largely disappear in his mature work—a function of Derrida's deepening understanding of Heidegger, as I also show (this being another major vector of Derrida's thought, which begins to be tracked in this chapter). Nevertheless, in *Le problème* Derrida had already aimed at a kind of radicality foreshadowing his later thought; and in order to set this out, chapter 4 focuses first in *Le problème* on a moment when this standpoint becomes readily visible: Derrida's discussion of Husserl's genetic phenomenology program. What genetic phenomenology means in Husserl, as well as its significance for Heidegger's break with Husserl, is explained; and against this background, Derrida's singular intentions toward phenomenology (and philosophy), which even at the age of twenty-four strikingly anticipate those in his later work, are made clear. At this moment in his text, Derrida, explicitly contrasting his own views with those of Heidegger and other heterodox phenomenologists, declares his intention to stay with Husserl's brand of phenomenology to the very end—affirming Husserl's essentialism, his rationalism, his claim to have discovered a new kind of philosophical apriori—yet, *at the same time,* insists that this will permit an unsurpassingly radical reversal of Husserl's thought, will let a genuinely radical notion of genesis come forward, toward which other criticisms of Husserl, such as Heidegger's, tend, yet which Derrida alone successfully executes.[11] In *Le problème* Derrida thus articulates a strategy of deferral that clearly foreshadows his mature stance: philosophy and its rights are to be given authentic recognition, a break with them is to be postponed; yet this postponement will make possible, in turn, a questioning of philosophy of unheard-of radicality—the invocation, among other things, of what Derrida here will call "absolute alterity"—a schema which, despite all the changes it undergoes, is clearly significant for all of Derrida's future work.

In addition to this "signature" strategy of Derrida already visible in *Le problème,* chapter 4 sets out another baseline for Derrida's mature thought to be found in this work, which also undergoes further transformation (development ultimately implying both continuity and discontinuity): Derrida's embrace of Husserl's transcendental attitude. Considerations stemming from Husserl's transcendental reduction play a central role up through Derrida's first deconstructions, and by way of a discussion of Eugen Fink's well-known essay comparing Husserl's and Kant's versions of transcendental inquiry, I show that as far back as *Le problème* Derrida's break with Husserl is also a response to a problem implicit in Husserl's own thought, to a problem with the transcendental reduction itself. The problematic of genesis is meant to shore up Husserl's program even as it brings it into doubt in *Le problème*—a gesture of break *and* restitution that remains visible in Derrida's mature writing, albeit in a different form.[12]

With both these aspects of *Le problème* in tow, finally, chapter 4 frames an overview of the totality of Derrida's intentions in his first deconstructive writings. The different sets of concerns that inform Derrida's two earliest works on Husserl intersect in Derrida's first deconstructive works. Derrida's oldest aim, already present in *Le problème*—to expose a contamination of and at the origin ("origin" here ultimately referring to Husserl's own transcendental attitude)—will be overlaid in the 1967 writings by the new demands of writing and language-oriented themes. The broadest framework shared by the two book-length works of 1967 is provided by these two earlier projects and their interaction, and within this framework, the difference as well as the similarity between Derrida's 1967 writings for the first time can fully come into view. Both *Speech* and *Of Grammatology* mount operations of the sort just described, aiming to capture a new, more general writing, and reworking Husserlian transcendentality in a fashion reminiscent of *Le problème*. Yet even in 1967, it must be seen, Derrida cannot set out this new, more general writing in its own right; he will never be able to think it as such—just such an "as such" being what the "Introduction" already showed this writing always eludes. To simulate this more general writing, then, to capture the force of this new perspective, Derrida in 1967 must instead take these two more limited starting points—mundane empirical writing, on the one hand, and Husserl's transcendental conception, on the other—and show they give way to the "same" or parallel deconstructions. *Of Grammatology* and *Speech*, consequently, are to be seen as complements: Derrida starting from a mundane, empirical conception of writing in one, and returning to that transcendental-phenomenological notion of writing and language that he encountered in the "Introduction" in the other, in order to arrive at the "same" outcome across both works.

Chapter 5 turns next to *Speech and Phenomena*, the concerns of which are more closely in line with our discussion so far, though *Of Grammatology* was probably Derrida's next work chronologically. Chapter 5, "Husserl's Circuit of Expression and the Phenomenological Voice in *Speech and Phenomena*," starts by sketching the structure of *Speech* as a whole—the first such sketch to my knowledge—in which *Speech* is shown to consist of two large-scale gestures. The first, occupying roughly its first three chapters, tries to show that Husserl's doctrine of the sign is determinative for the rest of Husserl's views on language (a claim Husserl scholars have often found vexed, and not wholly without reason), in order that Derrida may demonstrate that Husserl's entire treatment of language—

sign, discourse, meaning—is tributary to a teleology of presence that is said to characterize "metaphysics" as an "epoch" (Derrida now having moved closer to Heidegger in this regard). A second gesture, in *Speech*'s chapters 4–7, aims to articulate a "beyond" of this value of presence, and to begin to free the sign from these metaphysical appurtenances from which its concept and all related ones derive in Derrida's eyes. Since, however, as we have anticipated, Derrida himself *can never* put a positive version of signification, writing, or language in place, since he is at best able to delimit negatively Husserl's sign concept (and all that depends on it), the axis of Derrida's own argument, across the central chapters of *Speech*, eventually swings back toward Husserl's own models of language, discourse, and meaning, returning us to some of those same concerns in regard to the sign as spiritual corporeality that were already broached in the "Introduction."

This shift accords with the movement of *Speech* as a whole—which starts, as will be shown, from an outside edge of Husserl's work, a marginal interest of Husserl's, and then moves back toward the center of phenomenology and Husserl's own concerns, in order to pass from there to what Derrida alone believes to be a really radical outside: a thought beyond both Husserl's thought and the totality to which it pertains. In chapter 4 of *Speech*, more specifically, Derrida begins to pass over to this second "internal" phase of discussion by taking up a model, drawn largely from *Ideas I*, of the "circuit of expression" within phenomenological interiority: an interpretation of expression (and discourse and language) in which a wholly *prelinguistic* sense, a *Sinn*, comes to pass through conceptual meanings *(Bedeutungen)* into ideal objectivity (in a first expression)—conceptual meanings, which, in turn, are themselves to be expressed again in linguistic expressions proper (the *bedeutsamen Ausdrücke*, the discursively significant expressions, of *Logical Investigations* II).

This analysis proves crucial for everything else Derrida will subsequently do in *Speech*, particularly *Speech*'s chapter 6, which is the final focus of my fifth chapter. Following Derrida, I here explicate, perhaps for the first time, what precisely *la voix*, "the voice," of *La voix et le phénomène* designates (*Speech and Phenomena*'s original title being better translated as *Voice and Phenomenon*), and with that, set out the exact character of the final deconstruction of Husserlian phenomenology, and of philosophy generally, that Derrida mounts in *Speech*. The phenomenological voice, it turns out, is what structurally allows sense to stay close to itself, even as it passes beyond itself (toward the infinity of ideality)—what keeps this circuit of expression intact, this circulation limited. At the same time, this voice, as Derrida ultimately analyzes it, remains a *phenomenon*, a *phenome-*

nological voice: only to be arrived at by way of the reductions, and implying Husserl's standpoint throughout. The voice is thus a radical *simulacrum* of self-expression and self-proximity within transcendental phenomenological subjectivity: it is an ultimate ground, a last instance,
referring back to nothing other than itself, and the deconstruction of
the voice that Derrida accomplishes must pass through this subjectivity,
and through Husserl's thought, rather than rejecting Husserl's standpoint entirely. Derrida thus deconstructs Husserlian phenomenology by
arguing that the phenomenological voice in the end is more primary than
consciousness itself; it at once disguises, and indicates, a radical auto-
affection, a radical self-relation bearing difference within it—thereby escaping the value of presence. Derrida is also careful to stipulate, however,
that a *pure* difference remains in question in this self-relation, and the
radical outside at which Derrida finally arrives here ends up being an expansion of Husserl's transcendental attitude as well as a questioning of it,
in the style that *Le problème* had already foreshadowed. Indeed, the deconstruction of Husserlian phenomenology comes about not insofar as
writing takes the place of the voice—certainly not writing as any known
linguistics or meditation on language reveals it—but rather insofar as the
phenomenological voice itself is already an instance, the sole known to
date, of what Derrida sometimes calls *archi-writing:* itself the unique work
of *différance,* and of a spacing, already to be found within phenomenological interiority, bearing reference to a radical outside.

  In chapter 6, my discussion returns to the first text with which we
began, the first half of *Of Grammatology.* In this final chapter, "Essential
History: Derrida's Reading of Saussure, and His Reworking of Heideggerean History," I start out by comparing the views on language of phenomenology and structural linguistics: a vexed field of inquiry even before Derrida's intervention, and one that has scarcely been explored since
in the literature. The congruence some have seen between Husserl's
standpoint toward language and Saussure's is merely apparent, I argue,
and thus in *Of Grammatology,* given the treatment of language at issue, Derrida crucially lacks that point of transcendental contact that was available
to him in *Speech and Phenomena.* Readers of *Of Grammatology,* despite the
enormous amount of discussion devoted to this text, have repeatedly
failed to realize how deeply foreign the terrain supplied by Saussure's linguistics is to any sort of transcendental concerns. Saussure's own goal is to
establish a regional science of language, an ongoing empirical field of
research that has language as its well-defined object of study, and thus
Saussure himself is, and must necessarily be, agnostic about everything
that lies beyond this field and beyond a strictly empirical inquiry—in-

cluding such issues as the ultimate status of consciousness, whether language is prior to it or no, as well as the status of linguistic differences themselves, how they stand apart from their status as social, collective facts.

This is the cause, moreover, of that breakdown of the operation of deconstruction which I started out by presenting. This dissonance, between the empiricist terrain from which Derrida begins in *Of Grammatology* and the transcendental perspective he himself introduces, largely accounts for that incoherence in the reception of Derrida, and in Derrida's own thought. In *Of Grammatology,* that is, the moment of reinscription, entailing recourse to a transcendental standpoint, proves far more problematic than in *Speech,* since Derrida finally has no footing within Saussure himself to reintroduce transcendental concerns, and because Derrida's discourse has already moved in the direction of skepticism, in part thanks to his starting point in Saussure's own empiricism. Whatever the ultimate disposition of these issues, however, they are at least partly made good, in turn, by the fact that Derrida is finally not interested in supplying a theory of language or writing of his own (as I have already shown) and that Derrida's key interlocutor in *Of Grammatology* is not finally Husserl himself, but Heidegger (though Husserl's transcendental standpoint will be explicitly invoked). As in *Speech,* so too in *Of Grammatology,* Derrida finally only intends to negatively delimit Saussure's language doctrine; he does not wish to put a new theory of writing or language in its place, and Derrida's *express positive* intention in this work is to bring together Heidegger's meditation on To Be (*Sein*) with concerns that modern linguistics raises (*G* 18–24)—his focus on *Heidegger* thus accounting for that more empirical ground on which Derrida's discourse now finds itself.

Consequently, in the second half of my last chapter, I turn to these issues, and to the final piece of the puzzle concerning Derrida's development that has been held in abeyance up until now: namely, Derrida's changing stance toward history between 1962 and 1967, and his corresponding movement toward Heidegger's positions. Even now in 1967, even with this talk of an epoch of metaphysics, I emphasize, Derrida does not want to embrace without reserve what some take to be Heidegger's historicism. In *Of Grammatology,* in fact, it is fair to say that Derrida once more aims at reconciling Husserl and Heidegger, while going beyond them both—now repeating *Le problème*'s project *except in respect to history,* rather than genesis. Nevertheless, Derrida's thinking has undergone an important shift by 1967; in 1962 he still endorsed the teleology of Husserl's transcendental history and historicity outright (even if he had begun to probe it in places), something he now denies. And in the final phase of my discussion, I focus on the moment at which Derrida passes to its unequivocal rejection—a transition visible in Derrida's two most important early essays, on Foucault and on Levinas. Examining Derrida's twin rejections—on the one hand, of Foucault's historicism (a position itself deeply indebted to Heidegger) and, on the other, of an absolute transcendence of history on the part of Levinas's Other—the significance of the eventual disappearance of "history" as an explicit theme in Derrida's 1967 works can be tracked down, along with the force of Derrida's claim that deconstruction embodies an unparalleled historicity. Derrida affirms that his 1967 writings, and deconstruction generally, embody a radical nonhistorical, or nonhistoricist, historicity; and by placing this final thematic feature in the broader context of Derrida's development, what such a claim really entails can come forward, as well as questions concerning whether and to what degree it is really viable.

The examination of Derrida's encounters with Foucault and Levinas shows, more specifically, that Derrida continues to be in debt to Husserl's late work on history even as he breaks with it. A submerged dependence, almost a species of *Aufhebung*, sets the stage for history's disappearance in 1967, and this swerve away from Husserl's late work on history, which nevertheless leaves much of Husserl's scaffolding in place, establishes the place of politics, ethics, and similar themes in Derrida's thought thereafter. Without at all wanting to deny the provocative character and importance of Derrida's numerous specific analyses, it remains the case that these topics for Derrida can only ever be addressed on the far side of the deconstruction of Husserl's late teleological history, on the far side of a singular rapprochement of this history with Heidegger's epochal intentions—and thus in an absolutely singular hyperspace, whose recognition must prompt a reexamination of the viability of that political-historical responsibility (deemed by Derrida himself a species of the "impossible") that Derrida came to impute ever more urgently to deconstruction.

ESSENTIAL HISTORY

1

The Success of Deconstruction: Derrida, Rorty, Gasché, Bennington, and the Quasi-Transcendental

The ultimate aim of this book is to set out a new interpretation of Derrida's core thought, in particular his two book-length 1967 works, *Speech and Phenomena* and *Of Grammatology*—the works for which Derrida remains best known even today. In this chapter, I begin from some of Derrida's best interpreters in order to demonstrate the need for this new approach. I take up the debate between Derrida's quasi-transcendental interpreters (primarily Rodolphe Gasché, but also Geoff Bennington) and Richard Rorty in order to show that deconstruction in the way it has been taken to operate—as it is described by Derrida himself and by his readers, seemingly in conformity with some of Derrida's best-known texts—does not fully function as Derrida intended.[1] Deconstruction, at least in its usual constructions, is not able to maintain the various sides of its operation that Derrida wished to bring into play, and this demonstration, in turn, motivates and orients the project I subsequently bring forward. Due to the inability of Derrida's work to fully perform as he had hoped, a new way of treating Derrida's key texts proves to be needed: one that approaches deconstruction through its development.

The eventual site on which this breakdown is exposed in this chapter will be Derrida's discussion of Saussure in *Of Grammatology*'s first half. This remains the signature topos of Derridean deconstruction—the text of Derrida most widely cited and read, for better or worse. However, before turning to *Of Grammatology* and to the debate in the commentary—to Gasché, Bennington, and Rorty—I must begin by briefly making clear what is at stake in Derrida's own enterprise. Indeed, not only is it necessary to show that deconstruction does not function as Derrida himself wished, in order to reframe our understanding of this operation and our approach to Derrida's text and corpus—but since I am about to criticize Derrida's project in certain respects, while devoting the remainder of this book to its explication, it ought to be made clear first of all what in my eyes remains urgent about Derrida's thought: what remains compelling about Derrida's project as a whole.

I will thus start by briefly distinguishing Derrida's views on deconstruction from the sort of radical undecidable skepticism with which it is most often identified, in order to show what Derrida intended deconstruction to accomplish and why such work potentially remains so pressing. Derrida, I will argue, wished deconstruction to remain far closer to philosophy than many acknowledge even today, in the sense that he wanted deconstruction to fulfill that "responsibility to thought" that philosophy alone from Derrida's perspective so far has instantiated.

To be sure, this is a tricky matter, since the interpretation of deconstruction I am contrasting with this one, deconstruction as an undecidably radical skepticism, itself demands ongoing contact with philosophy, with fundamental thinking, and its traditions, just as would the honoring of real responsibility to them. Deconstruction, in fact, has long been seen as undecidable on just this account: due to this apparent retention of thought, due to the appearance of recognizing both the rights of thought and their renunciation at once.[2]

On this construal of deconstruction, Derrida's work indeed is believed to continually find itself speaking from a position of philosophical authority and knowledge, even while aiming to leave these behind. Because reason, thought, and philosophy brook no stable or permanent opposition, according to this account, because they allow for no permanent escape, no authoritative other, Derridean deconstruction must necessarily have repeated recourse to thought's authority, to philosophy's positions, in order to take leave from them radically, to break decisively with reflection and philosophy (albeit only for a time). Compressing an account of deconstruction that is today widely known, and hence readily recognizable: thought, reason, are believed to be a sort of enclosure or trap—such that only by remaining within them in the right way, by acknowledging the inevitability of ongoing recourse to them and recontainment by them, is any sort of meaningful escape to be had.

These are the claims and premises of the most common construal of Derridean deconstruction: deconstruction as undecidable, and therefore truly radical, skepticism. Yet so far from such a scenario retaining any real recognition of thought's claims, all genuine contact with thought and genuine responsibility to it is hollowed out by this construal in advance, it must be seen. Compelled to turn to reason, *while already wishing to escape from it,* the appeal to reason and thought here *originates* on a wholly irrational ground. The demand to turn to reason *from the first* is an unjustified and violent one—reason being known not to be authoritative, but only impossible to avoid. Making reason, or thought, compulsory or unavoidable in this way thus removes any trace of genuine responsibility from recourse to thought, since interaction with reason or thought in this scenario can indeed only represent "an unwarrantable involvement" with them—as Jonathan Culler puts it, in his treatment of the workings of this same undecidable radical skepticism (Culler 1982, 88).[3]

Here, then, the continuing appeal to thought or reason can only ever be a sign of their total and absolute illegitimacy—rooted, as it is, in the premise that an escape from reason is somehow known in advance to be both warranted and desirable. And it should be no surprise that once this strategy was promulgated and the limits of thought were believed established by Derrida himself, if only for a time—and even if these limits were supposed to pass through thought, as well as around it, to require intra-, as well as circum-scription—that all these strategies immediately slipped from view, and only their outcomes, postulating the most radical sort of skepticism, even nihilism, remained.

By contrast to the standard account, then, and this brings us to the crux of the matter, Derrida's own aims, his own responsibility to thought, to the question, to philosophy, it was argued—both by a second group of critics, as well as by Derrida himself—necessarily went beyond this type of backhanded endorsement. Derrida himself had decided on undecidability, it was often emphasized; and Derrida had made this decision in the name of something like thought's own goals—in the name of a continuation, a broadening out, of this responsibility. Derrida doubtless did engage with all that seemed to bring thought and philosophy into doubt, but Derrida did so not for its own sake, but with the goal of fashioning new modes of thought and finding new ways to fulfill thought's underlying responsibility, or at least some transformed version of it.[4]

Derrida himself has always insisted on this construal of his own project. He has denied from the start that he is a skeptic in any sense and has maintained that he rejects "skepticism, empiricism, even nihilism," terms that Derrida repeatedly groups together ("AED" 137). Moreover, Derrida has insisted that the totality of his thinking answers to the living ethos of thought, indeed that of philosophy itself (which he at times invokes by name), even as it may question radically some of philosophy's own aims and operations.

Thus Derrida in 1996 avowed not only that he is "a philosopher," but "that I want to remain a philosopher and that this philosophical responsibility is something that commands me" (Mouffe 1996, 81). And in another, even more recent discussion of his own work, Derrida both espouses his ongoing passion for Plato and Aristotle—"however old I am, I am on the threshold of reading Plato and Aristotle. I love them and I feel

I have to start again and again and again"—and also goes on to make clear that he believes his deconstruction of these authors, his analysis "of the functioning and disfunctioning of his [Plato's] work," is itself "a sign of love and respect for Plato," a way "to be true to Plato" (*DN* 9).

Derrida's deconstruction of Plato—his claims about this work's "*disfunctioning*" as well as its "*functioning*"—are intended "to be true to Plato," according to Derrida. Deconstruction as a whole even at this late date thus intends to be true to philosophy, to thought—that side of deconstruction that may appear to stand perilously close to skepticism included. From first to last, Derrida, then, has seen his work in this way: Derrida, by his own testimony, engages with the unthought of philosophy, but this ultimately in order to carry on thought and its responsibility, not abandon it altogether. His is a vital renovation of thought, a renewed and transformed commitment to the living responsibility that philosophy alone has previously instantiated—and this indeed at a time in the present day when the possibility of maintaining or fulfilling such a commitment has appeared most in doubt.

These, I maintain, are the real stakes of Derrida's endeavor. The question of whether thought has a future today is more urgent than ever. In this promise to carry on the legacy of thought, to honor it, transform it—to continue to honor this "responsibility that commands him"—consists the deepest import, the true pith, of Derrida's enterprise.

At the same time, what this entire chapter will show, and in the name of just this responsibility Derrida wishes to acknowledge, is that deconstruction in its most canonical form was never able to entirely fulfill its own stated aims. This end comprises the singular importance, the urgency, of Derrida's project. Yet at least in its most widely read text, and according to a construal of his work that Derrida himself offers, Derrida's thought does not fully satisfy this responsibility in a way that he himself had hoped. Deconstruction does not wholly succeed at keeping this responsibility to thought alive in the way that Derrida himself intended, and seeing this will lead to the recognition that a new manner of approaching Derrida's work is necessary, a new way of construing Derrida's project must be found, more in line with his own intentions. At present, deconstruction represents the most sophisticated matrix that we have for carrying on the project of thought, even while recognizing what brings it into doubt; and I will eventually explore whether a new perspective on this work, perhaps one also always Derrida's own, albeit implicitly or tacitly, can better bring to light the total work of deconstruction, such that it fulfills Derrida's own ongoing attempt to give continued life to thinking.

I will start from the debate among some of Derrida's best interpreters, then, in order to discover more precisely where Derrida's project falls down; why Derrida's thought has so rarely been understood in the way just described; why the very different sides of Derrida's intentions have rarely been brought together within a single treatment. What in Derrida's own work accounts for the fact, more specifically, that the phase of deconstruction that urges thought further is repeatedly neglected, and the one that appears to abandon it is emphasized? Why does Derrida's work remain known as the latest, highest-octane brand of skepticism, despite his own repeated denials? And why, when such recognition has not been missing, perhaps most notably in the work of Rodolphe Gasché, has it not then been able to take a fully credible form and never managed to sway those holding alternative views?

* * *

In truth, I have a long way to go, since my actual criticisms of deconstruction, my specific diagnosis of this problem, will come forward only in the next section of this chapter. Indeed, how much of the present problem is owed to the commentators and how much is owed to Derrida himself is at this moment impossible to say, since part of the problem is that we have no satisfactory way to bring the totality of aims of Derrida's work before us at present, no way that takes the spectrum of Derrida's intentions really into account—but also no way to easily distinguish a breakdown of Derrida's execution from a failure in our understanding of him. The two, Derrida's writings and the commentary on them, presently exist together in a kind of colloidal suspension whose separation may only slowly be brought about. The present state of engagement with Derrida demands approaching this problem, then, through the commentary; and such an approach will also let us see the mark these problems have left in Derrida's text more clearly by way of that which they have made upon the texts of his interpreters.

Let me begin, then, by giving a brief account of Richard Rorty's role in the present chapter. Much of the remainder of the present section focuses on Rodolphe Gasché's interpretation of Derrida in his early essay "Deconstruction as Criticism." Rorty's place in the whole of this first chapter is, however, even more crucial than Gasché's in some respects; Rorty brings forward the issues most decisive for our discussion, since in effect I will argue that Rorty's criticisms of deconstruction are right.

The centrality of Rorty for my argument may at first appear surprising, however, given how little commentary Rorty has offered on specific works by Derrida. And while this apparently rather disengaged style of Rorty's Derrida interpretation will be discussed in a moment, right now it must be recognized that Rorty, despite this, is one of Derrida's canniest critics. Rorty's *proximity* to Derrida's own standpoint, I believe, accounts for this fact—setting aside Rorty's own considerable philosophical acuity. Indeed, Rorty is one of the very few working philosophers who has written on Derrida whose concerns genuinely parallel Derrida's own, and yet who has himself not been influenced by Derrida's own thought in any significant way.

Rorty has devoted a great deal of consideration, after all, to a set of problems that Wittgenstein's famous figure of the ladder at the end of the *Tractatus* may serve to indicate: problems pertaining to philosophy's ability to make statements about the limits of its own projects, what sort of limits these may be, and what such pronouncements might entail, if anything, for whatever successor discourse to philosophy one might attempt to imagine.

These questions lie at the heart of Rorty's own investigations and they abut Derrida's program as well; and they have thus put Rorty in an almost unique position to question Derrida's enterprise. All Rorty's criticisms of Derrida focus on the moment—or membrane, if you will—in deconstruction between philosophy and some alternative discourse, a moment to which Rorty's own work has sensitized him, and these will eventually help us to show that deconstruction as usually construed is not able to balance all its goals successfully: to give heed to what lies beyond philosophy and fulfill its promise to philosophical responsibility at once.

Rorty's criticisms of Derrida's interpreters thus prove cogent when viewed as criticisms of Derrida himself (which is how, I take it, Rorty himself ultimately intends them), and it will, in fact, turn out that Rorty in some sense has already shown what this first chapter seeks to prove. At the same time, however, if Rorty proves to be right on the essentials, we have some way to go before seeing in what way this is really so. This is due to the above-mentioned issue: the apparent thinness of Rorty's descriptions of Derrida's work, the sometimes flickering character of Rorty's presentation of Derrida's thought.

Rorty's own work proceeds through what he sometimes calls "recontextualizations" or "redescriptions" in reference to Derrida's own writings—the presentation of the thought of another author through a conceptuality different from their own, ultimately for the sake of presenting his, Rorty's, own views.[5] Due to this way of working, an apparent distance of Rorty's commentary from Derrida's text arises, and though this is largely deliberate, Rorty's criticisms of Derrida and Derrida's interpreters, accordingly, require a translation device before their real pertinence and force may be seen. Paradoxically enough, just because Rorty and Derrida are genuinely concerned with the same things, at least as Rorty understands this—with the conditions and limits of philosophical discussion— they end up in Rorty's text appearing not to speak the same language:

Rorty everywhere redescribing Derrida's redescriptions in turn. A recourse to those commentators Rorty criticizes must first be had, then, a schema of translation put in place, for mapping Rorty's essays back on to Derrida's own text, so that the validity of Rorty's critique as applied to Derrida himself may emerge.

A bit of stage business, then, a bit of preparation turns out to be needed, if what Rorty for the most part really only hints at in respect to deconstruction is to rise anywhere near to the level of demonstration and our claims about deconstruction's partial, potential failure are to be made good. And here Gasché's work in particular becomes crucial. To be sure, Gasché's interpretation of Derrida is highly significant in its own right; were it not itself pathbreaking, it could not do most of what is being asked of it here.

Gasché, in fact, has gone furthest in advocating and defending just the view of Derrida that Rorty most wants to question: the same view of Derrida that I myself began by endorsing as philosophically responsible, as furthering the tradition's aims. Rorty and Gasché are thus both concerned with Derrida's active, living relation to philosophy in a single-minded way that few other commentators on Derrida are—and this is why Rorty has so often ended up engaging with versions of deconstruction that stem from Gasché, even without always recognizing this is the case.

Gasché's account of deconstruction has indeed gone furthest at just the point where Rorty has the most doubts, and into this clash I wish eventually to insert myself. In the end I side with Gasché, as well as Rorty. For if I believe some of Rorty's criticisms are cogent, I also believe Gasché is right about Derrida's own intentions, and I invoke Rorty's criticisms, then, not to take leave from philosophy all the more radically or effectively than Derrida, as does Rorty himself, but to bring forward a new way of approaching this work more in line with Derrida's deepest aims, those aims which I believe Gasché has largely rightly identified.

Gasché's early account of deconstruction in his article "Deconstruction as Criticism" (hereafter "Deconstruction") will most concern us here; I believe it still to be one of the single best pieces devoted to Derrida that we have. Rorty's criticisms of Gasché and of interpreters with similar approaches, however, have been framed for the most part in terms of Gasché's 1986 work *The Tain of the Mirror,* specifically in reference to the notion Gasché first sets out there of the "quasi-transcendental"—and thus it is necessary briefly to see first how Gasché's talk of the quasi-transcendentals in *Tain* accords with his discussion of Derrida's project in his earlier essay.

The issue of the quasi-transcendental is important here in any case, since it brings us back to some of the largest issues of this chapter, indeed of this book, and the quasi-transcendental will be our focus again later, when possible remedies to the problem I am currently on my way to presenting start to be found. As I have begun to mention, the singular contribution of Gasché's work on the whole is that it allowed, or appeared to allow, Gasché to set out Derrida's complex relation to philosophical responsibility in some detail, to show how this concretely worked in Derrida's own texts. And in particular, thanks to this notion of the quasi-transcendental, to the idea of something that is a condition of both possibility and impossibility at once, Gasché was able to argue in *Tain* that all those aspects of Derrida's texts which seem to border on skepticism—in which Derrida seems to declare that philosophy has run its course—are ultimately subordinated by Derrida to a larger project that expands philosophy's aims and carries on its singular ambitions.

Gasché conceded, more specifically, that items like "archi-writing" or "mark" do not simply forgo all skeptical claims—they do not forgo all resonances delegitimating of philosophy—and for this reason such notions indeed function *quasi*-transcendentally, not transcendentally merely. Yet, in turn, as quasi-*transcendentals,* these same formations still carry out a *transcendental* function, Gasché insisted. They are finally presumed to have some kind of a priori or necessary force and they instantiate forms of argument only philosophy can make. These terms, such quasi-transcendental infrastructures as "*différance*" or "spacing," thus designate what impedes philosophy, what contests philosophy's values—they designate outlaw instances, as far as "philosophy itself" is concerned; yet they also perform a transcendental labor of a sort, in a style only philosophy can envision, and thus, according to Gasché, Derridean deconstruction, the notions it "produces" or "inscribes," ultimately fulfills an overarching commitment to philosophy and the ethos of thought, even while questioning in key respects philosophy's rights.

Tain, then, provided a view of deconstruction, one of the very few available in the literature even today, that tried to capture all that in deconstruction brings philosophy into doubt, all that borders on skepticism in it—deconstruction's talk of logocentrism and phonocentrism, its insistence on privileging writing, the text, and the sign—without, however, giving over the totality of Derrida's work to something other than thought, to a radical skepticism or nihilism of any sort. And, to come closer to the immediate matter at hand, Gasché had already started out on this course in "Deconstruction as Criticism." In this work Gasché had already argued that deconstruction, while recognizing such seemingly skeptical concerns, subordinated them to philosophical or quasi-philosophical ends, and Gasché's approach in "Deconstruction" thus already provided a preview of the argument he was to make in *Tain.*

In "Deconstruction," however, equally crucially, while pursuing a strategy parallel to *Tain*'s, rather than focusing on the schema of the quasi-transcendental—a notion whose importance is largely owed to Gasché himself—Gasché had examined Derrida's own description of deconstruction as an operation of reversal and reinscription (first offered by Derrida in *Dissemination,* and one commented on further in *Positions*); and so too, in "Deconstruction," Gasché had ultimately framed his article as an interpretation of a specific Derridean text: Derrida's reading of Saussure in *Of Grammatology*'s first half. Gasché's talk of quasi-transcendentals in *Tain*, then, is in fact a continuation and a broadening out of Gasché's discussion of reversal and reinscription in the first half of *Of Grammatology* in "Deconstruction," and this proves key to our translation schema here, since Rorty discusses Derrida almost exclusively in *Tain*'s terms, terms really at one remove from Derrida's own discourse.

Indeed, more specifically, Gasché had begun "Deconstruction as Criticism," his first published work on Derrida in English, by arguing against the then-current literary critical interpretation of deconstruction that saw it as a kind of radical skepticism, and Gasché had done this by insisting that these critics paid attention only to what he there identified as deconstruction's first phase, namely "reversal." Critics who took deconstruction as criticism, and also as skepticism, according to Gasché, thus overlooked "reinscription," the more crucial second phase of deconstruction.[6] Gasché's argument in "Deconstruction," in this way tempering the skeptical side of Derrida's project and presenting it in a larger context, accordingly anticipates the one Gasché makes in *Tain* about quasi-transcendentals, and recognizing this allows us to bring the two sets of terms in question here together. The "quasi-" side of the quasi-transcendental, signaling what borders on skepticism and what brings philosophy's project into doubt, clearly answers to this moment of reversal; while in turn, reinscription—for Gasché indicating an expansion and continuing loyalty to thought—corresponds to the *transcendental* functioning of the quasi-transcendental infrastructures that he will later set out.

In "Deconstruction" and in *Tain,* Gasché essentially adopts the same standpoint; the two works largely share a common argument strategy; and the notions of reversal and reinscription upon which Gasché initially relied can thus be seen to correspond to the *quasi-* and the quasi-*transcendental,* respectively. In turn, this permits the central matter that concerns us here to start to come forward: how reversal and reinscription is specifically understood by Derrida himself and how it applies to Derrida's own text, the same text Gasché takes as his example in "Deconstruction," namely, the first half of *Of Grammatology.* Indeed, we now start to be in a position to see how Derrida's own description of deconstruction as reversal and reinscription, and Gasché's schema of quasi-transcendentals, which will later be taken up by Rorty, map on to one and the same text.[7]

To begin with this first phase, reversal: both Gasché and Derrida speak of it as an overturning, a contrary privileging, of one of two terms supposed to compose a set of binary oppositions, "a hierarchy of dual oppositions" (*P* 42), as Derrida puts it—oppositions that almost always pertain to language in Derrida's early writings. Derrida, as well as Gasché, emphasize that "reversal" means taking a term like "writing" or "the sign" and giving it pride of place over and against another previously privileged term: Gasché speaks of a "reprivileging of the sign" (1994a, 46) in the example of reversal that he first brings forward in "Deconstruction," and Derrida himself, in the best-known account of these operations, offers an instance of such "overturning" in respect to "the hierarchy speech/writing" (*P* 42).

Reversal thus represents a reprivileging of one term of a supposed set of hierarchized oppositions, a term usually related to language—and not only does Derrida indicate this in the citation from *Positions,* but Derrida clearly has in mind in this same citation the work that he himself had actually performed in *Of Grammatology*'s first half in respect to the hierarchy of speech/writing. This moment of reversal, however, the "overturning of the hierarchy speech/writing" in *Of Grammatology,* is the moment most attended to by commentators, and thus it does not require much further discussion here. Suffice it to note that this overturning takes place at the beginning of the section of *Of Grammatology* entitled "The Inside Is the Outside." There Derrida argues that Saussure, having already excluded writing from language and from the work of linguistics as such, brings it back, later on, in order to explicate the internal functioning of language as a system of arbitrary signs—an apparent contradiction that lets Derrida "re-privilege" the term "writing": to speak of writing as integral to language and its work, and thus even as "prior" to speech, insofar as all speech, any instance of discourse, already presupposes some language to which "writing" has now been shown to be intrinsic. As Derrida puts it, previewing this phase of his argument as a whole: "Something which was never spoken and which is nothing other than writing itself as the origin of language writes itself within Saussure's discourse" (*G* 44).

Derrida thus does "overturn this hierarchy" in *Of Grammatology*'s first half. More crucial, however, is the other operation that Derrida stipulates as belonging to deconstruction: the moment of reinscription, one that we have already seen Gasché claim was overlooked in *Of Grammatology*'s interpretation and which Gasché himself was one of the first commentators to explore. Reversal covers the opening phases of Derrida's reading of Saussure in *Of Grammatology,* leading up to this first phase of

"The Inside Is the Outside"; reinscription pertains to the far murkier work Derrida's text goes on to do, particularly in the next section called "The Hinge." And what such reinscription actually entails—as well as the fact that Derrida indeed has shifted from "reversal" at this moment in his treatment—is perhaps most economically shown by attending to an imaginary dialogue with Hjelmslev that Derrida conducts near the end of "The Inside Is the Outside," which prepares the way for Derrida's discussion in the next section.

Hjelmslev's innovation in linguistics, which he called glossematics, entailed that the distinction between writing and speech ceased to have any significance, any relevance at all in his system, and thus Hjelmslev would seem immune to the sort of concerns, and the notion of writing, that Derrida brought forward in the case of Saussure. Nevertheless, Derrida is forced to confess at this crucial moment that even so, "he [Hjelmslev] would not have understood why the name writing continues to be used for that X which becomes so different from what has always been called 'writing'" (G 70).

The term "writing" has indeed undergone an operation other than reversal; it has, more specifically, come to be reinscribed in the text of *Of Grammatology*. Writing at this point has begun "to be used" for an "X"—for something far "different from what has always been called writing," something that has no proper name, no proper referent of its own and that even Hjelmslev, who escapes Saussure's phonocentrism, would not recognize.

Derrida's comments here should be compared with what he says about reinscription more generally in *Positions*, in particular, later on in the same interview already cited, where Derrida develops this notion further under the related topic of paleonymy, the new use of old names. Having already spoken of the necessity for reinscription earlier in *Positions* in the place cited above, "we must also mark the . . . eruptive emergence of a new 'concept,' a concept that can no longer be, and never could be included in the previous regime" (P 42)—a description that clearly answers to Hjelmslev's failure to recognize writing in *Of Grammatology*—Derrida a little later in this interview specifies that this emergence takes place through "the delimitation, the grafting and regulated extension" of an already existing "conceptual structure" bearing a predicate "named X" (P 71).

The term "writing," then, is indeed such an X at this point in *Of Grammatology:* it has become a paleonym, an old name designating something new. It has broken entirely with its customary referent, its traditional designation, as this talk of paleonymy indicates, and writing, now, this X, designates something utterly foreign to its usual meaning, something no linguist could recognize by Derrida's own avowal.

Equally important, however, are the grounds that Derrida himself adduces for this claim: what he specifies as the motor of such reinscription and why he believes all this has become so foreign to Hjelmslev and linguistics generally. For Derrida indeed goes on to relate this incomprehension on the part of Hjelmslev precisely to the role that is to be played here by transcendental experience: to the recourse reinscription has to an "experience," an experience dependent on "that transcendentality I [Derrida] elsewhere put into question" (*P* 61). Thanks to the introduction of a transcendental perspective, then, to a possibility of inquiry Derrida himself specifies as "transcendental," writing has been rendered unrecognizable to Hjelmslev and its reinscription has been achieved. Derrida makes clear that the notion of transcendental experience he has in mind is that of Husserl, and what is in question here, then, at the core of this operation of reinscription pertains to Husserl's transcendental phenomenological reduction: to a field of inquiry, a field of experience and indeed a nonworldly, nonmundane, subjectivity, entirely different from any an empirical science could access.

For Derrida doubtless is right: Hjelmslev would not understand this reinscribed "writing": he would not grasp why "writing" continues to be employed here as a name for this X at all, and this is due to the role these transcendental considerations play. "Writing" is indeed a newly grafted predicate and has built into it this singular reliance on such a transcendental perspective, on this sort of specifically philosophical concern and viewpoint.

Here, then, the legacy of philosophy that has been in question all along, what Derrida continues to owe to the tradition, steps forward most visibly. The side of Derrida's project that most answers to this commitment to thought and its ongoing and expanded life has emerged in this moment of reinscription, and seeing this we are in position to move back to Rorty's treatments of Derrida, and identify the issue between them. For indeed, we can now clearly see what has ultimately been aimed at all along: that reversal and reinscription, the quasi-transcendental and Derrida's treatment of writing in *Of Grammatology,* all agree. Derrida does draw on transcendental concerns at this moment, after drawing the rights of philosophy into doubt; and the work of reinscription may thus be said to result in what Gasché later would call a "quasi-transcendental" infrastructure, a formation unthinkable apart from philosophy's legacy and rights—in this case embodying the "quasi" of the reversal of speech/writing, as well as Husserl's own "transcendental," in what is here specifically known as "archi-writing."

* * *

Turning to Richard Rorty and his objections to Derrida's quasi-transcendental readers, Rorty repeatedly poses two main objections to

Derrida and his interpreters, in accordance with Rorty's own complex views on how to depart from philosophy. And while the second will prove important later, the first objection, the more general one that Rorty makes, sets out the problem with Derridean deconstruction that here concerns us above all.

Rorty's first objection takes the form of a "dilemma" which Rorty repeatedly claims that Derrida and his readers face. Rorty brings up this dilemma on numerous occasions when he comments on the literature on Derrida, and in his 1984 "Deconstruction and Circumvention," the first published piece Rorty devotes to these interpretations, to Jonathan Culler's in particular, Rorty describes this dilemma. He sets out his first objection as follows: "One horn of the dilemma I have been sketching consists in not saying anything about philosophy but instead showing what literature looks like once it is freed from philosophy. The other horn of the dilemma consists in outdoing the philosophers at their own game by finding a general criticism of their activity something comparable to Parmenides . . . or Kant's . . . grasping the second horn will produce one more philosophical closure, one more metavocabulary which claims superior status, whereas grasping the former horn will give us openness but more openness than we really want" (Rorty 1991, 94).[8]

Thanks to our previous section, we can see that Rorty's dilemma focuses on just those two different sides of deconstruction that have already come forward in Gasché's and Derrida's accounts. One side, Rorty's second horn, consists in "outdoing the philosophers at their own game" through "an activity comparable to . . . Kant's," and this horn thus answers to the transcendental side of the quasi-transcendental, the moment of reinscription: that moment when Derrida takes up the tools of philosophy and heeds considerations philosophy alone can present. In turn, the other side, the first horn, represents a break from philosophy, a moment entirely disqualifying of its viewpoint, which Rorty here calls "literature."

Rorty's essay was written in 1984, when the skeptical reading of Derrida was prevalent, especially among literary critics, and with his talk of "literature," Rorty clearly has this reading in mind (as well as his own prior discussion of Derrida's work as presenting "philosophy as a kind of writing"). "Literature" thus represents all that considers thought and philosophy as in doubt in deconstruction, and Rorty's first horn, this first pole, answers to the moment of reversal, and to the "quasi" side of the quasi-transcendental.

Rorty's two horns, his two poles, thus correspond to the two sides of deconstruction that we have seen come forward in more canonical accounts. And Rorty's first objection, his dilemma, is a serious one. For Rorty's dilemma, his first broad strategic objection to Derrida, poses the problem of *why* Derrida would actually want to do *both* of these things: to adopt a skeptical standpoint, from which all philosophy appears simply as a kind of writing, as literature, as a mere functionary "in the metaphysics of essence and presence," as Rorty elsewhere puts it (1991, 336), yet also continue to go on and try to "beat the philosophers at their own game," by bringing transcendental and quasi-transcendental considerations forward. Given this first gesture, this first horn, identifiable in deconstruction itself and in *Of Grammatology* in particular, as consisting of an appeal to a set of binary oppositions (and bearing the radically disqualifying stance toward philosophy that Derrida's accompanying talk of logocentrism and phonocentrism entails)—how do the apparent aims of this standpoint, of this first phase of reversal, in any way comport with those of the other horn: the return or reappeal to philosophy, to a (quasi-) transcendental practice that Derrida announces in his second phase?

This is the gist of Rorty's first objection; yet its import goes even further. Rorty's dilemma, this objection, raises the problem not only of why—why *have* both horns, reversal and reinscription, skepticism and responsibility to philosophy—but *how*. How *after* this operation of reversal, more specifically, *can* Derrida proceed to this moment of reinscription, even assuming his motives for doing so are good? Even granting that it makes sense to want what Derrida wants, how *could* Derrida or anyone do what Derrida wants: invoke a moment that depends on philosophy for its own authority, undertake this second transcendental or quasi-transcendental phase, if we assume that the initial reversal, this first literary or skeptical phase, holds good and these considerations relating to writing, language, logocentrism, and phonocentrism have force?

The first phase of the deconstruction of Saussure devoted to the sign and its differential functioning has already been traversed, when "writing" begins to stand for an X that Hjelmslev could not grasp, when recourse to transcendental experience is to be had. But, Rorty goads us to ask, once these initial considerations, the logos itself, reason as such, have already been radically cast into doubt, indeed, have already been portrayed as a function of something called logocentrism, by what authority are the knowledge, the argument-structures, the concerns specific to philosophy now invoked—by what right can one appeal, as Derrida does, to transcendental experience at all at this moment?

Put otherwise: the first phase of deconstruction, reversal, by Derrida's own avowal, is associated with a notion of writing that indicates an unflagging difference at work within all language, all discourse and speech—one which blindly conditions all philosophy and which all "metaphysics" represses.[9] But if any of this is even slightly plausible, how *can* transcendental considerations of any sort (whether Husserl's or Kant's or anyone else's) retain validity, retain any authoritative status, once the logos, reason, and philosophical truth have been denied all principled legitimacy?

Nor do Derrida's own intentions finally have any effect at all on this issue, it can readily be seen: whether Derrida ultimately *intends* deconstruction to be skeptical or not, or some combination of both, has no pertinence here. Rorty's objection, at its deepest stratum, makes plain that a part/whole problem with respect to the role transcendental concerns are called on to play affects the strategy of deconstruction in totality—a role that we have indeed already seen at work in Derrida's own text, in Derrida's formulations of deconstruction and in those of Derrida's interpreters. In all these cases—the first half of *Of Grammatology,* reversal and reinscription, the quasi-transcendental—this same problem arises: How does Derrida have access to these concerns at that point when he comes to them in his text? How has the philosophical branch upon which Derrida and deconstruction need to stand in this second phase already not been cut off by what deconstruction accomplishes in the first? And the literary critical interpretation of Derrida as a skeptic, then, while mistaken about deconstruction's aims, may finally not have been so wrong, when it comes to the workings of Derrida's own texts.[10]

Rorty, as I said, turns out to be right; in effect, his criticism is a good one. And the central conclusion this entire chapter sets out to reach has thus been shown. There simply is no obvious way on the usual construals of deconstruction for Derrida's text to function as he had hoped, at least in this key instance. There is just no way that this second moment can be taken seriously—not ironically, as Rorty himself everywhere treats it—given the results that deconstruction first brings forward and given the description of its own operation it supplies. Deconstruction indeed inadvertently falls into the pit of radical skepticism before it ever arrives anywhere else; and to this feature is owed much of deconstruction's ongoing interpretation in the literature—its perception as a radically skepticist, even relativist, enterprise—an interpretation which ends up not being simply unwarranted.[11]

Of course, I do not mean at all, let me hasten to add, in bringing such considerations forward, to imply that all further work on Derrida should therefore cease, that his thought should henceforth not be taken into account, that his project simply loses all interest or becomes an impossible one on account of this impasse. Not only does it apply to a single Derridean text taken in isolation, for one thing, but generally speaking, I believe Rorty's critique rather opens the door to a new approach to Derrida's thought; it invites us to explore new ways of viewing this work, new possibilities for understanding Derrida's project, in a manner more in line with Derrida's own aims.

Derrida himself, after all, was concretely aware of the problem just brought forward. This singular construction embodied in deconstruction's operation, this unparalleled way of working, as I will show, was not unknown to Derrida, and much of his development turns on it. Thus, how Derrida himself has all along viewed his own work, why he believed this singular way of working, mapped by such notions as reversal and reinscription, was needed (even if some of these descriptions, like reversal and reinscription itself, may finally fail to meet Derrida's or our own purposes), also arise as questions. Did Derrida, perhaps, have a way of viewing his own deconstructive work—in a tacit context, with a specific problem in mind—that mitigated these issues? Had he not perhaps himself always implicitly seen his work in a still unexposed light, which would lend it greater legitimacy, since, after all, Derrida had always intended to carry on this responsibility to thought, and he always believed that his work managed to do this?

Such questions, as will eventually become clearer, are the ones that inform my approach here and indeed all that this book subsequently does. I will seek to view deconstruction, the writings, the texts, of 1967 in a new light, from a new perspective, one that Derrida himself may have himself tacitly brought to this work. A hitherto unrecognized standpoint on these writings that brings them closer to Derrida's own aims for them may already be implied in Derrida's own views, due to that "singular putting into perspective" which any new idea necessarily brings with it—a feature of all innovation that Derrida himself first pinpointed in his early work on Husserl (*LOG* 107/*IOG* 104).[12]

Moreover, to remain still with the literature, I should hasten to add that while the approach I will be proposing is new, it is not radically novel, or as different from some of the work already done, as it may at first appear. This sort of tack, or some of its important premises, have already begun to come forward in the commentary, albeit often partially. And the rest of this chapter, in fact, will stay with the literature on Derrida— this debate over quasi-transcendentals between Gasché, Rorty, and also Bennington—in order to bring forward some key anticipations of my own enterprise.

* * *

Gasché himself, it is important to note, in *Tain* had already made something of a start on a response to Rorty's problem—he had in fact been forced to do so. Gasché wrote *Tain,* let us recall, at the moment when the interpretation of deconstruction as a novel and radical form of skepticism was at its height; he composed it specifically in response to interpreters who foregrounded the skeptical side of Derrida's project. And since, as we have just seen, deconstruction offers a foothold to views of this sort,

Gasché in *Tain* was already implicitly faced with the impasse that Rorty identified. He perforce found himself addressing this problem as he worked with Derrida's texts aiming to rebut their skeptical interpretation.

In *Tain*, Gasché had already tacitly confronted Rorty's problem, and the important thing here is the innovation this forced upon Gasché, one which lets the first important anticipation of my own project emerge. For Gasché in *Tain* deviated from Derrida's own stated method in at least one significant way: Gasché gave himself a starting point markedly different from Derrida's own in the 1967 works. Derrida, in the two book-length writings of 1967, takes up philosophy second, as we have seen, and begins from what appear to be regional, even empirical, concerns (concerns associated with language, writing, and the sign). By contrast, in *Tain* Gasché starts from philosophy, from a prior setting and achievement in philosophy, in order to supply a different, perhaps broader, context in which to view deconstruction as a whole. Gasché, in *Tain*, before even turning to Derrida's own texts, began not from language, but from philosophy in totality—specifically, from what Gasché calls the "philosophy of reflection" and its supposedly successful self-completion at the hands of Hegel and others—and he did this, I would argue, in order to meet the problem with the operation of deconstruction that Rorty has helped us to identify.

This tack, moreover—Gasché's appeal to a previously existing philosophy of reflection—though it has a negative as well as a positive side, as we shall shortly see, was a good one: it provides an important clue to meeting Rorty's problem and presenting a version of deconstruction that does not inadvertently succumb to skepticism. For, were all the work of deconstruction, both of Rorty's horns, to answer to some previously existing necessity or demand in respect to philosophy, as in the scenario Gasché puts forward, deconstruction as a whole could indeed be seen as part of a larger endeavor, of a single whole comprised of philosophy and itself, and this first phase might no longer block all access to the second. If some sort of problem, some occasion, in philosophy and its problematic—something in reason or thought in whatever form—had already called for this sort of treatment, the operation of deconstruction *in totality* might appear to be warranted, and its first side cease to squelch the second, permitting the responsibility to thought of Derrida's enterprise to be fulfilled.

The strategy of *Tain*, then, generally speaking, is on the right track, and Gasché's recourse to a prior philosophical context in *Tain* is warranted, once Rorty's problem comes squarely to the fore. Yet while such a scenario is indeed promising at a distance, it also proves to be far more difficult to execute successfully than it may initially appear. What sort of philosophical problem could actually motivate philosophy's deconstruction—in respect to what version of philosophy, conceived in what form, and under what conditions—is very hard to know. And I myself will eventually find it necessary to turn to that philosophical endeavor that stands prior to deconstruction both in fact and in principle in order to seek a specific occasion, a problem wholly unique, that might provide deconstruction's warrant.

Here, then, important ways in which I differ from Gasché, as well as side with him, begin to come into view, and with that a very difficult issue in *Tain*, as well as in respect to making progress on Rorty's problem more generally, emerges. Speaking still at a highly provisional level, the issue of what sort of philosophy generally *could* provide a precursor or context for the operation of its own deconstruction is far from clear. What sort of philosophical milieu is able to grant any kind of philosophical validity to deconstruction, even as deconstruction goes about exceeding it, is a thorny issue, and raising it here, in the context Gasché's *Tain* provides, will indicate the second broad guideline for responding to Rorty's problem that my final discussion (of Rorty and Bennington) aims to set out: my identification of the type of philosophy that alone is really able to play this role.

In addition to motivating my own work here, this last issue proves important in itself, given how widespread in the literature is the understanding of Derrida as a quasi-transcendental philosopher, in the basically Kantian sense that Gasché lays out, an interpretation essentially stemming from *Tain*. This construal is prevalent among many of Derrida's best commentators, who follow Gasché in attempting to see deconstruction as other than a new form of skepticism.

Nevertheless, this interpretation of the philosophy that deconstruction is thought to presuppose is just where *Tain* itself proves most problematic. Gasché's attempt to show deconstruction as meeting its commitment to philosophy on the basis of philosophy of reflection, and through an operation akin to Kant's transcendental argumentation, despite the progress it allows Gasché to make—the important mapping of Derrida's thought it makes possible—ultimately runs aground, goes awry. This happens most visibly at the very moment in *Tain* that Gasché turns away from his discussion of this philosophy of reflection (and of people like Hegel and Herbert Schnadelbach who, Gasché believes, have brought this philosophy to completion, showing it can form a total working self-consistent body of knowledge) in order to take up Derrida's own work and begins to address deconstruction more directly.[13]

For at this moment, when he is about to turn to Derrida's own texts for the first time in *Tain* (or at least that species of thought, heterology, under which Gasché believes they fall), Gasché makes the following rather startling admission. "From a traditional philosophical perspective," Gasché writes, about to speak of the way of working that he himself is generally attributing to Derrida, "this approach makes no sense. Indeed, as we shall see, the approach I shall be concerned with escapes the norms and expectations classically associated with the discourse of philosophy" (Gasché 1986, 80–81).

The size of the concession that Gasché makes here must not be underestimated—with it, a problem that runs like a fault line beneath *Tain* emerges. After all, Gasché's project is precisely to show the philosophical cogency, to bring forward the philosophical responsibility, of deconstruction: this is the hallmark of his commentary and indeed the source of its considerable value. As Gasché himself puts it in his introduction to *Tain,* in the very first pages of his work, his aim is to provide an "interpretation [of Derrida that] is philosophical; . . . focuses on Derrida's relation to the philosophical tradition, emphasizes the manner in which his writings address particular philosophical problems [and] . . . the philosophical itself" (Gasché 1986, 2).

And what then have become of these admirable ambitions, it must be asked, at this moment in *Tain,* at the very moment Gasché in fact turns to Derrida's work? Why bother with the philosophy of reflection at all and the first seventy-five pages of *Tain,* if this discussion of deconstruction is to make "no sense" "from a traditional philosophical perspective"?[14]

At the moment he embarks on his discussion of deconstruction in *Tain,* Gasché is forced to forfeit the most central goal of his entire undertaking, and the larger point ought not to be lost from sight. For Gasché's concession bears important witness to the main argument of this chapter: it shows how deep a mark the problem Rorty identified has left on Derrida's commentators, to such an extent that arguably Derrida's most responsible interpreter, the one most devoted to debunking the skeptical account of Derrida's thought, is forced to fall into absurdity and essentially relinquish this aim at the moment he turns to Derrida's own text.[15]

Beyond that, however, *Tain*'s breakdown serves to indicate that the sort of philosophy Gasché envisions—a philosophy of reflection that has its roots in Kant and blossoms in Hegel—can never play a real role in deconstruction as a precursor or context of any sort. This is a deep and thorny matter and ultimately extends well beyond Gasché's treatment. Suffice it to note, however, that as part and parcel of Gasché's commitment to a philosophy of reflection in *Tain*—one absent in his earlier "Deconstruction as Criticism," by the way—and his related, essentially Kantian, construal of the transcendental (as a condition of a conditioned, whether of possibility or impossibility), Gasché puts enormous weight on the notion of a system in *Tain:* both on philosophy as a system, as well as in his talk of "system" in respect to the results that deconstruction brings. Gasché repeatedly refers to the outcomes of deconstruction as forming a "system of infrastructures," and this emphasis on system is consonant with the rest of Gasché's approach. It stems from Gasché's construal of philosophy, of philosophy in its completion, as a philosophy of reflection.

Yet philosophy understood in this fashion, as Gasché's own turn away from it above attests, can never do the work that Gasché wants. Such a version of philosophy is essentially a static one, wherein philosophy itself must already be complete—indeed, a total system—before it can perform the task Gasché assigns to it: providing the object for deconstruction (the conditioned of deconstruction's conditions), as well as the tools deconstruction employs (deconstruction's own transcendental arguments—philosophy thus conditioning deconstruction, in turn). For Gasché, philosophy is conceived as both the conditioned of deconstruction (the conditioned of the quasi-transcendental conditions that deconstruction uniquely articulates) and the condition of deconstruction (the premise for the sort of work deconstruction does in its singularity, which Gasché believes ties it uniquely back to philosophy). Yet only a philosophy that frames its inquiry, its knowledge, in some form other than a system can really hope to do this sort of work. Only a philosophy that is more dynamic and that does not in fact construe the transcendental simply as a ground, as a condition of a conditioned in any primary sense, and thus gives it a more open-ended, dynamic form—in which the transcendental is itself framed as an experience, for example—can provide an occasion for deconstruction in this fashion to arise, to respond to Rorty's problem, or even, it could be shown, to perform the specific work assigned to the transcendental in Derrida's texts.

After all, speaking generally, if there is successful philosophy, true philosophical knowledge, if Schnadelbach, Hegel, or anyone else has indeed brought "philosophy to successful completion"—which would indeed be big news—why bother to deconstruct it at all? Were philosophy truly a completed system, what within it could conceivably call for its deconstruction? Yet if it is not complete, if the system of philosophy fails, how can we move on *to* deconstruction *from* philosophy? If there are problems with philosophy, why do these not warrant further and better philosophy, rather than the sort of radical discontinuous alternative that in some way deconstruction represents?

This problem of how to motivate deconstruction on the basis of philosophy, in fact, often besets *Tain,* and it surfaces in the passage just cited when Gasché must affirm the "success" of philosophy, even as he claims to question that "very successfulness," thus himself falling into absurdity, affirming what makes "no sense." Indeed, throughout *Tain,* in line with this static conception of deconstruction and philosophy, Gasché will tack back and forth between these alternatives, attributing prior "success" to philosophy in order to justify deconstruction's philosophical credentials, yet forced to deny such success, in turn, when it is a matter of motivating deconstruction itself.[16]

A more dynamic understanding of philosophical knowledge and philosophical practice alone holds out hope, then, for what Gasché wants: to provide some sort of philosophical discovery or ground that may yet point the way beyond philosophy, and provide deconstruction with its philosophical bona fides. Accordingly, the need for the next guideline here begins to come forward; for this guideline will indeed begin to specify the sort of philosophy that deconstruction must and does presuppose.

Of course, it is to Gasché's credit, let us not forget, to have attempted to make real arguments concerning all of this—to have tried to *demonstrate* that deconstruction is not a form of skepticism. And even if this has partially gone awry, perhaps Gasché alone has gone this far in fulfilling his own responsibility to thought. On that score, in addition to so many others, we remain in his debt. Yet only by transplanting Gasché's strategy, and perhaps transforming it, by bringing it back to the actual soil on which deconstruction arose, does a real chance exist for successfully executing Gasché's original intention.

* * *

Our final look at Gasché has brought us to the impossibility of construing philosophy as Gasché suggests in *Tain,* as philosophy of reflection, and have it still function in the way Gasché wants, as a platform for deconstruction. I now want to turn to Bennington, and back to Rorty, in order to identify how, in a broader, more familiar context, philosophy as deconstruction in its 1967 form has always presupposed it and in some way understood it, and make clear the importance of this fact. The second guideline here indeed concerns the way in which philosophical knowledge has actually been believed to function by Derrida himself, and our examination of another of Derrida's best readers, Geoff Bennington, will help set this out.

In addition to providing a second anticipation of my approach, however, my discussion of Bennington and Rorty will let my treatment of Rorty be completed, since this identification, as well as its actual significance, only become visible through the interchange, the interaction, between Bennington and Rorty that we are here about to follow out. Bringing forward this second orienting guideline, my discussion of Rorty's role will be concluded, a discussion in which a number of matters still remain outstanding.

Rorty, after all, as we have already noted at the start of the preceding section, has not one but two objections to deconstruction. And while his first objection, examined above, was a more strategic, general one—asking how these two phases of deconstruction fit together—Rorty's second objection actually questions the functioning of one of them, namely, the capacity of this second phase of deconstruction to make transcendental arguments at all. Rorty's second objection is meant to raise the issue of whether the second, philosophical or quasi-transcendental, phase of deconstruction is really valid, insofar as it is understood by Gasché and Bennington to rely on transcendental arguments of a Kantian type, a position in philosophy that Rorty believes to be finally untenable.

Not Rorty's arguments against Kantian transcendentals per se, however, but these arguments insofar as they concern the related issue of how philosophy is to be done, how this field is to be understood in the first place, will prove to be the focus of this debate and of our attention. Because Gasché and Bennington take Derrida to be arriving at quasi-transcendental considerations in respect to philosophy generally, Rorty addresses the issue of the transcendental in the context of the more general question of what methods in philosophy are appropriate and how philosophy is to be construed, and this point is the most central one: how philosophy is understood as a field of inquiry, in Bennington's account and Derrida's, as opposed to Rorty's own.

Let us turn to Rorty's second objection with an eye on this issue of philosophy, as this objection comes forward in Rorty's treatment of Bennington in Rorty's "Derrida and the Philosophical Tradition," Rorty's last discussion of quasi-transcendental interpretations of Derrida to date. The portion of Rorty's essay in which he makes his objection responds to a claim that Bennington had made about the status of philosophy and its relation to the other disciplines in the section entitled "The Series: (Quasi-) Transcendental Questions" in Bennington's "Derridabase," which comprises one half of *Jacques Derrida*. I will cite Bennington's passage first, in which he describes philosophy as he believes deconstruction presupposes it, and then cite Rorty's comments on it immediately after.

Bennington declares: "Any attempt to unseat philosophy from a classically defined region can only replace in the final instance something which will play the part of philosophy without having the means to do so. Thinking one can do without philosophy one will in fact be doing bad philosophy" (Bennington 1993, 283).

And Rorty, in turn, commented on this as follows—in one of the very few places in all of Rorty's published work where he appears to grow angry—his tone rising to an ever more impassioned pitch: "How, without turning back into phallogocentrists, can we know as much about the inescapability of philosophy—and about the presuppositions other people have whether they admit them or not—as Bennington claims to know. Isn't the condition of possibility of knowing that sort of thing precisely the metaphysics of presence and essence that deconstruction was supposed to help us wiggle free from? Couldn't the different species of anti-metaphysicians . . . at least agree on the need to be nominalists? . . . Shouldn't we stop rummaging through texts in a hunt for 'transcendental contraband'?" (Rorty 1998, 335).

Rorty is here criticizing what he takes to be deconstruction's transcendental labors, specifically as applying to philosophy itself. Rorty thinks Bennington's argument—that the work of philosophy cannot be replaced by any other discipline—depends on a Kant-style transcendental analysis of concepts, as Rorty's ironic invocation "of the condition of possibility of knowing this sort of thing" and his reference to "transcendental contraband" here attest. Since, however, Kant is not the original source of these claims,[17] what is really of interest at the heart of this critique is the more general role of the concept that Rorty believes is implied here: the imputation of an illegitimate metaphysical, fantastic power to concepts, one that Rorty believes thrusts Derrida and his interpreters back into metaphysics, into that "metaphysics of presence and essence" and that "phallogocentr[ism]" which deconstruction is supposed to avoid.

The weight of Rorty's objection falls on the role given here to concepts, and with that Rorty brings into play his own views on how philosophy should proceed. Rorty's objection indeed pertains, above all, to the way in which he believes philosophy's work is to be construed in the first place: what methods are appropriate to it, what goals are its own—and specifically to Rorty's preference for a starting point for philosophy in a philosophy of language over and against all other possible beginnings. Throughout these debates this is a constant refrain of Rorty's. A supposedly metaphysical or phantasmatic life of concepts, a treatment of concepts as "quasi-persons," as Rorty puts this elsewhere in his essay, underlies the construal of the transcendental upon which Bennington and Gasché and others depend (Rorty 1998, 330). By contrast, Rorty repeatedly insists, as he does here, that Derrida and his interpreters join him in making what is sometimes called the linguistic turn—in a kind of clean, stripped-down, "methodological nominalism" in particular.[18]

The whole thrust of Rorty's complaint, we can now more readily see, thus falls on this issue of whether philosophy should take its starting point in language, as Rorty himself proposes.[19] A more sweeping complaint, or suggestion, underlies Rorty's second objection—a version of the issue that we already encountered in our discussion of Gasché—as to the style of philosophical work deconstruction presupposes; and this indeed brings us nearer to the core of my own concerns here.

For the construal of philosophy by Bennington that Rorty is attacking, it must be stressed, *is a genuinely Derridean one*—more so than Gasché's reconstruction of a completed philosophy of reflection. And thanks to this understanding of philosophy's status, Bennington is able to make a signal advance over Gasché in formulating the work of deconstruction as a whole. Indeed, earlier on, in this same section, Bennington had described the outcome at which deconstruction aims as follows, and here we find an actual breakthrough on Bennington's part.

Bennington, earlier in the section "The Series: (Quasi-) Transcendental Questions," described deconstruction as resulting in a kind of spiraling reversal, more specifically, a movement both "upward" and "downward," encompassing both philosophical knowledge and the other regions of inquiry and their rival knowledge claims. Thus Bennington capped off his description of the quasi-transcendental result of deconstruction: the situation of philosophy as deconstruction brings it about by "formaliz[ing]" it in "the proposition 'the empirical is the transcendental of the transcendental ["of the empirical"]'" (Bennington 1993, 278).

Bennington, then, conceiving of the quasi-transcendental as a movement—in which philosophy's own (quasi-transcendental) conditions are drawn from the other empirical branches of knowledge, even as philosophy's claims maintain their rights over these in turn—makes progress over Gasché's systematic conception, and this description, as Rorty recognizes, remains perhaps the best single formulation of deconstruction's work we have. Bennington is right in the first place about this issue of where philosophy initially stands for Derrida himself, and thanks to this, Bennington can chart a more fluid interaction between philosophy and its others, one focused on the interaction between the transcendental and empirical sides of Derrida's discourse, offering a description, it seems to me, that indeed hews closer to the actual movement of Derrida's texts than Gasché's talk of infrastructures.[20]

Especially important, then, is that Derrida does see philosophy in this way, in the manner that Bennington portrays and that informs Bennington's insight here. Philosophy for Derrida is indeed to be taken as situated amidst rival branches of knowledge, as Bennington presents it in the passage first cited above. So, too, Derrida himself believes that the "attempt to unseat philosophy" can only replace it with more philosophy, and thus is convinced philosophy can maintain its rights against all other knowledge claims.

Such a construal of philosophy, moreover, is ultimately the key difference between Rorty and Derrida themselves. Leaving aside for the moment who is right on this point, not only do Derrida and Rorty recognize different starting points for philosophy, but this is the source of their very different modes of departing from philosophy, in turn. Rorty, in line with his commitment to the linguistic turn and his insistence on methodological nominalism, here and everywhere, would depart from philosophy, would break with "the metaphysics of essence and presence," as he puts it, in favor of just that empiricism and historicism that Derrida elsewhere rejects.[21] Rorty essentially joins in the neo-positivist program that sees philosophy as ultimately having no subject matter or field specific to itself—no mode of argument, discourse, or decision proper to it in its specificity. In accord with his other commitments in the philosophy of language, Rorty advocates a radical positivist pragmatism that would, as it were, push to evanescence, that severe diminution of philosophy as a working discipline to which much of Anglo-American philosophy already subscribes.

And what, then, of Rorty's objection itself, having begun to fix on its stakes and the object to which it actually applies: what of this issue concerning the construal of philosophy lying at the root of deconstruction and of Derrida's ability to initially insist on philosophy's rights, to resist all forms of positivism and empiricism and to maintain some distance from the linguistic turn, to defer it or depart from it in some fashion? How is Derrida able to argue that philosophy is irreplaceable and insist on the rights of something like a transcendental apriori, even if this does not take the form of a transcendental deduction of concepts? For these claims about philosophy's positioning, we start to see, are indeed the source of the singular work that deconstruction envisions; to them a large part of the singular power of deconstruction's project originally accrues.

Once again, then, Rorty's feel for the issues at stake proves sound; his question, at least, once more proves urgent. Rorty is quite correct, in my view: any starting point for philosophy other than one in language remains in doubt, and whether philosophy really can maintain the epistemological priority on which both Bennington and Derrida insist is a genuine question. More broadly, it is very difficult to know how the work of philosophy today is to be construed: if philosophy has any proper activity at all—any sort of field or knowledge of its own—whether it can stand up to the ever-mounting prestige and authority of the sciences, and consequently what sort of future, if any, it has.

It must also be recognized before proceeding any further, however, that just such questions concerning the status of philosophy which I, along with Rorty, believe to be the most pressing for philosophy today are the ones that Rorty's own approach forever bars us from seriously discussing. Indeed, to bring my discussion of Rorty to a close here, Rorty's question to everyone with whom he undertakes something like dialogue is, how is philosophy to be conceived seriously as a discipline now and going forward? Rorty's own way of working, however, I would suggest, prevents any further serious discussion of this genuinely pressing matter, even to the point of preventing Rorty's own views from being treated with the gravity I believe they deserve, since Rorty's radically ironic stance tends ultimately to swallow up his own assertions, as well as those of his opponents.[22]

After all, on Rorty's own account of these matters, on his pragmatist construal of discourse, and his methodological nominalism, the conditions under which it is alone meaningful to engage in a discussion of terms and what they may designate (as, in the present instance, the term "philosophy") are when a preexisting consensus exists concerning the aims of that discourse in which the term is used. The "inferential connection" between sentences in which such terms are found, as Rorty puts it— what statement would make another one true or false—must be agreed on in advance by the participants in order for such "sub-propositional" discussion to be meaningful.[23]

Since, however, Rorty stands alone—since no one else in these debates, none of his interlocutors, shares Rorty's own aims—he, as far as I can make out, everywhere finds himself involved in a manifest petitio principii, a self-contradiction, which is, in part, to what this strategy of recontextualization seems ultimately to amount. Rorty repeatedly claims, in an initial phase of his work, the authority of certain presumed results within philosophy (here, for example, these findings in philosophy of language over against Bennington's or Gasché's reliance on the concept) in order to argue in a second phase that philosophy has no mission, purpose, or role generally, including the specific form in which his interlocutors present it (as, here, that there is no purpose to maintaining such talk of quasi-transcendentals). But this is to say that Rorty in one phase of his discussion only *appears* to be arguing with his interlocutors, according to the conditions that he himself stipulates for argument—agreement with his interlocutors about the means and ends of discourse—and that Rorty subsequently denies that this is what he has actually been doing: quite self-consciously and indeed ironically denouncing the pertinence of the very activity in which he has been engaged.

This is how Rorty's strategy of redescriptions or recontextualizations functions, as far as I can make out—thus promoting that "circumvention" of philosophy that he believes to be the only intellectually honest way to break with philosophical discussion. Practicing a kind of Socratic irony in reverse, Rorty quite consciously intends to motivate the abandonment of philosophy by appearing to engage in philosophical discussion, only to subsequently announce that he was only pretending to do so, and affirming that there is thus really nothing left to discuss, that he was in effect engaged in a very sophisticated joke.[24]

Rorty's ironic exit from philosophy provides the ultimate parameters for his own project, then, and this is of course the ultimate ground for Rorty's attention to Derrida. Rorty's singular situation spurs him to scrutinize Derrida's work on just these points, to hone in on Derrida's own claim that he believes he has found a happier mode of leave-taking from philosophy than Rorty himself.

What is crucial for us to see for our purposes here, since the gyrations of Rorty's discourse cannot be pursued beyond this point, remains again Rorty's question, not his outcomes. Rorty's belief that philosophy must be abandoned may not finally be persuasive in the form he sets it out; yet the issue raised by Rorty while doing so remains a serious one: how Derrida is able to construe the work of philosophy in a way other than Rorty's own, in the way that we have begun to describe. If Derrida does not take the linguistic turn simply, yet does not, à la Gasché, subscribe to a completed philosophy of reflection in the form of Schnadelbach, or even Hegel, how does Derrida maintain philosophy's primacy in the first place at all?[25]

Doubtless Bennington is right: Derrida sees philosophy in this fashion, Derrida upholds philosophy's prerogatives and rights—and believes that philosophy cannot be replaced by any form of empirical knowledge à la Rorty. Bennington himself, however, remains unaware, it turns out, of the grounds that Derrida actually has for holding these views, even as Bennington brings them forward. This is an equally important piece of the puzzle, since Bennington's failure to grasp the actual arguments underlying the view of the philosophy that he rightfully identifies as Derrida's once more attests to the corrosive power of the skeptical side of Derrida's writings that has been a central theme here. Just as Gasché, employing this inappropriate model of the philosophy of reflection, was forced to succumb to irrationalism or misology even as he attempted to ward it off, so too, Bennington, another outstanding interpreter of Derrida, is not able genuinely to identify the philosophical argument for the construal of philosophy he rightfully attributes to Derrida, even at the very moment it permits him to make his greatest breakthrough in presenting deconstruction.

Yet it was in fact Edmund Husserl who first set forth this argument, in 1900, concerning philosophy's position—and it is thus not an "entirely classical philosophical argument," as we have seen Bennington aver.[26] In the face of the growing prestige and success of the positive sciences, as well as new discoveries in logic, Husserl in the first volume of *Logical Investigations* argued that no empirical branch of knowledge can ever supplant philosophy, and that its work remains authoritative for all other disciplines. All the sciences and their findings, according to Husserl, presuppose truth or knowledge, both as a goal already given and an idea already known, and thus not any one of them, but philosophy alone, can ultimately clarify scientific activity and knowledge.

More specifically, any branch of knowledge that would claim to account for truth, that would presume to take over philosophy's work, Husserl argued, could do so only on the condition that its knowledge were true, and thus must presuppose that into which philosophy alone can inquire: the vocation, meaning, and validity of knowledge and truth. (Neurobiology, for example, just like history or sociology, can claim to account for human, even scientific, behavior, only insofar as its researches are true; but then the validity of truth, truth's authoritative status, must be given in advance of these researches, not through them.)[27]

And whatever one may think ultimately about the persuasiveness of this argument, the important point, whose significance we are really only now in a position to see, is that Derrida himself has always believed these claims. Derrida in fact has always subscribed to Husserl's account of philosophy and its work, has always subscribed to Husserl's rebuttal of empiricism and naturalism in *Logical Investigations* I, and all of deconstruction in Derrida's mind already presupposes such a demonstration.

Matters here come full circle; the very same passages that I brought forward at the outset, in which Derrida affirms his own commitment to the responsibility of philosophy and thought, are those in which Derrida also explicitly invokes Husserl's name and Husserl's own arguments about philosophy, in order to keep the kind of historicism and empiricism upon which Rorty insists at a distance. "Something that I learned from the great figures in the history of philosophy, *from Husserl in particular,* is . . . not to be held within the fragility of an incompetent empiricist discourse," stated Derrida in 1996 (Mouffe 1996, 81; my emphasis). "I have . . . drunk my mother's milk on the breast of transcendental phenomenology, which first of all was a rigorous critique of relativism, empiricism, skepticism, and historicism" ("AA" 83). "Husserl has shown better than anyone else, relativism, like all its derivatives, remains a philosophical position in contradiction with itself" ("AED" 137). And even earlier, in the very interview in *Positions* in which Derrida brings forward the formulation of reversal and reinscription of which we have made so much, in fact in that very same interview in which that formula is set out, the following may be found in a footnote appended later: "I had forgotten that Scarpetta's question also named historicism. Of course the critique of historicism in all its forms seems to me indispensable. What I first learned about this critique in Husserl . . . seems to me valid in its argumentative framework" (*P* 58n32).

Derrida, then, has indeed always subscribed to Husserl's view of philosophy's primacy, its unavoidability and irreplaceability; and moreover,

Derrida has repeatedly stated that it is this that keeps his own thought at a distance from all historicism, relativism, empiricism, naturalism, and positivism. Derrida has in truth always wished deconstruction to honor this commitment to philosophy, one whose form Derrida believes Husserl most successfully set out and defined.

The work of this section, of this chapter, is thus complete. Our second guideline, as well as our first, both stand confirmed. Not only is it necessary to follow the overall argument structure of *Tain*, and see deconstruction in light of a preexisting philosophical context and problem, but, as Bennington's work begins to indicate, the true philosophical precursor to deconstruction is not Kantian or Hegelian reflection, but Husserlian phenomenology. This philosophy, and this philosophy alone, in fact, and in principle, stands at the root of Derrida's own conception of philosophy's work, his responsibility to that work, and the renewed, transformed responsibility to thought that Derrida believes that deconstruction will fashion.

By way of an admittedly circuitous route, working both with Derrida and his commentators and against them, we have begun to make plain the unique importance of Husserl for Derrida, as well as the necessity for something like a return to the roots of Derridean deconstruction in phenomenology, thus opening the possibility of a developmental approach to the 1967 work. Spurred by Rorty's powerful objections, by Gasché's breakthrough interpretation of Derrida's work (thanks to which alone the force of Rorty's objection can really be grasped), and assisted by Bennington's important supplement to Gasché, we can now begin to turn back to Husserl's thought and Derrida's engagement with it, to seek a new approach to Derrida's 1967 texts more in line with Derrida's own avowed intentions for them.

2

"A Consistent Problematic of Writing and the Trace": The Debate in Derrida/Husserl Studies and the Problem of Derrida's Development

Chapter 1 started from the debates in the literature to bring forward a problem with deconstruction's operation, and from these debates, I set out two guidelines that pointed a way toward a remedy. These guidelines, however, as some readers may have already sensed, contain an implicit tension, if not an outright contradiction, which it is now time to explicitly discuss. The first guideline, after all, points toward a new way of looking at Derrida, one so far unrealized in the literature and potentially foreign even to Derrida himself. By contrast, the second relies on statements made by Derrida himself and asserts that Derrida has already made explicit the singular privilege of Husserl's thought, on which it insists. The first guideline, then, turns away from Derrida, at least to a point, and heads in a decidedly new direction, while the second invokes Derrida's own authority and calls on the role Husserl is already supposed to play to get this new approach off the ground.

I emphasize this tension because in it, across its different pulls, emerges the notion of Derrida's development as it will be at issue here, and it thus lets me sketch more concretely the approach I will subsequently take. A decidedly new perspective, an additional frame encompassing both of Derrida's first deconstructive works, will indeed come about, thanks to a return to Husserl and Derrida's writings on him. Recourse will be had to Husserl's thought and its primacy for deconstruction, in accord with Derrida's own statements and in line with certain construals long extant in the literature; yet a developmental slant will be taken through these works—a previously unrecognized diachronic cut made through Derrida's early writings—in order to bring forward a perspective on the 1967 works that is itself new: one not wholly coincident with their own self-presentation, yet permitting each to be interpreted in detail in a manner ultimately in line with Derrida's own intentions.

Of course, the novelty of this resulting standpoint, this frame that a diachronic perspective alone makes available, does not cancel what also began to come forward earlier: namely, the possibility that Derrida himself in some way always tacitly viewed his own writings in this light, always saw his work through the singular optics implicit in its development. Nevertheless, I wish to stress the novelty of this perspective—that if Derrida has always somehow implicitly viewed the 1967 writings in this way, such a standpoint has remained just that, implicit, tacit at best. And I want to emphasize the novelty of this frame, for not only has it so far remained undisclosed, but that from which it derives, the fact of there even being real development across Derrida's thought, has until now gone unrecognized.[1]

The question of whether there is in fact significant development in Derrida's standpoint between 1952 and 1967 is thus my present concern, and it is indeed a very large problem, among other reasons because Derrida's own remarks have at times appeared to give support to the view that such development does not take place. That Derrida spent his early years working on Husserl and through this brought forward the work for which he became best known is widely acknowledged. Yet the notion of anything like deep change across this period—that Derrida's own project, as well as his reading of Husserl, would differ in 1967 in significant ways from its form in 1962 or even in 1954—by no means finds agreement today, and Derrida's own statements, as we shall see, are in part responsible for this fact.

The case must be made in the first place, then, for real development in Derrida's thought. And I propose to start with the literature once more, this time the literature on Derrida and Husserl, to make this case. For just as the premise of my previous chapter was that there is still no real consensus about what Derrida wants deconstruction as a whole to accomplish or how it really operates, so, too, in the particular case of Derrida's Husserl interpretation, an equivalent, indeed, an even greater, controversy currently rages.

An enormous impasse still exists today concerning Derrida's reading of Husserl; critics are at absolute loggerheads about whether Derrida's Husserl interpretation is valid, whether it is successful or convincing. The present chapter will show that only with real development in Derrida's writings on Husserl being recognized is there hope of sorting this out. Only by reckoning on quite significant, deep change across Derrida's early writings, it will become clear, can these controversies even locate a starting point from which their disputes may someday successfully be resolved.

Hence, the demonstration that real development takes place in Derrida's thought begins from the debate on Husserl and Derrida. It will, however, give way later in this chapter to the question of development more broadly, as seen in the context of all of Derrida's early writings, including *Of Grammatology* and *Writing and Difference,* and this broader issue will prove to be the more decisive one in some respects. Nevertheless, the impasse I start by examining here concerning Derrida's Husserl treatment is deeply important in its own right, since, in part for the reasons laid out in chapter 1, the philosophical bona fides of deconstruction finally reside within Derrida's fifteen-year engagement with phenomenology. These claims, too, hinge on how Derrida's Husserl interpretation is viewed: on whether significant development takes place across the four different works Derrida wrote on Husserl over the course of fifteen years.

In sum, then, I will start to make the case for development more broadly, by starting with these debates in the Husserl/Derrida literature in order to show that such a hypothesis alone holds out hope for resolving the current impasse there. The question of Derrida's credentials as a Husserlian will be shown to rest on whether real development affects this work. In turn, this raises the possibility that Derrida's thought may undergo significant alteration through all his early writings on the way to deconstruction. It is this hypothesis that begins to introduce my developmental perspective on the 1967 writings and this new frame through which they will be viewed in subsequent chapters.

* * *

Let me begin, then, by turning to this debate in Derrida/Husserl studies and the impasse that still exists there. The absence of a developmental perspective on Derrida's Husserl writings has led even the best commentators astray, I will argue, and has led to an irresoluble roadblock in these discussions, at least so far. At the same time, by diving into the debate on Husserl and Derrida, an additional issue, equally important for my project, also comes into view, one that has remained largely on the sidelines so far. Reference has been made more than once to the controversy surrounding Derrida's deconstructive works: that no consensus exists about their most basic aims, their fundamental themes, or whether these works are successful at whatever it is they actually do. Just to limn this a little further, whether Derrida's work is primarily about language or something else, whether it aims at a new form of skepticism or no, whether its claims are even prima facie convincing or merely the latest in a series of hoaxes (which commentators always somehow seem to label "French")—not to mention this work's political valence, whether it is a genuinely progressive, politically potent, mode of thought—about all of this, no agreement exists in the literature, even after more than thirty years of discussion.

The impasse in Husserl/Derrida studies that I am about to explore can help get to the roots of all these disagreements, since much of the controversy surrounding Derrida's project, I will argue, is traceable to a more general hermeneutic problem that stems from Derrida's own function as a commentator in his mature works. Interpreting Derrida has everywhere proved hard due to the difficulties implicit in commenting on an author whose own thoughts are of primary interest (and startling novelty), yet whose work always proceeds through reading or commenting on the writings of another. And this problem is further compounded by the innovative uses to which Derrida puts the standpoint of commentary itself.[2]

Indeed, just to give a highly provisional idea of these difficulties, one that obviously will prove important later on, let me recall for a moment the singular purpose Derrida assigns commentary in his 1967 work on Husserl, *Speech and Phenomena.* Derrida elsewhere declares that between 1963 and 1968 he invented a new "strategic device . . . for reading and writing and interpretation" ("TT" 40). And in line with this, at the end of his introduction to *Speech,* Derrida announces that his discussion of Husserl aims to exhibit "a hold" over Husserl's thought at work in his writing, which "is neither simply operative nor directly thematic," "neither central nor peripheral" (*SP* 16/ *VP* 16). Derrida himself thus stipulates at the outset of *Speech* that he intends to bring forward a set of considerations that play no obvious role in Husserl's own work, and that his interpretation, as Derrida himself puts it, correspondingly remains "poorly conceived in the concepts traditionally associated with the philosophy of the history of philosophy"—by which Derrida means those concepts governing interpretation or commentary in the traditional sense (*SP* 16/ *VP* 16).

The kind of interpretive work that Derrida intends to do here, his stance as a commentator, is thus unlike any other, by his own avowal; his focus is on a matter neither "operative nor thematic," "neither central nor peripheral," and to be elaborated through an innovation in "interpretation" that breaks with "the concepts traditionally associated" with reading. This dimension of *Speech,* one at work in all of Derrida's mature work, has never been fully confronted, much less mastered, in the literature.[3]

What this innovation in commentary more specifically entails, how critics are to respond to it, will be dealt with further as I explore the current controversy in Husserl studies. Let me be clear from the outset, however: by no means do I wish to suggest in the one case or the other—in *Speech* or in Derrida's deconstructive writings generally—that these works are finally illegible or ultimately indecipherable in some way. In fact, my final chapters will be devoted to just the sort of extended interpretation of *Speech,* as well as *Of Grammatology,* that so far has too often failed to come about—a failure that already gives some indication of the problem we are confronting, given the extent to which these works have been previously discussed.[4]

So, too, such hermeneutic considerations should not suggest that a number of other causes are not also at work in the ongoing controversy that surrounds Derrida's Husserl interpretation. Indeed, controversy has been especially vehement in respect to Derrida's work on Husserl, and circumstantial reasons doubtless account for this at least in part. Commentators who have devoted years of study to one author, namely Husserl, clash with those who have shown the same devotion to another, Derrida, and insufficient respect for each other's labor has at times been the result—a clash made all the harsher due to the very different philosophical reference points that each camp brings to these debates.

In the case of the Husserlians, in particular, it is worthwhile noting how Husserl studies in the United States were positioned prior to these discussions and at what distance their own concerns stood from those of most Derrideans. In the United States, Husserl studies have long been the area of "Continental" philosophy most closely in contact with analytic philosophy (as opposed to work on Heidegger, or Habermas, or perhaps even Kant). Commentators on Husserl, often starting from the same considerations in logic as Anglo-American philosophers of language, have competed with this school for title to the most comprehensive working version of philosophical rationality—each approach at times fecundating, as well as differing with, the other.[5] American Husserlians and Derrideans, then, largely inhabited very different philosophical universes prior to their meeting in these debates, and surely this is a further reason for the bitterness of their impasse. The broader stakes that inform my own work here also gleam through at this moment—since by showing that Derrida's thought is able to hold its own in contemporary Husserl circles, that it can measure up to this scrutiny, I hope it may be brought more within the mainstream of Anglo-American philosophical discourse from which it even today remains largely excluded.[6]

To stay with the narrower point, however, while concomitant causes, these different starting points and orientations among discussants, have clearly added fuel to these controversies, such differences have overflowed their occasions, and thus point to a further cause at work in the writings themselves. The debates concerning Derrida's work on Husserl portray a disconnect so profound, so singular a failure of communication between the two sides involved, that it marks them off for special notice even in a field so traditionally contentious as philosophy, and this indicates that something more than merely occasional is implied here, something specific to Derrida's own works.[7]

This "something" is the issue already raised: the problem of the "hermeneutics of deconstruction." Commentators on Derrida and Husserl turn out to be divided, above all, by an interpretative dispute as to how debate itself should proceed, about how the interpretation of Derrida's in-terpretation of Husserl should be conducted in the first place.

More specifically, participants in these debates largely break down into two camps. In the first camp are mainly Husserl scholars, often late-comers to Derrida's thought. These tend to prefer argument as their pri-mary mode of discussion, and they concentrate on detailed individual positions, single problems, in a particular text or corpus—sometimes in isolation from broader interpretive concerns. For such critics Derrida's role as an interpreter of Husserl is the most important thing, the most de-cisive issue in all discussions of Derrida's Husserl work.[8] These commen-tators imply that the validity of Derrida's Husserl reading is the sine qua non for all work on Derrida and Husserl. This is the specific interpretive assumption that this camp makes: to know whether Derrida's reading of Husserl is right is the first thing to be determined, and this can be done, this first camp believes, even in the absence of a thorough confrontation with Derrida's own thought, before a full-fledged understanding of Der-rida's own aims has been achieved.[9]

By contrast, in the other camp stand commentators who tend to read rather than argue; these critics have more care for the broadest aims of the author under discussion, at least if this author happens to be Derrida. This camp is most concerned with what Derrida thinks; Derrida's *intentions* are key for this camp, and these readers have often tended to give short shrift to Husserl's own thought, it must be conceded.[10] The hermeneutic prem-ise informing this camp's approach is thus precisely the opposite of the first camp. Understanding Derrida, not Husserl, is the sine qua non for making any progress in these debates, this camp asserts. Derrida's own thinking and aims for them are the first thing to be understood, and this can be done, they believe, even prior to evaluating Derrida's role as a com-mentator on Husserl. As this was recently put by one participant in these debates, in response to the claims of the first camp, "if one cannot recog-nize the issue . . . [that] organizes Derrida's thought, then it is impossible to identify Derrida's readings as distortions" (Lawlor 1998, 192).

At the core of this conflict concerning Derrida's reading of Husserl, then, stands a specifically hermeneutic dispute, a fundamental discon-nect, in regard to how the interpretation of Derrida's work on Husserl should proceed. To be sure, these two sides disagree about much else, in-deed, about almost everything; they don't read one another often, and when they do, they tend not to understand or convince each other. Yet at the heart of their conflict lies a disagreement about interpretation: specif-ically, concerning how one should go about interpreting Derrida's writ-ings on Husserl and where discussion should begin. One camp believes that Husserl's teachings, and the accuracy of Derrida's understanding of these, are to be established first; the other that Derrida's thought is to be grasped before anything else—and each camp believes its aims can be achieved largely in the absence of the other's.

This dispute, in turn, sets in relief a more general problem with how Derrida's works are constructed and operate: the "hermeneutics of deconstruction," as I call it, understood more broadly (though for the moment this problem will continue to be viewed within the frame of Derrida's reading of Husserl). For not only is Derrida's own role as a commentator first and foremost at issue here—the manner in which Husserl is positioned in Derrida's own text being essentially problematic, such that each side wishes to start from a different end of the semantic stick: one from Derrida's report on what Husserl is saying, the other from the discourse of Husserl himself. Furthermore, this divide is exacerbated by the correlative fact that previously emerged: namely, that Derrida's own discourse in *Speech and Phenomena* aims at a theme *in principle inaccessible to Husserl himself*. As we began to see earlier, this "hold" at which the entirety of Derrida's interpretation aims stands at an oblique angle to Husserl's own enterprise; and part of its very point is that Husserl could never acknowledge it or integrate it into his own thought *even in theory*. Derrida's entire work deliberately targets something that Husserl could never foresee or address—and to the degree that this is so, to the extent that Husserl and Derrida themselves aim to treat such radically different matters, it is indeed difficult to know where interpretation should begin.

Critics have thus been forced, as it were, to fall on one side or the other throughout these debates, to turn to Husserl or Derrida exclusively, due to the novel use to which Derrida puts commentary, and the problems inherent in commenting on commentary as such. Each camp attributes exclusivity to its own starting point, due to the ambiguous status of commentary itself, as well as to the unique status of Derrida's commentary in particular, and this is the deepest source of the controversy surrounding Derrida's Husserl interpretation, accounting for its singular virulence.

Nevertheless, recognizing this general problem—a problem that all interpretation of Derrida's mature work arguably faces—the solution to it, at least in principle, is rather easily known. Most simply stated, both camps are right: Husserl's claims, as well as Derrida's aims, must both be respected. Whatever else it does, Derrida's thought does present itself as commentary; and so judging independently whether Derrida gets Husserl right must form a part of any serious analysis of his thought. At the same time, Derrida is finally the primary author here—no other Husserl commentary, no matter how important, receives this level of attention—and thus Derrida's own aims, self-avowedly independent of Husserl's, must be honored. This is even the ultimate condition for what the first camp wants to do, for judging the accuracy of Derrida's grasp of Husserl's thought, I would suggest.[11]

Both camps are in some way right, then, and this fact, the outcome of these debates, supplies us with a sort of measuring stick, a standard, for the interpretation of Derrida in this case, as well as more generally. Indeed, every serious confrontation with Derrida's mature thought must finally strive to do "justice," as it is sometimes put, to both Derrida's own thought and that of the author he reads. Without in any way denying that Derrida himself may have already done this—though this also must not be taken for granted—the interpreter must strive to pass judgment *in his or her own right*, making independent judgments about Derrida's readings that do not take his conclusions for granted, as well as judgments setting forth Derrida's own complex intentions.

Such an approach, heeding Derrida's aims and his author's claims simultaneously, perhaps may appear self-evident. Yet the unique character of Derrida's interpretation makes it far from so. Rather, Derrida's stance as a commentator and the uses to which he puts this require that Derrida's own interpreter each time find a unique starting point, a singular common ground shared by Derrida and the author in question, from which to approach this work. Such a standpoint must indeed be discovered individually, independently, and uniquely by the commentator—it cannot be taken for granted—and it must be secured from the start, if both viewpoints are really to be honored at once.[12]

This is the challenge that all interpreters of Derrida face, and it is thus not insoluble in principle, even if the demands of interpreting deconstruction generally have not been adequately reflected on before, and even if such a solution has all too rarely actually been found.[13] Yet given that some of Derrida's best interpreters are to be found on both sides of these debates, and that discussion has so often failed here when it comes to Derrida's Husserl writings, an additional impasse, a further practical problem, I would suggest, is also at work, which has kept greater progress from being made. In this case, if anywhere, such common ground should have become readily evident in a practical, working way—a more successful standpoint from which to comment on Derrida and Husserl should have emerged—had not a further opacity held back even the strongest commentators from arriving at truly definitive results.

Indeed, features unique to Derrida's engagement with Husserl, I want to suggest, have aggravated the difficulties faced by all interpreters in commenting on Derrida's commentaries. And I highlight these, not only because they prove critical to the current impasse in Husserl/Derrida studies, but also because I believe that these same singularities may eventually show us a way out, both from these impasses in interpreting Derrida on Husserl and in respect to Derrida's mature works generally. What makes Derrida's engagement with Husserl uniquely problematic, when viewed in the proper light, can help resolve the problems with interpreting many of his individual works, and these ambiguous features will also eventually bring squarely to the fore the issue of Derrida's development.

Two aspects in particular of Derrida's reading of Husserl have made it especially difficult for critics to comment successfully on *Speech and Phenomena*, then. The first is the fact that Derrida offered at least one, if not two, total interpretations of Husserl's thought prior to his best-known work on Husserl, *Speech*. This has aggravated the problems everywhere inherent in Derrida's way of working. Even in the simplest case, after all, Derrida's basic approach entails that the thought of the author he reads undergoes significant compression. Derrida has to squeeze into a single frame, as it were, both the standard work of commentary and his own extraordinarily complex and innovative thinking, and not only does this mean that Derrida often approaches his author from a highly unusual direction, but it leaves Derrida's actual interpretation especially open to what is called "sedimentation"—the technical term (in fact coined by Husserl) for the burial of an original intention due to repeated recursions, both temporal and logical, in the course of its being built on further.

Such compression and its corresponding sedimentation are particularly aggravated, however, in the case of *Speech* due to facts surrounding its composition of which we have only recently been made fully aware. Fifteen years before *Speech,* Derrida had written one work surveying the totality of Husserl's corpus available at that time; and five years before *Speech,* in 1962, Derrida had written another work on Husserl's late writings, which may also be seen to offer a new interpretation of Husserl as a whole.[14]

In *Speech*, then, Derrida often takes for granted all the earlier reading of Husserl that he has done, and his account of Husserl there is especially sedimented and compressed as a result. Derrida repeatedly assumes the basic working interpretations of phenomenology that he has elsewhere set forth; his actual analysis builds on this prior interpretation, at times starts from a point where he had earlier left off, and appears to do so not always wholly consciously.[15] The compression and sedimentation that is everywhere endemic to Derrida's commentary has thus been especially acute in the case of Husserl due to Derrida's prior interpretations, and this has made it even more difficult to find the standpoint from which to honor both Derrida and his subject that subsequent commentators need in order to approach Derrida's work successfully.

This apparent distance between Derrida and his subject—the failure of a working common ground for commentary to manifest itself—has been further compounded by another related factor pertaining to the situation of Derrida's reading in *Speech,* and again one unique to Derrida's engagement with Husserl. This further aggravating feature has been *Speech*'s place in Derrida's own itinerary. As the sequence of his writings just sketched lets us see, in *Speech* Derrida approaches Husserl's first properly phenomenological work last. Derrida, that is, comments on Husserl's first properly phenomenological writing, the *Logical Investigations,* only at the termination of Derrida's own engagement with Husserlian phenomenology. This, too, has clearly made it harder for subsequent critics to find that perspective needed for successful commentary on *Speech,* that common ground from which both Derrida's and Husserl's projects may be respected.[16]

These conditions most notably, though others could be brought forward, have aggravated the difficulties with Derrida's interpretation of Husserl in *Speech;* they have made it more problematic than in any other instance of Derrida's mature work for readers to find that working common ground, that unique practical profile shared by Derrida and Husserl, that would allow both their enterprises to be simultaneously respected.

At the same time, just these same aggravating conditions may offer hope for mitigating these difficulties, both here and in the rest of Derrida's mature writings. In *Speech,* taken on its own, a genuinely adequate proximity between Derrida and Husserl has yet to come forward, genuinely common ground between Derrida and Husserl has indeed proved lacking—and this is perhaps a fault, or flaw, which to some degree must ultimately be laid at the doorstep of *Speech* itself, even if it does not simply invalidate Derrida's enterprise there or deprive it of continuing interest.[17]

It is not only the case that a renewed scrutiny of Derrida's earlier works on Husserl (with attention to what I call Derrida's "development" in a weak sense) may finally offer what is needed to orient commentary on *Speech.* An appreciation of the history of Derrida's engagement with Husserl might do a similar service for commentary on deconstruction generally, as well.

Here Richard Rorty's problem that I brought forward in chapter 1 returns. Rorty's objection (aimed at how deconstruction's first phase of reversal is to be integrated into Derrida's deconstructive intentions as a whole) entails that many of Derrida's mature commentaries begin from a swerve away from those he reads, from a distance and a different perspective from those on whom he comments, at least as regards authors in the philosophical tradition.[18] On account of Derrida's starting from language-related, quasi-skeptical concerns at the outset of his readings, Derrida's commentaries often talk about something different from what his subject is talking about, even if Derrida's commentary at other essential points may ultimately be sound.[19] Deconstruction's operation, by its own avowal, in this first phase of reversal brings to bear a set of concerns foreign to philosophy. And this, tied to Derrida's novel employment of commentary, doubtless has impeded truly successful global interpretations aimed at once at Derrida and those he reads. It has held back from being implemented in practice that general hermeneutic standpoint for interpreting Derrida so easy to grasp in theory, which was set out above.

If, however, the overarching congruence between deconstruction's aims and philosophy's claims had already been in some larger way established, if Derrida's original, core *philosophical* concerns had indeed become manifest and were generally known, in the case of any given text or reading it would be far easier to find an appropriate starting point for this kind of truly judicious commentary. In turn, this is just what attention to Derrida's early work on Husserl promises, what engagement with his development through phenomenology might permit.

After all, the "Introduction" and *Le problème* were composed before Derrida's avowed innovation in reading and his explicit invention of deconstruction. In fact, *only* Derrida's commentaries on Husserl show us Derrida treating a philosopher *pre-deconstructively*. Only in Husserl's case do we have writings on an author that start from within philosophy and move outward to approach it in totality, rather than proceed from Derrida's views on philosophy as a whole and move inward toward the author. These writings thus offer an opportunity to see not only where Derrida's and Husserl's thinking coincide, but where Derrida's concerns and philosophy's do so most broadly—a coincidence, an overlap, which alone may not only provide a definitive orientation for further work on *Speech*, but for many of Derrida's other mature texts as well. An awareness of Derrida's pre-deconstructive engagement with Husserl could thus turn out to be the unique preparation, the singular propaideutic to future, more concrete interpretations of Derrida's deconstructive works.

Yet with this claim, the question toward which I have been making my way all along emerges: namely, that of the actual development of Derrida's thought. The role for Derrida's early work on Husserl just sketched assumes that some sort of real change occurs among Derrida's early works: both across his fifteen-year-long encounter with Husserl and at the time of the 1967 writings. The works on Husserl before 1967 would indeed have to be viewed as presenting significant stages in Derrida's thought, not simply considered as footnotes to Derrida's 1967 text; a development with real depth would now be acknowledged, taking place in three dimensions, as it were, rather than in the margins of Derrida's 1967 writings. Important differences would exist among these early works. And these works, and with them Derrida's own thinking, would thus be open to a genuinely diachronic treatment, a mapping of the complex changes in Derrida's standpoint across time.

Indeed, not only would significant variation extend across the line of works on Husserl, but real development, discontinuity of some deeply significant sort, would indeed have to take place between the 1967 writings and all that came before. A genuine division would exist between Derrida's pre-deconstructive and deconstructive standpoints, one fashioned largely through Derrida's Husserl reading.

Yet if all this is so, why has such development been recognized so rarely, and been so infrequently taken into account? Why has the impression persisted in the literature for so long that no real change takes place among Derrida's first writings?[20]

To see what stands at the heart of this issue, it is necessary to see that two different sets of assumptions lie behind this neglect. One has already begun to be discussed. *Speech* has been taken to provide the teleological culmination of all of Derrida's Husserl writings. Even if all these works have not simply been seen as identical in every respect, they have been thought to tend toward the same conclusions, the same outcomes as *Speech*—the single aim that *Speech* most authoritatively fulfills. And to this degree the relation among these works has been flattened out, as we have already seen—differences, even significant differences, between them being repeatedly ignored by commentators, or downplayed on the occasions when they have been noticed.[21]

In addition, however, and here we come to the crux of the matter, a broader assumption about all of Derrida's early writings, not just his writings on Husserl, has functioned beneath this first one and provided its real support. All of Derrida's early writings have been believed to form a single whole, to reflect an underlying unified aim, and this broader assumption has tacitly overflowed into the narrower discussion, informing commentators' views of Derrida's work on Husserl. This conviction of the essential coherence of all of Derrida's early work has been so profound that the question as such has rarely been put concerning the changes of Derrida's standpoint in respect to Husserl; and even those authors who recognize profound differences among Derrida's writings on Husserl— some of the very best to participate in these debates—have shied away from their ultimate significance, due to this belief concerning the underlying unity of Derrida's early corpus.

The primary assumption concerning Derrida's development, the main ground for its denial as a major factor, then, has been this assumption concerning the totality of Derrida's early corpus. This assumption, however, is traceable to some extent back to Derrida himself.[22] The crux of the matter lies with *Of Grammatology* and its relation to the "Introduction"—not with *Speech* (for example, *Speech*'s relation to *Le problème*—a complex issue in its own right). The belief has long been held in the literature, in part due to occasional comments on his corpus that Derrida himself made, that the "Introduction" and *Of Grammatology* share the same subject matter—that the writing Derrida discusses in the 1962 "Introduction" and the writing that comes forward from the very first pages of the 1967 (or 1965) *Of Grammatology* are in fact the same. Derrida himself has seemed to suggest that the "Introduction" and *Of Grammatology* offer substantially the same doctrine on key points and thus that no significant development among his early works takes place, including his early works on Husserl. The belief in the essential unity of Derrida's corpus across 1962 and 1967, between Derrida's work on Husserl and his less specialized concerns, thus recurs to Derrida's own statements, and to these I must now turn.

* * *

Derrida seems to downplay the differences among his early works, in particular, in the first of two discussions of his corpus he has offered. Two authoritative accounts of Derrida's early work exist. The first occurs in a 1967 interview later republished in *Positions;* a second that Derrida provided nearly fifteen years later on the occasion of his thesis defense (which comes at a much later stage of one's career in France) first appeared in English as "The Time of a Thesis: Punctuations" (1983). "Time of a Thesis" discusses Derrida's early work at far greater length than does *Positions,* and from "Time of a Thesis" eventually results the outcomes concerning where Derrida stands on his corpus that are most decisive for my own work.

The interview in *Positions,* which is the first I will take up here, on account of its being prior chronologically, has proved to be far more influential, even though less detailed, than Derrida's remarks in "Time of a Thesis." The *Positions* account established the view of Derrida's corpus that has held sway ever since, in particular the identification between the "Introduction" and *Of Grammatology* which I just set out; and thus, though Derrida's remarks in *Positions* are rather scanty, a good deal of attention must be paid to them.

In this 1967 interview, in the course of giving an account of how his "books . . . are organized" (*P* 3), Derrida makes those comments from which the belief that all his early works agree has largely been derived. More specifically, Derrida asserts, after a discussion of his 1967 works, that "in this essay," that is, in his 1962 "Introduction," "the problematic of writing was already in place as such, bound to the irreducible structure of 'deferral' in its relationships to consciousness, presence, history and the history of science, the disappearance or delay of origins, etc." (*P* 5).

These claims and what they seem to imply have led commentators to view the totality of Derrida's early works as undifferentiated, as essentially one in most important respects. In 1967 Derrida declared that "the problematic of writing" was already "in place" in the "Introduction"; Derrida in the "Introduction" had already connected writing to "deferral," "consciousness, presence," "the . . . delay of origins." Both the "Introduction" and the 1967 works have the same theme, Derrida seems to suggest; in them Derrida treats the same subject matter, "writing," and in the same way.

Nevertheless, questions remain as to whether Derrida is in fact saying what readers believe him to be saying here: whether in these statements Derrida is denying all discontinuity, any real significant development, across these early works. Derrida does, of course, state that a problematic of writing, appearing first in the "Introduction," was subsequently taken up in the 1967 works. Yet the role this problematic plays, and the standpoint Derrida adopts toward it, do not necessarily have to be the same in each of these texts on that account, nor is Derrida necessarily claiming this is so. The "Introduction" and the 1967 writings may have two very different contexts, two very different outlooks and orientations, in each of which the problematic of writing distinctly surfaces. For no one doubts, of course, that Derrida first encountered writing as a theme in his analysis of Husserl's *Origin of Geometry*, nor even that this spurred Derrida in some fashion to his subsequent project—the "absolute novelty" of Husserl's own approach to writing being something to which Derrida will always attest (*VP* 91/*SP* 81).

The problem of Derrida's development thus depends on knowing whether Derrida takes the same attitude toward this problematic and whether it plays substantially the same role and serves a similar function in 1962 and 1965 (or 1967). Here, however, I can begin to bring forward some of the key features of Derrida's presentation of his work in this interview that raise doubts about whether the standard account of Derrida's comments is in fact correct. Two such features, in particular, draw this into question.

First, in this interview, the discussion of the "Introduction" and the remarks that I have quoted concerning it follow Derrida's discussion of *Speech*—they do not precede it—and *Speech* itself, in turn, is introduced in a singular fashion, one that finds interesting echoes some fifteen years later in "Time of a Thesis." Derrida, before speaking of either the "Introduction" or *Speech*, that is, had been asked by his interviewer about how *all* his 1967 works relate. The topic of Derrida's present corpus and organization was thus the first one taken up, yet in this initial survey of his 1967 works Derrida comes to realize he "forgot" *Speech* (*P* 3). Derrida only speaks of *Speech* at all in *Positions* after being prompted by his interviewer, even though, once prompted, Derrida identifies *Speech* as "perhaps the essay" he "likes most" (*P*4), as well as the essay which "in a classical philosophical architecture" "would come first" (*P*5). And not only will Derrida do something like this again in "Time of a Thesis," but this forgetting informs the introduction and discussion of the "Introduction."

This is the second feature of Derrida's presentation of his work that should be highlighted. Derrida forgot *Speech* initially, spoke about it only after being reminded of it, and in turn, Derrida also brings up the "Introduction" on the fly, connecting it with *Speech* in a way that has much to say about the "Introduction's" relation to *Speech* and the 1967 works generally. The "Introduction" is introduced as follows. *Speech*, Derrida states, "can also be read as the other side (recto or verso, as you wish) of another essay, published in 1962, as the introduction to Husserl's *The Origin of Geometry*" (*P*5). The "Introduction" arises as a topic at all—and it is immediately after this that the remarks first quoted above come—as the other side of *Speech*, as "recto" to its "verso" (or vice versa), and in respect to the question now before us, as to whether Derrida asserts that a single context, a single framework, belongs to the "Introduction" and *Speech*, the "Introduction" and all the 1967 works, his comment is highly significant.

Derrida's remark indicates, after all, that he wishes in some fashion to distinguish these works, that he does recognize some difference between them, even as he goes on to assimilate the "Introduction" and *Speech* to one another. Two sides of one coin imply not only identification (the single coin), but also differentiation between the two sides. Yet this difference (and identity) here remain unclear. Derrida does not gloss his figure further in this interview; he says no more about the relation of these works in *Positions*, and no definitive conclusions, then, may be drawn about whether Derrida's thought develops or not on the basis of the interview in *Positions*.

Of course, the tenor of Derrida's own remarks, the tone of his comments on this occasion, have inclined readers to take these remarks as denying significant development altogether, and were it not for what Derrida says in "Time of a Thesis," even having raised these doubts, this view might well be convincing. This characteristic of downplaying whatever difference Derrida may recognize among his early writings, it should be noted, also will not be absent in "Time of a Thesis." In both works, Derrida does wish to minimize any discontinuity among his early works; he stresses those works' similarities. But whether Derrida is actually denying significant development, or simply providing a quick, foreshortened sketch of his works' total accomplishment even while recognizing that change does take place, becomes much more of a question in "Time of a Thesis."

Let me turn, then, to "Time of a Thesis" itself. Its more complex and detailed account will make clear that the problems and questions that *Positions* has begun to raise are real ones. Even "Time of a Thesis," however, we must be clear, will not unequivocally decide this matter. Final resolution, as I pointed out at the start of this chapter, will only come when I turn to Derrida's own writings, in particular the "Introduction," and examine these issues in their own right. Besides a confirmation of the fact that this problem is a problem—that whether Derrida does or does not deny development is a real question—what is wanted from "Time of a Thesis" is not a decision but a *criterion,* a measuring stick, by dint of which we ourselves can finally decide whether or not significant development takes place across these works.

No more than in *Positions,* then, does Derrida in "Time of a Thesis" unreservedly affirm the existence of significant shifts in his own thought. And indeed, at first glance "Time of a Thesis" may seem to swing even further in the opposite direction, away from development, than did the *Positions* interview, since in "Time of a Thesis" Derrida's account of the "Introduction" appears to recognize no difference at all between it and the later work, between the "Introduction" and *Speech* in particular.

Let me cite a long section from the paragraph in which Derrida starts to remark on the "Introduction." Here is the beginning of it:

> Following this first work [*Le problème*], my Introduction to the *Origin of Geometry* enabled me to approach something like the un-thought out axiomatics of Husserlian phenomenology, its principles of principles, that is to say its intuitionism, the absolute privilege of the living present, the lack of attention paid to the problem of its own phenomenological enunciation, to transcendental discourse itself, as Fink used to say, to the necessity of recourse, in transcendental or eidetic description, to a language that could not itself be submitted to the epoche—without itself being in the world—thus to a language which remained naïve, even though it was by virtue of this very language that all phenomenological bracketings and parentheses were made possible. This unthought axiomatics seemed to me to limit the scope of a consistent problematic of writing and the trace, even though the necessity of such a problematic had been marked out by the *Origin of Geometry* with a rigor no doubt unprecedented in the history of philosophy. ("TT" 39/"PTT" 445)

Here in "Time of a Thesis," unlike in *Positions,* Derrida comes to the "Introduction" by way of his earlier work, the 1954 *Le problème* ("following this first work"), and Derrida, to confine myself just to this first sentence, indeed the first part of the first sentence, introduces this 1962 work, the "Introduction," by referring to "an unthought axiomatics of Husserlian phenomenology," an unthought axiomatic which Derrida specifies in clauses that follow ("the privilege of the living present," etc.).

This passage is, to be sure, marked by the more turbulent side of Derrida's style, and it is thus necessary for us to approach slowly what Derrida is saying. The "Introduction" permitted Derrida to approach an "unthought axiomatic of Husserlian phenomenology" and Derrida will specify this axiomatic under three headings: (1) "intuitionism," (2) "the absolute privilege of the living present," and (3) themes related to the problem of "phenomenological enunciation," "transcendental discourse," and "language" more generally. This work, as so enumerated, appears very close to what Derrida will do in *Speech*, and Derrida's statements as they are initially encountered in the course of "Time of a Thesis" might thus seem to confirm the standard reading of the *Positions* interview, and to identify Derrida's accomplishments in the "Introduction" with those of his later work generally, indeed perhaps even more unequivocally than the earlier interview itself.

This is so much the case, however—there is such a total absence of daylight between the "Introduction" and *Speech*, as these remarks present the "Introduction"—that one can also wonder whether Derrida is not repeating a very different feature of the *Positions* interview: namely, whether he has not somehow forgotten *Speech* again as he appears to report on his earlier writings and his own intellectual itinerary. In "Time of a Thesis" Derrida, in fact, makes no explicit comments about *Speech* at all—despite having previously deemed it the work he "likes most"—apart from including it under "the triple publications of 1967" and that innovation "in reading, interpretation and writing" that I have already discussed.

Has *Speech* been forgotten again? One may ask this, especially since the topics Derrida invokes at this moment would indeed seem to apply far more immediately to *Speech* than they do to the "Introduction" itself. *Speech*'s declared goal, after all, is to set out precisely what could be called an "unthought axiomatics" of the sort Derrida here announces. From its introduction forward, as we have already seen, *Speech*'s explicit aim is to lay out a system of presuppositions, a "hold" at work on the entirety of phenomenology, which remains unknown and inaccessible to Husserl himself. *Speech* is to disclose a set of presuppositions which has phenomenology in its grasp, yet nothing like this is ever mentioned as the explicit aim of the "Introduction"; such an "unthought axiomatic" is nowhere in its foreground, and it would be surprising if it were, given that the "Introduction" is the introduction to Derrida's own translation of Husserl's *Origin*, still the standard one in French.

So, too, the topics Derrida enumerates under this heading, intuitionism and the privilege of the living present—and even language as the condition of the reduction—stand front and center in *Speech,* and do not have an equivalent status in the "Introduction." While all of these themes are in some way touched on in this work, the "Introduction's" central concerns obviously lie with Husserl's transcendental or intentional history, and its first half consists mainly of a defense of Husserl's highly challenging late approach to this topic. The privilege of the living present, in particular, due to Derrida's affirmation of Husserl's historical standpoint, is relied on in this early work far more than it is questioned, and the first two issues only emerge as problems very late in the "Introduction's" proceedings.[23]

Fortunately, however, far more support than simply these arguments is available for my suggestion that Derrida may ultimately not be giving here the kind of account of his own work that it at first may appear, that he may not be presenting his works in any genuinely diachronic fashion at all, nor, then, addressing his development in any real sense. Indeed, this support is provided by Derrida himself, by the wording of his own remarks. At the start of the paragraph which I have been discussing, Derrida does not say that the "Introduction" achieved all this, after all—that it accomplished this unthought axiomatic and so forth—but rather, he literally says that the "Introduction" "enabled" him (in the current English translation), it would have "permitted [him] *to approach* something like the unthought-out axiomatics of Husserlian phenomenology" ("m'avait permis d'approcher quelque chose comme l'axiomatique impensée" ["TT" 39; "PTT" 445; my emphasis]). Derrida himself never actually claims that the "Introduction" on its own simply arrived at this axiomatic, that the "Introduction" itself presented this "unthought" of all of Husserl's thought. Rather, Derrida says the "Introduction" let him *approach* all this: that the "Introduction," in a fashion yet to be specified, let Derrida draw near to the possibility of such work. And the implication, of course, is that Derrida genuinely arrived at what the "Introduction" let him approach, genuinely accomplished these outcomes, only subsequently, elsewhere, on another occasion.

Indeed, we find ourselves once more back in *Positions,* since the perspective of "recto" and "verso" may here again be at work, albeit now tacitly. Derrida's own discourse, his language and wording at this point in "Time of a Thesis," do not rule out the possibility that he is thinking of the "Introduction" and *Speech* together—*Speech,* never mentioned, having indeed perhaps been forgotten once more. In both this account and the one in *Positions,* Derrida would thus be taking the "Introduction" and *Speech* as parts of a single whole and presenting the "Introduction" itself in the light of what Derrida was later able to accomplish elsewhere thanks to its work. That is, Derrida may not be intending to offer an actual account in "real time" of the "Introduction" at all, of what he actually achieved there, but instead only a retrospective view, essentially teleological in character. Though Derrida's remarks tend initially to present themselves otherwise, the "Introduction" is perhaps being seen here in the light of all it later permitted (of what "it allowed" Derrida "to have approached")—thus entailing that what the "Introduction," taken singly, in actuality did or did not do may not be in question at all.

Of course, again, that this is not the way matters appear at first in either "Time of a Thesis" or *Positions* must be conceded; nor, let me be clear, am I insisting that either this passage or the other must necessarily be read in this way. My overall point, rather, is that Derrida's remarks in both "Time of a Thesis" and *Positions* are at the very least deeply ambiguous, radically equivocal. What is certain, if nothing else, is that what Derrida means to report about his own development in either of these texts is fundamentally obscure—whether he denies or affirms real development remains unknown—since whether Derrida means to report anything at all about his development in the first place in these passages remains unclear. Whether he aims to report on the history of his thought as it comes to find its footing, or whether he is only offering a retrospective sketch of his work, one that views the earliest writings along with those that follow in the light of his later achievements, teleologically, is not known; and thus whether Derrida in these remarks ultimately affirms or denies significant development across his early work cannot be answered by appealing to either text.

"Time of a Thesis" does, however, permit a step beyond this. Not only does it confirm that the question of Derrida's development remains far more open than many critics have recognized, and more open than *Positions* alone taken on its face would suggest; beyond this, perhaps equally important, "Time of a Thesis" provides a guidepost to a possible solution of this problem, a criterion for deciding this issue. Along with confirming that the status of Derrida's development as presented in his own occasional remarks is ambiguous, "Time of a Thesis" makes available a measuring stick for resolving this dispute, one for which there is clearly a need.

Let me turn to the end of the passage quoted, to the second sentence of Derrida's remarks in this paragraph, to make this plain. This sentence furnishes a continuation of Derrida's first remark; it provides closure to Derrida's thought, and in this closure lies a key clue to the guidelines we are seeking. Derrida began, as we have seen, by speaking of Husserl's "unthought axiomatics," and specifying this axiomatics further. In turn, in his next sentence Derrida links this theme to what he calls "a consistent problematic of writing and the trace." He connects this "unthought axiomatics" to the "problematic of writing and trace," and this linkage is key.

"This unthought axiomatics seemed to me to limit the scope of a consistent problematic of writing and the trace," Derrida states, "even though the necessity of such a problematic had been marked out by the *Origin of Geometry* with a rigor no doubt unprecedented in the history of philosophy." According to Derrida here, Husserl in his *Origin* went further than all other philosophers in giving writing its due. In his *Origin,* Husserl "marked out" the necessity for a problematic of writing "with a rigor no doubt unprecedented in the history of philosophy." Yet, due to this unthought axiomatic, Derrida continues, due to this unsuspected set of premises which holds all phenomenology in its grasp, Husserl himself could never think this problematic of writing and the trace consistently: "This unthought axiomatics seemed to me to limit the scope of a consistent problematic of writing and the trace."

The critical question, then, is this. Is the problematic of writing that Derrida sets out in the "Introduction" a *consistent* problematic in the sense that Derrida himself stipulates here: one that sketches an unthought axiomatic of Husserlian phenomenology, in order to decisively go beyond even Husserl's own "breakthrough" in respect to writing? This passage indeed establishes such an equivalence: thinking the unthought axiomatic of Husserlian phenomenology turns out to be necessary, according to Derrida, if a consistent problematic of writing and the trace is to be thought. Without thinking the unthought axiomatic of Husserlian phenomenology, it is impossible to arrive at a truly consistent problematic of writing, Derrida suggests.

And this, then, is the criterion, the guideline, that can be applied to Derrida's own work, to his 1962 "Introduction," in order to decide these issues. Were these conditions in fact fulfilled by Derrida in 1962? Did Derrida himself already think "this unthought axiomatic" of all phenomenology in the "Introduction" to a degree sufficient to set forth such a truly consistent problematic of writing? Did Derrida manage to think writing in a way decisively different from Husserl himself already in 1962?

Or did Derrida perhaps only begin to *approach* all these outcomes, as another possible reading of "Time of a Thesis" suggests? Did Derrida perhaps start to see in the "Introduction" that such a fully consistent problematic of writing was absent from Husserl, despite the pathbreaking character of Husserl's work—even though Derrida himself was still unable to frame this in any other terms? So too, in the "Introduction," did Derrida begin to see that something in Husserl's own thought held it back from complete radicality when it came to writing, and thus begin to discern that something like an unthought axiomatic was at work in Husserl of the sort that only Derrida's mature work would really be able to articulate?

In the "Introduction" Derrida may well have already begun to glimpse the terrain that he would subsequently cover. And while all of these would be significant, important discoveries, all would still necessitate the recognition of a good deal more development in Derrida's thought, a good deal more difference among his early works, than has so far been acknowledged, which of course remains the essential point here.

This alternative scenario may differ only in certain nuances from the one presented in Derrida's own remarks as these are usually understood. And clearly the matter would not be one of denying all continuity. Development implies continuity, as well as discontinuity—only in this way is the theme or problem brought forward as being "in development" conceivable. And these nuances, these slight differences, might well indicate authentic change, real development, continuity and discontinuity both, in respect to Derrida's relation to Husserl, as well as in respect to Derrida's conception of this key theme of writing. Finally, should such development have to be acknowledged, should Derrida's relation to Husserl and to writing undergo genuine alteration, this could also alter the way all Derrida's works are viewed, significantly transforming how the works of 1967, and *Speech and Phenomena* in particular, are seen, along the lines that the end of the first part of this chapter began to indicate.

Right now, however, this hypothesis must be tested, this criterion applied, to see firsthand whether significant differences do exist in the "Introduction," as well as potentially of what sort. Did Derrida already think a consistent problematic of writing and the trace in the "Introduction," or did he perhaps only take the initial step toward doing so? Did Derrida in the "Introduction" break with Husserl, depart from the terrain of Husserl's thinking in the way talk of an "unthought axiomatics" implies, or did Derrida himself remain—to a far greater extent than has been usually recognized—in the grip of this axiomatics, even as he was beginning, perhaps, to sense from the inside the form of this hold?

Derrida's 1962 Interpretation of Writing and Truth: Writing in the "Introduction" to Husserl's *Origin of Geometry*

I am about to turn to section 7 of the "Introduction" to Husserl's *Origin of Geometry,* in which Derrida discusses writing for the first time in his published corpus, in order to answer the question that has emerged as decisive for adjudicating whether Derrida's thought develops significantly: Is the problematic of writing in the "Introduction's" section 7 essentially the same as that in the 1967 works? Does Derrida, by dint of having recourse to "the unthought axiomatic of Husserl's thought" (as he puts it in "Time of a Thesis"), arrive at a truly consistent problematic of writing in the "Introduction," passing beyond that breakthrough in regard to writing that Husserl himself had already accomplished?

As we will see, these are quite thorny issues. Some of Derrida's best interpreters, including some leading phenomenologists, have believed the answer to be yes.[1] They have interpreted the "Introduction" as presenting an account of writing the same as that of the 1967 works in all essentials, perhaps in part because they were convinced that Derrida himself had already asserted this in his remarks examined in the last chapter.

In addition to this obscurity in Derrida's comments, however, the text of section 7 itself is remarkably dense—perhaps another reason commentators have been led to precipitous conclusions. Moreover, adding to the difficulties with following Derrida's argument in section 7 is that this section has so often been seen in isolation from the rest of the "Introduction." The "Introduction" itself has rarely been understood in its own right—what it accomplishes grasped on its own—and section 7 has been deprived of context, doubtless thanks to these same assumptions concerning Derrida's development that we have just brought forward.[2]

Derrida, however, was only a few years past thirty when the "Introduction" went to press, and he had published nothing else prior to it at the time. Even "Genesis and Structure," which we now know is essentially an abbreviated reworking of Derrida's 1954 *Le problème,* had not yet seen print (though "Genesis" had already been delivered as a conference paper in 1958—at a highly prestigious three-day gathering organized by Maurice de Gandillac, apparently one of Derrida's early mentors, and by Jean Piaget and Lucien Goldmann).

The "Introduction" was Derrida's first publication anywhere, and it indeed stands as the introduction to Derrida's own French translation of one of Husserl's very last writings, *Die Frage nach dem Ursprung der Geometrie als intentional-historisches Problem* (a title given to this fragment by Eugen Fink). Derrida's, in fact, remains the standard French translation of this work even today.

I would like first of all, before turning to section 7, to step back and take a brief look at the "Introduction" as a whole. I wish to specify the overall philosophical position Derrida took in this work, in order to better orient our discussion of section 7. Viewing the "Introduction" as a whole will also accomplish something else: it will let another theme important for all that follows, namely history, come forward. History, and issues related to it, are a further touchstone of Derrida's development. Two thematic threads—one related to language, the other to history—are ultimately crucial for discerning whether significant development takes place in Derrida's thought (and of what sort); and reviewing the work of the "Introduction" as a whole will introduce this second theme.

The main concern of Husserl's *Origin of Geometry,* after all, is history, not language; and this is ultimately true of the "Introduction" as well. The *Origin* comes at the close of what is widely considered to be the final phase of Husserl's thought, a phase that the Vienna and Prague lectures inaugurated, in which Husserl rather surprisingly turned to the theme of history. Apparently long allergic to historical considerations (a fact of which Derrida makes much in *Le problème*),[3] Husserl now extends his transcendental phenomenological researches into this area: he makes history a theme of transcendental inquiry, and he attempts to incorporate some kind of historical standpoint into his own work and to propound a philosophy of history.

The "Introduction," taken as a whole, has Husserl's late encounter with history as its topic; and in 1962 the "Introduction" represented a major intervention into this field and in phenomenological discourse generally, as this subject even today remains a vexed one, a difficult field of study relatively rarely attended to in the Husserl literature even at present.[4] Not only does Derrida's "Introduction" offer one of the few accounts treating this phase of Husserl's thought in depth, but it offers a defense of Husserl's late history program. The "Introduction" makes a sustained argument for the validity of Husserl's approach to history, though this has rarely been appreciated in retrospect. It takes Husserl's side at nearly every turn, and Derrida indeed broke with the prevailing wisdom at the time in order to do so.[5]

Let me unfold all this a little further, in order to gain the broader orientation being sought. The most rapid way to see where the "Introduction" stands in respect to Husserl's late treatment of history is to compare Derrida's stance with three major treatments of these same late writings that had appeared in France prior to the "Introduction's" publication, to all of which the "Introduction" refers. The "Introduction" explicitly sets itself against the interpretation that two renowned phenomenologists, Paul Ricoeur and Maurice Merleau-Ponty, offer of this phase of Husserl's thought, as well as that of Jean Cavaillès, a more idiosyncratic, eclectic, less well-known philosopher, whose influence on Derrida's very early work was nevertheless quite large (something also true of a number of Derrida's contemporaries, most notably Michel Foucault).[6]

Situating the "Introduction's" treatment of Husserl first in respect to Ricoeur's: Derrida refers positively to Ricoeur's essay "Husserl and the Sense of History" throughout the "Introduction" (*IOG* 29n8, 128n148), and this essay indeed remains one of the best introductions to this entire phase of Husserl's thought. Ricoeur's treatment had been deeply skeptical of at least one aspect of Husserl's late work, however: its capacity to measure up to what Ricoeur called "the historicity of history," the openness of all history to change and transformation (Ricoeur 1967, 170), and Derrida in the "Introduction" differs with Ricoeur on just this point.[7] One of the "Introduction's" main themes is the success of this very feature of Husserl's late work, of its thematization of historicity, and the rights of Husserl's historical apriori (*IOG* 63–64, 109–10, 118, 132).[8]

Derrida's differences with Merleau-Ponty are even more profound, with implications for all of Derrida's subsequent work, including deconstruction—though, as we shall see, the results of this critique and the one of Ricoeur ultimately dovetail. Merleau-Ponty viewed Husserl's late work largely as buttressing his own: as lending support to the modified form of phenomenological inquiry that he himself had come to forge, in which empiricist and essentialist claims, mundane and transcendental concerns, consorted together (Merleau-Ponty 1974, 273–74). Focusing on Husserl's 1932 letter to the anthropologist Lucien Lévy-Bruhl, Merleau-Ponty, in a series of essays to which Derrida refers in the "Introduction," had argued that Husserl's late work indicated a radical change of standpoint on Husserl's part—one that brought Husserl closer to Merleau-Ponty's own methodology (*IOG* 77n77; see also Merleau-Ponty 1964, 109–11).

In the "Introduction," however, Derrida violently rejects Merleau-

Ponty's interpretation of Husserl's late thought. Specifically, in section 8 of the "Introduction," Derrida explicitly defends Husserl's essentialism—the continuity of Husserl's understanding of the apriori, as well as its rights—over and against Merleau-Ponty's claim that Husserl eventually reconsidered its status in favor of a standpoint that would begin by acknowledging a certain "'relativism'" (Merleau-Ponty 1964, 108). So too, Derrida defends Husserl's ability to apply this apriori to history as such and to speak of a European Idea (*IOG* 111–17).[9]

Moreover, Derrida's critiques of Merleau-Ponty's and Ricoeur's positions ultimately dovetail. Derrida's most emphatic denial of Merleau-Ponty's position comes when he is arguing against Merleau-Ponty's suggestion that Husserl opened phenomenological research to historical factuality in his late thought: that Husserl had seen that "abstract phenomenology" had "to come into contact with the facts" (Merleau-Ponty 1974, 275). If Husserl's treatment omits anything, however, Derrida responds, it is just such historical factuality (*IOG* 116). What Husserl primarily elucidates instead is the historicity of history. Husserl's account of historicality, of the conditions that make history possible, not any factual history as such, is the single most powerful contribution made by his late thought—and Derrida thus ends up insisting on the same point upon which his difference from Ricoeur rests: the primacy of Husserl's treatment of historicity.

Derrida advocates Husserl's notion of historicity and even defends Husserl's philosophy of history in section 8, closing off a sequence that had begun in section 6 and in whose midst the section on writing, section 7, falls. The entire center of the "Introduction," in fact, from sections 2 through 9, including the discussions of language and writing, offers a staunch defense of Husserl's late work. Derrida defends the apriori that Husserl claims undergirds all history; he stands up for Husserl's historicity, and he even defends Husserl's philosophy of history, as well as Husserl's right to speak of history itself, earlier in the "Introduction."[10] The "Introduction" taken as a whole shows Derrida siding with Husserl's treatment of history and historicity, then, to a hitherto unprecedented degree, and shows him breaking with some of the most prominent interpreters of Husserl in France at the time to arrive at these positions.[11]

So siding with Husserl, Derrida moreover breaks with his own earlier interpretation of Husserl's work on history as well. Here Jean Cavaillès, and the third contemporaneous interpretation of Husserl's late thought, becomes relevant. In *Le problème* Derrida had already offered an interpretation of the *Origin of Geometry*—a matter which will be discussed further later in reference to Derrida's overall development. Now, however, what we need to see is that Derrida had drawn heavily on Cavaillès's criticism in

Le problème. Yet the "Introduction," rejecting Cavaillès's views, rejects Derrida's own earlier standpoint as well.[12]

Indeed, in the penultimate portion of *Le problème*'s final section, Derrida, having already deemed the *Origin of Geometry* one of Husserl's "most beautiful" works (*LPG* 260/*PG* 162), nevertheless follows Cavaillès in asserting that in it Husserl has recourse to empiricist and technicist concerns of doubtful validity. According to Cavaillès, in place of science's own genetic logic, Husserl had substituted extraneous prescientific considerations, neglecting a becoming internal to science as such (Cavaillès 1997, 80–81, 89). Derrida, in turn, in *Le problème* specifies Cavaillès's critique further: in the *Origin,* he argues, two different strands of Husserl's thought—an "empiricism," corresponding to Cavaillès's comments, and a certain "formalism"—come asunder. In the *Origin,* Derrida claims in 1954, an individual, empirical, pre-predicative intuition is artificially and unsuccessfully coordinated by Husserl with an overly static, rigidly idealistic version of (mathematical) truth. And for Derrida this disassociation is one of the final proofs of the incapacity of the entirety of phenomenology to think genesis authentically—the main theme of *Le problème.* It seals the failure of Husserlian phenomenology to come to grips with a genesis of the transcendental, as well as with a true transcendental genesis (*LPG* 266/*PG* 166).[13]

By the time of the "Introduction," then, *Le problème*'s criticisms have clearly ceased to be valid for Derrida, since the "Introduction" as a whole, in contrast with *Le problème,* asserts the fundamental validity of Husserl's project in the *Origin.* Indeed, in the closing sections of the "Introduction," where Derrida returns to these themes and traces out the movement of infinitization by which geometrical idealities are first brought to light, he now explicitly rejects Cavaillès's charge (and his own earlier one) of an illicit empiricism and formalism (*IOG* 133 ff.). Derrida, to be sure, also raises a new set of questions about the workings of Husserl's project at this juncture—specifically, about the evidence pertaining to this infinity—with important relation to Derrida's later thought (*IOG* 137–38). Yet, to an extraordinary degree, even these questions presuppose that Husserl is right: that Husserl's late work on history and his late philosophy of science are valid.[14] Derrida now affirms Husserl's account of the institution of mathematical, geometrical truth in a way decisively different than he had in *Le problème.* And near the end of the "Introduction," when Derrida asserts that the "absolute is passage," which has also been taken to anticipate his later thought, he makes this statement on the basis of an explicit rebuttal of Cavaillès and his critique of Husserl's late work ("why should we choose, as Cavaillès thought" [*IOG* 143]).[15]

A decisive shift in Derrida's own position in respect to Husserl's work on history has taken place in the "Introduction," then, in tandem with the "Introduction's" departure from the evaluations of Husserl's project that were common at the time—and these themes of history and historicity thus turn out to be much more of a wild card than has so far been recognized.[16] Derrida's treatment of writing in the "Introduction's" section 7 must be seen in this larger context, which will prove to be absolutely decisive as we proceed. Having gotten a first orienting glimpse of the work of the "Introduction" on its own terms, then, let me turn to section 7 of the "Introduction" and Derrida's discussion of writing there.

* * *

The narrower questions now before us—the status of writing itself and the related one of Derrida's development between 1962 and 1967—still remain undecided. Derrida's thought may undergo real change in respect to history between 1954 and 1962; however, this does not establish the fate of writing between 1962 and 1967. And while grounds may have arisen for believing some change takes place across Derrida's early works, what the status of writing truly is in section 7, what Derrida actually says about it there, and how this relates to his mature thought still need to be set out.

Writing is discussed exclusively in the "Introduction" in section 7; indeed, it appears as a theme there for the first time in all Derrida's published writings—and Derrida never speaks about it again in the "Introduction," including, importantly, in the final sections of this work.[17] The identification that commentators have made between Derrida's stance in the "Introduction" and in his later works rests on section 7, then, and in particular, stems from the opening lines of the section.

Derrida starts section 7 by declaring: "A decisive step remains to be taken" (IOG 87), and he subsequently invokes the "possibility of writing" as this next step, as what moves Husserl's discussion onward at this point. "The possibility of writing," Derrida continues at the start of his next paragraph, "will assure the absolute traditionalization of the object, its absolute ideal objectivity" (LOG 83/IOG 87).

"Absolute ideal objectivity" in a Husserlian context is another name for truth, for absolute theoretical or scientific truth, and most readers, on the basis of section 7's opening, have thus taken Derrida to be claiming that writing conditions truth: that truth's mode of being depends on writing for its own possibility.[18] So, too, critics have affirmed that no really deep development occurs between the "Introduction" and the 1967 texts on these grounds, insofar as writing plays this role as the condition not only of knowledge, but of *truth itself*, both here and afterward. At the crux of all Derrida's 1967 deconstructions lies the dependence of truth on writing that has just come forward at the start of section 7, it is believed—an unlikely correlation of truth and writing which indeed opens the door to the advent of a new era of the *gramme,* of the program, the grapheme, and so forth, as well as the deconstruction of all the values with which knowledge and thought are traditionally associated in the "West."

Here, however, the larger context in which Derrida's remarks are made—the overall argument of the "Introduction" that has already begun to be restored—proves crucial. One major impediment to understanding what precisely Derrida is saying at this moment (a second will be brought forward later) has been that section 7 begins in medias res. The majority of commentators have overlooked this; they have failed to realize that Derrida's claims about writing emerge in the aftermath of section 6's discussion, not of writing, but of *language* (a development that began in section 5), and readers have perhaps wrongly assimilated Derrida's remarks here to his later work as a consequence.[19]

Let me begin by restoring this context, then, in order to make clear what this "decisive step," this recourse to writing at the outset of section 7, represents, and thus start to arrive at a definitive answer to the question of whether a consistent problematic of writing and the trace, the same as in the 1967 works, is already to be found in the "Introduction." At the outset of section 6, Derrida had already spoken of a "surprising" "turnabout" on the part of Husserl prior to this "decisive step" taken at the start of section 7. This "turnabout" at the beginning of section 6 pertains to the role of language, rather than simply writing: it concerns how "ideality . . . comes to objectivity" now "'by means of language'" (*IOG* 76).

At the outset of section 6, then, Derrida had already made a connection between truth and language; yet this is also, it must be noted, where that polemic with Merleau-Ponty to which I have already referred gets under way. Accordingly, a set of stipulations will soon be introduced in regard to language that will also apply to writing—stipulations that get ignored when the opening of section 7 is taken in isolation.

Derrida, more specifically—introducing this connection between language and truth, and aware to what extent such a claim might appear to be at odds with much else in Husserl's thought—asks whether Husserl is not here coming "back to language, culture and history, all of which he reduced in order to have the pure possibility of truth emerge," and whether Husserl will thus "not be compelled to remove all the reductions" and "to recover finally the *real* text of historical experience" (*IOG* 76; his emphasis).

At the outset of section 6, faced with the argument Husserl seems to be making that truth depends on language, on linguistic incarnation, even before it is said to depend on inscription as such, Derrida wonders if this does not tie Husserl's thought to *empirical culture and language,* forcing

Husserl to succumb to a historicism that he has always denied—whether, as Derrida puts it on the next page, this recourse to language does not "revolutioniz[e] Husserl's thought," and "contradict a previous philosophy of language," thus, in fact, bringing it more in line with that view of phenomenology held by Merleau-Ponty already canvassed above; for that a revolutionary turn had been taken by Husserl at this moment was indeed Merleau-Ponty's claim (*IOG* 77; compare Merleau-Ponty 1964, 84–85).

Not only, however, does Derrida deny flat out that this is the case— "Husserl does exactly the opposite"—but he argues that a set of stipulations must be seen in place at this moment in respect to language *that keep Husserl's thought from coming into contradiction with itself,* preserving it from just the sort of revolutionary consequences Merleau-Ponty envisioned— stipulations that keep Husserl from having to lift the eidetic and transcendental reductions above all else. Only "a juridical and transcendental dependence" of truth on language is at issue at this moment, Derrida accordingly declares; only the "*pure* possibility of an information in a *pure* language" is envisioned by Husserl, not any "particular and factical linguistic hold" nor "a subject speaking a determined language and belonging to a determined cultural community" (*LOG* 70/*IOG* 76–77; my emphases).

Language, then, insofar as it contributes to truth, is envisioned only as a "pure possibility." Only a "juridical and transcendental dependence" on language is at issue in Husserl's work, Derrida insists. And these same stipulations, it is worth noting in anticipation, also apply to writing. Language and writing, insofar as they have any hand in truth, will both be viewed exclusively from within the parameters of Husserl's transcendental project, in consonance with the optics of Husserl's own phenomenology, at no point violating Husserl's transcendental, phenomenological, or eidetic reductions. Derrida himself, in fact, explicitly has recourse to the term "transcendental language" at this moment in section 6 in recognition of this: he explains that he uses the term not only to indicate that language has a "constitutive role" in "ideal objectivity," but also because language as it is in question here "is not to be confused in its pure possibility with any empirical language of fact" (*LOG* 71n1/*IOG* 77n76).[20]

To my leading question—does Derrida arrive at a thought of writing and the trace decisively beyond Husserl's in the "Introduction"; does Derrida bring forward an unthought axiomatic of Husserl's thought, and fashion a view of language and writing already more consistent, more radical, than Husserl's, which can be identified with that in his 1967 works?—the answer at this moment seems to be no. Though still at a provisional phase, if what has proven true about language indeed proves true about writing, if both these themes in the "Introduction" are treated within Husserl's framework, according to these transcendental-phenomenological stipulations, a decisive difference between the conception of language (and writing) here and in Derrida's subsequent work would have to be affirmed.

This is not to say, let me be clear, that in the "Introduction" Derrida is not impressed by this turn Husserl's thought has taken. Already here in section 6 Derrida declares that "speech [*parole*]" has been shown by Husserl in the *Origin* to "constitute[s] the object," and he is clearly intrigued by the possibility that "a transcendental language" would be "constituting in respect to ideal objectivity" (*IOG* 77/*LOG* 70). Transcendental discourse no longer merely expresses an object or truth already there, which Derrida indeed believes is a breakthrough; and Derrida even says that this transcendental role of language may indicate that the "transcendental" itself needs to be "rethought." Yet my present concern remains whether Derrida himself goes decisively beyond Husserl on these points. Derrida always maintained that Husserl's own standpoint represented a breakthrough, indeed had the status of an "absolute novelty" with respect to the tradition (*VP* 91/*SP* 81), and the question, then, is whether Derrida himself decisively and definitively goes beyond Husserl in respect to writing and language anywhere in the "Introduction."

Derrida's rejection of Merleau-Ponty thus begins to look crucial. Husserl's enterprise, phenomenology, even at the last would never be revolutionized by a language whose functioning and status we otherwise know, or whose provenance would break with the underlying tenets of Husserl's thought, as Merleau-Ponty had indeed suggested. Thanks to the stipulations Derrida brings forward, language, once again, is "transcendental language." "Pure" and "juridical," its empirical factuality is not at all in question, and should these same stipulations genuinely apply to writing here, significant development would indeed take place between 1962 and 1967: important change would occur and the appearance of continuity with the later works would be just that, an appearance.[21]

Let me make my way back to section 7 to confirm that this is so, that these same stipulations apply; and in so doing, let me get a still clearer view of the actual argument that Derrida is engaged in making in these sections of the "Introduction." Not just Derrida's statements, or even Husserl's, but the things themselves, the matters at hand, make it evident that only language and writing understood from Husserl's standpoint, seen from within the brackets, from within a transcendental-phenomenological perspective, can perform the functions assigned to them here. Thus, to identify language (or writing) in a transcendental context with these in any other sense—as factical, historical, real empirical language, as a linguistics or any other philosophy of language might treat it—is simply not possible.[22]

To grasp the broader analysis in which Derrida is engaged at this moment, it is necessary to refer back to the role of history and historicity more generally in Husserl's late thought. Derrida affirms from the start of the "Introduction" that in the *Origin of Geometry* Husserl had found a way to speak of an "essential history," a history of essences and of the apriori: an "intrinsic becoming," not just of knowledge, but of the *objects* knowledge knows (*IOG* 47). The truths of mathematics, for example, which Husserl believed were a priori from very early on, are thought to refer to a history all their own. This history is of a very special sort, however, since it by no means cancels the a priori rights of geometry, but rather presupposes these—and indeed these "historical" analyses themselves are supposed to have an "essential" or "a priori" force.[23]

What is in question, then, in the *Origin* is a new form of essential (and transcendental) knowledge *of the essential* that can also be said to be *historical;* and that feels no need to decide between the two. And to the extent that history in some sense nevertheless remains in question here, it becomes meaningful in Husserl's late thought to speak, in particular, of a moment when truth comes to be founded, inaugurated—to be instituted *for the first time* (*IOG* 48). A *transcendental inauguration* or *production* of essences, a transcendental historical constitution of essences, at this phase of Husserl's work now becomes thinkable—one entailing an ideal first time, an incipient moment of their appearance—though this production itself is always guided by an anticipatory insight into a truth also "already there," and cannot be performed arbitrarily (*IOG* 135).[24]

In section 6, then, where we have already joined Derrida, he is in the course of tracing out ever-widening circles of *transcendental subjective* conditions that must be in place, if the type of objectivity appropriate to this sort of essential, omnitemporal or eternal, truth can register as such. The Pythagorean theorem, for example, along with the objects that this theorem concerns (the triangles of geometry), are instances of "absolute ideal objectivity": they are truths, objects of knowledge that in themselves never change. Nevertheless, a community of transcendental inquirers must stand over against them, as well as a correlative set of transcendental subjective conditions without which these objects could otherwise not register or *appear* as these objects and truths at all.

And in section 6 Derrida has begun to elaborate these conditions. Assuming the reductions are in place, and that the essences pertaining to geometry have already been produced,[25] section 6 starts out by arguing, more specifically, not only that there must have been a first protogeometer, a protogeometrical consciousness, able to generate these ideal formations and return to them within his or her own ongoing intentionality as the same, but that the pure possibility of a pure language must also have been available at the moment of geometry's inception, permitting this protogeometrical insight to find its way into concepts, to be given logical expression in *Bedeutungen,* themselves ideal—thus stabilizing this originating insight and allowing it to be expressed and repeated among a wider community of inquirers. All objectivity, Husserl has come to believe, all truth, from the moment of its apprehension, implies a potential community of transcendental subjects for whom it is also valid; and thus the objectivity of absolute ideality demands as a transcendental subjective correlate what Derrida will call at the outset of section 7 *langage oral,* an "oral language," ensuring the availability of the originating insight of the protogeometer to an implicit transcendental intersubjectivity (*LOG* 84/*IOG* 87).[26]

Something more is needed on a transcendental plane, however, for this type of eternal validity to register and function as such, and here we rejoin Derrida's discussion of writing at the start of section 7. This initial insight of the protogeometer must be able in principle to go beyond not just the protogeometer, but any finite community of transcendental subjects: it must be able to circulate without bounds, to undergo an infinite transcendental transmission, if the style of objectivity appropriate to it, absolute validity, is to be fully meaningful. This is writing's role: transcendental writing's transcendental role. There must in principle be something like a total transcendental availability of this founding insight, a potential for it to circulate across an unbounded, even infinite, range of transcendental subjects—corresponding to this objectivity's omnitemporality or eternity—thus permitting the sense of this insight's truth *as* valid at all times and places to be registered. This is the "decisive step" that writing alone makes possible in the form it is here conceived, the step to which we have already seen Derrida refer at the outset of section 7. Precisely because what is in question is absolute ideal objectivity—truths whose validity is supposed to extend beyond any given time or place, any single community of interpreters or any given world—a medium must be available correlative to this power, one which the transcendental possibility of not just language, but specifically writing alone can provide.

Writing's function at the start of section 7, then, is to ensure an infinite transcendental availability of that insight founding or inaugurating the absolute, ideal, essential truths of geometry, and this is why those same stipulations that we have already seen apply to language necessarily apply to writing as well. Only as pure and juridical *can* writing play this role in the constitution of truth; and Derrida himself, accordingly, brings forward in section 7 the very same stipulations that we have already encountered in section 6, now in respect to writing, some six paragraphs into his discussion—a fact which seems to have provoked a good deal of misunderstanding. Nevertheless, Derrida explicitly declares at this moment that these stipulations apply to his entire *preceding* discussion in section 7. Derrida himself clearly states that these same stipulations which he earlier brought forth in respect to language have also been presupposed all along in respect to writing as well. "But, all this," Derrida asserts at the beginning of the sixth paragraph of section 7, referring to the analysis of writing that has come before, "*only can be said* [*tout cela ne peut se dire qu'*] on the basis of an intentional analysis which retains from writing nothing but writing's pure relation to a consciousness which grounds it as such, and not its factuality, which, left to itself, is totally insignificant" (my emphasis). And he states in this same paragraph: "If there is no purely juridical possibility of it [the written text] being intelligible for a transcendental subject in general, then there is no more in the vacuity of its soul than a chaotic literalness or the sensible opacity of a defunct designation, a designation deprived of its transcendental function" (*LOG* 85/*IOG* 88).[27]

Derrida himself affirms that the same terms, the same transcendental-phenomenological stipulations that governed language, must also govern writing. Writing, again, is being considered only as a pure possibility—and only so understood, in "*pure* relation to a consciousness which grounds it" ("pure" meaning without reference to what factually exists), and within the purview of Husserl's *transcendental* subjectivity ("as intelligible for a transcendental subject in general"), does it perform transcendental labor, or take on a transcendental role. Writing is deprived of all transcendental status otherwise, Derrida avows; writing is but "a sensible opacity," "a defunct designation," "a chaotic literalness," when seen in terms other than Husserl's, and as such, as fact, it is "totality insignificant." Factual writing, writing in any actual language (in French, or German, etc.), is not at all in question here, Derrida makes plain, and only writing seen exclusively from a transcendental-phenomenological angle, everywhere subordinated to Husserl's transcendental-phenomenological optics, has any role to play in section 7's account of truth, just as was the case for language in section 6.[28]

Significant change thus does take place, it can be affirmed, between the "Introduction" and Derrida's 1967 works, since clearly none of these stipulations remain in Derrida's better known writings. Derrida in 1962 hews rigorously to Husserl's own framework, he concedes all of Husserl's distinctions, he is in accord with Husserl's own axiomatic (whether thought or unthought)—and thus major development will take place hereafter: the "Introduction's" "problematic of writing" itself having to be deemed "inconsistent," if Derrida's own later criteria were to be applied.

Fundamental differences thus exist between Derrida's approach to writing (and language) in the "Introduction" and in his 1967 texts, with enormous consequences for how all of Derrida's early thought is to be construed. Moreover, the common assimilation of Derrida's stance in the "Introduction" to that in the 1967 writings makes it impossible to grasp the very insight that led Derrida to focus on writing so extensively later on. Only if Husserl's stipulations are in place, and recognized as such, *can* the absolutely novel specificity of writing as a medium be identified as this initially showed itself to Derrida thanks to Husserl's own breakthrough. If writing here is assimilated with writing in 1967, the advances *Husserl* made in respect to writing and language are impossible to grasp, the breakthrough with which Derrida always credited Husserl and which spurred Derrida's own later work itself becomes wholly obscured.

The power of *langage graphique,* "graphic language," as opposed to "oral language" (for the issue will never be whether such-and-such an utterance happens to be written down, but of inscription as a possibility of the totality of a language—whether *any* utterance *can* be written down), we can now see, turns out to be this extension of the availability of meaning to "infinity." The power Derrida ever after imputes to the written medium is the ability to carry truth and meaning out beyond any finite community, any finite sphere. Yet just this power of writing, which Derrida will indeed come to identify with that of an infinite repeatability or iterability, could never emerge were the validity of these ideal objects and this apriori also not able to be affirmed. Were Husserl's framework not in place, there would be no eternal, supratemporal, omnitemporal truths at all, only finite communities, empirical formations, limited beliefs—and the infinitizing capacity that Derrida assigns to writing henceforth could never have even initially appeared.

Writing, then, only shows its power as a medium, as a unique dimension of language with powers distinct from any other in the closest proximity to truth—a moment that assumes the validity of Husserl's essential historical-intentional analysis and which would lose all legitimacy if Husserl's claims to this sort of knowledge were canceled. This is not to deny, let me be clear, that Derrida subsequently finds aspects of Husserl's own treatment problematic, or even to deny that Derrida already does so here: already in the "Introduction" Derrida starts to raise questions about writing and its functioning that seem never to have bothered Husserl. To say that Derrida in section 7 of the "Introduction" was not already intrigued and fascinated by the possibility that Husserl's text here exposes—that Derrida did not even somehow start to see beyond the limits of Husserl's own thought, or suspect that there were such limits—would be wrong, even if one must affirm that significant development does indeed occur. Derrida does raise questions about Husserl's account of writing, he does raise concerns about Husserl's stipulation even in section 7, as he first takes heed of Husserl's own insight—and these tentative steps of Derrida's have indeed caused problems for commentators attempting to come to grips with his stance in 1962.

Yet these questions that Derrida raises in 1962, as I am about to show, are far different from those he will raise in 1967. As should already be plain, they proceed on a very different footing, and, for this reason, this first attempt on Derrida's part to question Husserl in the second half of the "Introduction's" section 7 in fact goes awry. Derrida *does* attempt to go beyond Husserl in section 7, to pose questions in opposition to Husserl's own philosophical tendencies; yet, as we are about to see, Derrida continues to proceed on the basis of Husserl's own thought; he draws even further on Husserl's own conceptuality at the moment that he wishes to initiate this questioning—with the result that Derrida's steps in this direction falter, lending a tentative, even unstable quality to much of Derrida's own discussion at this moment.

This is the significance that section 7 of the "Introduction" has from the perspective of Derrida's development taken as a whole. In 1962 Derrida recognized Husserl's breakthrough, Husserl's insight in respect to writing, and even started to see beyond this; to glimpse what he later comes to believe is an "inconsistency" in Husserl's own thought. Yet, as we shall see, Derrida encountered irresoluble difficulties in trying to go beyond Husserl's own insight in section 7, and just this impasse, in fact, will prove to be that unique problem that we have been seeking all along: that unparalleled motivating instance that prompted Derrida to "invent" deconstruction in the first place, that led him to devise his own singular way of working—his new device for "reading, writing, and interpretation"—and which alone may supply its intra-philosophical credentials.

* * *

So Derrida does already wonder in the 1962 writings about the implications of the novel role of writing in Husserl (in part due to the earlier work Derrida had already done on Husserl).[29] He wonders if writing's role does not point beyond Husserl's own treatment and even beyond phenomenology as a whole, and this has indeed been the second large-scale impediment to an accurate understanding of Derrida's intentions in all of section 7, an impediment with which the remainder of this chapter will be occupied. What I call the last "half" of section 7, the last fifteen of the twenty pages that comprise it, is devoted to a kind of thought experiment concerning the implications of this new role of writing for the rest of Husserl's thought, and for Husserl's treatment of history in particular. This discussion culminates in the now-famous comparison between Husserl and Joyce. It starts from the premise that the role assigned to writing by Husserl would indeed somehow lead, against Husserl's own express intentions, to "truth's disappearance" and to "empiricism and nonphilosophy" (*IOG* 92–93); and the existence of this long sequence has misled readers as to what goes on in section 7.[30]

Derrida at this moment in section 7, embarking on its second half, here appears to give voice to that linguistic or scriptural relativism that most readers already expect to find. And not only has this spurred commentators to ignore the large differences in the way writing is thematized—in the presuppositions of Derrida's discussion of writing at this moment and in the rest of section 7—but it has also encouraged them to believe that Derrida arrives at essentially the same results here in the "Introduction" as in 1967: that the hypotheses he pursues in the remainder of section 7, moving in a direction contrary to Husserl's intentions, are in effect already equivalent to the deconstruction that the 1967 work undertakes.

This is far from being the case, however, and establishing this will show yet more clearly to what extent Derrida's thought about writing develops and what directions this takes. To explore this more closely, at the conclusion of the first portion of section 7, of its first five pages devoted to specifying writing's transcendental role (pages in which numerous other indications are to be found of the distance between Derrida's treatment of writing here and in 1967, most notably the role of the book), Derrida is preparing to turn to the hypothesis of truth's disappearance, of which much has often been made in earlier interpretations of this work. He concludes this phase of his discussion by stipulating that Husserl's argumentation permits two distinct ways of viewing writing and language. And while the core of a good deal of the confusion about Derrida's intentions lies in this statement, since many commentators have believed these two versions of language rather unproblematically may be seen as one,[31] Derrida here is careful to specify that these two versions of language (and writing) are to be taken as coordinated *temporally* across the "moment" of the transcendental inauguration of truth, the transcendental historical constitution of absolute ideality.

Elucidating in what way writing should be seen as "admitting and completing the ambiguity of all language," Derrida declares:

> Movement of essential and constituting incorporability, it [writing] is also the place of factical and contingent incorporation for every absolutely ideal object, that is to say for truth; this [truth], inversely, has its origin in a pure right to speech and to writing [*un droit pur à la parole et à l'écriture*], but once constituted, it [truth] conditions, in turn, the expression as an empirical fact. It depends on the pure possibility of speaking and of writing, but it is independent of the spoken and the

written insofar as they are in the world. (*LOG* 90/*IOG* 92; translation
altered)

At this moment, then, at the end of section 7's first half, Derrida clearly
continues to honor Husserl's distinctions. Writing and language, at the
moment of truth's inauguration, stand on one side, the constituting side.
Still understood as pure possibilities, as a pure right to speech and writing, they alone permit absolute ideality at the moment of its appearance
to find its proper transcendental objectivity and, in principle, to be at the
disposal of an infinite community of transcendental interpreters. In turn,
however, Derrida goes on to say, "once this comes to pass [*une fois constituée*]," "once truth has been so constituted," it supersedes all of its actual
expressions, everything actually "spoken and written [*du dit et de l'écrit*],"
and conditions them all as finite and worldly, in turn, everywhere announcing its own principled independence.

Derrida continues to maintain in all rigor, then, Husserl's distinctions between the juridical and the factical, the transcendental and the
worldly, in respect to writing, language, and speech.[32] Moreover, Derrida
only now makes a *further* argument to bring these two together—and on
this basis, and only on this basis, will he introduce the key notion of a disappearance of truth at writing's hands. This is the critical thing for us at
this juncture. Derrida, having begun from this divide that falls straight out
of Husserl's own analysis and program—a divide between constituting
and constituted language and writing nowhere visible in Derrida's 1967
works—only now seeks to find a way to bridge this gap, to bring these two
views of writing together and to consider whether writing, globally conceived, has implications that ultimately run against the grain of Husserl's
own program.

On what basis does Derrida join these two versions of language and
writing together at this moment? Thanks to what concept will Derrida
attempt to think a more comprehensive notion of writing than Husserl
himself in 1962, and bring Husserl's thought into question from one direction? None other than *Husserl's own interpretation of the sign:* Husserl's
discussion of what Derrida calls the "'sign expression,'" Husserl's definition of the expression as *bedeutsam Zeichen*, as a "significant sign," at the
start of *Logical Investigations* II (*LOG* 90n3/*IOG* 92n96). Husserl's own understanding of the sign, at this key juncture, is to bridge the gap between
constituting and constituted writing and language, and on its basis, Derrida argues for an *ongoing* connection between the sensible spatiotemporality of factical, empirical writing and its pure possibility, even *after* the
inauguration of absolute ideal objectivity.

Derrida begins the following paragraph by bringing in the notion of the sign (the first place this notion is explicitly mentioned in section 7), and by footnoting Husserl's own discussion in *Logical Investigations* II: "*From then on* as is prescribed to it, sense is received into a *sign*, this becomes the mundane and exposed residence of an unthought truth," Derrida declares (*LOG* 90–91/*IOG* 92; my emphasis). Only now, by dint of this recourse to signification, will the truths that the pure possibilities of writing and language are supposed to vehiculate be claimed to be caught up decisively in factual worldliness and said to come into danger. More specifically, a little later on in this same paragraph, referring to the notion of the sign and the worldly sensible spatiotemporality that Derrida has just said this notion entails, he states: "Since, in order to escape mundaneity, sense *must* from the first *be able* to be gathered back into the world and lodged in sensible spatiotemporality, it is necessary to put in peril its pure intentional ideality, that is to say its sense of truth." And, Derrida concludes, "one thus sees" emerge "a possibility which here only accords with empiricism and nonphilosophy: the disappearance of truth" (*LOG* 91/*IOG* 92–93).

Thanks to Husserl's own notion of the sign, Derrida argues that the possibility of a *pure* writing and language rests on a principled possibility of *worldly* signification—and only now, on this basis, will Derrida postulate a disappearance of truth at the hands of writing. Language and inscription function successfully at the moment of truth's inauguration as pure possibilities; these pure possibilities, however, conceal a further reference to a worldly system of signification, to sensible spatiotemporal signs— "sense *must be able* to be received in the world" and appear in a "sensible spatiotemporality"—now raising the possibility that their "sense of truth," or "truth sense [*sens de vérité*]" itself be "put in peril" (*LOG* 91/*IOG* 92).

In section 7 of the "Introduction," then, the sign is indeed the bridge between constituting and constituted writing and language; the sign is the bond between the "essential and constituting incorporability" of the "pure right to speech and writing," on the one hand, and the sensible spatiotemporality of "the written and the spoken," on the other. Accordingly, it should come as no surprise, not in retrospect at least, that Derrida's argument will encounter significant difficulties from this point going forward—as I will shortly confirm—nor that he will eventually turn to just this theme, Husserl's treatment of the sign, when he revisits Husserl's thought some five years later.

Derrida has heretofore consistently maintained Husserl's distinctions—in both sections 6 and 7—and only attempted to question or lift them at this moment. But this attempt henceforth will not succeed, and cannot do so on these terms. Truth will never disappear or even be seriously threatened along the lines that Derrida has just laid out. Though

Derrida's own presentation in section 7 is a tortuous one—and there are good reasons that commentators have gotten lost in its twists and turns— the factical worldly body of the sign turns out to have no effect whatsoever on the sense of truth and on the pure juridical possibility of language and writing that incorporates it. Thus, not only will Husserl's framework finally be affirmed by Derrida himself once more here in 1962; but this is indeed why in 1967 Derrida subsequently elucidates not a new *theory* of writing and language, but undertakes their *deconstruction:* a deconstruction of the totality of the conceptuality through which writing and language have always been approached (at least in Derrida's eyes), including in the work of Husserl.

Derrida, it should already be clear, has by no means just embarked on the deconstruction of writing or the sign in a way identifiable with his later thought, whatever else may be coming to pass at this moment in the "Introduction's" section 7. Rather, Derrida has turned to Husserl's own notion of the sign itself for whatever sort of undoing or question of truth at writing's hands is supposed to come about, in order to call into question Husserl's own distinctions between constituting and constituted writing and language. This is why Derrida's effort here falters; and it in part accounts for why in 1967 Derrida begins from the conviction that a certain "metaphysics" has hold of Husserl's thought, and why Derrida focuses on just this same Husserlian definition of the sign at the start of *Speech* in order to elaborate this "hold" (*SP* 16). In 1967, having devised a new way of working soon to be known as deconstruction, Derrida starts from just this notion of the sign and asserts that metaphysics and its legacy have hold of the totality of Husserl's (language-related) conceptuality—a presupposition whose underlying motivation (long opaque to some) clearly stems from Derrida's experience earlier here: from Derrida's reliance on Husserl's notion of the sign in 1962 and Derrida's failure to get decisively beyond Husserl's own framework in the "Introduction's" section 7 on its terms.

* * *

Let me next establish that these claims are correct: that in the remainder of section 7, Derrida, on the basis just set out, will never be able to impugn the transcendental function of writing—never be able to really question constitutive writing and its truth-sense thanks to the embodied worldly sign; and that Derrida will in fact be forced to affirm just the opposite: that the empirical factical body of the written sign can have no effect whatsoever on writing's pure juridical functioning and thus all of Husserl's transcendental history of truth.

Derrida dedicates the remainder of section 7 to exploring the possibility of "truth's disappearance" and to that of an "empiricism and nonphilosophy" that has just come forward, supposedly contrary to Husserl's own thought. In section 7, more specifically, Derrida goes on to explore these possibilities counter to phenomenology according to three different scenarios, which Derrida explicitly enumerates. These three scenarios arise dialectically from one another in section 7's second half; each scenario of truth's disappearance emerges through the rejection of the prior one, and this alone should have made clear to readers that Derrida's initial claim is far more vexed than has been suspected, since of the three, only the third hypothesis has even a chance of being right, given how Derrida's argument is structured.[33]

A further twist has made Derrida's conclusions in the second portion of section 7 even more difficult to grasp, however: the second scenario turns out to entertain a hypothesis identical to that which launches the entire sequence. Showing this can indeed confirm that Derrida backpedals: having envisioned a disappearance of truth at the hands of a worldly, empirical writing—a peril coming to truth from the sensible, spatiotemporal sign—Derrida must deny that such a possibility is significant even before proceeding to scenario three, the only one that has any chance of working out. This development, understandably, has led to much confusion in the literature, which is another reason to focus on it here. Just because scenario two contemplates those very terms on which this whole sequence arose, and because this scenario states what most readers have expected to hear in any case, what Derrida has to say about this second scenario, his unequivocal rejection of it, so decisive for the interpretation of the second half of section 7, has almost always been denied.

Let me, then, explore scenario two in more detail in order to confirm that Derrida *rejects* the possible disappearance of truth at the hands of mundane inscription, thanks to the worldly, sensibly spatiotemporal body of the sign. Having summarily dismissed scenario one, having dismissed the disappearance of truth within the individual intending ego— "once sense appeared in egological consciousness, its total annihilation becomes impossible" (*IOG* 93)—Derrida moves on to this second scenario, which is thus no longer egological, but "historical." "The graphic sign," Derrida begins, "pledge [*caution*] of objectivity, can also be utterly destroyed *in fact*. This peril is inherent in the factical worldliness of inscription itself, and nothing can preserve it [inscription] from it [destruction] definitively" (*LOG* 92/*IOG* 94; his emphasis).

The disappearance of truth at writing's hand in scenario two proceeds, then, according to the same premise which launches this entire sequence. Derrida again invokes worldly sensible spatiotemporality, the "factical worldliness of inscription," and the destruction to which it is open, which Derrida here claims cannot be "avoided definitively." Even today, most readers think Derrida (not to mention Husserl) affirms truth's disappearance on just these terms. A wide variety of Derrida's readers affirm that *truth* (not just human knowledge) really is threatened through the worldly destruction of writing's signs, thanks to the perils to which writing's worldly materiality exposes it.[34]

Derrida, however, explicitly *rejects* this hypothesis according to which writing makes truth itself disappear—the hypothesis which Derrida himself has just formulated and the one most commonly believed today—in terms that leave absolutely no room for doubt. The "destruction of the 'archive'" is the phrase sometimes used to refer to such a possibility, and Derrida himself gives voice to such a scenario, imagining "a worldwide conflagration of libraries" near the beginning of scenario two (*IOG* 94). Yet Derrida rejects the claim that this possibility has any significance for truth itself, unequivocally and without reserve, first of all in Husserl's name. "The hypothesis of such a factual destruction does not interest Husserl at all," Derrida begins his next paragraph. "While completely recognizing the terrifying reality of the current risk, Husserl would deny it any . . . philosophical significance" (*IOG* 94).

Such a denial holds good for Derrida himself as well, however, as the remainder of scenario two's discussion makes clear. Indeed, the bulk of this scenario is devoted to a thought experiment conducted "analogously to the famous analysis of section 49 of *Ideas I*" (*IOG* 95)—an analysis which showed that the rights of pure consciousness withstood even the complete and total annihilation of the world—and Derrida's own thought experiment here (for nothing like this is to be found in Husserl's text) is meant to demonstrate, analogously, that absolute ideality withstands a total destruction of truth's worldly signs, the complete annihilation of the archive. Accordingly, at the end of scenario two, Derrida himself explicitly renounces this hypothesis—explicitly denies that a destruction of the written sign might have any effect whatsoever on absolute truth, on ideal objectivity. Derrida, clearly in his own voice, says at the end of scenario two: "No worldly catastrophe can put truth *itself* in danger . . . Even if all geometrical 'documents'—and, as well, all actual geometers—had come to ruin one day, to speak of this as an event *'of'* geometry would be to commit a very serious confusion of sense and to abdicate responsibility for all rigorous discourse" (*IOG* 97/*LOG* 97).

Derrida explicitly denounces as "confusion" and "abdication of responsibility" the notion that the destruction of factical writing could threaten truth, that the annihilation of the totality of geometrical truth's worldly signs could in any way be considered an event of "geometry," despite what some of his best commentators have seemed to believe. And in doing so, Derrida denies the very premise upon which this entire sequence has started out. The fate of writing in the real—the factical worldly body of the sign—can have no effect whatsoever on truth. The hypothesis, thanks to which pure language and writing, by referring back to the worldly sign, put into peril that truth which they help to constitute, is rejected by Derrida himself at this moment, even as he continues to affirm that Husserl's transcendental history of geometrical truth is valid (the "Introduction's" commentary continues for nearly another eighty pages). And thus Derrida continues to affirm the constitutive role of pure writing and language themselves even as he denies that they have any significant relation to the worldly empirical sign.

Derrida at this moment, then, returns to the fold; he returns to the framework within which Husserl all along has understood the transcendental role of writing and language. Derrida's rejection of scenario two bears witness to this, as does also the footing on which he now pursues his next scenario, three. Derrida begins scenario three by explicitly embracing Husserl's own terms once more. Thanks to what Derrida will call a "new reduction," he affirms writing and language as "properly constituting" (*IOG* 97)—and he himself concludes that the disappearance, the forgetfulness, of truth "will never be . . . radical" (*IOG* 98).

The entire hypothesis of truth's disappearance at the hands of worldly empirical writing thus collapses at the end of scenario two: its affirmation, Derrida himself is forced to recognize, finally entails simple relativism, rendering Husserl's own thought incoherent. Moreover, as I have begun to suggest, were scenario two correct, it would also make the practice of deconstruction itself irrelevant, superfluous. The need for deconstruction, what demands a deconstruction of all linguistic-related conceptuality, is wholly obscured, if one does not see that scenario two's hypothesis must be rejected and that no danger can come to writing and language functioning transcendentally from their worldly instances. *No* straight way, *no* standard form of argument, it here turns out, *can* permit passage from constitutive to constituted writing and language, while preserving Husserl's insight into their transcendental functioning—none can allow moving from the pure, transcendental possibility of incorporation to actual instances incorporated in factical worldly language—and only because this is so did deconstruction have to be invented. The reason Derrida contrives deconstruction, this unparalleled way of working, in 1966 or thereabouts is to capture the force of a writing and language which Derrida here glimpsed in 1962—a writing and language genuinely constituting and constituted *at once,* truly simultaneously the condition of truth's appearance and its disappearance—a more comprehensive, global writing and language (more "consistent," if you wish), yet one that indeed eluded Derrida's own grasp here. Alternatively, if Husserl's view of constituting writing and language could have been more tightly linked to writing and language as empirical worldly entities by philosophical means, if scenario two had not failed, there would be no need for deconstruction at all, and Derrida's own thought would never have had to finally transgress the confines of philosophy and philosophical argumentation.[35]

This, then, is the problem that has been sought all along, the unique intra-philosophical motivation for Derrida's new, unparalleled way of working in his first mature works. The impossibility within previously known forms of thought to rigorously think that more general language and writing (a writing and language "without reserve") that he had here begun to glimpse led Derrida to invent deconstruction. The impossibility of so proceeding philosophically grounds Derrida's belief that a certain metaphysics has hold of all language-related conceptuality, and it pointed the way toward those considerations that would permit the undoing of those restrictions within which Derrida's thought found itself confined in 1962.

* * *

Finally, scenario three confirms this as well. Scenario three, the only one that ever had a chance of being right, shows clearly that in the "Introduction" Derrida is never able to think transcendental and mundane, constituting and constituted writing together, while it also makes clearer the specific task Derrida will subsequently face, the labor deconstruction will have to perform. Scenario three, culminating in the comparison of Husserl and Joyce, has been assigned great importance in the literature, and rightfully so. Scenario three does point the way toward Derrida's future work, toward some of the key themes and issues upon which deconstruction will turn—most notably a certain infinitization and the role of the idea in a Kantian sense—especially when taken with the end of the "Introduction," sections 10 and 11, where these themes again become prominent. Derrida, perhaps not surprisingly, is able to go furthest in mounting a genuine criticism of Husserl in soliciting, shaking, his thought in scenario three—just because Derrida again proceeds on those terms that are genuinely Husserl's own. Yet Derrida's criticism of Husserl in scenario three, for these same reasons, it must be stressed, remains wholly immanent; in the end Derrida affirms the prerogatives of Husserl's philosophy, indeed the rights of the idea itself and of an infinite teleology of truth, and only by seeing this does the reason why Derrida turns to the *deconstruction of philosophy*, and how, emerge.

At the start of scenario three, then, to begin to explore its workings more closely, Derrida abandons the very premise from which this entire sequence began and explicitly operates on new terms. More specifically, at the end of scenario two, as a result of the argument that has just been laid out, Derrida had declared that "all factual peril . . . stops at the threshold of its [geometry's] internal historicity" (*LOG* 97/*IOG* 97). And Derrida now returns to his earlier distinctions, to a pure juridical constitutive writing, at the start of scenario three—a return thanks to which alone he is able to move his argument forward. "We would be fully convinced," Derrida says of two's outcome, "but did we not just find out that writing inasmuch as it was founding, or contributed to founding, the absolute objectivity of truth, was not simply a constituted sensible body *(Körper)*, but also a constituting body proper *(Leib)*, the intentional originarity of a Here-Now of truth?" (*LOG* 97/*IOG* 97).

Derrida now brings writing as "constituting," as the "intentional originarity . . . of truth" (as opposed to a "sensible body") back into the picture—making reference to an earlier interchange with Fink.[36] Pure constitutive writing once more will be the focal point of Derrida's discussion. Indeed, Derrida goes on to invoke what he calls "a new reduction" on Husserl's part, which will finally and definitively establish the relation between constituted and constituting writing and language. A new reduction will "isolat[e] once and for all the intentional act that constitutes the *Körper* into *Leib* and maintains it in its *Leiblichkeit*, its living sense of truth," and this reduction, according to Derrida, now lets emerge a "danger which menaces truth" thanks to "constitutive writing or speech" alone (*IOG* 98).

As far as I am able to discern, there is actually little evidence in Husserl's own text that a reduction of any great degree of novelty is performed by Husserl at this point in the *Origin*. Yet the most important points for our discussion remain valid in any case, and they are as follows.[37] First, the danger to truth in scenario three, as Derrida himself now states, *exclusively comes from constitutive writing and speech*. Not the sensible spatiotemporality of the worldly empirical sign, but rather these alone pose a threat to truth. Second, and just as important, Derrida links this distinction that has been crucial all along, between constituting and constituted writing and language, to another: to the difference between *Leib* and *Körper*, between a "living body," or "flesh" *(Leib)*, and body, a simple material or physical entity *(Körper)*.

This distinction between *Leib* and *Körper*, which is standard in German, here applies to the sign itself, and it is an important component of all of Husserl's thinking on speech, writing, and language—though at this moment the *graphic* sign, linguistic *inscription*, is most specifically in question. It will be met with again and again in what follows; and thus let me dwell on this development at some length before returning to scenario three, which my discussion of this difference will also prepare me to treat.

For Husserl, as Derrida indicates, all signs of language ultimately owe their ability to signify to a certain *Verleiblichung* ("enfleshing" or "embodiment"): to their being enlivened by the meanings which they embody in turn.[38] Hewing to his own stipulations about how philosophy must proceed, Husserl, as far as I am aware, never spoke about the ultimate ontological relations between thought and speech, language and meaning—which was ultimately prior to which, or whether one could ultimately do without the other.[39] Husserl did embrace, however, what could be called a phenomenological view of signification or linguistic semiosis, which comes forward here, tracing the ultimate meaningfulness of the sign to its use.[40] Linguistic signs, whether written or spoken, owe their signifying capacity, according to Husserl, to the meanings that animate them in their employment, and ultimately, then, to the (subjective) intentional acts at the root of such meanings. Only through such animating acts of intention, thanks to participating in discourse, do linguistic signs ultimately function as signs for Husserl—only then taking on sense and sometimes reference, ceasing to be mere physical bodies *(Körper)*, ink or sound, and becoming *Leib*, "flesh," live media of signification.[41]

Husserl's views on language, speech, and signification will be discussed further as we continue. Most important at this moment is that Husserl's baseline view of discursive signification is indeed the complement to those transcendental stipulations attached to writing and language already discussed, and thus these views have been implied here all along. The entire realm of language and writing, that is, *can* be subordinated to Husserl's transcendental framework in the way that we have seen—these *can* be taken as mere pure possibilities and juridical instances—precisely because Husserl views the signifying function of language in writing and speech as owed to animating acts, to a consciousness, an intentional subject: because Husserl believes that lacking these, signs fail to authentically function as signs at all.

Derrida himself, it must be stressed, is aware of this throughout the course of section 7, and not only here at its end—a fact which further buttresses the claim that a decisive distance between constituted and constitutive writing and language is at work throughout the section.

Right after where my discussion of writing broke off at the beginning of section 7—right after Derrida had spoken in paragraph six of the need to see writing "in pure relation to a consciousness which grounds it as such" and as "intelligible for a transcendental subject"—Derrida went on to invoke just these distinctions which emerge again at the outset of scenario three. "When considering the de jure purity of intentional animation," Derrida writes, "Husserl always says that the linguistic or graphic body is a flesh, a proper body *(Leib)*, or a spiritual corporeality. From then on, writing is no longer only a worldly and mnemotechnical aid to a truth whose own being sense would dispense with all writing down. The possibility or necessity of being incarnated in a graphic sign is no longer or simply extrinsic and factual . . . it is the condition sine qua non of Objectivity's internal completion" (*IOG* 89).

Derrida himself has thus been aware of these stipulations all along, of the role played by writing phenomenologically understood, and whatever the ultimate disposition of these distinctions in Derrida's own thought at the beginning of scenario three—whether this talk of a new reduction in part loses sight of Derrida's own earlier stipulations or not—it should now be clear that such phenomenological stipulations do indeed hold. They are everywhere affirmed by Husserl himself along with his transcendental ones, and Derrida himself repeatedly recognizes them, both at the outset and at the end of section 7.[42]

More narrowly, then, on these terms alone, everything else in scenario three takes place. Thanks to this reduction which brings the meaning-embodying, be-souled sign, the spiritually animated flesh *(Leib)*, back into view, an "intrinsic threat" to truth for the first time emerges (truth becomes "intrinsically threatened"; *LOG* 98/ *IOG* 98). The comparison between Joyce and Husserl takes place on these grounds: with regard to writing now understood purely as constituting, as *Leib,* and solely as the subject of an intentional animation—no longer as *Körper,* sensible spatio-temporality playing no role at all—and thus once more grasped wholly within the framework of Husserl's late thought.

Consequently, it could be expected, as already suggested, that the outcome of this discussion could never be radical; scenario three, for these reasons, will in no way have the radicality some have imputed to it, one equivalent to Derrida's later deconstructive stance. Having returned to Husserl's own transcendental-phenomenological framework, Derrida cannot be expected to thematize and thus break decisively with Husserl's "unthought axiomatic." Yet at the same time, just because of this renewed immanence—because in three, of all the scenarios in the second half of section 7, Derrida hews most closely to Husserl—Derrida's criticism at this juncture does indeed also come closest to genuinely questioning Husserl's thought. Here, if anywhere, something at least approximating a disappearance of truth is to be found, and this will let us see the direction in which Derrida's thought will eventually go.

Derrida's starting point in scenario three thus has a double-edged character—both closer to Husserl himself, but *for this reason* able to cut more deeply—and this is readily visible in the issue which Derrida pursues from the outset of three: namely, equivocation. With equivocation, the locus of Derrida's questioning now moves back to the subject's own intentions. The failure of truth, Derrida now indicates, will occur only through "an abdication of responsibility" on the part of the subject in imparting or gathering meaning from its writing and signs. Writing and language are again here to be seen exclusively from within Husserl's own framework, and now that sensible spatiotemporality has been ruled out as a factor, the disappearance of truth can indeed "never be radical" and will take place by dint of a failure on the part of the subject alone (*LOG* 98/ *IOG* 98).

At the same time, this conception of writing purely as *Leib* returns us to Husserl's transcendental-phenomenological *historical* framework as well, and Derrida can now broach a version of the problem of equivocation far thornier than is usual in the philosophical tradition. The presupposition of a pure transcendental history and historicity of truth having been restored, to compress a much longer discussion, Derrida now, and only now, can argue that insofar as this pure history remains a history, and is still *under way*, the *Urstiftung* (the "Ur-foundation," original founding, the first inauguration) of geometrical knowledge will not have reached its final form, its *Endstiftung* (its "end-foundation"), with the result that *a singular play of meaning* must in principle be recognized across the unfolding of this pure intentional history. Singular "puttings into perspective" *(mises en perspectives)* will necessarily exist inherent in this history's own pure movement in the absence of a definite arrival at its objects, on account of its incompletion, giving purchase to an *unavoidable, structural* equivocity. An "enriching, renascent equivocity" must be admitted by Husserl himself, Derrida eventually concludes (*IOG* 103)—both absolute equivocity and absolute univocity paralyzing once and for all even a transcendental history (*IOG* 101–2).

The closest thing to a genuine disappearance of truth begins to come forward at this moment along with such structural equivocity—a moment eventually answering to what Husserl himself indeed designated as crisis (to which the work of that title also ultimately owes its name).[43] Such structural equivocation has as its correlate what Husserl called sedimentation: the covering over, or burial, of the originating intention (e.g., the founding intentions of the protogeometer instituting mathematics), and because such transcendental history, as dependent on *Leib*, is now traced back to an intention of the subject, and because as still ongoing it is potentially equivocal, such history never remains free of sedimentation—prior intentions, indeed defining ones, coming to be lost (in the sense of being covered over, withdrawn into palimpsest) as this history proceeds.

"A sort of pure equivocity grows in the very rhythms of science," Derrida thus states (*IOG* 104); a pure equivocity waxes alongside the unfolding of truth, increasing within the movement of the transcendental history of knowledge itself; and in the final two pages of section 7, building on this notion of a pure renascent equivocity—"the problem of univocity echoes immediately upon its reactivation" (*IOG* 105)—Derrida points out that because such history is also infinite, sedimentation and crisis in fact will never be able to be definitively avoided, even on the transcendental plane. Within transcendental history itself the transmission and recovery of sense may always fail; crisis remains unavoidable, and this is indeed the nearest thing to a disappearance of truth at the hands of writing that is to be found throughout Derrida's discourse in section 7 of the "Introduction." Within pure history itself a transcendental equivalent of empiricity thus emerges: a finitude, an opacity, having the *force* of fact *internal* to the unfolding of this transcendental history as such.

So, too, correspondingly, an appeal will be made at this moment to an idea in a Kantian sense, to an infinite idea—the evidence for which will come into question at the end of the "Introduction" in a manner that Derrida already anticipates here. Such infinite sedimentation and potentially growing equivocity require a further "reduction" on Husserl's part, Derrida claims; the capacity for reactivation is at first finite, and only an appeal to the infinitization of the idea allows for this factuality to be definitively overcome. Crisis in the face of a transcendental finitude can only be definitively overcome by a further infinitization, a further idealization, which has as its reference the absolute idea of truth that *opened* all philosophy, knowledge, and transcendental history in the first place.

In turn, however, all of this presupposes Husserl's own treatment of language—everything here still being traced back to the intentions of a founding subject. Even at the moment of this failure, the very notion of sedimentation points back toward the construal of the written sign solely as *Leib*. Correspondingly, it must also be emphasized that Derrida, even at this moment, never denies the primacy of Husserl's principles as principles; he never rejects the rights of the Idea or the absolute value of this telos of univocity as such. The possibility of this factual disappearance may not be able to be definitively overcome (barring a further idealization); at the same time, truth itself will never be thought to definitively disappear, or such reactivation become simply impossible, which is why the further operation Husserl undertakes at this point is by no means illicit on its own terms, nor does Derrida suggest it is as such.

Never within the "Introduction," then, will Derrida assert the rights of equivocity over and against univocity, or even suggest that they are equivalent, stand on the same footing, occupy a single plane as equals. Here the famous, and much misunderstood, comparison between Husserl and Joyce becomes crucial. I have already been commenting on it: Derrida having argued—where I have just cited him as bringing forward such pure renascent equivocity—that Husserl must recognize the "same relativity as Joyce" (*IOG* 103). Both Joyce and Husserl must recognize equivocity as well as univocity, on a mundane and a transcendental plane, respectively, claims Derrida, and this is what opens the door to that sedimentation, that crisis in the reactivation of meaning that has proven unavoidable even within pure transcendental history.[44] Because the projects of Husserl and Joyce share the "same relativity," an ongoing infinitely expanding sedimentation challenging any finite capacity for reactivation necessarily appears even on the transcendental plane.

Yet Derrida goes on to insist that a single aim, a single axiom, governs Joyce's program as well as Husserl's—and that *only Husserl's project sets forth this axiom as such*. A single telos, that of univocity, governs Joyce's undertaking as well as Husserl's, and only Husserl sets out this aim in its own right—cashes out the "absolute horizon" of that relativity governing empirical as well as transcendental history, empirical as well as transcendental writing and languages. "If the univocity investigated by Husserl and the equivocation generalized by Joyce are in fact relative, they are, therefore, not so *symmetrically*," Derrida writes. "For the common *telos*, the positive value of univocity is *immediately* revealed only within the relativity that Husserl defined. Univocity is also the absolute horizon of equivocity" (*IOG* 104).

Univocity as a telos provides the absolute horizon common to both Husserl and Joyce, then; under its aegis alone do their parallel tasks take on significance, and univocity thus remains presupposed as true, as a genuine telos, even if the factical failure of reactivation in the transcendental sphere itself may also be affirmed. Crisis, thus, will never be irremediable. Derrida may ask about Husserl's assurance as to the reactivatability of this sedimentation, yet even this renascent pure equivocity remains immanent to Husserl's framework; it continues to pertain to this single horizon of truth's recovery and to recognize in principle the rights of the eventual reappearance of sense. Thus, again, never within the "Introduction's" section 7 do Husserl's project, Husserl's axioms, come radically into question. Even here at the most extreme verge of this questioning, poised beyond the destruction of the world and of all worldly signs, the rights of univocity will continue to be recognized by Derrida himself, truth will never radically disappear: the reactivation of its sense will always be presumed and be presupposed possible as such.

What transpires in scenario three thus confirms everything else that we have seen in section 7, and again, does not conform to Derrida's later thought. By no means are the rights of univocity decisively overturned at this moment, nor is this infinite teleology of truth questioned from a point definitively beyond itself or inaccessible to Husserl's own thought—an outcome that was indeed to be expected, insofar as Husserl's own notion of writing as *Leib,* and the restoration of the entirety of his earlier transcendental-phenomenological stipulations, made this entire development possible in the first place. Scenario three continues to confirm the distance that has emerged between Derrida's stance in 1962 and 1967, the difference between constituted and constituting writing and language, empirical and transcendental history—even as scenario three also comes closest, doubtless, to questioning the totality of Husserl's thought, and, in so questioning, giving us the clearest glimpse of the turn Derrida's thought takes when he arrives at deconstruction.

Indeed, it begins to become clear here—along with why Derrida starts in 1967 from the sign—that Derrida will later also see Husserl's own stipulations pertaining to writing and language as one with this infinite idea and its teleology, which is what Derrida failed to do here. That is, Derrida will come to believe that the decisions Husserl made about language and writing are everywhere tied to this infinite teleology itself, and thus that this teleology blocks the thought of a truly comprehensive and finally novel language and writing—a language and writing at once the root of the radical appearance and disappearance of truth, of both the infinite circulation of sense and of its profound disappearance. In turn, the removal of these restrictions will pave the way for taking this idea itself as but one possibility among others—for seeing the infinite idea of truth itself as a moment of reserve in a more general unrestricted economy of signs, thought, meanings, intentionality, and objects.

Derrida thus prepares the way for his later thought in 1962, though by no means arriving at it here. More narrowly, though perhaps as important, it can also be seen that an entire grid of reference points—pertaining to writing and language, as well as thought, meaning, and objectivity—is implied in Derrida's 1967 deconstructive problematic, a set of reference points beyond this notion of the sign as such. An entire transcendental-phenomenological matrix of interpretations has here come forward: a network of stipulations pertaining to writing, language, speech, discourse, thought, objectivity, signification, and their relations. These are everywhere bound up with the rest of Husserl's thought, as we have seen, and upon them falls the brunt of Derrida's 1967 deconstruction. This gridwork turns out to be the real object of Derrida's deconstruction of language, providing the axis of his work on Husserl in *Speech,* as my treatment of this will confirm. The discussion of the sign is but the opening sally (though for the reasons that we have discovered here, perhaps a critical one) of the deconstruction of the totality of Husserlian phenomenology in *Speech and Phenomena,* which fixes on this entire set of distinctions. And only with this matrix in view, I would suggest, can the work Derrida does in *Speech* be precisely grasped, especially in respect to the critical topic of the voice.

These more narrow conclusions, while being held in reserve for now, must remain finally provisional. More work still needs be done pertaining to Derrida's early development. The "Introduction," of course, is not Derrida's only early work on Husserl. Other early writings by Derrida on Husserl exist, and these must first be taken into account, especially since their claims have often been seen by interpreters to lead in a direction specifically at odds with the one set out here: toward greater continuity of Derrida's early thought and his 1967 works.

That significant development does take place in Derrida's thought, however, has been demonstrated decisively, I believe—indeed, according to Derrida's own criteria. Nowhere in section 7 of the "Introduction" does Derrida ever manage to offer "a problematic of writing and the trace" "more consistent" than Husserl's, or definitively break with the "unthought axiomatic" of all of Husserlian phenomenology (though both this unthought and this inconsistency may well have started to come within Derrida's notice there). Yet the current interpretation is not wholly wrong: Derrida, as we are about to see, had already taken an attitude toward phenomenological orthodoxy in his other early writings that is closer to his mature works in some respects. Though by no means envisioning a break as profound or decisive as the 1967 works, and having a very different focus, Derrida's other early writings do anticipate his later thought in important ways, and this too must be taken into account. To this I now turn, the fact of development having been secured. Only after *Le problème* and "Genesis and Structure" have been brought into the picture and their results coordinated with what takes place here in the "Introduction" will a complete overview of Derrida's development be at hand, and only then may Derrida's mature thought, the 1967 writings, be approached by way of his development as a whole.

The Development of Deconstruction as a Whole and the Role of *Le problème de la genèse dans la philosophie de Husserl*

Significant development does take place in Derrida's treatment of writing between 1962 and 1967, as well as in his thought more generally, it has now been shown. Derrida came upon the theme of writing for the first time in the "Introduction" within the framework of Husserl's late historical analysis, and in the "Introduction" writing thus remains viewed on Husserl's terms, from his transcendental-phenomenological perspective, as *Leib*, and as subject to an animating transcendental intentionality. Derrida doubtless also poses significant questions to Husserl in 1962; he probes the limits of Husserl's thought in the "Introduction" in respect to writing, as well as to Husserl's late historical teleology. Yet Derrida stands on a very different footing in 1962 than he will later: his questioning everywhere proceeds from within Husserl's framework, and nowhere does it attain the radicality that distinguishes his mature thought. In 1962, it is not impossible to claim, Derrida was still a Husserlian, albeit a rather unorthodox one; and the sweeping break with Husserl and indeed all philosophy that Derrida later undertakes is notably absent in the "Introduction"—a break of the sort indicated by Derrida's talk of "logocentric metaphysics" having reached its own "exhaustion" at the start of *Of Grammatology* (*G* 8), or Derrida's announcement at the end of *Speech* that "the history of being as presence . . . is closed" (*SP* 102).

The "Introduction" adopts far more restrained positions, as I have demonstrated, in respect to Husserl's thought as a whole than anything Derrida writes thereafter. Nevertheless, where Derrida stands in 1962, and what exactly the "Introduction" represents for his own thinking—leaving aside the ambiguity of Derrida's occasional remarks—is not so easily settled due to the other work Derrida had engaged in by the time of the "Introduction's" composition. *Le problème de la genèse dans la philosophie de Husserl* suggests that Derrida had already conceived of a project at a considerably greater distance from phenomenology than the "Introduction" as early as 1954; and though *Le problème* has only somewhat recently been published, another work, "'Genèse et structure' et la phénoménologie" ("'Genesis and Structure' and Phenomenology," hereafter "Genesis"), has long made it difficult to come to a clear view of where Derrida stands even at this early juncture.[1]

How "Genesis," as well as *Le problème,* fit into the picture of Derrida's development must be clarified, then, if such development is to be established as convincingly and clearly as possible. The notion of development implies continuity as well as discontinuity—identity of interest and theme, as well as significant differences in standpoint—and that some sort of baseline continuity exists among Derrida's early works is not to be doubted. This continuity, as shall be confirmed, is most readily found in *Le problème* and in "Genesis" (which turns out largely to be a précis of this earlier work). At the same time, as points that came forward at the start of my last chapter show, as well as some specific to "Genesis" itself, Derrida eventually repudiated aspects of "Genesis" (along with some of what it has in common with *Le problème*). Thus, after I bring these indices out, after I clarify this repudiation further, I will turn back to *Le problème* in order to establish Derrida's initial positions more precisely: to make clear how near, and how far, the project that *Le problème* and "Genesis" both share stands to Derrida's mature thought.

Let me first turn to the issue of how "Genesis" and the "Introduction" are related, and from which positions in "Genesis" (and *Le problème*) Derrida distances himself in the "Introduction." Whether Derrida's views in the "Introduction" or in "Genesis" were more recent, and which were finally valid, was impossible to know prior to *Le problème*'s seeing print in 1990. Because of the publication history of "Genesis" already mentioned—because "'Genèse et structure' et la phénoménologie" was delivered as a lecture in 1959 *prior* to the "Introduction's" publication, yet only appeared in an anthology three years *after* the "Introduction" in 1965—where Derrida stood at this period immediately preceding his first deconstructive works could not be determined on the basis of the "Introduction" and "Genesis" alone.[2]

For significant differences do exist between "Genesis" and the "Introduction": differences in theme and in Derrida's stance toward Husserl. Above all, however, perhaps the major difference between the two works concerns the organization of Husserl's corpus. Though this has rarely been recognized, "Genesis" takes a far more standard view of the organization of Husserl's late work than does the "Introduction." In "Genesis" Husserl's late *history* writings are said unequivocally to fall under the category of *genetic* phenomenology. When in "Genesis" Derrida turns to "the enormous problems of genetic phenomenology," he includes without reservation Husserl's writings on history: these works represent one of "three lines" along which "the profound unity of this genetic description is diffracted, without being dispersed" (*WD* 164).[3]

By contrast, Derrida paints a quite different portrait of the relations of Husserl's writings on history to Husserl's genetic phenomenology program in the "Introduction." In it Husserl's history project, according to Derrida, inaugurates "a new form of radicality." Derrida makes this claim in the very first section of the "Introduction," and the rest of the "Introduction's" argument presupposes it. History in general as a theme no longer simply answers to an already existing "phenomenology" in the late writings in the "Introduction," even while referring back to earlier phases of Husserl's analysis; instead it has a novel specificity of its own that "engages phenomenology completely." As Derrida writes: "Remaining completely within a determined relativity, history in general no less completely engages phenomenology with all its possibilities and responsibilities, its original techniques and attitudes" (*IOG* 30).[4]

In "Genesis," Derrida claims a comprehensive identity between Husserl's genetic and historical writings; these ultimately belong to a single genus. The "Introduction" denies this, and only *Le problème*'s publication makes clear that the view of Husserl's corpus in "Genesis" essentially belongs to an earlier phase of Derrida's thought, since *Le problème* takes the same stance as "Genesis."[5] *Le problème*, Like "Genesis," and unlike the "Introduction," subordinates Husserl's late history to Husserl's genetic phenomenology and to Husserl's treatment of genesis generally. Derrida takes the same approach to Husserl's corpus in "Genesis" as he did in the 1954 *Le problème*, and the "Introduction" thus represents a shift on Derrida's part: a more recent evaluation of these same matters.

Nor are these variations in Derrida's construal of Husserl's corpus trivial. Everything else that Derrida does in the "Introduction" depends on this way of viewing Husserl's corpus, as I have indicated, and only in the "Introduction" arise those themes that will provide Derrida's starting points in his first deconstructions—writing and history. Writing (language, and the sign), as well as history, are the twin nonphilosophical, nontranscendental reference points—the two *worldly* themes, in a Husserlian scheme—from which considerations different from philosophy's own emerge in Derrida's 1967 works. These themes are wholly absent from *Le problème* and from "Genesis." Derrida discovers them in the "Introduction" on the basis of his new reading of Husserl, a reading possible only if the history writings are taken to be novel in the way the "Introduction" argues, and Derrida's previous work denies.

"Genesis" importantly bears marks of an earlier phase of Derrida's thinking, then, which is not to say that Derrida in "Genesis" has in no way altered his stance since writing *Le problème;* nor does it mean, more crucially, that no important anticipations of Derrida's mature thought are to be found in this phase of his work, speaking broadly—anticipations which *Le problème* first presents and which "Genesis" fine-tunes.[6] I will thus embark on bringing these anticipations forward—this baseline intention common to both *Le problème* and "Genesis"—though I will do so solely through *Le problème,* since it is the more comprehensive work, and in it Derrida first worked out these positions in depth. *Le problème* does point the way toward Derrida's mature thought in important respects, and examining it gives us a different view of Derrida's early ambitions than does the "Introduction." In fact, *Le problème* shows us a more radical side of Derrida's thought than any that has so far emerged. Any comprehensive view of Derrida's development must take into account these factors—bearing the continuity of Derrida's intentions with them—as well as those that make its discontinuity plain.

Moreover, in the final analysis, the "Introduction" itself, it turns out, supervenes on a project already under way, transforming it significantly. Accordingly, later in this chapter, after fleshing out Derrida's baseline intentions in *Le problème,* I will resume my discussion of the "Introduction." I will turn to it to situate the "Introduction's" breakthrough in this new larger setting that *Le problème* provides, in order to capture both the continuity and discontinuity of Derrida's development. The incorporation of *Le problème* into my sketch of Derrida's development thus ultimately proceeds in two steps or phases: first, setting out what remains continuous across all Derrida's early thought; and second, stressing what changes through the "Introduction's" intervention—and this more complete overview will finally give us what has been sought all along: the most general framework of Derrida's development, through which the 1967 works may then be approached.

* * *

Taking *Le problème* into account, even in this first way, simply showing in a relatively straightforward manner how it anticipates Derrida's mature thought, is itself a complex undertaking. Not only is *Le problème de la genèse dans la philosophie de Husserl* a vast work, but a number of different vectors lead from it to Derrida's mature writings. *Le problème,* most centrally, anticipates Derrida's later work in not one, but two important respects: first, its *strategy*—Derrida already sketches in *Le problème* a wholly unparalleled way of working which will remain his "signature" ever after; and second, *thematically*—*Le problème*'s central concerns continue to be a motivating force in Derrida's later work, even as they undergo considerable transformation.

Treating *Le problème* is made even more complex, however, insofar as the reasons Derrida had for abandoning this work in the wake of its composition must also be examined. Reasons internal to *Le problème* itself account for why Derrida did not let it be published at the time that he wrote it. In his 1990 "Avertissement" Derrida tells us that Jean Hyppolite "encouraged [him] to prepare [*Le problème*] for publication" in 1955 (*LPG* VI/ *PG* xiv); but why at that time Derrida was not inclined to let *Le problème* go to press, he does not say.[7] The problems internal to Derrida's own thought, what may have kept Derrida from publishing *Le problème* at the time, need to be specified on the basis of a reading of *Le problème* itself, then—these internal problems also clearly being an important feature of the development of Derrida's thought.

Finally, in attempting to grasp the deepest underlying ambition extending from Derrida's early thought through to his more mature writings, one more new matter must be reckoned with, one that will be followed up extensively in my final chapter: namely, Derrida's relation to Heidegger. *Le problème*'s program, as I have begun to indicate, is more comprehensive, more ambitious, than the "Introduction's"—its aim is more radical in some ways. Whenever Derrida announces concerns distinctly foreign to Husserl's phenomenology (in his early writings), or to philosophy's more generally (in his later ones), however, Heidegger's project is never far off.[8]

As we shall see, this matter of Derrida's relation to Heidegger also proves to be something of a wild card. Derrida's situation vis-à-vis Heidegger, setting forth the more radical side of Derrida's project, is an especially difficult issue to pin down—in part due to the relative immaturity of Derrida's own thinking in this regard in *Le problème*. Derrida in 1954, at the age of twenty-four, is already a more than respectable Husserlian, I would suggest. Derrida's understanding of Heidegger at this time is visibly less well developed, however, and does not, I believe, measure up to his grasp of Husserl's thought.[9] Derrida in 1954 has a view of Heidegger's thinking as focused on existence, as a kind of existentialism (as I will further confirm). Yet just here, in turn—in his proximity to his reworking of Heidegger—is where the more radical aspect of Derrida's undertaking resides, with the result that this aspect of Derrida's project is the one that will undergo the greatest change as his thought matures. The most volatile aspect in the evolution of Derrida's thought is Derrida's relation to Heidegger, and this presents obvious difficulties for interpretation, especially given how volatile Heidegger's own doctrines tend to be.

Numerous complexities thus accompany my attempt to extend my account of Derrida's development to *Le problème*, which is not surprising given the density of *Le problème* itself, a work that still holds many unmined treasures. *Le problème* is a vast, enormously ambitious work; it treats every phase of Husserl's corpus, every one of Husserl's writings available to Derrida at the time, as well as some of the *inédits* (the unedited *Nachlass*).[10] In *Le problème* Derrida offers a total interpretation of Husserlian phenomenology, an interpretation which gestures toward an interpretation of philosophy as a whole—ultimately, toward a total interpretation of the structural strengths and fault lines of philosophy as such (for which Husserlian phenomenology provides the defining instance) that clearly prefigures Derrida's later thought in important ways.

This chapter, among other things, thus hopes to serve as an introduction to *Le problème*, to the specific standpoints and themes of this work only recently translated into English (all translations here are my own), which, accordingly, have yet to really find their way into the literature. Given the vast scope of *Le problème*, however, I must here restrict myself to but a few moments in it—initially, to a single development that will introduce us to Derrida's intentions in the totality of this work. And this single development, by letting Derrida's strategy in *Le problème* emerge, offers the first important anticipation of Derrida's later thought.

This single moment has not been arbitrarily chosen, however; any reader might seize on it as encapsulating *Le problème*'s aims. *Le problème*'s theme is the problem of genesis—as its title states, the problem of genesis in Husserl's philosophy—and the most ready access to where Derrida stands toward this problem is supplied in the section about to be taken up, in which Derrida discusses Husserl's own explicit treatment of genesis: the "Phenomenological Theme of Genesis," as part 3 of *Le problème* is titled.

More specifically, due to the particular status that genesis has in Husserl's early writings (after his *Philosophy of Arithmetic,* not yet itself a properly phenomenological study, Husserl turned away from the topic of genesis for many years), Derrida in *Le problème* initially introduces phenomenology's treatment of genesis by way of its *omission:* through a discussion of the "neutralization" of genesis in *Logical Investigations, Ideas I,* and the *Phenomenology of Internal Time-Consciousness* (parts of which argument I look at below). Only in the second half of *Le problème,* consequently, in part 3, does Derrida take up Husserl's own phenomenological treatment of genesis in its *positivity.* Derrida, in part 3, examines Husserl's *Experience and Judgment* and the *Cartesian Meditations*—and, in the latter, specifically in *Cartesian Meditations* 4, Husserl famously first laid out his genetic phenomenology program, thus providing an apt and ready site for a comparison with Derrida's views.

The swath of Husserl's text to which I am about to turn, on which Derrida will be seen to comment, is thus the locus classicus for the statement of Husserl's own phenomenological turn (or return) to genesis. It also proves critical in a further respect. Husserl's genetic phenomenology is the locus where the question of *Heidegger's* relation to Husserl becomes especially visible. Here most plainly emerge the themes that Heidegger first contested in Husserl's thought (this, in part, because Heidegger was aware of some of Husserl's researches and drew on them himself). Turning to this discussion, and taking into account in what follows both Husserl's and Heidegger's positions as well as Derrida's own, I will not only be able to ascertain where Derrida stood toward Husserl and the theme of genesis in 1954, but also begin to sketch Derrida's early relation to Heidegger.[11]

I will eventually join Derrida as he examines Husserl's first presentation of genetic phenomenology in *Cartesian Meditations* 4 (§30, 65ff.) in a section of chapter 2 of part 3 of *Le problème* that Derrida titles "The Contradiction of Active Genesis." Most broadly, Derrida there hopes to set forth a notion of genesis that he claims was presupposed by all of Husserl's thought, by all phenomenology's work, yet one not graspable within Husserlian phenomenology—a genesis that lies beyond Husserl's compass even at this juncture when Husserl himself turns to genesis and makes it an explicit theme.[12] And with this gesture, Derrida indeed anticipates his more mature way of working, achieves something that some might even call a proto-deconstruction of Husserlian phenomenology (though not philosophy as a whole): one that *never* contests Husserl's thought intra-phenomenologically, however, but positions it uniquely as the gateway to what lies beyond it.

In turn, Husserl (to take a step back and prepare ourselves for a more detailed examination of Derrida's treatment) was led to propound what he would call genetic phenomenology—the reidentification of "phenomenology as a whole" as the explication of "the self-constitution of the monadic ego," as he puts it early in *Cartesian Meditations* 4 (Husserl 1960, 68)—largely through his prior genetic researches into the phenomenology of the object, of the individual thing given in perception (now collected in *Experience and Judgment,* among other places). Husserl's new vision of phenomenological exposition as an exposition focused on *genesis* was inspired, in particular, by the growing importance taken on by horizonal consciousness, that of the world especially, in the wake of Husserl's inquiries into the spatiotemporally individuated existent.[13]

To compress a much longer argument, crucial in its own right, to which I unfortunately cannot do justice here, suffice it to note that Husserl's researches into the individual existent had shown that taking this up had a broader array of commitments than he had previously acknowledged. Specifically, the perception which gave this existent "in person" implied (a) grasping it as *already there* prior to the ego's active awareness of it; (b) understanding it *as already being there for others* and not just the subject (thus implying a community of subjects); and finally, (c) certain sorts of expectations pertaining to its further recognition and understanding. The thing in perception, in sum, was implicated in what Husserl called both internal and external horizons: overflowing structural anticipations concerning what the thing itself was and would further show itself to be, and also concerning the overall situation in which it was encountered.[14]

This phase pertaining to the existent, in turn, led Husserl to investigate *egological* genesis, the development of the transcendental ego itself, in part to account for the ability of individuals to be meaningfully encountered in this way: to account for these horizons and accompanying structures through which the individual's situatedness prior to being actively taken up was given, through which the subject's future interaction with it was anticipated, and its co-availability for a host of other subjects secured.

Genetic phenomenology, as it was called, thus aimed to explore new capacities of the subject which corresponded to Husserl's new (more genetic) understanding of individual existing things—as arising in a single, already understood, common world—and this, in turn, is where Heidegger's contestation of Husserl arguably most centrally begins.[15] Heidegger doubted that even this new, more radical approach to the existent—one which was rooted in a model of consciousness that Husserl, with an eye on theoretical and logical interests, had elaborated earlier in *Ideas I*—was sufficiently penetrating to permit an authentic account of these existents in their most primary modes of being and givenness.[16] Moreover, Heidegger believed that Husserl could not give an adequate account of the other themes whose importance he was now led to recognize: namely, those of a world and others, and with them, the subject, the ego itself, explicitly understood in the form of a *person*.

Husserl's genetic phenomenology program, at the moment that I am about to examine Derrida addressing it, indeed focuses above all on features specific to *personhood*—to an ego now conceived with an individual history, and habits, as well as prior and ongoing acquisitions.[17] These are all now thought to develop in stages around an identical ego pole, to refer back and forth to one another—facets of an agglomerating personal identity (some of which Husserl had already begun to sketch in *Ideas II*), which now take on specifically transcendental functions. These potentialities and stages informing the ego's own self-formation are the correlatives of those structures that allow the existent thing to appear as existing.[18] The ego itself now has a "history," and this history—with its implications backward and forward, its internal developmental structures—ultimately makes possible the ongoing givenness of the world, as well as that of intersubjectivity, both of which, in turn, underlie the perceived individual's existence construed phenomenologically.[19]

The problem this turns out to pose, however, put in a highly abbre-viated fashion, is how such recourse to the person and the movement of its self-formation—whose structure and internal relations carry with it the brunt of these possibilities—how this self-formation is to conform to Husserl's longstanding claim that philosophical knowledge can and must be a priori. The self-constitution of what Husserl calls the transcendental monad is to embody and ultimately make possible *common* meanings and referents. Yet how this is to be conceived such that these decisive egologi-cal formations, these stages of development, finally specific to *personhood,* are to be effectuated *apart from all prior factuality*—how these sequences comprising the ego's own development are to be determined solely with reference to a *pure* ego—is far from clear.[20] Just by dint of the wider-ranging implications that egological self-genesis now bears—to the ex-tent that what is to be constituted is a *person* bringing with it a world, im-plying acquisitions and patterns of understanding of everything in that world, for itself as well as others—it becomes all the more difficult to en-vision *even in principle* how such self-genesis might ever attain to that a pri-ori essential status that Husserl always believed philosophical knowledge must possess.[21]

Heidegger, accordingly, turns to just these issues to mount his break with Husserl. Heidegger, as I began to note, believed that Husserl's model of consciousness was illegitimately influenced by the modern epistemo-logical tradition, that it had been tailored to ensure apodictic starting points for foundational knowledge; and this commitment to apodicticity, Heidegger asserted, made it impossible for Husserl to authentically dis-close what had emerged at this juncture in Husserl's own researches: the status of personhood, the basic character of world, of others, the always-already being together of things, persons, and understanding, and so on.

Given this prior contestation by Heidegger, it is far from surprising to find Derrida taking up the problem of genesis in *Le problème* in 1953 and 1954, as the site of *his* own break: to see him deciding that this will be the crossroads at which to lay out his own most radical ambitions, his most radical questioning of Husserl's thought. Genetic phenomenology—at least as it appears in *Cartesian Meditations* 4, as stretched between models and frameworks taken from Husserl's earlier thought and challenges to these assumptions his own discoveries had begun to raise—had already emerged as the preeminent locus for questions and reservations in re-spect to Husserl's own endeavor, indeed by phenomenologists of many stripes, preeminently Heidegger, but also Merleau-Ponty and Tran Duc Thao. Derrida, choosing this issue of genesis to focus on in *Le problème,* thus hews to a longstanding set of debates within phenomenology itself.

Derrida's interest in genesis may thus not be surprising. Something quite unexpected does transpire at this juncture, however, something determinative for all Derrida's future thought and for his place in the phe-nomenological tradition generally, I believe. Though Derrida at the age of twenty-four follows, in some respects, an already well-trodden path in his departure from Husserl, the form this takes, the *manner* in which Der-rida intends to break with Husserl, turns out to be wholly unparalleled, unlike that of any previous thinker, among all other heterodox phenom-enologists—and in this way, as a strategy, it indeed prefigures Derrida's mature thought.

More specifically, Derrida, wishing to contest this moment of gene-sis, will *retain* Husserl's stance *longer* than Heidegger and Merleau-Ponty. He will *refuse to break* with Husserl initially on any of the grounds just noted: these issues of world, others, persons, and even that of consciousness and its tie to foundationalism. Derrida instead insists on the continuing co-gency of Husserl's philosophy—that Husserl is *right,* as far as phenome-nology itself is concerned—and that Husserl's project can only be broken with at the end, at the limit, "dialectically," as Derrida puts it in *Le problème.*

Stated otherwise, Derrida here sides with Husserl more completely than any of his precursors; yet this also finally permits him, Derrrida in-sists, to break *more radically* with Husserl than anyone else—ultimately, in the name of a structural impossibility endemic to thought itself. By defer-ring every break, by staying with Husserl to the end, Derrida claims that he also conceives of a departure from phenomenology more radical than anyone else's, and, in this way, Derrida's mature thought indeed already shows through here like a watermark.[22]

Let me just cite a long passage, then, where all this becomes plain; it is the one toward which I have been proceeding all along.

> The necessities of this preparatory eidetic are in the eyes of Husserl . . .
> methodological. If one does not start from an a priori description of
> essences, one will never be able to attain to any rigor. Existence itself, in
> its most original uprising, would never be able to appear to a philosophi-
> cal gaze. Thus, every reproach addressed to Husserlian essentialism in
> the name of an empirical or existential originarity or of some anterior
> moment of genesis, in order to have a sense, would imply an already con-
> stituted eidetic . . . This is what authorizes us to speak of a dialectical phi-
> losophy as the sole possible philosophy of genesis . . . The sense of gene-
> sis is produced by a sense whose genesis is only accessible in its being,
> possible in its apparition, if one starts from the originality of its sense. All
> philosophy is condemned to traverse in the opposite direction the effec-
> tive itinerary of all becoming. Every critique (that, notably, of Heidegger
> and Tran Duc Thao, otherwise very different) tends to a radical reversal
> of which one does not see that it assumes the problematic defined and
> resolved by Husserl. (*LPG* 225–26/*PG* 137–38)[23]

Derrida in part 3 of *Le problème,* addressing Husserl's own account of genesis, first insists on the rights of Husserl's philosophy, on the legitimacy of Husserl's own "sense of genesis," an insistence which we now know carries a quite heavy cache of philosophical and phenomenological commitments. Derrida starts by identifying his concerns as "methodological"; and it is precisely method, Husserl's methods, that most come into question at this juncture. As this passage makes plain, however, for Derrida, Husserl's essentialism even now is not to be rejected, at least not in the first instance. Derrida has no concern that Husserl *can* "begin by a description of essences a priori"; he doesn't doubt that *philosophical knowledge* of these matters *can be attained in the form that Husserl always conceived it.* Husserl's methodology does not simply give way to an "anterior genesis." Thus, the rights of "sense"—the *sense* of the ego, of the person, and of genesis itself—must continue to be recognized, in a fashion that Husserl's analysis alone would provide, in the face of the objections of Heidegger and Tran Duc Thao.

Derrida's approach at this moment first represents a *defense* of Husserl's standpoint—most profoundly, of Husserl's determination of consciousness, the model of the subject, and the correlation noesis-noema.[24] Whatever else transpires, these will never be subject to interrogation on their own terms. Their birthright in the modern epistemological project, in the desire to find apodictic foundations for all knowledge, and their Cartesian legacy, which Heidegger so adamantly wished to question, are not issues for Derrida now (or in the future, I would suggest). Derrida retains Husserl's model of consciousness, of subject-object, his reductions; and indeed nothing that comes after, as far as I can tell, will alter this set of decisions as such.[25]

Of course, this does not mean that Derrida himself does not also aim to depart from Husserl's standpoint at this moment—indeed with unparalleled radicality, according to his own account. Though Derrida's defense of Husserl must be genuine if all that follows is to hold, though Husserl must really be right philosophically speaking (otherwise the route of Heidegger, or Merleau-Ponty, or Tran Duc Thao, or indeed simple skepticism, immediately supplant all else Derrida hopes to do), nevertheless, the retention of Husserl's rationalism is also intended to be the first step in a break, a departure from Husserl, that Derrida, even at this early point, claims for just this reason, thanks to holding to Husserl's perspective, will also turn out to be more radical than any previously conceived. The interdependence of these two results is ultimately the most urgent thing to see more clearly, then—again, its singular dynamic prefiguring Derrida's future thought, in it a strategy here becoming visible that in some way will always remain Derrida's own.

Having first defended the starting point of Husserl's project, having acknowledged what is due to "the sense of genesis," Derrida, in the second half of this citation, will claim that such "sense" must be seen to have been "produced by a genesis." A radical genesis, proceeding "from the inverse direction" of thought, *anterior* to Husserl's eidetics of genesis (and to the transcendental monad and its self-constitution), now and only now will be said to be productive of all sense, to be a condition, at least in part, of both the pure ego and the transcendental subject themselves—with Derrida himself, in fact, soon raising some of the problems already brought forward here.[26]

Having affirmed Husserl's thought in its entirety, having defended the prerogatives of essence, Derrida goes on to sketch a predicament of thought of unheard-of radicality, he claims. Thought itself, all thought, runs a course radically opposed to being—the *ordo essendi* and the *ordo cognoscendi* will forever be implacably opposed. And thus after embracing Husserl's thought all the way to the end, after affirming that "problematic [which only] Husserl defined and resolved," a condition of these conditions (of the apriori itself), an other of thought, a certain radical alterity, can and must be taken into account. Derrida at the end of this passage gestures toward a "radical reversal" of Husserl: a self-consciously vertiginous dialectical moment (further elaborated at other junctures in *Le problème*), wherein the condition (the a priori sense of genesis) turns out to be the conditioned of its own conditioned (a genesis of this sense), in a spiral without end, at once the ruin of the thought and the moment of its greatest extension and completion—a result toward which the projects of Heidegger and Tran Duc Thao already "tend," yet which Derrida alone genuinely achieves.[27]

The total intention of Derrida here in *Le problème* thus comes into view: an intention that indeed anticipates Derrida's mature work in important ways, and remains as vexed as it is unparalleled. For Derrida's work will always be marked by a double movement of the sort that has come forward here, even as Derrida further complicates it in ways that I begin to make clear below. In this passage, Derrida already sketches a program that proceeds in two rather disjunct phases, two distinct steps: a first that insists on the *retention* of Husserl's rationalist starting point, and a second that outstrips Heidegger and all other nonorthodox phenomenologists—and something like this will always be the case in Derrida's work. In 1954, that is, Derrida proposed to break with Husserl and phenomenology radically by staying with it longer, just as Derrida later honors philosophical reason, recognizes the rights of the logos longer than his rivals (such as Foucault, Levinas, or Lévi-Strauss), in order to break with it all the more boldly. Derrida's aim here in *Le problème*—to combine the retention of Husserl's philosophy and the rights of phenomenology with the setting forth of a radicality parallel to (or greater than) Heidegger's—foreshadows, then, the "logic" of deconstruction.

The strategic combination that Derrida proposes here permits an important adjustment of our usual view of Derrida, moreover (one that has in part been presupposed here all along). For it entails a profound, definitively *nonskeptical* undecidability which always marks Derrida's work. Derrida doubtless from the first wished to question thought, or phenomenology, radically, it can now be seen; at the same time, however, this most radical questioning was equally intended to preserve the rights of philosophy, and even in a certain way to extend them—to extend the reach of thought, by bringing within its compass a presupposition of thought itself previously impossible to think. The two—exceeding thought and extending its own borders—have always gone in hand in hand for Derrida, and this again makes clear that Derrida never aimed to abandon thought entirely, or simply transgress it as such.[28]

Put in different terms (terms which will prove useful as my discussion proceeds), from the first, it could be said, as this passage also attests, that Derrida has always wished to get what's right in Husserl and what's right in Heidegger right together. Not only has Derrida always aimed to build on Heidegger's project, even radicalize it further, as John Caputo and others emphasize; he has also wished to maintain contact with Husserl's endeavor, with Husserl's commitment to rationality, modernity, and his specifically modern theoretical perspective. Derrida's deflection of the usual phenomenological heterodoxy (of Heidegger's thought as he came to understand it) indeed has the effect of moderating or tempering the antimodern, antirationalist aspects of Heidegger's program, even as Derrida also claims to embrace and extend Heidegger's standpoint.

This is the side of Derrida's project that my first chapter began to highlight, the side which indeed first drew some of us to Derrida's work. For Derrida would be doing a tremendous service to thought, to philosophy and the tradition, were he right, should this combination now or later in any way prove truly possible. Finding a way to maintain Husserl's rationalism alongside Heidegger's questioning of the final stability of all foundations, to acknowledge the rights of Husserl's descriptions alongside a "radical alterity" (a term we already find Derrida employing in *Le problème*), Derrida could indeed secure for thought a future—a way to remain authoritative while acknowledging what draws it into doubt—at a time when any possibility of thinking fundamentally, of genuinely radical philosophical achievements of any sort (including Derrida's own first step, Husserl's phenomenology), remain gravely in question.

No final evaluation of the success of Derrida's endeavor can be reached at this initial juncture, of course. Only after the transformations that Derrida's initial ambitions undergo have been traced, and they have been explored in the context in which Derrida alone believes they are fulfilled, can the ultimate success or failure of Derrida's project be judged. *Le problème* in its strategy does provide a baseline for Derrida's future thought as a whole; nevertheless, Derrida's thought will change in important ways from this point going forward, and only after these shifts have been taken into account may any final evaluation of the success of Derrida's urgent project come about.

Such change in Derrida's standpoint is thus the next matter that needs to be taken up. While Derrida's intentions, his reference points, always owe much to Husserl, as well as Heidegger, while Derrida could always be said to aim at a navigation that includes them both—meaning that his thought will always be undecidable in this nonskeptical sense— how Derrida proposes to do this also alters over time. The result of this change, to cast a provisional glance forward, will be that Derrida's project swerves in a distinctly Heideggerean direction. Derrida will never want to abandon entirely these starting points provided by Husserlian rationality, even as he multiplies their implications, sometimes in directions far different from Husserl's, as I readily acknowledge.[29] Yet as his thought unfolds, Derrida's overall project will draw nearer to Heidegger's intentions, and this, among other things, may have obscured Derrida's loyalty to Husserl's rethinking of the Cartesian starting point, which Derrida himself seems never to have entirely disavowed.

Perhaps the most puzzling thing, however, is that this movement toward Heidegger and away from Husserl which marks Derrida's later work turns out to go by way of Husserl himself. The "Introduction" itself, it will turn out, is the vehicle for the corresponding transformation of Derrida's thinking, this movement toward a more profound incorporation of Heideggerean concerns. The "Introduction," the work in which Derrida arguably stands closest to Husserl, plays a crucial role in the transformation of Derrida's thinking, its further incorporation of Heidegger, as Derrida's interpretation of Heidegger deepens. And this paradox is itself bound up, in turn, with another important theme here: the problem that Derrida encountered in *Le problème* that may have kept it from publication (since this problem provides the setting for Derrida's eventual reinterpretation of Husserl's project and of his own in the "Introduction").

Lingering one more moment with the "Introduction" itself, however, let me recall a fact that I began to bring forward earlier, since this will set the stage for my further discussion of *Le problème*. In the "Introduction," as I earlier noted, Derrida embraces Husserl's history writings in a way that he had not done before. Derrida himself, moreover, specifically indicates that he changed his mind on this score—in respect to history, historicity, or as Derrida is about to put it here, "traditionality"—shortly after *Le problème*'s composition; he makes this point in one of the very few new notes that he allowed to become part of *Le problème* in 1990. Late in *Le problème,* in the course of his discussion of Husserl's *Origin,* next to his claim that "'traditionality' is always defined by Husserl as an empirical phenomenon," Derrida in 1990 added a footnote, telling us that he soon afterward wrote "'no, look again!' across from these lines" (*LPG* 264n12/ *PG* 164n12).[30]

The "Introduction," then, to establish this once and for all, clearly heralded a new interpretation of Husserl's work on history on Derrida's part, by Derrida's own avowal. What's more, Derrida, in embracing these themes, also began to move into a region closer to the core of Heidegger's thought. Once again to speak provisionally, the question of Being in its difference from beings (the *Seinsfrage,* the ultimate goal of Heidegger's inquiry as presented in *Being and Time*) is indeed first and foremost a historial and epochal question, and Derrida thus drew himself into the vicinity of Heidegger's real concerns by turning to the theme of history in the "Introduction"—a fact which also accounts for the disappearance, or demotion, of genesis as an issue in Derrida's mature thought.[31]

The works of 1967 indeed all start from concerns related to history, not genesis—from "phonocentrism," "logocentrism," "epochality," and the "system and history of metaphysics"—issues wholly absent from *Le problème;* and this indicates a new, further appropriation of Heidegger's thought on Derrida's part. This is not to say, of course, that none of Derrida's previous interests is discernible here; yet the writings of 1967 can be seen, provisionally speaking, as a repetition of Derrida's project in *Le problème* on new and deeper Heideggerean ground. In 1967, Derrida will again attempt to temper Heidegger's thought with Husserl's more rationalist and modern perspective, while still claiming a greater radicality than Heidegger in some respects—yet now with regard to history, historiality, and historicity, along with what Derrida too has begun, with Heidegger, to call "metaphysics."[32]

To begin to grasp the real force of this movement, to take the measure of this shift, it is necessary to confront the problem Derrida encountered in *Le problème* that seems to have kept him from publishing it at the time, along with the terms on which Derrida mounted his first Heidegger interpretation, since these matters will eventually return me to the extraordinary role of the "Introduction," allowing me to determine it more precisely. The "Introduction" and Derrida's new interpretation of Heidegger both, as I began to note, respond to a problem that Derrida faced in *Le problème,* a problem bound up with the inchoate state of Derrida's interpretation of Heidegger there.

To begin from this last, from the status of Derrida's Heidegger reading, then, Derrida understands Heidegger's intervention at the epoch of
Le problème, as we have already begun to witness, mainly in terms of a radical *tode ti,* an empirical facticity that Husserl's thinking can never ultimately take into account. Derrida's understanding of Heidegger is here at
its very earliest phase, and, accordingly, Derrida takes the Heideggerean
problematic to be focused on radical facticity—Derrida even repeatedly
speaks of the "real" in this context (a term that will drop from his vocabu-
lary immediately hereafter).[33] Derrida, focusing on the existent for the
thrust of his break with Husserl at this time, in 1954 thus interprets Heidegger's project in an existentialist mode. What is at stake in Heidegger's
break with Husserl is finally "existence itself," as we have already seen Derrida put it (*LPG* 225/*PG* 137); and throughout *Le problème* the transgressive value associated with genesis is almost always assigned to an "ontological" genesis, to a genesis in the real that gives primacy to a radically
individuated empirical singularity, which Derrida believes captures the
force of Heidegger's concerns.

Such an interpretation of Heidegger is arguably somewhat weak in
itself, and much thinner than that found in Derrida's later thought; moreover, this understanding of Heidegger—and Derrida's designation of the
beyond of Husserlian phenomenology in accord with it—poses numerous problems for Derrida himself in *Le problème.*[34] Understanding the unthought, the beyond of Husserlian phenomenology, as consisting in a
radical facticity, in the individuality of the existent, Derrida's own account
runs into a sheaf of difficulties, which Derrida, I would suggest, soon
found insurmountable, and this indeed led him to delay *Le problème*'s publication for so long.

A large, interrelated set of difficulties here arises, and the quickest
way into them is to pose the following question (since certain nuances of
Derrida's own presentation have to be omitted, without changing its basic
tenor): namely, how, in the section just examined, is a dialectical "reversal" of Husserl's thought supposed to arrive in any case at "existence itself," at a radical facticity (in the sense that Derrida believed Heidegger
wanted to give it)? How can Derrida finally lay claim to a radical *factical*
genesis at this moment, rather than a simple conceptual negation of
Husserl's claims, something like a "not-ideal," or even a prior, more fundamental, *transcendental* genesis (which is something Husserl himself
seems at times to have considered)?[35]

This is by no means immediately clear at this juncture in Derrida's
text, especially since Derrida also insists on the "formal" character of the
starting point that he shares here with Husserl ("the absolute commencement of reflection" as "a formal commencement," claims Derrida, is the

price "paid for all philosophical rigor," as he puts it a little later [*LPG* 226/*PG* 138]), and such formality sits poorly with the supposed concreteness of this outcome in "an already constituted ontology," and "a world whose ontological structures [are] themselves produced in the unity of a history" (*LPG* 228/*PG* 139). Derrida's claim to arrive back at a prior worldly empiricity, a constituted ontology, on the basis of this reversal thus appears ungrounded; and such a passage through dialectic is also rendered questionable, insofar as it is obscure why such passage is needed, if its outcome is a worldliness already otherwise known and recognized.[36]

An answer does exist, however, concerning why Derrida believes he has a right to speak of radical facticity at this juncture—which response, however, is really only to be found in part 2 of *Le problème*. Derrida's talk of an ontological genesis here in part 3 ultimately has its ground in work done before: it refers back to Derrida's work in part 2. And seeing this, a larger issue pertaining to the structure of *Le problème* as a whole will emerge, one that also ultimately concerns Derrida's interpretation of Heidegger.

In *Le problème*, Derrida, proceeding chronologically through Husserl's corpus, intends to give an interpretation of the entirety of his thought, and in the service of this, as I have already noted, Derrida in *Le problème* construed the totality of Husserl's writings provisionally in terms of a first phase, in which the theme of genesis is avoided or neutralized, and a second, when this theme, like the repressed, returns.[37] The answer to the question of by what right a "reversal" of Husserl yields real genesis in part 3 of *Le problème*, then, finally depends on what Derrida has done in part 2, in this first phase in which genesis is said to be neutralized. Derrida's argument, that the reversal of Husserl's genetic phenomenology (and of the goal forms structuring all egological genesis) points back to an ultimately *real worldly* genesis of these structures in part 3, is only possible thanks to an argument Derrida had earlier made in *Le problème*, concerning Husserl's treatment of time and the role in this of radically empirical genesis and real facticity.

Indeed, Derrida in the first half of *Le problème* makes much of the fact that Husserl's famous lectures on time (from which the *Phenomenology of Internal Time-Consciousness* was eventually drawn) fall chronologically between *Logical Investigations* and *Ideas I*. Specifically, Derrida argues that Husserl had come across certain features in his analysis of time that already implied real ontological genesis on the way to assuming the standpoint Husserl set out in the latter work. Casting back to a moment of phenomenology when genesis had not been an issue at all for Husserl, in the phase of its "neutralization," Derrida argues, an authentic existent, a *real* precursor to the absolute synthesis of lived temporality, is already presupposed by Husserl's analyses. Prior contact with an other, an anterior real, itself neither pure nor transcendental, must be assumed, Derrida asserts, if the possibility of even inner time passing is to be made good, if temporality is ever to differ from itself and gather itself up again, in the ongoing movement of lived constituting time-consciousness.[38] A kernel of the real is necessary even for absolute time to gather itself up in its own self-constituting ("phenomenological temporality" being "founded at the origin," "upon . . . *reality*"; *LPG* 120/*PG* 62), and thanks to this recasting of Husserl's teaching on time in part 2, Derrida is ultimately able to speak of radically factical genesis in part 3 as the outcome of a radical dialectical reversal of Husserl's genetic phenomenology. Husserl's investigations of absolute temporality have already been shown to lead back to the real and to an "ontology already in place" (*LPG* 117/*PG* 60), and Derrida's arrival at "ontological structures" of "a world" in part 3 thus ultimately refers back to this moment.[39]

Setting aside some of the more provocative nuances of this discussion, however, this earlier analysis brings before us a tension structuring *Le problème* as a whole. Derrida differs with Husserl on his treatment of time, claiming this implies an ontological genesis and commerce with the real that Husserl rejects. Moreover, on this basis, in part 2, Derrida will go on to argue that the *omission* of this more radical temporal level and all it implies underlies the very architecture of transcendental phenomenology as Husserl sets it out in *Ideas I,* and that continues to serve him thereafter.[40] The reductions themselves, the notion of phenomenology as eidetic descriptions of the transcendentally reduced ego, the correlation of noesis and noema—the "reduction" to the *eidos* ego in particular, as Derrida calls it—all depend on Husserl's having *in the first place* illegitimately omitted these considerations in respect to both absolute temporality (an omission to which Husserl himself more innocently stipulates in *Ideas I* 193–94) and the genesis in the real that it brings with it, according to Derrida.

Yet this raises the question of how, later in part 3, where we have already joined Derrida's discussion, Derrida *can* take a stand against Heidegger and Tran Duc Thao, and *can* side with Husserl's phenomenology, more generally. Derrida himself has already argued that this radical dialectic of temporality renders the institution of the framework of phenomenology in *Ideas I* doubtful. Indeed, he has earlier declared that "the eidetic reduction appears insufficient for escaping the contradictions of genesis" (*PG* 130).[41] How, then, can Derrida at this later juncture claim that the reduction of the ego to its essence *should* be maintained (along with all of Husserl's other methodological strictures)? According to Derrida himself, this possibility has already been brought into doubt by a prior ontological genesis, a passage through the real, in the work on time, before this level of Husserl's analysis has even been reached?[42]

Accordingly, a structural tension underlies Derrida's treatment of the two main phases of phenomenology in *Le problème*, and this, as we have already begun to see, is the sign of a larger conceptual problem that affects Derrida's project as a whole in 1954. As the passage cited above showed, Derrida indeed wants what *precedes* Husserl's own program and calls it into question (genesis in the real) to be the unique *result* of Husserl's own thought (thus anticipating Derrida's mature strategy in important ways—in fact, anticipating what Derrida calls the "logic of the supplement"). Yet Derrida's understanding of Heidegger at this time entails the corresponding characterization of this result as the "real," "the worldly," and the "constituted." Due to this identification, Derrida is not yet able to control these different phases of his inquiry, not yet able to square his outcomes with his precursors. On account of Derrida's existentialist reading of Heidegger, the alterity that calls Husserlian phenomenology into doubt is ultimately assimilated to a *real* anteriority, a radical singular *facticity*. This identification of alterity with the real makes it impossible, however, for Derrida ultimately to explain how passage through Husserl's account is both possible and necessary, and thus for Derrida to maintain that Husserl's account's conditioned uniquely emerges only *afterward* as this account's condition.

Derrida's construal of this result here has a destabilizing effect on dialectic itself, on the totality of his own argument. And this is why, I believe, Derrida had finally to downgrade the achievement of *Le problème* within this text itself, as well as to eventually withhold it from publication. Derrida confesses at the start of his "Avant-propos" that *Le problème* has turned out to be but a "historical inquiry," a contribution to the history of philosophy, rather than the more definitive, "more dogmatic" account of all thought, all philosophy, at which he had initially aimed (*PG* 1n1). And this, I presume, is due to these unresolved tensions between Husserl's project and what ultimately called this project into question as understood by way of Heidegger. Derrida himself had to recognize that dialectic, intended to represent the very "idea of philosophy"—its culmination, completion, repetition, and undoing, all in one—instead at best ended up denoting a simple failure or lapse on Husserl's part as he had presented it.

Profound difficulties, indeed, dogged Derrida throughout *Le problème* (which is not to blunt the continuing fascination of many of these readings, not to mention that some of the nuances of Derrida's own analyses have here necessarily had to be blurred down). These having been recognized, the contribution of the "Introduction," the difference Derrida's next major engagement with Husserl makes, now can be better grasped. As we saw earlier, in the "Introduction" Derrida comes into contact with what he himself specifies as a *nonempirical* traditionality—a specifically transcendental history and historicity. The significance of this new set of concerns, we begin to see, lies in their ability to *resolve the problems* that Derrida encountered when he first invoked these issues of facticity or empiricity in *Le problème*.

Derrida will not simply give up on these themes, as is well known; he will not altogether renounce this interrogation of the distinction between the empirical and the transcendental by any means. Yet raising these problems on this new site, his work in the "Introduction" subsequently permits Derrida to take up these issues concerning the empirical and the transcendental (the whirling dialectic of the two) from the side of the *constituting* (as well as the constituted): to raise them as they *pertain to the subject* as well as the object (and thus in effect already from within the transcendental attitude, thanks to a position that Husserl's thought alone makes available).

History as well as language stand on this divide between constituted and constituting in Husserl's late writings, as I have already shown. Though differentiated, each is constituted and constituting, empirical fact *and* transcendental presupposition. Accordingly, Derrida, in the aftermath of the "Introduction," in turning to these domains, can simultaneously start from a problem focused on this *constituting* work, and thus only reachable by way of Husserl's project (not even conceivable otherwise, thereby preserving the necessity of a passage through Husserl's thought, through the reductions and phenomenological evidence), while already having another foot in a moment pertaining to the object and its facticity (language and history raising questions concerning their status as objects, as singular worldly facts—issues concerned with facticity, alterity, and anteriority, on the side of the constituted). Language and history (though matters become more complex in the latter instance), thanks to their novel roles in Husserl's late work, provide a unique set of sites, both constituting and constituted at once, that allow Derrida to raise these questions about the transcendental and its other (the conditioned that conditions its conditions) from a greater variety of directions than before, in a way different from anything that transpires in *Le problème*. Derrida can thus pursue the concerns he initially established in his examination of genesis, even as he finds a way to resolve some of the issues that I have just set out, and as he lets this theme, genesis, in all its explicitness drop from his consideration.

The "Introduction," then, lets Derrida further complicate the framework of *Le problème* (furnishing it with an additional internal and external fold, if you will), even as it also brings Derrida's ambitions more generally to a site closer to Heidegger's most comprehensive concerns: since Heidegger's focus, falling on the difference between Being and beings, finally also in its own way falls on the "constituting" side, on the operation of transcendental difference, rather than on the simple existence of the existent as such. Since Husserl's last writings bring forward a transcendental historicity (as well as a pure history, underlying all real history), along with the possible transcendental achievements of pure language, as we have seen in chapter 3 (including even considerations related to Europe as an Idea), these thematics give Derrida a new set of Husserlian considerations parallel to Heidegger's historial ones, issues related *in Husserl* to the history of thought as such. Accordingly, they can furnish a new jumping-off point for Derrida's project in *Le problème* of combining and outflanking Heidegger and Husserl both at once—radicalizing both their stances by bringing them unexpectedly back into contact with one another.

This brings me to the final point in this phase of my discussion devoted to the *continuity* of Derrida's early development: namely, the "Introduction's" total place in this movement, which indeed turns out to be absolutely singular. After all, from the first moment the "Introduction" was discussed, it has been said that in it Derrida moves closer to *Husserl,* that Derrida embraces a hitherto unsuspected aspect of Husserl's program, and affirms the late work on history that Derrida himself had previously doubted. It can now be seen that this embrace, this reaffirmation of Husserl's thought in the "Introduction," coming after Derrida aimed at a unique kind of break with it in *Le problème,* also turns out to be a launching pad for another attempt at such a break: the even more radical future departure from Husserl and all of philosophy that Derrida undertakes in 1967. Derrida's rapprochement with Husserl in the "Introduction" provides the vehicle for him to move away from Husserl more radically, and move yet closer to Heidegger. But this means, then, that the "Introduction's" role in Derrida's development itself supplies an instance of that singular strategy that we have just seen Derrida himself articulate in *Le problème.*

The "Introduction" as a whole, that is, when seen as a step in Derrida's development, accords with that singular "strategy" or "logic" that has already emerged as uniquely Derrida's own in *Le problème.* In it, Derrida can be viewed as staying with Husserl longer, longer than even Derrida previously believed possible, only to eventually break with his phenomenology all the more radically. In the "Introduction," Derrida finds a further outpost of Husserl's thought to which to hew; he stays with Husserl beyond what had been conceivable in *Le problème*—all this to depart from Husserl even more drastically subsequently.

The "Introduction" as a whole, viewed developmentally, is thus another instance of Derrida's singular way of working, an application of Derrida's signature strategy. So, too, this accounts for why the "Introduction's" role in Derrida's corpus has always been so hard to pin down—the

"Introduction" being inherently a wild card, an intrinsically unstable phase of Derrida's thought, as well as having important implications for all of Derrida's mature thought, as we shall see. For the "Introduction's" total role indeed suggests that a kind of reconciliation with, or even *Aufhebung* of, Husserl's late historical project remains concealed within all of Derrida's later thought (the works of 1967 going forward), thanks to Derrida's having arrived at this later thought through his earlier rapprochement with Husserl.

* * *

Derrida's mature project thus emerges according to the singular strategy already evident in *Le problème*. Bringing the themes of history and historicity within his ken through the "Introduction," Derrida arrives at his 1967 stance toward these topics, which is perhaps why genuine *history* (just as genesis had earlier in *Le problème*) proves to be ultimately unthinkable in any direct way in Derrida's mature writings. A further development, a final link, takes Derrida, however, from the "Introduction" to the 1967 writings. Derrida having come upon history (and language) in the "Introduction," this transformation of his own thought, the reorientation of *his own project* in respect to history specifically takes place subsequent to the "Introduction." This last step of Derrida's bringing him to his mature thought on these themes becomes visible in his encounter with Foucault and Levinas in the early 1960s. These works, too, thus prove transitional works, and in the final half of my final chapter, accordingly, I will map in detail the workings of this transformation of Derrida's thinking in respect to history in the wake of the "Introduction."

For now, however, Derrida's development in a broader sense must still continue to be set out with an eye on *Le problème*. Until now, the considerations in this chapter have stressed the continuity of Derrida's early writings: *Le problème* has, for the most part, been explicated as presenting the baseline of Derrida's mature thought. Development, however, as already stressed, implies discontinuity as well as continuity—constancy of intention *and* chance encounter. Accordingly, at this moment, it becomes necessary to examine the context that *Le problème* and "Genesis" provide from the perspective of discontinuity as well. In 1962, in the "Introduction," Derrida made a genuine discovery: writing and language, themes that he had never broached before, appeared to him in a new light. These themes serve as the gateway to the 1967 works, in turn; and to round out our view of the development of Derrida's thought, these novel considerations that the "Introduction" presents, the difference it brings to the table, must be brought back into the picture, and their place in the broader context established by *Le problème* set out.

Writing, or language (not genesis, or even history or historicity), after all, will be the most central topics through which Derrida finally carries out his longstanding ambitions. And not only did Derrida first encounter these subjects in the "Introduction," but with them he subsequently faced new sorts of problems as well. Let me briefly recall, then, where my previous discussion of the "Introduction" left off: this matrix of issues, the singular difficulty Derrida faced in the "Introduction" (which will supervene upon the enterprise he had embarked on in *Le problème*). This was Derrida's inability to find some way to coordinate the two very different accounts of writing and language entailed by his examination of Husserl in the "Introduction's" section 7. The "Introduction" bequeathed to Derrida the problem of how to bring together writing and language as conceived by Husserl (transcendentally understood, with an intrinsic role in the constitution of truth) with factical, worldly writing—the real spatio-temporal inscription of empirical-factual signs, which Derrida had made the center of his deliberations at the outset of section 7's second half.

The breakdown of the hypothesis of truth's disappearing, which underlies the final fifteen pages of section 7 (a breakdown discernible in particular when the second hypothesis of truth's disappearance had to be dismissed), made evident that it was far from clear how the transcendental contribution of writing to truth (Husserl's own breakthrough) was to be preserved, and a way nevertheless opened to a broader understanding of writing than Husserl's own—how Husserl's stipulations, restricting writing and language to their transcendental intelligibility, to their phenomenological purity, and to their status as living flesh *(Leib)*, are to be lifted, and Husserl's innovation still maintained. This is the most immediate cause for Derrida's invention of deconstruction in the years leading up to 1967.

This last fact should be emphasized, and it will receive further attention in my subsequent chapters: Derrida invents deconstruction, this absolutely unparalleled way of working, most directly as a response to this impasse in forming a total, global conception of writing and language— at once constituting and constituted, pure and worldly—that he encountered in the "Introduction." Specifically, Derrida fashions what he himself calls a novel "strategic device" for "reading, writing, and interpretation" between "1963 and 1968" ("TT" 40), whose discontinuity with Derrida's earlier work has here already been stressed. And he did this because, as we began to see in chapter 3, no traditional mode of argument, nor any sort of previously recognized style of knowledge, is able to bring these two versions of writing together. There just is no direct way to think a writing more general than Husserl's (extending beyond his transcendental phenomenological stipulations) without its transcendental functioning being forfeited, thus forcing writing's conception back to positions that fall short of what Husserl himself had already discovered in the *Origin of Geometry*.

A further step is necessary, however, for Derrida's project to reach maturity. If Derrida is to successfully resolve the dilemma that he confronted in the "Introduction," if he is to bring together these two views of writing—transcendental writing and writing as it is more generally understood—and still not shut down Husserl's breakthrough entirely and obscure writing's constitutive role, then Husserl's own conception of *transcendentality*, as well as the notions of writing and language generally, will have to undergo a sort of transformation. Neither the standard conceptions of writing and language (both Husserl's and those opposed to it) nor that of the transcendental and its functioning may remain in place if a broader understanding of writing and language than Husserl's, which still has some sort of transcendental pertinence, is to be thought.

These themes, Derrida's actual reconstrual of the Husserlian transcendental along with writing and language, are the subject of chapters 5 and 6, with both *Speech* and *Of Grammatology*, albeit differently, undertaking this task. These issues are also of present concern, however, since, although these considerations focused on language and writing look wholly forward (being new to the "Introduction"), this second aspect of what will be required of Derrida's thought, this rethinking of Husserl's transcendental attitude, indeed points backward: toward *Le problème*, and the project that Derrida conceived there. Without in any straightforward sense contesting Husserl's thought, without breaking with his dialectical stance already reviewed, Derrida had already attempted a rethinking, even a deepening, of Husserl's transcendental standpoint in *Le problème*. Indeed, the problematic explored earlier, the problem of genesis, is itself a direct result of this endeavor. Derrida's concern with this theme, as we shall further see, provides a groundwork for Derrida's mature thought. In this instance, however, this theme, Derrida's reworking of Hussel's transcendental standpoint, undergoes *the greatest discontinuity* as Derrida's development proceeds.

In *Le problème* Derrida had already been concerned to address—to shore up, even supplement (in a less charged sense than Derrida will subsequently give this term)—Husserl's own transcendental framework. Husserl's own standpoint, however, as well as the transformation of it Derrida initially contemplated in *Le problème*, are themselves large, complex topics (even setting aside the issue of its further development). Thus, to begin to bring these surpassingly difficult matters into view—both Husserl's own understanding of the transcendental and the complementary conception Derrida gives to it in *Le problème*—I want to briefly call on Eugen Fink's famous account of Husserl's transcendental program in his essay "The Phenomenological Philosophy of Edmund Husserl and Contemporary Criticism."

Fink was Husserl's last graduate assistant, and his work generally, as is well known, strongly influenced Derrida's early approach to Husserl, especially in *Le problème*.[43] Fink's essay lets both the unique power of Husserl's transcendental standpoint, as well as a singular set of problems intrinsic to Husserl's perspective, be glimpsed. And it proves particularly useful to me here, since historical grounds indeed exist for believing that Derrida was aware of Fink's interpretation and that Derrida himself from very early on wanted to address the particular issues that Fink raised.[44]

Let me, then, briefly turn to Fink's work. Fink's 1933 essay, written as a defense of Husserl against contemporary neo-Kantian critics, received Husserl's own imprimatur at the time of its publication. In it, Fink, after a long discussion of the neo-Kantians' objections, offers a restatement of Husserl's enterprise, which Fink expresses in the form of a rather startling paradox.

On the one hand, Husserl's philosophy, Fink insists rather unexpectedly, ultimately has the same aim as that of the most traditional philosophy (indeed traditional philosophy's most traditional task): namely, to disclose "the origin of the world," "to make the world comprehensible . . . in terms of the ultimate ground of its being" (Fink 1970, 97, 98).[45] Husserl's thought, according to Fink, goes beyond Kant's, in part because it addresses the question concerning the origin of the world posed by *cosmology*, which is arguably the most metaphysical branch of traditional philosophy.

On the other hand, Husserl's thought pursues this problem, Fink quickly adds, in a post-, not a pre-Kantian style. Husserl discloses such an origin entirely by way of a "methodological" shift, thanks to finding a "completely different orientation" from all previous thinking (Fink 1970, 100). A change of standpoint, a change of *attitude,* reveals this origin. And one sign of the singularity of this shift is that it continues to entail "the retention of the world" (Fink 1970, 99).

This is the first key twist that must be gathered from Fink's work, one which should already resonate with readers familiar with Derrida's writings. Husserl's work, his reduction, aims to disclose an *origin*, a radical origin, indeed the origin of the world as such; yet an origin of a wholly unparalleled sort, in no way to be identified with any previous sorts of origins, one that does not retreat from what it originates, and in some sense is even embedded in, or dependent on, the latter.

Indeed, Husserl, according to Fink, stands apart from all traditional metaphysics, precisely because this "world origin" does not stand in a "transcendent relation" to the world. It does not take the form of a world-creating god; nor does it consist of the revelation of "some other world" (such as that of the supposed Platonic forms, or even Kant's things-in-themselves [Fink 1970, 99]).[46] Rather, Fink declares, "just as the world is what it is only in terms of its 'origin,' so is this origin itself what it is *only with reference to the world*" (Fink 1970, 99–100; my emphasis).

Husserl's transcendental-phenomenological attitude thus does not have recourse to a special sort of entity or even any new types of rules or logics, but instead consists of a radical shift in perspective on the world itself and the beings already there (including consciousness and the subject). Such a change in attitude discloses a concrete yet functioning world-ground understood as an *absolute* constituting *intentional* matrix, one already at work in respect to the world—indeed in a sense already at work *in* the world—though previously wholly unrecognized.[47] In so doing, the reduction inaugurates a fundamentally new domain of specifically philosophical research, a new style of philosophical science, whose final form of knowledge, whose ultimate character or boundaries, have themselves yet to be fully grasped, according to Fink.

Fink's account clarifies the transcendental in the specific sense that Husserl conceived it, and it makes palpable the lure of Husserl's transcendental inquiry, the power of phenomenology to renew philosophy, which Derrida himself, I believe, also always felt. Derrida was drawn from the first by those features of Husserl's thought that become visible here, I would maintain: among others, its ability, thanks to the transcendental reduction, to offer a new *field* of *experiences,* of *absolute* experiences, which promise validation to philosophy as knowledge and assign to it its own proper "empiricism" (avoiding all arbitrary, ungrounded, or free postulations).[48] Thanks to this radically novel of construal of world-origin, a field of originary experiences is revealed specific to *philosophy* itself, proper to no other domain of inquiry, and themselves ultimately authoritative for all *other* forms of knowledge and knowledge claims.[49]

Inseparable from this power of Husserl's thought and in tandem with Husserl's unique renewal of philosophy, there arise problems, however, problems which Fink was one of the first to raise. Most important (to reduce these matters again to their most basic contours), precisely because transcendental phenomenology gathers its power solely from such a radical change of *standpoint* and avoids all ontological commitments and hypotheses, the question of the ongoing and total relation of this standpoint to what precedes it becomes especially vexed. Husserl's absolute *comes to itself:* it finds itself as already in relation to a world, and this thanks to a previously existing standpoint, a *nonabsolute* standpoint—a relative understanding of the world (the so-called natural attitude) which differs from it, yet upon which this *absolute itself supervenes.*

Put in other terms, the very novelty of this world-ground, the very power of this revelation that transcendental phenomenology uniquely discloses, is inseparable from the fact that it posits an *origin* that necessarily emerges in medias res. Husserl's thought can disclose an absolute world origin and still avoid traditional metaphysics because, as a radical change of standpoint, it takes over givens and relations *already there* (already inhering in worldly consciousness, existing between consciousness and the world). Yet the question inevitably arises of how this new standpoint relates to the old. How does this standpoint put *itself* forward as *the absolute* even while referring back to the old one, in which the world was first given and through which it is still retained (thus allowing transcendental philosophy to have an identifiable task and an actual explanandum). This is the best-known single problem associated with transcendental phenomenology and with the transcendental reduction in particular.[50]

How the transcendental and natural attitudes, worldly consciousness and originary consciousness, are to be thought in totality—and how the turn toward the absolute is to be made in the first place, what motivates it and what its final relation to all that precedes it may be—are by no means wholly transparent in Husserl's thought, as Fink himself in this same essay makes plain. Fink specifically is led to posit "three egos" at work here, all belonging "to the performance-structure of the phenomenological reduction," in order to specify the ultimate relations of the transcendental to what precedes it (Fink 1970, 115). Fink posits three distinct egos in an attempt to master this issue of how these various standpoints are to be coordinated—how the ego which is not absolute can be thought as becoming aware of itself as absolute, as well as how the ego supposed absolute continues to refer back to a world. Yet Fink himself must admit that all three egos possess a "unique identity," are themselves finally *ontically one* (Fink 1970, 115, 116), and that this poses a profound "problem" for Husserl's phenomenology, indeed a problem to which "entire disciplines of the phenomenological philosophy" will have to be devoted (Fink 1970, 116).

Fink's magisterial presentation of Husserl's transcendental phenomenology thus ends up in a suspiciously familiar-sounding triune mystery: three egos or persons, also somehow one, the ultimate ground of whose self-differentiation remains obscure.[51] And in subsequent writings, Fink continued to pursue these questions concerning the relation of Husserl's absolute and his transcendental attitude to what precedes it. In particular, Fink, in line with these same concerns, famously raises the question of the status of the *discourse* in which all this is to take place: of how that language in which transcendental inquiry is supposed to express its findings is related to its worldly operation. Fink indeed doubted whether transcendental and mundane discourse are really in any way finally translatable, and this, too, is part of the problem posed by the emergence of Husserl's transcendental attitude in medias res: how this attitude is to relate to a *precursor,* to a *prior* standpoint which it can never simply eliminate, yet which is also supposed to be its own product and *conditioned,* that whose absolute it itself is—a problem inseparable from Husserl's breakthrough, his discovery of a new sort of origin, and a radically new style of philosophical inquiry.

Fink had already surveyed a mass of problems, then, unique to Husserl's transcendental standpoint, inseparable from its singular capacity to provide a new path for thought and to promise some future for philosophy; and part of what Derrida (himself a reader of Fink and aware of these concerns) wished to do in *Le problème,* I would suggest, is to respond to these concerns.[52] The problem of genesis, in particular, it can now readily be seen thanks to Fink—of a genesis *of* the transcendental with one foot in the real—is in part crafted to account for Husserl's unique transcendental standpoint, for the singular emergence of this transcendental origin, in the midst of an ongoing world. Genesis beyond the transcendental is meant to answer how the transcendental attitude arises in the first place, and Derrida's dialectical stipulations concerning the former are meant to ensure the rights of the latter. Moreover, this will always remains true in some way of all that gives primacy to *difference* and somehow makes it "first" in Derrida. The transcendental standpoint, this world origin, is an absolute that in some way arises thanks to a difference from what is already there and what it explains, and Derrida's emphasis on difference always has this in mind, something that becomes apparent even in Derrida's later discussions of Husserl's philosophy.[53]

More specifically yet, staying with *Le problème,* this notion of a genesis anterior to the transcendental subject that Derrida wants to mount is meant to explain how there can be a prior field of reference, an explanandum in the form of the world (and worldly consciousness) prior to Husserl's origin, yet this origin still maintain its own absolute transcendental functioning. This other, this radical existent, this factical instance in the real, continues to rely on Husserl's own standpoint, on this radical world origin for its own identification and determination (as we have already seen Derrida insist in line with his resolve to proceed dialectically and remain longer with Husserl than Heidegger or others do). Thus, setting forth such an other, an unthought in *Le problème,* Derrida in part aims to shore up, even to extend Husserl's perspective, by showing how it may be in contact with a precursor even while retaining the validity of this standpoint in turn.

So, too, the issue that Derrida himself later identifies as the central one of all *Le problème* carries a similar charge. In his 1990 "Avertissement" Derrida asserts that an interest in an "originary complication of the origin" was the concern expressed in *Le problème* that will always remain his own across all his work (*PG* v). This concern, however, has its source in the issues that I have just been discussing. By dialectically, not phenomenologically, contesting the "purity" of Husserl's absolute standpoint, by investigating how Husserl's transcendental attitude can disclose "the origin of the world" (a formulation Derrida will repeatedly employ in many of his later writings) while emerging from a standpoint not itself originary—thus how the transcendental reduction yields an origin, yet an origin never itself simply entirely and unequivocally original—the theme of "contamination" or "complication" in *Le problème* that Derrida so prizes later emerges directly out of those problems specific to Husserl's transcendental standpoint. Husserl's origin, precisely because it is complex and implicated in, if not contaminated by, what it originates, will always have a concern for its own purity, which is but another name for its own philosophical standing and authority, and this is the very problem Derrida himself started out by addressing. In fact, the notion of "origin" in *Le problème*, it could quickly be shown, everywhere pertains *solely* to the transcendental in Husserl's sense. Thus, what Derrida is up to with this "contamination" or "complication" of it by an "other," as well as with his talk of more than one origin, both now and in the future, can never really be grasped without recognizing the singular status this theme already has in Husserl's unique interpretation of transcendentality.

In sum, Husserl's program, as has long been recognized in the literature, already had an inherently unstable side pertaining to the transcendental reduction in its specificity, and in *Le problème* Derrida, even as he contests Husserl's project (and intends to capture Heidegger's concerns as he then understands them) by aiming to set out a beyond, a radical existent, that Husserl himself is unable to think, also intends to buttress Husserl's singular endeavor, his unique transcendental perspective, by securing its relation to the nonabsolute (through expanding the scope of interaction between absolute subjectivity and the nonsubjective more generally)—thus furthering, not simply destroying, Husserl's standpoint. This aspect of *Le problème*, this ambition on Derrida's part, moreover, continues to be maintained by him up through the 1967 writings and thereafter: it is indeed another important thematic anticipation of Derrida's later thought to be found in *Le problème*, albeit one that undergoes the greatest alteration subsequently.

As to this latter fact, the change in Derrida's positioning of this theme—and here I rejoin the central concerns of my discussion above—the "Introduction" indeed brings to it new themes, new problems, the seeds of a new way of working. In doing so, it alters this motif of the transcendental in profound ways, even to the extent of sometimes making it difficult to straightforwardly identify this aspect of Derrida's ambitions in his later work. The "Introduction" and the new concerns it introduces indeed transform this problematic rather radically. And while the exact character of this transformation, the specific form Derrida's rethinking of Husserl's transcendental opening will take in his later works in the wake of the "Introduction" is in part the subject of the two chapters to come, here, recognizing this, those broader considerations toward which my discussion has been headed can finally arrive.

Even in 1967, it can already be affirmed, Derrida will be concerned with problems unique to Husserl's philosophical standpoint of the sort that have just been sketched (and to which he had already tried to respond in *Le problème*). Derrida will still wish to make room for or enlarge Husserl's thought of a radically new style of transcendental originariness, even while bringing this program otherwise into doubt. Yet thanks to the motifs bequeathed to him by the "Introduction" that we earlier identified, thanks to the need to think a newly conceived writing and language alongside a newly conceived transcendental attitude, this whole endeavor becomes further complicated, takes on a new concreteness and singularity, in a fashion that brings real discontinuity with it and makes it impossible, among other things, to continue to assign to Derrida's thought a single line of development.

More specifically, Derrida after the "Introduction" now starts with a different sort of thematic concern than genesis in the real, as I began to show above: language and writing, functioning at once on the subject and the object side of Husserl's program, representing both a transcendental and a worldly "empiricity." In addition, the premises pertaining to language and writing in each of Derrida's two book-length 1967 works become more complicated and necessarily differ *from one another,* in part thanks to the double standing of these themes themselves. As we saw in the "Introduction," Husserl's own stipulations in respect to writing cannot themselves simply be dissolved (and the usual views of writing and language come forward) and Husserl's breakthrough still be maintained. As a result, Derrida in 1967 perforce will have to begin, in two separate gestures, from each of these versions of writing and language—Husserl's views and the everyday ones, writing from within the confines of transcendental phenomenology taken as *Leib* and apart from Husserl's unique perspective—in order to pursue on more than one site the same more general notion of writing and language (radically constituting and constituted at once, simultaneously the possibility of both truth and its *radical* disappearance) that he had begun to glimpse in the "Introduction."

This is an important point, never taken into account before in the literature to my knowledge. Each of Derrida's book-length 1967 works, *Speech and Phenomena* and *Of Grammatology*, has a very different starting point in respect to language and writing, thanks to the impasse Derrida encountered in the "Introduction," even as he pursues in each the goals that first *Le problème* and then the "Introduction" bequeathed to him. In *Speech* Derrida clearly begins from Husserl's own views: from the phenomenological conception of writing and language as spiritual corporealities, as living flesh (and as thus open to a pure transcendental appropriation). In *Of Grammatology*, in turn, Derrida begins from the multiplicity of languages in their factuality, from language and inscription in the context offered by a mundane empirical science. And as a result, only when both the 1967 works are taken together will Derrida really achieve this thought of a more general writing and language at which he now aims, and which he had begun to glimpse in the "Introduction."[54]

My subsequent chapters will pursue these matters more deeply; what remains under consideration now, however, is the effect this has on the reworking of Husserl's transcendental standpoint—the other phase of Derrida's mature project that has become visible here. Put most broadly, while in some way continuing to be loyal to *Le problème*'s second set of thematic intentions, very different styles of rethinking Husserl's transcendental perspective become available to Derrida in 1967, thanks to the new themes of writing and language and the different starting points they bring. One style of pursuing these transcendental considerations will be more empirical and closer to Heidegger (in *Of Grammatology*, in line with Derrida's beginning there); another remains in greater proximity to Husserl's conception (in *Speech*, where Derrida maintains far more of the prerogatives of Husserl's philosophy than has often been recognized)—even as they themselves bear a complex relation to one another.

Derrida's different beginnings in respect to writing and language in each of these works thus further particularizes and individualizes his transformation of the transcendental that came forward originally in *Le problème*. They pave the way for the radical specificity and negativity of the practice of deconstruction (its movement through readings and writing) while also opening the door, it is worth noting, to the concerns my first chapter raised regarding whether Derrida can really bring this totality of his ambitions to a successful outcome—in *Of Grammatology* in particular, where he indeed starts from factical, worldly language. Whether the novel reworking of transcendentality that *Of Grammatology* proposes (more novel and radical than *Speech* in important respects, as may have started to become clear) can indeed maintain Derrida's intentions and not succumb to empiricism entirely, as Derrida himself hoped, is an issue already discussed here, and it stems from this doubling of Derrida's starting points in respect to language that is itself ultimately owed to the "Introduction."

My primary focus at the moment, however, is not on the outcomes of Derrida's intentions, but on these intentions themselves: the picture of Derrida's aims as whole in the 1967 works. Finally, that new frame, that overview of Derrida's first deconstructive undertaking in its entirety that has so long been sought, has emerged. In each of his 1967 works, to gather up all that has been said, Derrida will indeed face a single twofold task, even as he precedes from two different sites. Derrida will want to mount, first of all, a new, more general thought of writing and language (or at least a deconstruction of the teleology that confined the old, betokening a greater, more comprehensive, radicality). And second, Derrida will attempt to think Husserl's transcendental attitude anew: to carry forward, to *further expand* it, even as he also questions Husserl's novel notion of a world origin, and shows it to be implicated in a movement and history at least in part foreign to Husserl himself.[55]

Derrida thus maintains those aims from both *Le problème* and the "Introduction" even as he proceeds from two different sites, thanks to the discontinuity the "Introduction" introduces. His project thus becomes still more radically distinct, and further from Husserl's own, especially as it now incorporates that novel device for writing and reading which introduces the first properly deconstructive phase of his thought. Nevertheless, Derrida's deconstructive writings of 1967 are indeed *results,* we now know. And so by taking Derrida's development into account, a new, more precise look at the 1967 writings also becomes possible. Starting from this fourfold set of reference points that has here come into view (a twofold task starting from two different beginnings), full-fledged readings of these hallmark texts can now be undertaken, ones which will attend to their differences as well as their similarities, to their strengths as well as their weaknesses. My two final chapters pursue these readings, the question of Derrida's development now having been settled and an overview of its complex movement having been sketched.

5

Husserl's Circuit of Expression and the Phenomenological Voice in *Speech and Phenomena*

Having arrived at a developmental overview of Derrida's 1967 writings, I now wish to turn to *Speech and Phenomena*. Good reasons exist to think that *Of Grammatology*, or at least parts of it, were written before *Speech*—an earlier draft of the first half of *Of Grammatology* having appeared as an article in 1965. Nevertheless, insofar as Derrida's starting points in *Speech,* as well as his overall concerns there, are nearer to those we have already reviewed (*Speech* indeed closes out Derrida's engagement with Husserl, and it will not be until the next century that Derrida writes again on Husserlian phenomenology), *Speech* will be treated here first, and the break that *Of Grammatology* proposes, in some ways more radical than that of *Speech,* taken up last.[1]

Speech is, of course, the writing of Derrida on Husserl most familiar to Derrida's readers generally, as well as to Husserl scholars. *Speech* has often been the sole text studied when it comes to Derrida's relation to Husserl, or it has organized the understanding of the rest. So taken, however, *Speech* continues to generate a tremendous amount of controversy, and in bringing a developmental approach to bear on it, one of the main aims of this chapter, indeed of this book, is to resolve some of these longstanding difficulties.

Not only have commentators focused solely or largely on *Speech,* however; their reading has been tilted toward its first few chapters, which are devoted to Derrida's discussion of Husserl's comments on the sign (or else chapter 5, on time, has been taken in isolation), and this has contributed to much of the disagreement as well.[2] *Speech,* however, is not simply, or even primarily, a book about the distinctions that Husserl draws in the first few pages of *Logical Investigations* II; it is, as the work already done here allows us to recognize, a reprise of Derrida's intentions in *Le problème,* and aims once again at an interpretation of Husserl's thought as a whole.

Logical Investigations II.1 is the site for one final *global* interpretation of Husserl's thought on Derrida's part, and much of Derrida's commentary in *Speech,* especially as he gets further on in this work, is devoted to themes from *Ideas I* (noesis-noema, the phenomenological and transcendental reductions), the *Phenomenology of Internal Time-Consciousness,* the *Cartesian Meditations* (the reduction to a sphere of ownness in *Cartesian Meditations* 5), and *Formal and Transcendental Logic* (the interpretation of the linguistic sign as *Leib*), rather than to *Logical Investigations* II.1 itself.[3]

Of course, Derrida in *Speech* no longer wishes to proceed through Husserl's corpus step-by-step as he did in *Le problème.* In a more synchronic fashion he takes the opening moments of *Logical Investigations* II as the entryway to a discussion of Husserl's entire thought and corpus, and this clearly has to do with the initial thematic focus of Derrida's reading in *Speech.* Derrida does, however, intend to mount an interpretation of Husserl overall in this work, of all that Husserl has thought or attempted, a treatment on a par with, yet even more far-reaching than that of *Le problème.* Derrida's arguments or intentions in *Speech* thus cannot really be grasped without taking this aspect of *Speech* into account.[4]

In turn, this does not mean that no objections may be raised to Derrida's readings of Husserl—either of *Logical Investigations* II.1 itself or of the other texts that Derrida treats in *Speech.* In line with what I have argued in chapter 2, Husserl's intentions and his text must continue to be honored, as well as Derrida's specific intentions. Both Husserl's claims and Derrida's aims must be respected if an interpretation even potentially persuasive to all parties is to be mounted.

Granting, however, the necessity to acknowledge that Derrida's intentions pertain to *the totality of Husserl's thought,* as well as to Husserl's own specific interests in the opening pages of *Logical Investigations* II, where Derrida's aims lie in their own right is not easily established in *Speech,* especially in the absence of attention to Derrida's development of the sort that has been paid here. In part because of the artifice that organizes Derrida's approach—the extrapolation of matters concerned with the entirety of Husserl's corpus and every phase of his thought on the basis of a mere twenty pages of a single text (the first six chapters of *Speech,* some eighty pages in all, cover only eleven pages of *Logical Investigations* II.1)—Derrida's real differences from Husserl are by no means themselves always easy to discern on the surface of this work. Moreover, along with this singular interpretive standpoint—a standpoint only available thanks to Derrida's prior encounters with Husserl, and one that must be read in their light—*Speech,* it must be recognized, is very much a work in motion. In the course of *Speech,* as shall be further confirmed, Derrida's own perspective and the presuppositions of his own argument change, and this, too, has made it difficult to get clear about Derrida's aims in *Speech* as a whole, especially in its final chapters, which are the products of this shift.

Speech and Phenomena—to provisionally characterize this change of standpoint in more concrete terms—is composed of two distinct gestures: two different focal points, whose relations to one another are by no means straightforward. In the first three chapters of *Speech*, Derrida's focus is indeed on Husserl's treatment of the sign. The concerns of Derrida's own discussion directly relate to the distinctions that Husserl himself sets out at the start of *Logical Investigations* II.1 (though Derrida arguably sees these distinctions in a different light than Husserl himself and gives them different weight, as I shall later explain). In the last chapters of *Speech*, however, most notably in chapter 6, in line with his attempt at a total interpretation of Husserl's corpus, Derrida returns to what we now know to be some of his more longstanding preoccupations, and targets issues specific to transcendental subjectivity and transcendental experience as such—in a discussion largely relating to a later phase of Husserl's corpus than *Logical Investigations* II, and having different Husserlian presuppositions.

Derrida's focus thus alters in *Speech,* and the shape of this movement must be emphasized: moving, as it does, from the sign (and language) to transcendental subjectivity (and absolute temporality)—for here that rift once more becomes visible between language-related thematics and transcendental concerns, which has provided the guiding thread of my inquiry into Derrida's thought all along. Derrida's aims in *Speech* indeed shift overall from linguistic to transcendental concerns—by means of considerations pertaining to language largely stemming from *Ideas I* rather than from *Logical Investigations* itself, as I will later show—and as such, addressing the movement of *Speech,* those questions touching on the innovation, or methodology, of deconstruction as a whole that have already arisen will again have to be confronted.

Such problems concretely emerge in the movement of *Speech;* and the stakes of their resolution are even greater than has as yet appeared, since, corresponding to the question of the status of the movement of *Speech* itself, a further obscurity has taken hold pertaining to the voice, which is the one theme that does seem to provide a focus for the whole of *Speech. Speech* may be seen as composed of two different developments, two large-scale outcroppings (like the twin wings of a butterfly). The problematic of the voice emerges across these, however, and spans them both. The voice, *la voix,* in some way takes in both of *Speech*'s phases (though it also undergoes change, as we shall shortly see), and this problematic, and what Derrida intends by it, has been as little fully plumbed, finally, as the movement and structure of *Speech* itself.[5]

That problems pertaining to the interpretation of the voice coincide with those concerning deconstruction's methodology should be no surprise, however: the voice, after all, is a direct result of Derrida's development, just as is Derrida's new way of working in 1967. Considerations related to the voice and phonocentrism are absent even from the first three key transitional essays of *Writing and Difference* and are thus new to Derrida in *Speech* and *Of Grammatology*. With the advent of deconstruction, with this new way of organizing his texts, Derrida also struck upon concerns related to the voice and the *phone*, and both this theme and Derrida's innovation in approach ultimately pose the same set of problems.[6]

Neither of these themes has yet been made fully clear, however; and to stay solely with the voice for now, why Derrida introduced this theme, how his claims about it finally function, and what its relation to linguistics and other theories of language may finally be, is still not wholly grasped today. In part due to what I have just outlined—the complexity of *Speech* itself, its organization, and the difficulty of locating Derrida's intentions on the surface of his text—what actual phenomenon Derrida has in mind here remains obscure.[7] Accordingly, in what follows, I propose first and foremost to attempt to answer this question. Through attention to the structure of *Speech* as a whole, to the movement of Derrida's thought across the multiple sites it finds in this work, I will start to make plain what the voice represents through the various aspects of its privilege and the different phases of its presentation in *Speech*.

More concretely, I will first investigate the theme of the voice as it emerges in the first three chapters of *Speech,* in the context of Derrida's discussion of Husserl's treatment of the sign, a discussion which has proved especially problematic in the literature. In turn, I will explore the distinctly different functioning of the voice—that of the phenomenological voice in its specificity—in the last three chapters of *Speech,* and in chapter 6 in particular, where the actual referent of Derrida's talk of the voice, what phenomenon the voice really designates in *Speech,* finally emerges.[8] Chapter 6 represents the core achievement of *Speech,* a fact that has been difficult to see, insofar as the structure of this work as a whole and Derrida's ultimate aims in it have not been fully taken into account.[9]

Before turning to each of these developments, however—in the two subsequent parts of this chapter, respectively—let me make clearer this movement embracing *Speech* as a whole that I have begun to sketch and how it relates to those issues that my earlier examination of Derrida's development brought forward. For one, chapter 4 of *Speech* has yet to be mentioned here; however, it proves to be a critical turning point, in some respects—a moment in which Derrida's argument swerves in a decisive fashion from the first set of themes that underlies his discussion in *Speech* to the second. Especially when seen in the context of Husserl's corpus, in chapter 4 Derrida starts to move from these earlier language-related themes to concerns far more central to Husserl's own philosophy (the discussion of inner temporality following next in chapter 5)—and Derrida's argument in the body of *Speech* in fact runs a course parallel to the rather singular route Derrida follows in his introduction to this work, as I shall later discuss.

Chapter 4 is a turning point in *Speech,* then, and early on in it, Derrida makes an absolutely critical remark that bears on the shape of *Speech* as a whole, as well as on his own way of working here, giving a clue to where his development has now brought him. A crucial methodological consideration arises in respect to Derrida's intentions at this moment. Derrida insists, at this critical turning point in chapter 4, that *two disappearances* of the sign can be conceived, "two ways of eliminating the primordiality of the sign" are possible (*SP* 50), and that the route *Speech* subsequently follows chooses *one* of these ways. Though everything Derrida has previously said—namely, his criticisms of the limits of Husserl's approach to language and the sign—will have suggested that Derrida has in mind *a philosophy or theory of the sign and language of his own,* the rest of *Speech* will be engaged in what Derrida himself calls "eliminating the concept of the sign" and will turn to Husserl to do so.

A first disappearance of the sign may be conceived, more specifically, according to Derrida, "in the classical manner," in the name of an *"intuition and presence"* that "eliminate[s] signs by making them derivative"; a second, however, in turn, gives primacy to a *difference* associated with signitive *repetition* over and above the sign itself—though "these two ways," Derrida also acknowledges, "pass quickly and surreptitiously *into one another*" (*SP* 51; my emphasis).

Taking up project two, then Derrida cannot be interested, as has so often been claimed, in reducing all thought or truth to signs—since the sign as such is about to disappear as a theme in his work. Instead, Derrida (who is now about to turn to the core concerns of all Husserl's thought) intends to set out *something like* a possible originariness pertaining to the sign—an origin corresponding to the possibility the sign also entails— *which has always been eclipsed and never yet appeared as such,* and this from a position not falling short of, but starting from within, transcendental phenomenology.[10] Indeed, in a footnote at the end of chapter 3, Derrida had already made clear that "by reintroducing the difference of the sign at the heart of the 'originary,' it is not a matter of falling short of transcendental phenomenology" (*SP* 49n1); and in the second half of *Speech,* speaking broadly, Derrida aims to bring forward a *difference,* still in some important way related to Husserl's transcendental perspective—one also answering to the sign, yet not entailing a new account of it as such—a course in part made necessary, according to Derrida, insofar as every notion of the sign, every thought of it, all semiotic concepts heretofore, have been derived from "the metaphysics of presence" (*SP* 51).[11]

What this second development may look like, how this new nonclassical disappearance of the sign, supposed to restore a more originary difference corresponding to, or including within it, semiosis, is to function is by no means evident at this moment in Derrida's text, nor may it be extrapolated simply on the basis of Derrida's discussion up until this point. Indeed, what takes place in the second half of *Speech* is, as I will show, far more novel than has customarily been assumed—yet also far closer to Husserl in some respects. Derrida in these pages will attempt, among other things, to fulfill that aim at a dialectical reconfiguration of Husserl's transcendental attitude we already saw him undertake in *Le problème*. Derrida will once again attempt to both question and enlarge Husserl's transcendental attitude, to think anew Husserl's already unparalleled origin of the world, though now, to be sure, in a manner that also takes into account those problems of signification (writing and language) that arose in the "Introduction" (even as all the usual indices of this problematic—of language, writing, and the sign—become increasingly absent, and Husserl's own program comes increasingly to the fore), all the while sketching a notion of difference, albeit a transcendental difference, that finally would also be foreign to Husserl.

Correspondingly, that set of developmental considerations brought forward in my discussion of the "Introduction" will also make themselves felt in what follows. Thanks to them, it can be seen in advance that Derrida's initial encounter with Husserl's treatment of language in *Speech* must end on a radically negative note. Derrida does not, and cannot, simply offer an alternative theory of language, or a new notion of semiosis as such. Derrida will make highly novel claims, not finally about language and signs themselves, but rather about the restrictions that the conceptualization of these stand under—offering a meta-reflection on the thematization of language and signification generally, a second-order hermeneutics bringing forward the "metaphysical" history and system dominating all such thematics in advance—a treatment necessitated and motivated by those problems with fashioning a more global transcendental view of language than Husserl's own that Derrida had already encountered in 1962.

I emphasize this now because, to the degree that this is so, these language-related themes, so often assumed crucial to Derrida's 1967 breakthrough, ultimately turn out to be floating signifiers of sorts, and this has particular bearing on the voice: the one such theme that does seem to remain in view across the scope of *Speech*. The voice, too, will finally undergo a shift, in accord with the rest of the text of *Speech*. Participating in the motion of Derrida's argument as a whole that I have just set out, for which chapter 4 provides the pivot, the voice also does not fall short of Husserl's transcendental perspective, but ultimately works within it, in order to open a way beyond it. The voice in chapter 6, the legatee of all Derrida's earlier discussions, is indeed a phenomenological voice in its specificity, and it is itself finally thinkable on the terms of Husserl's thought alone, even as it points the way beyond them.[12]

* * *

Let me now, then, follow out each of these two gestures that I have just sketched, these two different manifestations of the voice, across the different stances taken by Derrida toward Husserl's thought in the course of *Speech and Phenomena*. Derrida's concerns related to the philosophy of language and semiotics will be examined initially (and the voice as it appears in proximity to these), an examination whose focus ultimately falls on *Speech*'s chapter 3. In turn, moving to the more central concerns of Husserl's own transcendental project, the phenomenological voice in its specificity will come forward in the second phase of my discussion, a discussion that ultimately focuses on chapter 6.

The first part of my discussion here eventually wants to focus on Derrida's analysis of expressions *(Ausdrücke)* in chapter 3; this is the crux of the controversy that has surrounded Derrida's work in the first half of *Speech*, and it will also eventually prove key for establishing a linkage to *Speech*'s second half—and thus for my interpretation of the voice in chapter 6 as well. Before turning there, however, I must begin by attending to another move that Derrida makes in chapter 4, in the same chapter in which he distinguishes these two disappearances of the sign. In chapter 4, as we have already begun to see, the first, specifically linguistic, side of Derrida's work in *Speech* arrives at this, its rather unexpected "completion," and at this moment, Derrida's discussion also focuses on the key theme of ideality. Having claimed, on the basis of his previous discussion of language and the sign, that "we thus come—against Husserl's express intention—to make the *Vorstellung* [representation] itself . . . depend on the possibility of repetition, and the most simple *Vorstellung*, presentation *(Gegenwärtigung)*, depend on re-presentation *(Vergegenwärtigung)*," Derrida goes on to state, "the concept of ideality naturally has to be at the center of such a problematic" (*VP* 58/ *SP* 52).

Derrida is here commenting on the following claim of Husserl's: because a merely *imagined* sign may be employed in soliloquy, its function, Husserl had argued, can only be to abet the work of conceptual or logical representation (falling under the broader category that Husserl calls *Vorstellung*), rather than to participate in any sort of communication. *Vorstel-*

lung is the standard German word for "representation" (coming from *vorstellen*, "to place something before"); in Husserl it connotes any presentation of an object to consciousness. And Derrida here, by drawing on a second set of Husserlian distinctions besides that pertaining to *Vorstellung*—between *Gegenwärtigung* ("making present," as well as *Präsentation*, the "presentation" of a thing in person), over and against *Vergegenwärtigung* (the "representation" of a previous presentation through memory or imagination)—is questioning whether these distinctions may be applied to language at all: whether Husserl, distinguishing between real (presented by way of *Präsentation*) and imagined instances (presented through *Vergegenwärtigung*) *within language*, will really be able to isolate a specifically logical or discursive work of linguistic representation, and with that, finally, distinguish the work of representation in consciousness generally *(Vorstellung)* from all other possibilities of presentation, including those pertaining to language and signs more generally.

Much of what Derrida has to say on this score will be taken up in the second phase of our discussion when we turn to the voice's role in Husserl's transcendental project. Yet, beginning here in chapter 4, a crux in the critical literature confronts us, which I want to first take into account. For Derrida's defenders and attackers alike often attribute the belief to him that ideality (as well as the transcendental subject and its rights) originates from linguistic and semiotic systems, and the origin of this belief is to be found in developments stemming from Derrida's declarations here.[13] Derrida, in reversing the roles of *Vorstellung*, the genus of primarily conscious representation (conceptualization, perception), and the derivative making-present *(Vergegenwärtigung)* of the imagined sign (and having earlier claimed that the "sign is never an event," it "implies representation: as *Vorstellung*, . . . as *Vergegenwärtigung* . . . and as *Repräsentation*" [*SP* 50]), indeed seems to be asserting that the ideality of logical representation (itself tied to the priority of *Vorstellung* as a function of consciousness)—and with that the *Bedeutungen* ("logical meanings") or ideal contents of discursive representation (what in other contexts are sometimes called propositions as opposed to sentences)—should be reduced to the work of signs and language.[14]

Now, it cannot be doubted that Derrida here and throughout *Speech* wishes in some form to raise questions about ideality, the timeless inexistence pertaining to conceptual and other cultural or spiritual *(geistig)* meanings. In particular, he will repeatedly claim that the ultimate rights of Husserl's principle of principles (phenomenology's founding dictum that only what is given in person, at first hand, to the phenomenological inquirer may be granted authoritative status as knowledge) are brought into question by dint of that infinite teleology, that idea in a Kantian sense, that Derrida claims ideality ultimately implies.[15] Nor can it be disputed, in respect not to ends, but to beginnings, that Derrida wishes to argue that Husserl's notion of origin (his transcendental subject and attitude) is implicated in a power of radical repetition that Derrida wants associated in some fashion with language, signification (and later writing)—as I have already begun to indicate.

Nevertheless, the common claim that Derrida subsumes outright the entire class of what Husserl called *Bedeutungen*—ideal logical or conceptual meanings, the selfsame contents of statements—into the functioning of language and signs as such, is not correct. Harshly questioning the totality of Husserl's distinctions in the first three chapters of *Speech,* as I will shortly discuss, Derrida may well seem to have in mind a matrix of distinctions pertaining to signs, language, and meaning significantly different than those Husserl sets out in *Logical Investigations;* a matrix in which ideality (and ideal meanings, *Bedeutungen*) would be identical to linguistic expressions *(Ausdrücke),* the expressive to other functions of language, and, finally, linguistic signs generally to indications *(Anzeichen).* It is worth noting, however, that Husserl himself while drawing such distinctions never established once and for all the ultimate relations between these terms, especially in respect to the conditions of their actual existence (a question ultimately beyond the bounds of phenomenological research)—producing an uncertainty of which Derrida clearly makes much in both "Form and Meaning" and *Speech,* in order to argue for a tighter connection between ideal meaning and linguistic expression than some Husserlians would allow.[16] Furthermore, it is also the case, importantly, that the work of *Speech*'s three opening chapters is not aimed at a first-order thesis about language (or semiosis) at all. Derrida, as we shall see, does not contest Husserl's distinctions with the aim of removing them and replacing them with others. In truth, Derrida never intends a simple first-order criticism, one which would lead to his own positively conceived versions of these matters.

The "de-" of deconstruction indeed derives from this unflaggingly negative stance that is soon to become visible in Derrida's opening phase of argument here, one that is too readily confused with philosophical critique or even commentary, though some identification of this sort may ultimately be unavoidable.[17] Nevertheless, even as the discourse in question, in this instance Husserl's, is brought radically into doubt, Derrida continues to hew to it in other respects, continues to acknowledge the *local* functioning of all its distinctions, putting no others in its place, and this is necessary since Derrida only comes to a new further "construction" on the basis of Husserl's own claims, claims which have thus been questioned, or departed from, in a wholly singular way.[18] Deconstruction relies on those theses it also questions, as witnessed by the trajectory of Derrida's argument as a whole. This finally results in the project of repeating otherwise the classical *disappearance* of the sign (as I earlier emphasized), in a new elimination of this concept, not in any sort of novel semiotics or linguistics.

Husserl's own decisions, then, turn out not to be corrigible in Derrida's eyes—even though Derrida perhaps inevitably finds himself treating them as such, a matter that will be considered later—because Derrida's real goal in the preceding chapters has been to show that an illicit teleology commands *all* discourse pertaining to language and signs. Husserl's thought does not and cannot finally be replaced with another better one, on this account, and thus will itself remain in some unexpected fashion the premise of all that Derrida later does in *Speech*.

Derrida's continuing reliance on Husserl's own thought becomes explicit in chapter 4 as well, and it is to this in particular that I want to draw attention. It was indeed already implied by my earlier claims concerning the structure of *Speech*'s argument as a whole. And more narrowly, near the start of chapter 4, we find Derrida himself posing the following objection to his own argument, which points the way to this dependence.

Early on in chapter 4, Derrida raises the objection that he has "formulated [his] question [concerning the role of the sign in soliloquy] with Husserlian concepts"—and to this he responds, "certainly" (*VP* 56/*SP* 50). Derrida concedes at this moment his continued reliance on Husserl's own distinctions and terminology, even as he plots his "departure" from Husserl. Indeed, Derrida's characterization of linguistic signification itself— the very model of the sign and the signifier Derrida employs, which was at the basis of the argument concerning ideality that I just reviewed—is taken directly from Husserl, as Derrida here stipulates. The account of the sign itself that was in question above—though it seemed to suggest that ideal meanings, *Bedeutungen,* might be founded directly on *Vergegenwärtigung,* and in some way rely on semiosis and language—turns out to be wholly Husserlian, and indeed, most tellingly, itself depends on asserting *the sign's own ideality.*

Derrida's account of the sign itself at this point is in fact wholly indistinguishable from the description that as proper a Husserlian as Dorion Cairns (the English translator of *Cartesian Meditations* and *Formal and Transcendental Logic,* among other contributions) set out in a pathbreaking article in 1941. In the passage that I earlier began to quote, Derrida insists that "a purely idiomatic sign would not be a sign," that "a signifier (in general) must be formally recognizable," and though it "is necessarily always to some extent different each time . . . it can function as a sign, and in general as language, only if a formal identity enables it to be issued again and to be recognized" (*SP* 50).[19]

Derrida here, just as Cairns earlier, asserts the *ideality* of the *signifier*, even to the extent of claiming that it implies a prior *Vorstellung*, an apparently prior *conscious* representation. ("This identity," Derrida continues, "is necessarily ideal. It thus necessarily implies representation: as *Vorstellung*, the locus of ideality in general, as *Vergegenwärtigung*, the possibility of reproductive repetition in general, and as *Repräsentation*" [*SP* 50].) Derrida thus wholly retains Husserl's own distinctions (even as he intends to question them in certain other respects). The sign is here led back, more specifically, *to a set of functions originally specific to consciousness:* to *Vorstellung*, *Gegenwärtigung*, and *Vergegenwärtigung* taken as a whole, and this has tremendous implications for all that Derrida will go on to do in the remainder of *Speech*, as well as elsewhere.

For the very same twist, the appeal to the ideality of signifier, as we will see, will allow Derrida to open the door to Husserl's own transcendental concerns in the midst of the first half of *Of Grammatology*. And this pivotal move in chapter 4 is telling with respect to Derridean deconstruction's place in philosophy overall. Starting from a Husserlian perspective on the signifier, as he does here, Derrida continues to give at least equal primacy in his analyses to structures (or terms) stemming from consciousness as he does to those more directly pertaining to language. Seen in this light, Derrida's own treatment of language indeed joins Husserl's in keeping a distance from what is known as the linguistic turn, and in fact remains closer to Husserl than most other prominent twentieth-century thinkers in regard to this matter.[20]

Of course, there can be no doubt that Derrida is also contesting Husserl's own thought at this moment in his own singular way, and this example can let us see how Derrida accomplishes this shift from the outside to the inside—how he manages to tack back toward the core of Husserl's thought in chapter 4 after having posed a set of questions in the first three chapters, to which we are soon about to come. After all, in putting forward this analysis that still relies on the *sign's ideality*, Derrida has brought Husserl's own distinctions *further to bear*, on to a realm to which Husserl himself did not necessarily think they applied (at least not in 1901). Derrida, that is, in chapter 4, by dint of focusing on the sign, and showing ideality and its structures already to be unexpectedly at work there, argues that the *Vorstellung* of consciousness (its representative capacity) derives from a general possibility of repetition, not the reverse (though this general possibility now also includes the *Vorstellung* of the sign itself, which retains a role for consciousness)—thus extending Husserl's own framework, his distinctions, back a step beyond where Husserl at this moment currently applies it. Derrida contests Husserl's thought, then, in chapter 4 by *overflowing* the borders assigned to Husserl's own notions, not by replacing them with other ones; and this permits Derrida *at once* continued access to Husserl's optics and framework, even while these are otherwise called into doubt.

So, too, correspondingly, in this way Derrida shifts gears and comes to switch from the outside to the inside of Husserl's own concerns. By dint of this maneuver, which contests Husserl's own priorities even as it continues to invoke Husserl's conceptuality, Derrida here moves his analysis on to the inside of Husserl's text, subsequently permitting him to take up themes more central to Husserl (those of the reduction, and absolute temporality)—doubtless to question them, to depart from them perhaps all the more radically in Derrida's eyes, but in a wholly novel style, one whose novelty, as well as its proximity to Husserl, remains still not wholly recognized even today.

It should be noted that the work of chapter 5 of *Speech*, a chapter that I will not otherwise discuss here, directly follows from this: from the transitional work done by the argument of chapter 4. That is, because in chapter 4 Derrida has pushed Husserl's own distinctions back a step—claiming that the *Vergegenwärtigung* that makes possible language and semiosis must precede the *Vorstellung* of consciousness, without claiming anything one way or another about the ultimate provenance or origin of this *Vergegenwärtigung* itself—Derrida can follow up the issue of conscious representation *(Vorstellung)* generally within Husserl's thought by turning to its seat in Husserl's analysis of absolute temporality, now to assert a priority of re-presentation *(Ver-gegenwärtigung)* within the making present *(Gegenwärtigung)* of the absolute present, yet without finally putting forward any other known area or region of being (such as language or signification) instead of consciousness as a locus for such repetition's functioning. Radical repetition will indeed begin to be conceived in chapter 5, for which the preceding chapter is in many ways a draft, in respect to *the region of absolute being as such.* Yet this region, let me emphasize again, can only be broached on the basis of Husserl's thought—it can in no way be envisioned apart from Husserlian phenomenology—no matter how strongly Derrida will contest some of Husserl's own premises concerning it at this moment.[21]

In chapter 4, then, the ideality that Husserl believes pertains uniquely to consciousness is indeed questioned, and its (logical) intentions traced back to a repetition which Derrida doubtless wants *associated* in some fashion with language and the sign (as also clearly remains the case in chapter 5).[22] Yet no identity is finally asserted here, and in fact Derrida only mounts this questioning by dint of employing Husserl's own terms, as we have seen, by dint of grasping language and signification themselves as *idealities* with corresponding intentional possibilities and correlates. The linkage Derrida makes in chapter 4 thus brings him onto the inside of

Husserl's thought, by taking him to the theme of absolute consciousness and temporality, even as it carries on in some fashion the force of Derrida's radical "criticism" of Husserl in his earlier chapters.

Chapter 4 thus establishes a transition crucial for the work of *Speech* as a whole. The actual work Derrida does in this chapter too often has been missed, however, largely because of all that comes before it in *Speech*. Without questioning where Derrida ultimately comes out in chapter 4, and where he subsequently intends to go, a potentially corrosive skepticism does indeed appear to occupy the earlier pages of *Speech,* pertaining to all of Husserl's own initial language-related distinctions, and this may easily obscure what takes place in chapter 4 (as well as Derrida's proximity to Husserl in the second half of this work, and his true goals there), not to mention potentially rendering problematic Derrida's own subsequent argument.

Before turning to *Speech*'s second half, then, it is worthwhile investigating this sequence more closely: to see what Derrida really has in mind, to determine more precisely how it relates to all that follows, and also in order to do justice to Husserl's own thought and views at the outset of *Logical Investigations* II.1. What does Derrida do with language and semiosis in the opening three chapters of *Speech and Phenomena*—chapters which have proved perhaps the most controversial in his corpus? How skeptical is Derrida's treatment there, and what relation do his comments have to the rest of *Speech*? Finally, what is the role of the voice in this opening progression, the single overriding concern of *Speech* as a whole?

Derrida starts *Speech,* as is well known, by following Husserl across an initial set of distinctions pertaining to the domain of the signitive (the realm of signs) and the linguistic (the realm of linguistic signification proper). Husserl's goal at the outset of *Logical Investigations* II is to introduce the eventual focus of his logical studies: namely, those *Bedeutungen,* specifically logical or conceptual meanings, to which I have already referred, as well as the *bedeuten,* the acts that intend them (see Husserl 1960, 1:322ff. [1984, 2.1.§29]).[23] The *Bedeutungen* and *bedeuten* are initially to come forward in their specificity thanks to highlighting the difference between linguistic and all other kinds of signs, since linguistic signs alone, according to Husserl, are able to express these sorts of acts and meanings (Husserl 1960, 1:269 [1984, 2.1.§1]).

In turn, *Speech* starts by questioning every one of Husserl's opening distinctions. In these chapters, Derrida first contests that distinction drawn by Husserl *between* the signs of language *(Ausdrücke)* and other sorts of signs (indications, *Anzeichen)*—"we know . . . already that, in fact, the discursive sign . . . is always . . . *held* in an indicative system; held, that is to say, contaminated" (*VP* 20–21/ *SP* 20)—with Derrida ultimately arguing that Husserl has ignored the larger question of "the structure of the sign in general" and what it may designate (*VP* 23/*SP* 23). Second, building on this, Derrida disputes the different functions Husserl distinguishes *within* language (that of communication from expression, intimation from assertion, imagined from real discourse, etc.), claiming that none of these can be legitimately disassociated in the way that Husserl intends.

Derrida in his first two chapters appears to find every one of Husserl's claims illegitimate, and the stakes of his disagreement with Husserl are by no means small. Husserl, following on the heels of his contention in *Logical Investigations* II.1.1 that *Zeichen* (signs) do not form a single proper class or genus (embracing both expressions proper, *Ausdrücke*, and indications, *Anzeichen*), will assert in *Logical Investigations* II.1.2 that indications and indicative motivation (*hinweisen*, in which a belief in one existent, such as a flag, motivates the belief in another, such as the army camped nearby) form a unitary essence distinct from expressions and expression's demonstrative capacity (*beweisen*, the expression's ability to demonstrate something *about* something, for example, that in a right triangle the squares on its two other sides must be equal to that on the hypotenuse)— a total argument that Derrida dubs the "reduction of indication." Derrida, moreover, concludes his own chapter 2 by arguing that in this reduction lies "the possibility of all the reductions to come, be they eidetic or transcendental." "The whole future problematic of the reduction," Derrida goes on to state, "and all the conceptual differences through which it is pronounced (fact/essence, transcendentality/ mundaneity . . .) would deploy themselves in a separation [*écart*] between two types of signs" (*VP* 31–32/*SP* 30; see also *VP* 21/*SP* 21).

Derrida's strong pronouncements at the end of chapter 2 thus resurrect those issues that I treated back in my chapter 1. A possible radical skepticism on the part of Derrida and deconstruction emerges here, as well as those problems that the quasi-transcendental account of deconstruction offered by critics ran into: attempting to resolve this problem and falling prey to it all over again. After all, according to Derrida here, not only is the core of Husserl's philosophy—the phenomenological and transcendental reductions—supposed to depend on a distinction between two types of signs, an assertion already provocative enough, but this distinction is itself not legitimate in Derrida's eyes. Derrida's whole point in these opening pages appears to be not only that all that follows in Husserl's philosophy depends on these distinctions pertaining to the sign (the linguistic sign and the indicative sign and their respective functioning), but that these distinctions are not valid in themselves. And since, in Derrida's eyes, they are illegitimate, a pyrrhonic skepticism indeed threatens to emerge at this moment, overwhelming all of Husserl's thought.

This deep skepticism, apparently bordering on nihilism, may well be what has angered so many Husserlians taking up *Speech,* provoking them to treat Derrida in a tone as harsh as they believe Derrida's treatment of Husserl is here, as well as leading the vast majority of critics to overlook the extraordinary closeness to Husserl in the second half of *Speech* that I have begun to bring forward.[24] Not only is such skepticism problematic in itself, considering how often Derrida has claimed he is not a skeptic, but more narrowly, just in the context of *Speech,* it does indeed seem to abolish the access to Husserl's thought that Derrida himself requires in the second half of *Speech*—to remove the opportunity for Derrida to invoke Husserl's transcendental attitude, or to make use of his thought more generally, along the paths that I have started to sketch.

My own chapter 1 has already rehearsed these difficulties; and my chapter 2 began to suggest that a singular hermeneutic standpoint, taking into account the intentions of both the author that Derrida reads and Derrida himself, needed to be found in order to address them. Thus, without wishing simply to deny the problematic character of these opening assertions, for Husserl's as well as Derrida's thought (a matter to which I will return), given how much is at stake here, the *validity* of Derrida's criticisms of Husserl should be examined further here, and indeed investigated more closely than has been the norm, at least among those sympathetic to Derrida.[25] The opening pages of *Speech,* as noted, are arguably the most controversial to be found in Derrida's corpus, and in turning to some of these objections, it may be asked whether Derrida is right about the illegitimacy of Husserl's opening arguments, and under what circumstances, if any, he might be construed as being so?

J. N. Mohanty's criticisms of Derrida's opening arguments in *Speech* can here stand for the vast number of criticisms Husserlians have raised against Derrida's readings over the years.[26] Of the four points Mohanty makes, I want to focus on his first objection, since so much turns out to rest on it in Derrida's own text. Derrida's initial rejection of Husserl's distinction of linguistic signs *(Ausdrücke)* from other signs (indications, *Anzeichen*) is first contested by Mohanty, who indeed argues that the *question of the sign in general,* upon which Derrida eventually puts so much pressure, is a false one. "As to [the] sign in general," Mohanty writes, "'indication'. . . is not the genus of expression; nor is indication a coordinate species (along with expression) coming under the genus 'sign' . . . The unity of sign is not a generic unity . . . To say as Derrida does, that Husserl does not tell us what a sign in general is, is to presuppose mistakenly that, on Husserl's view, 'sign in general' is a generic notion" (Mohanty 1997, 70).

For those familiar with Husserl's text, Mohanty's criticism that expressions are neither a species of indication, nor form with indication a single genus of signs—and that what is expressed by "sign" or *Zeichen* thus does not form a true unity for Husserl at all—is very difficult to dispute. To the extent that Derrida appears to suggest otherwise, Mohanty does seem right that Derrida's interpretation of Husserl at this key moment may be flawed.[27]

Let us grant that Mohanty is correct. Another issue lies latent here, however, that arguably pertains more deeply to the totality of Husserl's thought, and perhaps takes us closer to Derrida's own real concerns as well, one which might also prove more acceptable to Mohanty and other responsible Husserlians. Husserl doubtless does not believe the sign is a generic unity (and I will later return to the work that is supposed to be done by this claim, or something like it, in *Derrida's* text). Husserl, however, even in the *specific* instance in question here, *in the case of the linguistic sign alone,* never really focuses on the *sign function* as such. Husserl at the outset of *Logical Investigations* II does *not* inquire in any sustained way into the semiology of the linguistic sign that possibly underlies those discursive achievements upon which he is about to focus, nor will he ever give this prolonged investigation. To this extent, on account of this repeated omission on Husserl's part, Derrida, if not simply right, perhaps is also not simply wrong, even granting that Husserl's own distinctions taken locally may have the self-evidence that Husserl claims.[28] Indeed, ironically enough, what makes it doubtful in these opening chapters of *Speech* that Derrida's commentary on Husserl is everywhere correct is also what ultimately gives Derrida's "strong" interpretation a leg to stand on:[29] namely that Husserl does not really comment on these matters, the matters most of interest to Derrida himself, one way or another in *Logical Investigations* II.1, and that Husserl will repeatedly hereafter overlook the specifically linguistic and semiotic dimensions of his own thought.[30]

Derrida, focusing on language at the outset of *Speech,* thus focuses on a territory which Husserl himself neglected throughout his career (even in that sphere which Husserl does want to investigate, that of expression proper and logical meaning). In addition to the purchase this omission of Husserl's gives to Derrida's own inquiry (which others too have recognized to varying degrees), I especially want to stress that the semiotics of the *linguistic sign* should here be seen as the gateway to Derrida's *own* thought as well as to Husserl's. The *core* of Derrida's concerns in chapters 1 through 3 of *Speech* arguably is to be found in the status of this sort of sign, and the roles Husserl assigned, or failed to assign to this— not, in the first instance, in the sign generally—a focus that dovetails with those issues already brought forward as primary within Derrida's prior encounters with Husserl thanks to my canvass of Derrida's development.

Husserl's definition of the linguistic sign, his determination of the expression *(Ausdruck),* as he sets it out at the start of *Logical Investigations*

II.1—the focal point of these opening sections—played a decisive role, after all, when Derrida attempted to move beyond Husserl's own stipulations concerning writing and language in the "Introduction." Derrida drew on just this notion of the sign *proper to language* in the "Introduction" (*IOG* 92n96) in order to challenge the limitations Husserl had set on writing and language's transcendental functioning, and Derrida's own failure to break with Husserl's framework on this basis must be recognized as the most proximate cause, the deepest context, for *Speech,* especially these opening chapters where Derrida returns to precisely this same juncture in Husserl's corpus.

More specifically yet, undergirding Derrida's attempt to escape Husserl's restriction to language and inscription as pure nonempirical possibilities ("intelligible for a transcendental subject in general," on which account alone they did transcendental work) by appealing to the worldly body of the sign, lay a more comprehensive view of the linguistic sign and its operation, one drawn from Husserl himself, in which the linguistic sign owed its *capacity to signify,* its status in the first place as a *sign,* to acts of intentional animation. Signs, at least linguistic signs, really only were signs for Husserl, it became clear, due to their employment, their use, to what is called in other contexts a speech act. Apart from the animating intentions of a subject, which transformed their *Körper* (their mere material body) into *Leib* (living flesh), they failed to signify at all. Derrida relied on this version of the sign in the "Introduction" to mount his own questioning in the second half of the "Introduction's" section 7—a dependence that caused Derrida finally *to fail* to break with Husserl radically, and to be *unable* to conceive of a "disappearance of truth" at the hands of writing and language wholly on a par with its transcendental-historical "appearance."

In turn, this very same set of distinctions emerges tellingly enough at the climax of this first, more problematic phase of Derrida's argument in *Speech,* in the middle of chapter 3. The notion of *Geist,* and with it the transformation of *Körper* into *Leib,* arise at the center of Derrida's argument, and Derrida, as it happens, does a good deal of interpretive work to bring these themes to the fore, since these terms *(Geist, Körper, Leib)* are nowhere to be found in Husserl's own text, Husserl only introducing them later, above all in his published work in *Formal and Transcendental Logic.*[31]

Derrida is thus engaged in a total interpretation of Husserl's thought in respect to the sign and language in these opening chapters, I would suggest, one aimed at their repeated neglect throughout Husserl's own career, a neglect or omission whose seat appears to be this view of signification as owed to the transformation of the body of the linguistic sign into living spiritual flesh thanks to an intentional act. And the first thing to be remarked on this score, in respect to Derrida's demonstration at A.3 of chapter 3, is that Derrida indeed hearkens back to those earlier stipulations in the "Introduction" which limited writing and language to their pure, ideal functioning and which depend on this broader construal.

Derrida first comments here, more specifically, on *Logical Investigations* II.1.5: a paragraph in which Husserl himself is not primarily focused on language at all, but wants merely to distinguish a usage of the term "expression" not having to do with discourse (such as facial expressions and other sorts of gestures, which in German, as in English, answer to this term) from *Ausdrücke*, linguistic expressions as such. According to Derrida, however, Husserl, along with distinguishing such gestures (insofar as they merely *deuten*, "point out" a speaker's meaning or thoughts, and do not *bedeuten*, "mean"), would already at least implicitly go farther than this. Husserl would factor out here as well the "effectiveness of what is uttered," "the body of the word," indeed everything which, even *"in its ideality,"* belongs "to a determined empirical language" (*VP* 36/*SP* 34; my emphasis).

Whatever the status of Husserl's own discussion here, Derrida himself clearly wishes to locate all that belongs to empirical language, including its empirical *idealities,* its actual ideal signs, at this early threshold phase of Husserl's argument, and Derrida's own orientation thus hearkens back to his prior experience in the "Introduction." Derrida focuses on what in Husserl's construal of language and the sign eventually allows the empirical character of language to be bracketed out entirely, language and writing reduced to "pure possibilities," and it should be no surprise, then, that Derrida—believing he is already able to detect a certain privilege of the will, indeed "a voluntaristic metaphysics" on Husserl's part in this omission of facial expressions and gestures—immediately goes on to explicitly invoke this notion of *Geist,* and the construal of the linguistic sign as *geistige Leiblichkeit* that earlier emerged in the "Introduction," again despite the explicit absence of any such talk in Husserl's own text.

"This explains why everything that escapes the pure spiritual intention, the pure animation by *Geist* which is willed," Derrida goes on to write, "is excluded from the *bedeuten* [the act of meaning] and then from the expression." "The totality of the body and worldly inscription" are omitted by Husserl "inasmuch as they are not worked by *Geist,* by the will, by *Geistigkeit,* which, in the word as well as in the human body, transforms the *Körper* into *Leib* (into flesh)" (*VP* 37/*SP* 35).

Derrida in chapter 3, then, and arguably in the whole opening development of *Speech,* is concerned to track down and contest that privilege of spirit and the will in the realm of signification (specifically linguistic signification) with which he earlier became entangled in the "Introduction's" section 7, and which caused him so much trouble there. At the center of three, Derrida traces a whole network of Husserlian decisions back to *Geist* and the will, to the moment when the body of language, as well as the body generally, comes to be infused with Spirit and turned into living flesh *(Leib)*.

Of course, the contestation of *Geist* (residing at the deepest layer of Husserl's construal of language), it must also be recalled, was not so easy to mount, while still retaining a transcendental role for language or writing of any sort, which remained Husserl's own discovery. For this reason, as I have already begun to suggest, Derrida's contestation of Husserl takes an absolutely unparalleled form in a number of ways, and these, along with its primary object, must also be taken into account.

For one thing, *Geist* itself will not be attacked directly—nor even the claim that a *life* of some sort accompanies signs; this will never be flat-out denied by Derrida. Rather, throughout these first chapters, Derrida wants to knit together a broad range of Husserlian distinctions, heterogeneous in Husserl's own eyes (first between *Ausdrücke* and *Anzeichen,* and then between facial and linguistic expressions, communication and intimation, and so on), in order, in the first phase of this problematic, to depict them as part of a single unitary matrix, an unexpectedly systematic whole, itself the product of "the history of metaphysics," which indeed has *Geist* and the will at its core and which Derrida eventually wishes to call into question in totality.

On this account, because of this larger whole with which Derrida is here concerned, *Geist,* and even the sort of transcendental voluntarism it implies (Derrida has just declared on this basis that "all transcendental phenomenology" is "at bottom only a transcendental voluntarism" [*VP* 37/*SP* 35]), though central, also hold a somewhat eccentric place on the surface of Derrida's text, and doubtless this is why this strand of Derrida's argument has been relatively neglected or downplayed, even though it turns out to be impossible, it seems to me, to see what Derrida is really after here without it.[32]

The title of chapter 3 is "Meaning as Soliloquy" *("Le vouloir-dire* [*bedeuten*] *comme soliloque"),* and indeed this act, the *bedeuten,* which intends logical meanings, proves to be the theme that most explicitly stretches across the two subsections of Derrida's chapter. Derrida's aim even here, however, is not to reject the provenance of the *bedeuten* as such, but to *portray* it (and the *Bedeutungen*) as themselves part of this same larger system—as embedded in this matrix of distinctions Derrida is in the course of bringing forward, which have at their core this privilege of the will, *Geist,* and self-present representation—and thus the *bedeuten,* too, is taken up in the same sort of questioning as *Geist,* by way of its introduction into this larger matrix and its functioning.

Indeed, Derrida's highly provocative translation of *bedeuten* as *"vouloir-dire"* can only really be understood in this light. The *bedeuten* and *Bedeutungen* stand, in some way, at the apex of this network, at the pinnacle of this matrix. They are indeed those acts (and meanings) which ultimately provide life and spirit to these signs; they are what finally permit their transformation into signifying flesh; and from the very start of *Speech*, Derrida translates *bedeuten* ("to mean" in a conceptual or logical sense) as "wanting-to-say" *(vouloir-dire)* so as to highlight the role these concepts play in this larger system pertaining to spirit, as well as in their relation to language and signs more generally. Derrida sets out this translation, that is, to highlight the fact that *Bedeutungen* and *bedeuten*—that which makes signs, gives them life, coming by way of the *dire*, "speech"—are preassigned to this kind of work, across the otherwise arguably heterogeneous fields of expression, language, and semiosis generally. So, too, Derrida has this pre-scription in mind, declaring that "the *Bedeutung* is reserved to this which speaks [*parle*], and which speaks inasmuch as it says [*il dit*] what it *wants* to say [or means; *il veut dire*]" (*VP* 36/ *SP* 34). The *bedeuten* and the *Bedeutungen* have a vocation for doing certain kinds of work across a range of strata, hierarchically organizing those areas of language and semiosis which Husserl otherwise left essentially unresolved—and Derrida, then, in these opening chapters, in chapter 3 in particular, wants to contest them first and foremost by showing them as embedded in a larger network of decisions on Husserl's part, which he believes tributary to "metaphysics' history."

From this perspective too, on the basis of the *"dire"* of the *vouloir-dire*, we can finally understand the function of the voice in these opening chapters (with one exception concerning the phenomenological voice in its specificity, which will soon be taken up). Derrida translates Husserl's *bedeuten* as "wanting-to-say" insofar as it, and the meanings it intends (the *Bedeutungen*), are destined to express themselves, and come to animate the signs of language, specifically through discourse, speech *(Rede, dire)*. Derrida's talk of a privilege of the voice and orality, correspondingly, should be seen as focused on the role that the speech act plays here: the preference built into Husserl's treatment of these matters for the moment in which meanings *(Bedeutungen)* are imparted to language through *discourse*, as opposed to other possible aspects of language and semiosis (the reservoir of potential meanings language itself provides, the almost unconscious status of the signs themselves in semiosis, etc.). The voice in the first chapters of *Speech* primarily designates this preference for the speech *situation* generally, for language in use (thus maintaining the privilege of the will, the provenance of *Geist*) over and against other aspects also implied by linguistic signification—rather than indicating a privilege of any given *medium* of discourse over another, such as breath over ink. Clearly, Derrida wants to see these last as coupled; he wants to associate the medium of breath (the phonic, rather than the graphic) with the privilege given to language in use (speech or discourse) by Husserl. This connection is really a draft on an argument still to come, however, one only to be found in the second half of *Speech*—which had better be the case, since, as others have also pointed out, no actual preference for breath over ink, for the spoken character over the written one, is to be found at this moment in Husserl's own text.[33]

All this remains only the first phase of Derrida's contestation of Husserl, however, and all the problems raised earlier by Derrida's mode of proceeding reemerge along with this second phase, which must also be examined. Not only does Derrida want to claim, after all, that Husserl's distinctions form a single unperceived matrix or system oriented by *Geist* and the will, but he wants to go further, to argue that a *teleology*, an epochal predetermination, is responsible for the totality of this phase of Husserl's thought. Derrida thus must portray Husserl's distinctions not only as tending toward certain goals but as ultimately undermotivated, as finally illegitimate in themselves. Husserl himself, in the end, might finally agree with Derrida's first set of claims concerning *Geist*, especially given the role a certain notion of self-responsibility has always played in his thought. And Derrida must, then, not only show *Geist* at work across that network of distinctions comprising the threshold of Husserl's work, but he must *contest* this network in its totality, and each of these distinctions individually, in order finally to do what he had left undone in 1962.

Such contestation, the ultimate aim of the first three chapters of *Speech,* consequently entails the production of what may be called a backstory or background, which first and foremost portrays Husserl's concepts and distinctions as *products:* products of a prior *systematic* exclusion, as resulting from an illegitimate denial of other possible modes of functioning, on other sites. The teleology finally at issue here, Derrida's famous "metaphysics of presence," can only come forward in its own right if *Geist* and all that relates to it are shown to be *derived* from a series of prior exclusions— thus casting doubt on all Husserl has done and is about to do. And while Derrida's claims concerning the operation of metaphysics in Husserl have often been given due heed, the singular operation by which Derrida brings this forward, sketching in this backstory or background to Husserl's, and what it implies for Derrida's own arguments, as well as Husserl's, has too often been overlooked by both critics and defenders of Derrida alike.

For this ultimate phase of Derrida's argument in the first part of *Speech* is far more problematic than has been recognized. Through

Husserl's text Derrida wants to set out a phenomenon which *by definition* could never be an issue for Husserl himself, nor could ever be the object of Husserl's own intentions, and thus *can* never simply be unequivocally visible in his work. This phenomenon, however, can also never come forward in its own right anywhere else, can never show itself apart from Husserl and his writings, given Derrida's belief as to the thoroughgoing hegemony of this teleology, and the corresponding stipulations concerning the conditions under which it may be articulated. Derrida's demonstration must begin, then, by taking Husserl's work as a *symptom,* and already assuming it to be *questionable as a whole*—Derrida's argument everywhere thus proceeding *on the bias,* in the light of a more thoroughgoing hold already thought to come to pass on Husserl's thought—even though the only way to demonstrate such a hold, to make it appear in Husserl's text or anywhere else, is indeed to confront Husserl's distinctions one by one, treating each as if it could be valid, and contesting each of them in its own right.[34]

This strategy, which amounts to a *hermeneutic* of the concealed historial and systematic ground from which Husserl's thought will have already sprung, is evident at many moments in Derrida's text, starting with his argument about the structure of the sign in general (whose exclusion is indeed already supposed to be a sign of this formation). It may also be seen at work where I left off above, when I cited Derrida's comments on *Geist,* and the distinction between *Körper* and *Leib.*

> All this which escapes . . . the pure animation by *Geist* is excluded from the *bedeuten* and expression . . . the whole of the visible and the spatial as such. As such, that is to say, inasmuch as they are not worked by *Geist,* by the will, by the *Geistigkeit* which transforms the *Körper* into *Leib* (flesh). The opposition between body and soul is not only at the center of this doctrine of signification, it is confirmed by it . . . Visibility and spatiality as such could only lose the presence to self of will and spiritual animation which open up discourse. *They are literally the death of it.* (*VP* 35)

The complex gesture in which Derrida is engaged emerges here more clearly. The functioning of *Geist,* the opposition between body and soul, lies at "the center of this discourse." Nevertheless, it ultimately is supposed to derive, in turn, from a *prior* set of exclusions (of visibility, spatiality, death), all of which have been in play since the first moment of Derrida's discussion (this being the role of Derrida's original discussion of the sign in *Speech*'s first chapter). *Geist,* the soul, meanings, expressions, intentions, *Bedeutungen,* and even language as such have all emerged *in the first place* as identifiable *concepts* or *themes,* according to Derrida, only thanks to a previously unrecognized drive toward the denial of otherness—itself nameable *as* visibility, spatiality, absence, only on these same terms—a denial, a network of omissions, that is itself the manifestation of that teleological functioning (the epochal metaphysical privilege of presence and self-presence) which Derrida here ultimately aims to contest simply by setting it out, by making visible its hold.

Derrida's total mode of argument in the end does indeed possess a peculiarly deconstructive radicality which many readers, especially more traditional ones, might find rebarbative. The total result of these first chapters is to work backward toward a thematic presupposed to be at work, which is never available in its own right, which *by definition* could never be known or present to Husserl himself, and whose very setting out is supposed to call into question all Husserl's thought, indeed, effectively all thought hitherto. And Derrida might thus indeed appear to have plunged Husserl's project from the first into a skeptical abyss. What is central to see, however, is that Derrida's radically negative conclusions, their ultimately *nondialogic* character, so specific to deconstruction, also, oddly enough, have the effect of permitting Derrida to have continuing access of some sort to Husserl's philosophy, and to find a way back to the core of his thought in the second half of this work.

After all, as has been earlier emphasized, whatever else Derrida's deconstruction accomplishes, it never replaces Husserl's thought by another construal of these same problems. What is implied by this sweeping, structural style of deconstructive delegitimation, which might otherwise appear so problematic, is that no new set of distinctions or terms owed to Derrida or anyone else will ever be thought able to do the job better instead, and so are never to be introduced—and in this way Derrida, even as he everywhere delegitimates Husserl's thought in principle, continues to retain it in practice.

To remain a moment longer at the culmination of chapter 3: Derrida arguing against *Geist*, against the role of spirit and Husserl's doctrine of *bedeuten* and *Bedeutungen*, is not doing so in the style, let us say, of a Quine—with the intention of putting the sheer physical facts of language, or even an actually functioning semiosis (the real behavioral employment of empirical language), in place. Derrida, rather, has incorporated all these different possibilities, usually so opposed—Quine-like behaviorism, Husserl's insistence on *Geist*, and a transcendental will—into a previously unsuspected larger whole and has delegitimated them by arguing that they all derive *in totality* from a different value than one would expect, a value other than truth (namely, the privilege of presence). In a radically volatilizing gesture, a sort of negative version of Hegel's famous Bacchic dance of spirit's forms, Derrida has derived these terms as well as their others—indeed, *all that can be spoken and written on these subjects,* what in any way might still refer to language, thought, meaning, signs—from one and the same metaphysical privilege, one and the same denial of radical absence and alterity. And Derrida's treatment of Husserl thus proves to be so profoundly and asymmetrically delegitimating that it opens the way to a subsequent reappropriation of Husserl's terms and a further rapprochement with his standpoint.

Such a rapprochement, however—and this is the last point I want to make in this part of my chapter, bringing as it does my discussion of *Geist* to a close—goes beyond the formal possibility of taking up again in practice what in principle has been ruined. Derrida's discourse, with its initial focus on *Geist,* from the first can be seen to be aimed (thematically speaking, in terms of the results of this deconstruction) precisely at that notion which the "metaphysical" limitations of *Geist* itself may be thought to conceal: namely, life. Even as he undertakes such a resolutely negative labor, Derrida throughout the opening pages of *Speech* is finally interested, speaking positively, in *life,* first and foremost, including the life of signs and language. A *more generalized* functioning, or *economy,* of life, able to include that of signification and language, of which *Geist* as it functions semiologically in Husserl represents a more restricted form, is what Derrida aims to bring forward—and this concern alone, present from the first in *Speech,* is really compatible with the work done by Derrida in the second half of his book.

Derrida's aim at life, moreover, is visible not just in chapter 3, with its emphasis on *Geist* and *Geist*'s delimitation. In the very first chapter of *Speech,* Derrida had already brought forward "life" as related to "the historic destiny of phenomenology," and *contrasted* this destiny to the "classical metaphysics of presence," which has otherwise held Husserl's thought in check (*VP* 26–27/*SP* 25–26). A side of *Husserl's* project, an *internal* aspect of his thought, already opposes the metaphysical tendencies his project otherwise evinces (though Derrida is about to note that this contrast is more complex than it initially appears), and this first side is characterized by its treatment of life: by "the reduction of naïve ontology, the return . . . to the activity of *life* which produces truth and value in general across [*à travers*] its signs" (*VP* 26–27/*SP* 25).

In beginning *Speech,* then, Derrida already has the theme of life in mind—as it relates to signs and language, as well as more broadly—and this hearkens back to Derrida's introduction to *Speech,* which not only explicitly focuses at length on life, but in so doing also provides a representation in miniature of Derrida's entire argument across the whole of *Speech.*

The introduction to *Speech,* and the structural concerns it brings with it, have too often been overlooked in recent debates.[35] In the introduction itself, life has arguably an even more immediately central role than in the body of *Speech,* and in sketching this out, Derrida limns the path his argument will follow in the body of his work.

Derrida at first introduces concerns similar to those in his first three chapters, apparently radically disqualifying Husserl's project in the name of life. Thus, he begins by raising the question of what gives Husserl the right to characterize as a form of "life" all the transcendental achievements that he sets out.[36] Derrida initially broaches the question of "the unity of living, the focus of the *Lebendigkeit*" across all of Husserl's usages (the same question that Derrida poses concerning the "sign," the structure of signs in general, at the start of *Speech*). This unity, life itself, according to Derrida, "diffracts its focus in all the fundamental concepts of phenomenology," and to this extent, since life, this *Lebendigkeit*, including the life that gives meaning to signs, functions across the totality of Husserl's project, at every stage of Husserl's thought, life in general, the concept of life, initially appears to "escap[e] the transcendental reduction and, as unity of worldly life, even open[s] the way for it" (*SP* 11).

Life (including the term "life") thus first appears in the introduction to *Speech* as an unmasterable presupposition of Husserl's thought, calling into doubt Husserl's project from the first, just as we have seen it come into doubt in the first three chapters of *Speech* on the basis of concepts pertaining to (linguistic) signification. Derrida here, however, immediately swerves away from such an apparently radical dismissal of Husserl's work, and this, too, maps the course of Derrida's exposition in the body of *Speech*. The introduction in this way indeed offers a preview of *Speech* as a whole: for, so far from giving final weight to a life found in the world and embodied in language—to a pretranscendental concept of life—Derrida next insists on a passage *through* Husserl's thought, and immediately launches into a discussion, even a defense, of Husserl's late doctrine of a parallelism between the psychological and transcendental spheres. Derrida immediately reopens the question of life, now from within the unique context of Husserl's transcendental phenomenology, though even at this moment Derrida will not hew simply or wholly to Husserl's view of these matters. Indeed, in the course of his long analysis Derrida frames the singularly memorable dictum that "language preserves the difference that preserves language" (*VP* 13/*SP* 14)—a statement which, presenting in positive terms the role of language (in contrast to Derrida's discussion in the body of *Speech*), and linking to Husserl's own notion of transcendental consciousness (as "the difference that preserves language"), gives us perhaps the best single summary of Derrida's own views on language that we have.

This claim, arguably beyond Husserl's own purview, nevertheless comes in the course of affirming the "nothing that distinguishes the parallels" (between psychological and transcendental life), and thus affirms transcendental difference as a unique function of Husserl's "reduction" (*VP* 12/*SP* 12). Correspondingly, Derrida's discussion of life in the introduction concludes by introducing what he explicitly calls an "ultra-transcendental concept of life" (*VP* 14/*SP* 15): a "concept of life . . . which is no longer that of a pre-transcendental naïveté."

Derrida, in the introduction as in the body of *Speech*, thus at first evinces the appearance of skepticism, here pertaining to Husserl's pre-transcendental employment of the concept or term "life" and the possibility of its functioning generally. In turn, however, Derrida's treatment of "life" ends not by dispensing with Husserl's thought, but by arriving at an "ultra-transcendental life," which can be conceived solely by passing through Husserl's thought, embracing the reductions and even the singular parallelism between psychic and transcendental life. This ultra-transcendental life, moreover, it should be stressed, is very close to where Derrida will ultimately arrive in *Speech*, in chapter 6, not just in terms of the path that gets Derrida there, but thematically as well. Derrida is about to invoke a concept of "self-relation" *(rapport á soi),* which he stipulates can only come forward thanks to Husserl's transcendental position (even as it calls it into question in other respects), and such self-relation, clearly another name for "life," turns out to stand at the core of Derrida's discussion in chapter 6, at the moment when *différance* is treated at length for the first time, in the aftermath of Derrida's treatment of the phenomenological voice in its specificity. *Différance,* at least within the covers of *Speech,* appears as finally a version, or possibility, of such ultra-transcendental life, encompassing both the life of signs and Husserl's transcendental activity at once, and the project of rethinking life in general thus also structures the body of *Speech*. Both it and the introduction arrive at an ultra-transcendental conception of life and ultimately tread the same path in doing so. Starting from a radical criticism of Husserl's thought, a seemingly corrosive skepticism, Derrida in both cases swerves away from this to pass through Husserl's own thought, thus to arrive at a uniquely "ultra-transcendental" outcome that does not reject transcendental phenomenology in toto (relegating it to the scrap heap of metaphysics), but, rather, broadens it out, furthering Husserl's own insights and perhaps even his ends, while it also uniquely contests the limits of Husserl's conceptions.

* * *

Derrida's aim in the second half of *Speech*, then, is to bring forward this new, more radical differential relation to self, a quasi- or ultra-transcendental conception of life, at the center of whose setting out stands the voice, what Derrida calls the phenomenological voice in its specificity in *Speech*. The bulk of this demonstration comes to pass in chapter 6. To accomplish this, however, not only, as we have just seen, must Derrida refrain from substituting another (more empiricist or semiotic) treatment of language and signs for Husserl's own; Derrida also must and will retain an inner core of Husserlian considerations—a circuit, or circle of expression, touching on all the reference points central to transcendental phenomenology, a circuit that stems largely from *Ideas I,* rather than from *Logical Investigations* II itself. Even as Derrida's more general questioning proceeds in *Speech's* first three chapters to sweep away all Husserl's distinctions, Derrida will remain in contact with considerations at the core of Husserl's own thought, as his overarching strategy here demands.

To recall what was earlier set out in this regard, in these first three chapters, as may now be confirmed, Derrida opens up the problem of the "outside"—of visibility, spatiality, death, nonpresence—as they congregate on the threshold of Husserl's thought and text. Derrida, in turn, will again aim to arrive at a certain "outside" in the second half of *Speech*—one that does not emerge *prior* to Husserl's thought, however, but beyond it, in its wake, after passing through the *inside* of Husserl's program. Derrida will traverse the workings of transcendental experience in this second move to the outside—and, of course, not simply leave these in place. Nevertheless, what results from this second movement cannot be identified with the first, though undoubtedly gesturing back toward it in Derrida's own eyes, and Derrida thus must maintain access throughout *Speech,* across its entirety, to Husserl's thought—the brunt of which work turns out to be done by Derrida's discussion of expression in chapter 3 at A.1.

Preparatory to chapter 6, then, A.1 in chapter 3 must first be examined, and a further specificity of Husserl's own program, as well as the voice and all it entails, will begin to come forward here. The title of chapter 6 of *Speech* is "The Voice That Keeps Silence," and much of what happens there, in particular the notion of the phenomenological voice in its specificity, first emerges in 3.A.1 as a focus of Derrida's concern. Derrida, for the first and only time in the opening three chapters of *Speech,* to my knowledge, here speaks of the voice specific to Husserl's researches, internal to transcendental phenomenology—the phenomenological voice—and much of what Derrida will claim about the voice in chapter 6 is predicated on this prior moment, on the sketch of expression that Derrida offers in 3.A.1, commenting on *Logical Investigations* II.1§5 (where Husserl's *Ausdruck* is first introduced).

Derrida's arguments at the outset of chapter 3, under the subheading A.1, though compressed, present the most comprehensive picture of these issues internal to phenomenology and to the voice in its phenomenological specificity to be found in the first half of *Speech.* Let me make more plain precisely what Derrida establishes at this juncture.

Derrida is commenting on *Logical Investigations* II.1§5 and Husserl's definition of "Expressions [*Ausdrücke*] as meaningful signs [*als bedeutsame Zeichen*]." In particular, Derrida is attempting to answer the questions, "why 'expressions' and why 'meaningful' signs?" (*VP* 34/ *SP* 32). Why, that is, does Husserl invoke the notion of *expression* at the moment he distinguishes some signs from others by way of their capacity to be meaningful (*bedeutsame*), to convey those conceptual or logical meanings (*Bedeutungen*) that we have already begun to discuss (*VP* 34/ *SP* 32)?

In response, Derrida gives the following account:[37]

> Expression is exteriorization. It impresses [*imprime*] in a certain outside a sense [*sens*] which is found first of all in a certain inside . . . The *bedeuten* [act of meaning] intends an outside which is that of an ideal object. This outside is then ex-pressed, passes outside itself into another outside, which is always "in" consciousness . . . The expression as sign wanting-to-say [*comme signe voulant-dire;* as meaningful sign, *als bedeutsam Zeichen*] is therefore the double going out from itself of sense *(Sinn)* in itself, in consciousness, in the with-itself or the beside-itself that Husserl begins by determining as "solitary life of the soul" (*VP* 34–35/ *SP* 32–33).

Derrida's remarks here, though serving as the basis of an argument extending across almost the entirety of *Speech,* are at first glance rather cryptic and certainly highly compressed. The key to determining what Derrida is saying, to grasping "this double going outside of itself of sense in itself" which Derrida concludes lies at the basis of Husserl's choice of the term "ex-pression"—in addition to the notion of *Bedeutungen,* which we have already encountered, and I will soon further address—is another term decisively at work in this passage with which we have yet to meet up, namely, "sense" or *Sinn.* Derrida ends by speaking of a double going out of itself of sense *(Sinn)* in itself, and this results from a *first* passage outside, a first expression of *Sinn*—into *Bedeutungen,* conceptual meanings—and a *second* moment of expression pertaining to the *bedeuten* and *Bedeutungen* themselves. Thus, this notion of *Sinn* must first be clarified to grasp what Derrida has in mind here, as well as the distinction between *Sinn* and *Bedeutungen,* a notion and a distinction that hearken back, in turn, to §124 in *Ideas I,* as Derrida himself is about to indicate ("If by anticipation and for greater clarity, we refer to the corresponding sections of §124" [*VP* 35/ *SP* 33]).[38]

In *Ideas I* generally, to step back to Husserl's own text for a moment, Husserl inaugurates transcendental phenomenology in the strictest sense of the term by broadening out and extending many of the notions and insights that he had struck on in *Logical Investigations,* as well as further focusing on a host of methodological issues. At the center of this extension stands the notion of meaning. Indeed, transcendental consciousness as presented in *Ideas I* is, first and foremost, the site of an entirely inclusive intentional structure, the correlation noesis-noema, which brings before it everything, including individual beings, by way of different sorts of intendeds (noemata) and different types of intentionalities (noeses): a variety of intentional acts functioning in different "doxic modes" (such as memory, perception, imagination) which, according to Husserl, make accessible everything, all being, as what it is, and insofar as it is.

More specifically, in §124 of *Ideas,* in the passage to which Derrida has just alluded, Husserl, having in mind this broadening out of his own program, had famously declared that terms like "'to mean' *(bedeuten)* and meaning *(Bedeutung)* . . . originally . . . concerned only the linguistic sphere." "But one can scarcely avoid," Husserl continued, "and at the same time take an important cognitive step, extending the signification of these words . . . to all acts, be they now combined with expressive acts or not. Thus we . . . speak of 'sense' [*Sinn*] in the case of all intentive mental processes . . . for the sake of distinctness we shall prefer the term 'meaning' for the old concept and, in particular, in the complex locution 'logical' or 'expressive' meaning" (Husserl 1983, 294/Husserl 1950, 256; translation altered).

Sinn, then, is the term Husserl applies to all meanings, to meanings of any sort, but in particular, Husserl reserves the term for meanings that are not "combined with expressive acts," that is, nonconceptual meanings that do not pertain to acts that employ language, or logical expressions. *Sinn,* "sense," especially concerns what Husserl will also call pre-expressive *(vorausdrücklich)* acts, as he is about to make clear, going on to exemplify this notion of *Sinn* in the instance of an act of perception that takes up an object before anything is explicitly "thought or said." Clearly, then, what Derrida has in mind in the passage above, speaking of a sense in itself, a sense already on a certain inside which subsequently goes forth from itself, is this *Sinn,* or sense. And *Sinn,* sense, is thus "in itself," already on a certain "inside"—in line with the context of Husserl's own discussion—insofar, and only insofar, as it is already a function of certain transcendental intentional achievements.

This sense, *Sinn,* as we have already begun to see, lies at the base of the rest of the analysis that Derrida brings forward. It is subject to a double going outside: first, as taken up, expressed in *Bedeutungen*—as Derrida himself here puts it, "a pre-expressive intentionality aiming at sense . . . will be transformed consequently into a *Bedeutung* and into an *expression*" (*VP* 35/*SP* 33)—and second, through the *Bedeutungen* themselves, these logical or conceptual meanings, finding their way into expressions *(Ausdrücke)* proper.

Indeed, to begin to turn now to the *Bedeutungen,* these specifically logical or linguistic conceptualities, or meanings, are themselves ex-pressions, ex-pressions of this prior sense. Husserl in §124 of *Ideas I* still opposes the *Bedeutungen* to this *Sinn*—opposes conceptual or logical meanings *(Bedeutungen)* to a broader sense pertaining to all intentionali-ties of which consciousness is capable *(Sinn)*—and he explicitly asserts that these *Bedeutungen,* these conceptual meanings, are themselves ex-pressions of the former. ("Logical meaning is an expression"—as Derrida has earlier quoted Husserl as declaring in §124.)[39]

The *Bedeutungen* (conceptual or logical meanings) express in ideal-ity, in the form of ideal objects, then, this first pre-expressive sense *(Sinn),* and accounting for the first phase of this double going outside of sense in itself begins to answer Derrida's original question—why expression, why *Ausdruck?*—since the *Bedeutungen* that these further expressions (expres-sion proper, *Ausdruck*) embody prove to be already expressions in turn (of this first nonlinguistic, nonideal *Sinn*).

Before proceeding further, it must be emphasized that Derrida at A.1 of chapter 3 is in the course of presenting a matrix, a circuit of ex-pressions, of successive sorties or going forths of meaning, taking in the ar-chitecture squarely at the center of Husserl's own thought. This circuit of expression that Derrida is in the midst of outlining, this "double going forth of sense," brings forth a core set of operations proper to transcen-dental phenomenology alone, involving all Husserl's key notions, internal to Husserl's own thought, and assuming this thought's validity.[40] Derrida at this moment in his text, to take a step still further back, may be arguing, as we have already seen, that all of Husserl's distinctions are implicated in a supposedly illicit teleology; Derrida, however, also can and does continue here to maintain Husserl's own framework, to respect his most important notions, thus laying the ground for all Derrida will do in chapter 6.

Derrida himself alludes here to the centrality of what he is sketching both for Husserl and for his own work. In this same paragraph, in remarks previously omitted, Derrida, with an eye on the transcendental prove-nance of these distinctions just brought forward, speaks of an "absolutely original" inside and outside, and makes reference back to an earlier mo-ment in *Speech* when he had first raised this theme. "We have suggested above that this outside and this inside are absolutely original . . . we can now be more precise" (*VP* 34/ *SP* 32). Derrida's sketch at 3.A.1 is thus meant to substantiate and expand on an inside and outside unique to Husserl's philosophy that Derrida deems "absolutely original"—a term of approbation Derrida rarely applies, and only to thinkers to whom, and thoughts to which, he assigns the highest importance. And back in the previous passage, to which he now refers, Derrida claims this inside and

outside speak to "the phenomenological project in its essence." He there
goes on to declare: "Beyond the opposition of 'idealism' and 'realism,'
'subjectivism' and 'objectivism,' etc., transcendental phenomenological
idealism answers to the necessity of describing the objectivity of the object
(Gegenstand) . . . starting from an 'interiority,' or rather from a proximity
to self, or from an ownness *(Eigenheit)*, which is not a simple inside but the
intimate possibility of a relation to a beyond and an outside in general"
(*VP* 23/ *SP* 22).

Husserl's phenomenology will always have the role in Derrida's
thought that he affirms here: beyond all of the usual philosophical oppositions—beyond idealism and realism, subjectivism and objectivism—it
sets out "the possibility of a relation to a beyond and an outside in general," according to Derrida. Phenomenology makes known a respect for
otherness (not, by the way, of the Levinasian sort) that stands at the core
of all else *Derrida* himself will do—*including calling Husserl's own thought
into question for the sake of pushing this possibility further.* The relation to objectivity in general, for Derrida, thus remains the unique provenance of
Husserl's transcendental attitude, and Derrida, here at 3.A.1, expanding
on his earlier comments, has set out a unique circuit of expression embodying this insight. Cashing out the inner core of Husserl's thought, this
circuit continues to respect this singular membrane between outside and
inside which Husserl alone makes available, and to this Derrida will recur
in chapter 6.

One final concern remains to us, however, before turning to this latter chapter. Derrida there will eventually contest Husserl's thought, even as
it continues to play a key role of the kind set out here—in accord with that
singular trajectory of departure that we have already seen *Le problème* anticipate, in which Derrida defers his break to the end in order to attain an
unprecedented degree of radicality. Yet the voice, precisely that through
which such contestation will proceed, has yet to be discussed here. The
voice, however, does come forward for the first time at 3.A.1: at this third
and final layer pertaining to expression proper. In this second going forth
of sense, now of the *Bedeutungen* (ideal objectivities), into expressions
(Ausdrücke), what Derrida means by the voice, the phenomenological voice
in its specificity, appears for the first time in *Speech*.

"The *bedeuten*," Derrida notes in a sentence omitted earlier, *the act*
that intends *Bedeutungen* (conceptual meanings), aims at "a certain outside," which is not that of "nature, world, or real exteriority," but rather
that of an "ideal ob-ject." The *Bedeutungen* (conceptual meanings), as we
have seen, are themselves already expressions of *Sinn*, of sense, at least potentially; these (the *Bedeutungen*) also may be spoken of, it now becomes
clear, in terms of the aim at a certain outside (that of an *ideal* objectivity),

yet an outside singularly accessible to consciousness, not to be found in nature or real exteriority. This outside, in turn, moreover, finds itself expressed in a further outside, in the expression proper, in the *Ausdruck* as such—a further outside which all the while continues to let both the *Bedeutungen*, these ideal objects, and the *Sinn* they express, remain "within" consciousness. "This outside" (of the *Bedeutung*, of ideality), Derrida states in describing this second movement, "is then expressed, passes outside [of itself, of ideality] into another outside, which is always 'in' consciousness" (*VP* 34/ *SP* 32).[41]

Here emerges the issue that has received the most attention in Derrida's treatment of these matters: the status of these *Bedeutungen*, the ideal meanings that logic treats, and the correlation Derrida draws between them and the voice. This indeed turns out to be key, and is the goal toward which this entire phase of my discussion has been headed. The phenomenological voice is determined by Derrida as this final linguistic layer—or what permits this linguistic layer of expression proper, into which these idealities pass, to close off this circuit of exteriorization, this circulation of meaning, still keeping this whole circuit within the range of consciousness: keeping these successive goings-forth, involving a unique passage from a first outside *(Sinn)* to a second *(Bedeutung)*, and a second to a third *(Ausdruck)*, accessible to consciousness and consciousness's recuperation. "We wanted solely to note here what 'expression' means according to Husserl," Derrida concludes in 3.A.1, "the going outside of itself of an act, then of a sense, which is only able to remain in itself, however, in the voice, and in *the phenomenological voice*" (*VP* 35/ *SP* 33; my emphasis).

The sense, *Sinn,* is already the correlate of an intentional act, though usually bearing a temporal index; the *Bedeutungen,* the ideal meanings, which express these senses (and sometimes these acts), are themselves the objects of intentions aiming at what is atemporal; finally, these *Bedeutungen* are thought to find their way into speech or discourse of some sort (or at least are always accompanied by such a possibility). Correspondingly, Derrida introduces the voice *(la voix,* not "speech," as the English translation has it), the phenomenological voice, in its specificity *("la voix 'phénoménologique'")* to elucidate how this circuit might continue to function even while it extends to some form of language, some form of sign, which the term "expression" *(Ausdruck)* explicitly entails as Husserl uses it in *Logical Investigations* II.1.

The phenomenological voice is just what permits this last layer of a more general ex-pression to function in a manner congruent with the rest of Husserl's thought. The phenomenological voice, at this moment, is the final terminus of the passage of a sense outside itself: it is what permits this final "linguistic" layer to close off this circuit of exteriorization, all the while allowing these various outsides, these prior exteriorizations of both sense and meaning, to still remain "within" consciousness, in the sole sense that both the phenomenological-transcendental and the eidetic reductions would not thereby be drawn into question.[42]

When found in the midst of Derrida's other work in these chapters, and associated with this chain of exclusion, the voice might well seem to be aimed at calling into question all Husserl does and disputing the legitimacy of his thought, thanks to introducing a foreign externality—a type of signifying substance, an empirical system of language—into the system of Husserl's thought. Thus, it is certainly not unreasonable that even very good readers of *Speech* have understood Derrida to aim at something like such a sweeping critique. Yet, as we can already see, the phenomenological voice as such, in the specific sense it comes forward here—either as what permits this final level so to function or as this final layer itself insofar as it so functions—must be recognized as distinct from any actual vocal medium, any real act of speech. Indeed, Derrida himself, above where I first cited him, goes on to stipulate that this last layer of expression, of the *Ausdruck,* "of expressive discourse . . . has no need of being effectively offered in the world"; and the phenomenological voice, even as it first appears in *Speech,* taken in its own right, whatever else it may indicate, has nothing to do, at first blush, with orality or with a real signifying substance, with the voice as we know it or any actual vocalization of a real empirical language.

Not only is the phenomenological voice as it first appears here in 3.A.1 by no means a matter of voice as it is usually understood, but as we have already seen, the voice as 3.A.1 presents it can only appear at all, make any sense in its specificity (with the specificity Derrida himself assigns to it), insofar as this entirely Husserlian circuit of expression is supposed as valid. The voice works to cap or clinch this singular circuit of expression, and thus presupposes all the other phenomenological-transcendental distinctions this circuit implies (those pertaining to *Sinn* and *Bedeutung,* in particular). There could thus be no question of this voice at all if a real empirical voice, or even such a language, were to be understood here. As it is at issue here, the phenomenological voice in its specificity not only must be conceived apart from all actual vocal utterance, but further, it must even be able to do without all factual languages, and all real communities of speakers. Otherwise, it could not be envisioned as performing the function assigned to it, of letting meaning exteriorize itself while remaining in consciousness and close to itself (this possibility from the first already having been undone)—and this has been overlooked by too many of Derrida's readers, though, as I have noted, to some extent naturally enough.[43]

The distance of what Derrida is setting forth here from what is normally meant by language, speech, or discourse must not be neglected. The *phenomenological* voice may only be thought by way of Husserl's phenomenology and not the other way around. Of course, again, this does not mean that Derrida does not wish to contest this notion, and all of Husserl's other core conceptions as well. As we also noted, however, Derrida ultimately wants to do this starting from the *inside* of Husserl's thought and text; and it is now time, with this singular notion of the voice in view, to turn to chapter 6, in order to witness this unique contestation and to discover more clearly what Derrida means by this voice, what the phenomenological voice in its positivity genuinely connotes.

* * *

At the center of chapter 6 of *Speech and Phenomena*, then, we find Derrida's actual discussion of the phenomenological voice. Derrida here returns to the issue of idealization and the necessity of "the medium of expression," "to respect, restitute the presence of sense at once as the being-before of an object available to the gaze, and as proximity to itself in interiority" (*VP* 83/ *SP* 75)—thus revisiting the circle of expression that I have just sketched. Chapter 6, it should also be noted, itself falls into two phases corresponding to the two larger gestures defining *Speech* as a whole. Just as *Speech* itself consists of two broad movements—a first, represented by its initial three or four chapters calling Husserl's thought radically into doubt, and a second, taking up the remainder of *Speech,* and addressing itself to the inner core of Husserl's phenomenological teachings—so too, chapter 6, standing at the center of this last, at the culmination of this inside development, has two parts corresponding to each of the two larger ones in turn. In chapter 6 we find first an inside, answering to that earlier outside, to the movement of the first three chapters of *Speech* (and reprising some of its more radical teleologically-oriented concerns related to language and signification); and a second half, the culmination of this second larger movement, the inside of the inside, bringing forward an "ultra-transcendental" outside and Derrida's final word on Husserl's core doctrines.[44]

In the first half of chapter 6, then—to clarify the ground on which Derrida's talk of a phenomenological voice here reemerges, and on which the developments of the second half that most interest me take place— Derrida links his earlier concerns, his radically deconstructive undoing of all of Husserl's language-related terms, explicitly to Heidegger. Derrida returns once again to the end of *Logical Investigations* II.1.8 to pick up on Husserl's claim that in interior monologue speech serves no practical purpose, and he goes on to argue that a privilege of the proposition, or the theoretical statement—of the ability of linguistic signs to make claims of the form "S is P"—is to be found there. Derrida connects this privilege to Heidegger's assertion that the "metaphysical" interpretation of Being gives priority to the copula. When it comes to the infinitive "to be," the interpretation of Being that "philosophy" has always known mysteriously "starts from the third person singular of the present indicative" (*VP* 82/*SP* 74).

Derrida in the first part of chapter 6 thus further cashes out the illicit teleology that the first half of *Speech* as a whole had brought forward, relating this now to Heidegger, but also to what Derrida calls "logocentrism" (a certain interpretation of language that privileges its ability to say something about something, to furnish a logos, an account)—a conception at once supposed to extend, yet also to contest, Heidegger's own talk of an epochal metaphysics (*VP* 82n1/*SP* 74n4). In the 1967 writings taken together, moreover, logocentrism is always found paired with phonocentrism (a thesis concerning the privilege of one *signifying medium* over another, a privilege solidary, in Derrida's eyes, with the priority logocentrism gives to certain *functions* of signification rather than to others—seemingly apart from *medium*), and Derrida's introduction of the thematics of the voice, not surprisingly, follows directly after this setting out of a logocentrism at work in Husserl's thought.

Accordingly, Derrida, along with seeing a historial predetermination in Husserl's preference for the proposition, will now go on to announce that such preapprehension by the epoch of metaphysics extends to the privilege of the *phone* as well: that "the epoch of the *phone* is the epoch of being in the form of presence." Derrida, in bringing forth such phono- and logocentrism, it seems, even now wants to link that analysis of the circuit of expression that he is about to pursue and he has already introduced (functioning at the interior of Husserl's thought) to his initial claim that an illicit teleology stood at the threshold of all Husserl's thought—announcing that "between idealization and the voice, the complicity is indefeasible."

Yet the position of these assertions in chapter 6 as a whole is rather more nuanced than it may first seem, and Derrida's difference from Heidegger at this moment needs to be taken into account as well (along with his proximity), before too swiftly drawing conclusions about what precisely Derrida has in mind here. Derrida, after all, as he himself has repeatedly insisted, with his talk of phonocentrism and logocentrism ultimately aims to sketch metaphysics' *closure,* not its end, and intends to avoid Heidegger's historicism, as well as all linguistic relativism. In fact, according to Derrida, metaphysics *may never end,* though its limits, both internal and external, may now be beginning to be glimpsed. Thus, while Derrida may, at the start of chapter 6, seem interested in determining Husserl's philosophy from the outside, historically, in the name of an epoch now associated with the voice, what this voice, standing at the core of such phonocentrism, signifies in the first place—its original status as a referent—can only be found within Husserl's own thought, as Derrida himself is about to make clear. Thus, the simple priority of these Heideggerean concerns over Husserl's may not be taken for granted.

My assertion that the first half of chapter 6 presents the outside *of the inside* can now be better grasped. Derrida doubtless wants to suggest even now that some aspect of Husserl's thought extends beyond Husserl, that unknown to him phonocentrism and logocentrism have a hand in shaping his thought in some fashion. Here in chapter 6, however (as opposed to in the first three chapters), this finally proves to be a matter of casting *backward,* moving *outward* from Husserl's work and all it implies, to cash out these broader claims, which are themselves singularly at once linguistic and historical.

In fact, after the passage with which I have just been engaged, some two pages on in chapter 6—and this is what critics have too often failed to note, taking Derrida's opening remarks at face value—Derrida *only now* exhorts us to question Husserl as such, to interrogate "the phenomenological value of the voice." Were Derrida in his remarks just cited truly intending to derive Husserl's talk of idealization and the circuit of expression from the privilege of some actual vocal medium or real epochal history, however, there would be no need *later* to *go on* to question this privilege and this value. The "transcendent dignity" of the voice, as Derrida now puts it, would have *already* been brought into doubt had this movement of idealization, this circuit of expression, been shown to stem from a historical and linguistic outside, and Derrida, then, in these opening pages of chapter 6 has set out only a provisional set of reference points, a network of associations, indeed an outside of the inside (whose own core phenomenon and concerns have yet to be broached).

Derrida's exhortation to question the voice thus divides chapter 6 in two; it signals the move from this first phase, the first half of chapter 6, to the second, to the inside of the inside. So, too, correspondingly, Derrida himself at this key moment makes explicit the priority of Husserl's thinking going forward for all that is to be called the voice. Along with exhorting us to undertake such questioning, Derrida makes clear that the voice or the *phone* he wants to interrogate is not, nor ever can be, the matter of any regional or empirical science: the subject of a "phonetics, phonology, or the physiology of phonation" (*VP*84/*SP*79). In contrast to what Derrida seemed to suggest at the outset of chapter 6, then, no regional inquiry, no worldly science of vocalization, can bring the voice before us, just as Derrida, a little later in chapter 6, making his intentions even plainer, states that "an objective worldly science can certainly teach us nothing about the essence of the voice" (*VP* 89/*SP* 75).

The essential foreignness of the voice from all empirical inquiry that Derrida here highlights necessarily entails that Derrida rely on Husserl's thought first and foremost, on his unique transcendental-phenomenological perspective, both for the initial identification of the voice and for the questioning of it that is about to occur. A voice *originally* identified within phonology or linguistics (or some other worldly science) will *not* subsequently turn out to have consequences beyond its regional domain; rather, "nothing" is precisely what any objective worldly science can tell us about the voice, and only on the basis of the functioning of Husserl's own thought, then, and of the circuit of expression earlier sketched, can the voice at the center of chapter 6 really emerge.[45]

So, too, the central role of phenomenology for all that Derrida intends, for his actual setting forth and deconstruction of the voice that keeps silent, had already begun to become evident in the pages leading up to this transitional moment. The "phenomenon of the voice," as it is in question here, has already been stipulated to be the voice as it *"gives itself"* (*VP* 85/*SP* 76; his emphasis). "*Within phenomenological interiority,*" Derrida had declared, starting to focus on the status of the *phone*, "hearing oneself and seeing oneself" prove to be "radically different orders of self-relation" (*VP* 85/*SP* 76; my emphasis). The issue, the status of the voice in relation to the *phone* or the phoneme, then, already concerns only a *phenomenological* appearance, only the *appearance* of a signifier, not any actual phoneme as such—this is Derrida's specific focus as he makes his turn to the inside of the inside of Husserl's text.

Indeed, more narrowly yet, the priority of the *phoneme*, Derrida at this moment maintains, depends on its being viewed as "the *phenomenological* and *ideal* face of . . . [the] signifier," not as any real vocal medium, nor even as any instance actually pertaining to empirical speech or language (*VP* 85/*SP* 76; my emphasis). The priority of the phoneme over the grapheme stems from the fact that the grapheme provides an *appearance* of referring *to space or externality* within the phenomenological field itself—"in the (nonmundane) phenomenological sphere," as Derrida puts it—an *appearance* presumed absent in the *phone* ("nothing like this, *in appearance,* in the phenomenon of the voice" [*VP* 85/*SP* 76; my emphasis])—again, wholly apart from the real functioning of these media.

Even at this stage, then, even as he goes on to announce "the phoneme . . . as idealized mastery of the phenomenon" (*VP* 87/*SP* 78), Derrida continues to respect *Husserl's* views on linguistic signification. Not only does he treat the phoneme and the grapheme as *idealities,* but they are examined with an eye to their *constitution,* as well as their functioning, *within transcendental-phenomenological consciousness*—as *pure* phenomenological appearances, in which the issue is the reference to the world they bear "in appearance," not any actual worldliness, any genuine mundaneness, as such. And on this ground, and only on this ground, will Derrida finally assert the privilege within phenomenology of the "vocal" signifier or medium, of the phoneme or *phone* as such.[46]

The voice as Derrida brings it forward in these key transitional pages thus continues to presuppose Husserl's philosophy—to retain, not contest, all his phenomenological and even transcendental stipulations; and this indicates what will be the precise status of the voice in the second half of chapter 6, what the voice that keeps silence, the actual object of Derrida's deconstruction, finally designates. The voice emerges only "within phenomenological interiority"; and we can already begin to see that the phenomenological voice in its specificity will prove to be nothing other than a radical representation, an *absolute appearance* within transcendental phenomenological consciousness, initially without any other ground than that within Husserl's thought, nor with any direct reference beyond it. The phenomenological voice in its specificity indeed turns out to be an *absolute appearance,* arising at the third layer, the final station, of this circuit of expression, permitting the operation of this circuit wholly within "phenomenological self-proximity," that is, within the reductions. A pure ideal expressivity referring to *a possible linguistic medium in general,* not to any actual languages or real instances of their employment, the phenomenological voice is the final link in the chain, sealing this movement interior to transcendental phenomenology—this double going forth of sense from itself within transcendental consciousness that previously came forward—ensuring the terms on which Husserl supposes it to function.

Of course, none of this is to deny that Derrida, especially in the first half of chapter 6, also wants to claim that this absolute appearance, this *phenomenon* of the voice, only to be found within Husserl's thought, has reverberations or echoes beyond Husserl. Derrida indeed will want to extrapolate backward, as I have said, from this *absolute appearance*—first to the phoneme as it has always been understood, and ultimately to all distinctions relating to language and speech (both in respect to differences among types of signifiers, as well as between speech acts and language, and, also, all of these from other kinds of signs, and even nonsignitive entities). Derrida doubtless would claim that the possibility of the infinite mastery of ideality that the purely phenomenologically appearing "phoneme" is supposed to ensure (in the context of Husserl's late thought) and the epochal, Western interpretation of language, thought, and Being are ultimately one.

Nevertheless, none of this should obscure the fact that the phenomenon at the heart of these connections pertains to Husserl's thought alone—it is finally an absolutely *phenomenological* voice in its specificity, a pure phenomenon knowing no other ground than Husserl's own thought and distinctions, only able to become visible within them, and, to this extent, assuming their validity. Moreover, only having taken note of this, with the precise sense of the voice as Derrida understands it in view, is the actual deconstruction of Husserlian phenomenology that Derrida undertakes in the second half of chapter 6 able to be grasped.

Thus to finally directly confront this moment, let me turn to Derrida himself, in the second half of chapter 6, as he is about to mount his actual deconstruction of Husserl. There, he starts as follows: "*Considered from a purely phenomenological perspective, within the interior of the reduction,* the process of speech [*processus de la parole*] has the originality of already delivering itself as pure phenomenon . . . The operation of 'hearing oneself speak' is an auto-affection of a wholly unique type" (*VP* 88/*SP* 78; my emphasis).

Derrida is about to embark on his actual deconstruction of Husserlian phenomenology, one focused on this notion of an auto-affection, an auto-affection of a wholly unique type, which "hearing oneself speak" (*s'entendre-parler*) in "speech" (*parole*), taken within phenomenological interiority, initially lets come forward. Once again, everything about to take place, according to Derrida himself, depends, it must be emphasized, on the voice as seen from "a *purely phenomenological* point of view," and grasped "at the interior of *the reduction.*" This auto-affection thus emerges only in respect to a pure and ideal *semblance* of speech, a purely phenomenological voice and its operation. Not just the signifiers, the phonemes, at work in such hearing oneself speak must be taken from a Husserlian perspective, from the viewpoint of constituting transcendental-phenomenological consciousness (again from "within the reductions"), and thus as ideal, *pure* appearances; but the very signs themselves, both the signifiers and the signifieds, at work in this pure process of *parole* cannot be drawn from any real language, any empirical stock of conventional signs (and indeed must in Husserl's sense pertain only to a pure possibility of language and speech in general). A source other than this would immediately destroy the appearance of phenomenological proximity that this voice is supposed to ensure, since, after all, any real language (anything other than a pure possibility) would bear a reference to the world and its history much more surely than that which the mere *appearance* of *space* in the graphic signifier was earlier said to make, upon which Derrida's argument fixed above (compare *VP* 85).

The work of the voice as it is taken up here, of this unique pure auto-affection, is indeed to maintain the reductions. It is to allow within transcendental consciousness an appearance of discourse that, as Derrida will go on to say, itself seems to "have already suspended the natural attitude and the thesis of the existence of the world" (*VP* 88/*SP* 78).[47] Thus a pure and ideal *semblance* of expression, a radical *simulacrum* of the voice within phenomenology alone can be at issue, and it would be wrong to believe that Derrida's subsequent deconstruction of Husserl in any way depends on this auto-affection somehow being illicit, not really pure, somehow mundane.[48] Unique pure auto-affection arises within phenomenological interiority and must be seen to do so successfully. And accordingly, after having undertaken something like a phenomenology of the lived body (which subtends the functioning of the voice at this moment—now specified further as "lived as absolutely pure auto-affection" in this "hearing oneself speak" [*VP* 89/*SP* 79]) and having made a rather long detour through these issues raised earlier relating to the life of signs, their transformation into spiritual flesh, Derrida returns to this same notion of auto-affection and mounts his deconstruction of Husserl's thought as follows.

> Auto-affection as operation of the voice would suppose that a *pure* difference comes to divide presence to itself. It is in this *pure* difference that the possibility of all one believes able to exclude from auto-affection is rooted: space, outside, world, body . . . but it was necessary to pass through it [the transcendental reduction] in order to seize this difference in what is nearest to it: not in its identity, nor its purity, nor its origin. It has none of these. But in the movement of *différance*. (*VP* 92; my emphasis)

At this moment *différance* first emerges as a full-fledged theme in Derrida's text, and here, then, Derrida arrives at the outermost limits of his analysis of Husserl. Pure auto-affection, "auto-affection as operation of the voice," is still the issue, and the first thing to be noted is that, even now, this auto-affection will not be called into question as such. Derrida's departure from Husserl, here at the core of chapter 6, on the inside of the inside, at the moment *différance* is educed, does not take the form of denying the pure self-relation that the phenomenological voice and its operation implies; rather, having implicated all of consciousness' other functions in this operation by way of this circuit of expression, Derrida will now argue that this *absolute simulacrum* of pure vocal expression, this *lived experience* of absolute proximity, ultimately has *consequences* and *conditions* different than those Husserl affirms.

This unique auto-affection that surfaces within phenomenological interiority, more specifically, must itself be taken as the structural possibility of all that Husserl calls consciousness and subject—and to this degree, such a *self-relation* coming first, *prior to any entity or being as such,* it lets the role of difference, indeed a pure difference, become primary. Because a relation here stands not only at the basis of all talk of objects, but even at the basis of that entity (consciousness) with which the subject is identified, a *difference* (a "*pure* difference," Derrida is careful to state) turns out to be central to Husserl's own thinking; a pure difference, which as *difference,* and eventually *différance,* may also be said to lie at the root, and open the door to all that Husserl thought he could exclude from this domain—"space, outside, the world." Nevertheless, this pure difference that Derrida affirms here could only be reached by way of the transcendental reduction as what is closest to it, an option which must thus have been kept open, intact, and remained available here all along.

Différance too, more broadly, explicitly emerges here, along with this pure difference discovered at the heart of consciousness. It is itself brought forward by means of the operation of the voice within phenomenological interiority and the unique auto-affection it implies. All of Derrida's other "signature terms," moreover—"trace" (*VP* 95), "archi-writing" (*VP* 95), "spacing" (*VP* 96)—will soon follow in chapter 6 upon the introduction of *différance.* Accordingly, all these are (as had been earlier anticipated) versions of what is in effect a new, quasi- or ultra-transcendental *life* (life being, again, the notion to which the auto-affection that has come forward here corresponds). Including in them Husserl's own transcendental stipulations (now understood as transcendental difference), they also include all that Husserl himself would wish to exclude from such a conception, including at least in principle the possibility of mundane languages and signs.

Derrida, to put this in other terms, has here finally enacted that "dialectical reversal" of Husserl that he sketched so long ago in *Le problème:* postponing his break with Husserl until the end, deferring his departure until the last, he now reaches for a new more radical outside, which nevertheless has transcendental difference, the difference which allows beings to be and appear (something which Husserl alone authoritatively brings forward) as an aspect of its own operation—even as it overruns the limits Husserl himself assigns to this standpoint, though by no means rejecting it once and for all.

To be sure, even at this moment, as he announces *différance,* Derrida also declares that "no pure transcendental reduction is possible," and it would be wrong to deny that Derrida wishes *différance,* as well as these other terms, not only to capture the force of this passage from consciousness to the outside, this singular transcendental functioning, but also to capture the first half of *Speech,* in which all these distinctions were brought

156

ESSENTIAL HISTORY

into doubt. Nevertheless—and here a developmental perspective performs an invaluable service—not only does Derrida go out of his way to state that none of this could occur apart from Husserl's own thinking, thanks to his transcendental standpoint and passage through it; but moreover, this figure of departure obviously repeats the dialectic of *Le problème*. At its pinnacle, this indeed was supposed to *ruin* its own conditions, yet only at the moment it was brought forth. And this disruption of the reduction, Derrida's claim here about its impurity, must be understood in this sense.

So, too, in a similar vein, the role of the voice in all this has an important bearing on these issues, one I want to emphasize in closing. *Différance* may indeed represent a new, more general life, having Husserl's transcendental-phenomenological perspective at its semantic core, even as it ultimately brings into doubt all these differences and distinctions (sign, language, expression, *Bedeutung*, sense, intentionality) which in Derrida's eyes allowed Husserl to establish this standpoint, to set forth transcendental phenomenology in the first place. Yet the phenomenological voice itself, *la voix* of *La voix et la phénomène*, has proved to be the conduit to this outcome. This voice, not any other referent or concern foreign to Husserlian phenomenology, deconstructs Husserl's thought. In accordance with what was said earlier about an unprecedented "hold," the very presentation of the phenomenological voice as such (though obviously to be thought as also related to a host of other phenomena), this simulacrum itself, *as* functioning *within* transcendental-phenomenological consciousness, turns out *to be the deconstruction* of Husserlian phenomenology. And accordingly, it is the sole example here of the functioning of *différance*. It is the first and only example of the archi-writing that Derrida goes on to speak about, and the preeminent instance of the work of spacing. Because this is so, even as he exceeds and radically departs from Husserl's thought, nowhere within the covers of *Speech* may Derrida be thought to finally dispense with Husserl.

The phenomenological voice in its specificity alone finally permits Derrida to maintain a transformed transcendental attitude, to introduce his own talk of *différance*, archi-writing, and spacing, and it thus proves to be an unexpectedly autochthonous phenomenon, even as it draws phenomenology into question. This very fact, however, which establishes the centrality of Husserl's project to Derrida's thought, even as Derrida departs from him most radically, also raises questions about all that Derrida will or will not be able to do in *Of Grammatology*, when he takes up the other aspect of the program that the "Introduction" bequeathed to him in respect to language and writing more generally. In *Of Grammatology*, starting from a genuinely empirical and mundane science, Derrida will indeed approach language and signs on very different terrain than Husserl's own, and our treatment of the deconstruction of Husserl's thought in *Speech* thus raises a host of questions as to what Derrida can and does accomplish there. Can Derrida maintain the transcendental-phenomenological aperture that we now know is central to *différance* and all his other leading notions? How does Saussure's view of language comport with that of Husserl's? May they be reconciled—and on what grounds? And if not, what form does Derrida's deconstruction of Saussurean linguistics take there?

6

Essential History: Derrida's Reading of Saussure, and His Reworking of Heideggerean History

Derrida's encounter with Husserl has now been sketched: his thought's development through phenomenology—leading from Derrida's earliest writing, *Le problème,* to *Speech,* his last total interpretation of Husserl's thought—has arrived at completion. The deconstruction specific to Husserlian phenomenology by way of the voice has emerged, and what this operation, deconstruction, precisely entails, as well as what Derrida here means by the voice, has been clarified in detail, with specific reference to Husserl.

This line of development, as has already been discussed, has not one but two culminations, however, in which deconstruction emerges—two endpoints through which Derrida makes his break with philosophy and arrives, in the triple publications of 1967, at the core of his own project and his own way of working. *Of Grammatology* represents a second terminus on this same path. Accordingly, what Derrida intends and what he accomplishes in *Of Grammatology* must now be explored, if my overview of deconstruction and Derrida's development is to be complete.

In 1967 Derrida, to make good on the possibility he had glimpsed in the "Introduction" of a writing at once equally founding of truth and radical nontruth, faced the task of bringing writing and language out beyond the limits in which he had discovered them in Husserl, limits which entailed an infinitist teleology of truth, among a number of other factors. In *Speech,* accordingly, Derrida unwound Husserl's language commitments from within. As we have just seen, starting from Husserl's own thought and program, Derrida ultimately sketches a more radical wide-ranging ultra-transcendental standpoint than any conceived by Husserl himself—one which also thus fulfills Derrida's original intention in *Le problème.* In *Speech,* without ever simply opting for a different model of language and its operations than Husserl's own, Derrida both contests and expands

Husserl's transcendental project; he invalidates and then reworks Husserl's language and semiotic commitments in the name of a new, more comprehensive (transcendental) life and a generally functioning (transcendental) *difference*—pertaining to language as well as to thought, to intentional life *and* to the life of signs, thereby overflowing the borders of Husserl's own project.

To completely break free of that impasse from which his thought started out, however—to approximate that absolute radicality he had begun to glimpse in the "Introduction"—Derrida, in turn, must begin not only from Husserl, and from language and writing as Husserl conceives them, but from these taken apart from Husserl's singular conceptions: he must begin, that is, from empirical language, worldly writing, mundane inscription. Derrida doubtless wants to claim that one and the same teleology, one and the same "metaphysics of presence," holds *all* possible conceptions of language and signification in its grasp, including that of Husserl. To *demonstrate* this, however, Derrida must begin from diverse sets of starting points, and show that these fall prey to the same deconstruction—and from here, in part, arises the need for these iterations of this singular operation.

Accordingly, in *Of Grammatology*, Derrida begins from empirical language and mundane writing—these as linguistics, rather than Husserlian phenomenology, conceives them—to arrive at a result parallel to that which emerged in chapter 6 of *Speech*.[1] This different terrain on which Derrida starts in *Of Grammatology* presents challenges for his thought, however, as well as new opportunities.

Of course, given the resolutely negative results at which Derrida arrives in the first phase of *Speech,* it might at first seem that any such differences in starting points could never be decisive. Derrida's unique style of questioning Husserl's opening analyses in *Logical Investigations* II.1, which indeed finds a parallel in *Of Grammatology,* would apparently sweep away all distinctions pertaining to language—all that differentiates language from other sorts of signification, as well as all those that pertain to its different internal operations and aspects (communication and assertion, signifier and signified, etc.). Nevertheless, due to deconstruction's inherent reliance on the discourse of another for its work, which has already been exemplified in Derrida's treatment of Husserl, Derrida's starting point in *Of Grammatology* in fact proves to have critical consequences for the outcomes at which Derrida aims and for the success of his project.

Specifically, starting with language as it is precomprehended by a regional, empirical, worldly science—by Saussure's linguistics—will make it far more difficult for Derrida to successfully retain transcendental considerations of any sort. Saussure's discourse is itself utterly devoid of such concerns, as we shall see; and since Derrida continues to depend on this discourse, even as he calls it into doubt, he will have difficulty holding on to all the different phases of his own discussion and coordinating that diversity of standpoints—mundane and transcendental, empirical and essential—that he invokes at various points in his own work.

Nevertheless, whatever consequences these differences between Saussure and Husserl may ultimately have for Derrida's work in *Of Grammatology*, they do allow for a further phase of his thinking to become prominent there: they permit, indeed they almost *require* Derrida to take Heidegger, not Husserl, as his primary *philosophical* interlocutor in the opening half of *Of Grammatology* (and even arguably in this text as a whole).[2] Because of the empirical terrain on which he now finds himself, because Saussure's starting point is by no means a transcendental one, its discussion lets Derrida's relation to Heidegger come front and center— Heidegger himself having rejected Husserl's methodological stipulations—in a way, of course, that could not be expected in *Speech*.

Indeed, speaking generally, as my examination of Derrida's development has already made plain, by the time of *Of Grammatology* Derrida has moved much closer to Heidegger than he initially stood: he better grasps the core of Heidegger's project, and his own positions, accordingly, have moved much nearer to Heidegger's own. Derrida's invocation of such topoi as "historico-metaphysical epochs" (*G* 6) and the adventure of metaphysics ("all and all a short enough adventure" [*G* 8]) in the opening pages of *Of Grammatology* attests to how much nearer Derrida stands to Heidegger's project as a whole in 1967 than he did in 1954, 1959, or even 1962. Thus, any attempt to come to terms with *Of Grammatology* must take this new proximity into account, in the work where it becomes most evident.

Nevertheless, granting all this, even at this moment of perigee in respect to Derrida's and Heidegger's orbits, Derrida, I would argue, is still no Heideggerean: especially when it comes to these issues of the epoch and the totality of metaphysics—to themes that can be summed up as falling under the heading of history. Thus, along with getting a grip on Derrida's parallel deconstruction of Saussure's views on language (and its relation to Husserl's in *Speech and Phenomena*), and establishing Derrida's new understanding of Heidegger's thought and the role it plays in the 1967 writings, I will want to make precise where Derrida himself stands in respect to these matters.

Here the final phase of my developmental treatment and the final service it can perform steps to the fore. As I will show, much of Derrida's stance toward history in *Of Grammatology* emerges on the basis of two essays that he wrote prior to this work: his first essay on Levinas, "Violence and Metaphysics," and his first on Foucault, "Cogito and the History of

Madness" (both later collected in the 1967 *Writing and Difference*). The singular stance toward *history* that Derrida takes in *Of Grammatology*, at the moment of deconstruction's advent, comes about through this final phase of development that passes through Derrida's first engagements with Foucault and Levinas. Thus, this development, and Derrida's relation to the issue of history overall, is the last concern this chapter treats.[3]

By way of preview, let me emphasize that the title of the present work, *Essential History*, is meant to highlight the importance of this final developmental stage to all of Derrida's thought thereafter. This title was chosen, first, because Derrida's initial encounters with Levinas and Foucault, in which the theme of history is central, themselves turn out to be *essential history:* critical moments in the genesis of Derrida's mature thought. Moreover, as my examination of these works will make clear, Derrida's own understanding of history, even in his mature writings, owes more to Husserl's late historical thought than has previously been suspected. Husserl's thought, as we saw earlier, itself quite literally implies an *essential history*. Husserl in his last work, as Derrida reads him, presented a transcendental-intentional *history of essences* (such as those comprising geometry), and this project, which Derrida always believed decisive for philosophy's ultimate stance toward history, turns out to have an exemplary, albeit subterranean, significance in all of Derrida's future work. For this reason, too, the present text is aptly titled "essential history."

The current, perhaps overly capacious, chapter thus takes up all three themes: Derrida's deconstructive reworking of Saussure, his stance toward Heidegger, and the final phase of his development (visible in his first work on Foucault and Levinas) centered on history. Since, however, Derrida's new stance toward Heidegger is the factor that determines the architecture of this chapter as a whole—supplying the bridge between the other two themes—let me conclude this first section by dwelling at somewhat greater length on this point: by giving Derrida's new stance toward Heidegger in *Of Grammatology* a more extended treatment, and deferring the examination of Derrida's reading of Saussure (and the difference made by his empirical starting point) to the next phase of my discussion.

Doubtless, Derrida does appear to take a much more radical stance toward philosophy at the opening of *Of Grammatology* than any so far witnessed here—in particular, more radical than any to be found in *Speech*. Invoking this framework of the epochs and adventure of metaphysics, announcing what he calls a "new age of writing," Derrida at first glance may appear to have finally settled down in the camp of what some deem "Heideggerean historicism": the handing over of philosophy and its legacy to a new specifically historical or historial mode of dwelling (albeit in a history understood in no previously identifiable sense). Without wishing to deny that a novel strain is indeed heard here (for this will eventually be what I seek to ascertain: precisely what such talk of epochs and ages represents for Derrida), even at this point, Derrida's own stance, I believe, is more complex than it seems, the character of his intentions more equivocal than some of his statements might suggest. Thus, his relation to Heidegger and to history at this admittedly crucial juncture ought not to be too quickly surmised.

Getting to the end of how Derrida positions himself toward Heidegger at this stage of his thought—specifically, toward what I want to call Heideggerean history or even Heideggerean historicism (though these are admittedly partial misnomers)—will only be possible after Derrida's reading of Saussure has been examined (when Derrida's relation to Heideggerean Being can be treated) and Derrida's first works with Foucault and Levinas engaged (when Derrida's relation to this history as such will be broached).[4] I want to begin, however, by focusing on a sentence that comes a bit later in *Of Grammatology*'s introductory sections than the snippets already quoted, though still in chapter 1 (and thus prior to Derrida's actual engagement with Saussure's *Course* in *Of Grammatology*'s chapter 2). The sentence I have in mind is itself the conclusion of a somewhat lengthy development, which I will shortly review, and its importance lies in the fact that it offers a road map to where Derrida ultimately wants go in the first half of *Of Grammatology*. In fact, this characteristically complex utterance encapsulates Derrida's total intention toward Heidegger in *Of Grammatology:* how close Derrida now stands to Heideggerean positions, as well as the distance he maintains from these (including his interest in questioning Heidegger's own thought, apparently in rather novel ways). Indeed, the ultimate target of Derrida's work in the *first half* of *Of Grammatology* (and this has too often been overlooked), it here starts to become plain, is a singular engagement with *Heidegger's thought* (not simply or finally that of Saussure). Derrida writes as follows, providing what is in effect a topic sentence for the entire discussion of "grammatology" that is to come:

> To come to recognize not within but on the horizon of the Heideggerean paths, and yet in them, that the sense of being is not a transcendental or trans-epochal signified (even if it was always dissimulated within the epoch) but already, in a truly *unheard of* sense, a determined signifying trace, is to affirm that within the decisive concept of ontico-ontological difference *all is not to be thought at one go;* entity and being, ontic and ontological, "ontico-ontological," are, in an original style, derivative with regard to difference and with what I shall later call *différance,* an economic concept designating the production of differing/deferring. (*G* 23/*DG* 38)

In this dense and flowing pronouncement, Derrida makes clear, first of all, that his ultimate goal in the first half of *Of Grammatology* is to bring forth, by dint of relation to what he here calls "the Heideggerean pathways" the notion of *différance:* an "economic concept designating the production of differing/deferring." *Différance,* accordingly, will later emerge at the center of Derrida's concerns, at the culmination of his discussion of Saussure, in the third section of chapter 2—a development which I will take up and treat later in this chapter.

Along with the denomination of the ultimate goal of *Of Grammatology*'s first half, the uncharacteristic awkwardness or hesitation which appears to accompany Derrida's pronouncement in the text quoted ought not to go unnoticed. Not "*within* . . . the Heideggerean paths," "but on the[ir] horizon," Derrida begins by stipulating the recognition of his own claims will take place, only then to change his mind, it seems, as to where his results ultimately lie, and declare that such a recognition also occurs "yet *in* them" (my emphases).

Derrida's uncharacteristic change in positioning, if nothing else, should single out this sentence for attention. Not only does it seem to indicate a certain amount of hesitancy in respect to Heidegger's thought (as well the difficulty of finally knowing where Derrida and Heidegger end up standing in respect to one another, a point to which I will return); but, first and foremost, it makes visible the necessity of a *path* as such—the requirement that Derrida's thought, by dint of its own aims, traverse a *way,* as did Heidegger's own (and this necessity is the source of all the other uncertainties that arise here).

This is the first thing to be emphasized: that "all is not to be had at one go," as Derrida here insists, charting the course his thought will take. Thus, with this requirement, it can already be seen that in what follows Derrida will mount a departure from Heidegger, or a displacement of his thought, finally not so far from the one that we have witnessed in respect to Husserl. Heidegger's terms—"entity and being, ontic and ontological, 'ontico-ontological'"—Derrida here specifies, will be shown to be derivative from "difference" and *"différance,"* "in an original style"; and this "original style," Derrida makes clear a little later on, refers to the fact that only by passing through these terms, only by employing Heidegger's notions (specifically that of the ontico-ontological difference), will Derrida be able to bring forward his own thought of what is supposedly "more originary"—just as *différance* emerged in *Speech* only after Derrida had passed through Husserl's transcendental reduction "as what is closest to it."[5]

In the sentence right after the one I have just cited, Derrida announces that "*différance* . . . would be more 'originary'" than "the ontico-ontological difference" if "'origin' or 'ground'" were not "notions belonging essentially to the history of onto-theology." Derrida thus proposes at the outset of *Of Grammatology* to arrive at a more "originary" difference than Heidegger, *"différance,"* by passing through Heidegger's own notion in order to arrive at what would be a more fundamental origin—were the notion of "origin" itself not problematic, not tributary, in Derrida's eyes, to the "history of onto-theology."

The overall scope of Derrida's intentions in the first half of *Of Grammatology,* in the work on Saussure and grammatology, is thus to arrive at this sort of displacement of Heidegger's thought. In turn, the place of Saussure in all of this, the specific role played by his linguistics, next needs to be made plain. Derrida has already suggested, after all, that the force of this departure from Heidegger, this displacement of Heidegger, this arrival at a notion of *différance* close to, but more radical than, the ontico-ontological difference—somehow depends on Saussure. Derrida in the sentence just cited stipulates that the sense of Being henceforth is to be thought not as "a transcendental or a trans-epochal signified" but, in "an unheard-of sense," as "a determined signifying trace," and Derrida owes this differentiation of his own stance from Heidegger's to considerations stemming in some fashion from Saussure, pertaining to linguistic signification (signifiers and signifieds), notions clearly absent in Heidegger.

Announcing that the sense of Being is already in an unheard-of sense a determined signifying trace, Derrida here draws on an argument he just concluded leading up to this pronouncement, concerning the bearing Saussurean linguistics may or may not have on Heidegger's *Seins-frage* (question of Being). And having begun, then, to make clear the overall scope of Derrida's intentions in the first half of *Of Grammatology,* before turning to Derrida's treatment of Saussure in chapter 2, I want to focus a little more concretely on this prior discussion—first and foremost because it can clarify the problem raised at the outset and the one that ultimately most concerns us here: namely, the question of Derrida's specific relation to Heideggerean *history* and *historicism* at the time of *Of Grammatology.*

The issue of Derrida's relation to Heideggerean history is a particularly vertiginous one in *Of Grammatology,* it must be recognized. Everything transpires in these opening pages to suggest that Derrida, in turning to these considerations taken from Saussure and his linguistics (leading up to this thought of Being as signifying trace), aims to further Heidegger's own talk of an era or an epoch of metaphysics, to give this notion an even more comprehensive scope or sense than did Heidegger himself— a scope that would, in fact, include under its rubric even certain aspects of Heidegger's own thought (which is doubtless yet another reason, perhaps even the primary one, why Derrida above says his "recognition" occurs not "within" the Heideggerean pathways "yet in them").

Derrida would broaden out Heidegger's own concern with metaphysics as an epoch—a theme that, in Heidegger's case, at least, seems to be commensurable with historicism. Nevertheless, when the terms on which Derrida conducts this "extension" of Heidegger are examined more closely, and Heidegger's own discourse is recalled, the force of this putative extension of Heidegger's own problematic in Derrida's thought, especially in respect to the theme of history, turns out to be far less clear, far more vexed, than it may seem upon its first appearance.

Indeed, in the paragraphs leading up to the sentence quoted above, Derrida had earlier criticized Heidegger (if this is not too strong a term) by claiming that a previously unheralded phonocentrism and logocentrism were latent in Heidegger's thought. So, too, these notions of phonocentrism and logocentrism seem to be introduced by Derrida as an extension of Heidegger's own thesis concerning a metaphysical epoch, in regard to an era so far everywhere held under the sway of onto-theology and falling prey to the forgetfulness of Being, and this "indictment" of Heidegger directly accounts for that distance that we have already found Derrida putting between himself and Heidegger in the passage cited above.[6]

Derrida's delimitation of phonocentrism and logocentrism, as supposedly identified in Heidegger's own work, stems primarily from Derrida's earlier discussion of *Urworts* (originary words)—and Heidegger's notion of Being as an *Urwort*. "The word 'being,' or at any rate the word designating the sense of being in different languages," Derrida claims, is for Heidegger "an *Urwort*, the transcendental word assuring the possibility of being-word to all other words" (*G* 20). Heidegger's thought of Being thus is "tied," according to Derrida, "at least to the possibility of the word in general" (*G* 21), and Derrida will go on to pose the question of the relation of this dependence of Being (or the sense of Being) on *Urworts* (and thus on the word in general) to a "modern linguistics," presumably Saussure's, or at least to a structural linguistics generally, "that breaks with the privilege of the word"—this argument paving the way for Derrida's claim that Heidegger's thought is tributary to phono-logo-centrism.

Derrida suggests that both Heidegger's reliance on the word (his logocentrism) and his talk of a "voice of being" (his phonocentrism)—brought forward on the basis of a discussion of the role of the voice of conscience in *Being and Time* (*G* 20n10; a topos to which we now know Derrida will repeatedly return)—are drawn into doubt by modern linguistics (this linguistics "no longer having anything regional about it" once the question of Being is posed [*G* 21]). To this degree and to this extent, the appeal to linguistics shows that Heidegger's thought, perhaps "unknowingly," participates in that same metaphysics that Heidegger himself would otherwise question. ("Unknowingly because such [old] linguistics . . . has always had to share the presuppositions of metaphysics; the two operate on the same grounds" [G 21].)

However, when Heidegger's own positions are taken into account (the hermeneutic principle that must again be applied here, as with Husserl earlier)—as well as how all this plays out later in *Of Grammatology* itself, in Derrida's actual discussion of Saussure—this interaction, the actual dynamic between Derrida and Heidegger around these charges, seems to have quite different effects in respect to this notion of metaphysics as an epoch than Derrida's remarks immediately suggest.

More specifically, the issue arises, first, as to whether Heidegger himself ever really conceived of Being, or the sense of Being, as "a transcendental signified"—a term Heidegger himself, of course, would never use or allow—in a sense ultimately pertinent here. Heidegger may well speak of the word, and even *Urworts*, and may well have a far different precomprehension of language than that to be found in Saussure; none of this, in Heidegger, appears to enforce the suggestion that I take Derrida to be making by invoking this notion of a transcendental signified: that Being, or the sense of Being, for Heidegger, would take on the status of a sort of *universal*, one transcending all empirical languages, maintaining its identity across them all, and thus head in the direction of a signified standing apart from any and all signifiers.[7] In Heidegger himself, to the contrary, such insistence seems rather to tie thought and Being (the sense, or meaning, of Being and its questioning) all the more closely to *die Sprache*, to actual empirical language and the words to be found in them—and, indeed, with that, to something like empirical history. Nothing in Heidegger suggests, as far as I can tell, that his talk of *Urworts* is meant to present Being or the sense of Being as a self-sufficient or foundational *intended* in the way that the notion of a transcendental signified seems to suggest.[8]

Indeed, in the course of his argument here in *Of Grammatology*, Derrida a little later is eventually forced to concede just this point: "Heidegger . . . occasionally reminds us that 'being' is not a transcendental signified" (G 23). Thus, second, not only does it seem doubtful that Heidegger ever took Being as a *signified*, in any real sense, but more important, Derrida in thus raising these issues related to language and signification, in speaking of Being as *either* a transcendental *signified or* some sort of *signifying* trace—has in fact shifted the association of Heidegger's key notions *away from history to language*. The question of Being's, or the sense of Being's, relation to the sign in general, its status as a signifier or a signified, is first and foremost Derrida's own concern. The sense of Being must be thought as a signifying trace, Derrida says, and whatever else this entails, it makes clear that Derrida himself in *Of Grammatology* will "thematize" Being, or what ends up standing in the place of Heideggerean Being

(*différance*, archi-trace, archi-writing), in association with issues of signification and language—as these terms (archi-*trace*, archi-*writing*) themselves attest. Derrida is interested in the relation of Being (or something
like it) to language far more than is obviously the case in Heidegger's own
writings, certainly his early writings, where, from the moment in *Being and
Time* when phenomenology becomes hermeneutics (Heidegger 1993, 39),
going forward, the primary associations of Being in Heidegger's own
work are found with history, even real empirical history—with a thematic
of history and historicity that Heidegger himself identifies in *Being and
Time* with those of Nietzsche, Dilthey, and Count von Yorck (*Sein und Zeit*
§77; though admittedly this undergoes further complication, though not
cancellation, in the late writings in ways that Derrida himself has preemi-
nently helped us to recognize).[9]

Thus, in these opening pages (and in the discussion that follows)
of *Of Grammatology* Derrida intends to shift the force of the ontico-
ontological difference, or something like it, away from history, empirical
history (and thus away from historicism), and toward a thematics closer to
language—and indeed onto a general possibility of language, a genetico-
structural feature of linguistic signification—which is the role that Saussure most broadly plays in what follows. The detour through Saussure permits Derrida to bring forward a thought close to that of Heidegger's
Being (in its difference from beings), yet one far less obviously historical
than it, far more immediately embedded in theoretical problems concerning language in general than is the case for Heidegger himself.

Where does Derrida, then, finally come down in respect to this other
theme: in respect to history, to Heideggerean history and historicism, in
Of Grammatology? Indeed, the real question posed by Derrida's statement
of his intentions at this moment in the first half of *Of Grammatology,* his talk
of Heidegger's phono-logo-centrism, is: what does this finally mean for
Derrida's own construal of history, and for Heidegger's view of metaphysics as an epoch (to which Derrida seems so close at the outset of *Of
Grammatology*)? And this question is the one that I eventually want to pursue here.[10]

Before doing so, however, the other point raised earlier must first be
examined. A preview of the work to be done by Derrida's intervention in
Saussure's text and project has now come into view. Derrida's intervention, as we have started to see, is ultimately aimed at reworking Heidegger's thought of Being, displacing it in the direction of a signifying trace:
bringing forth an *economic* notion of *différance* that is somehow more originary, or older, as Derrida sometimes puts it, than that of the difference of
Being from beings. How Derrida accomplishes this, and how his starting
point in a regional science affects these outcomes at which he aims, must

now be explored. How does Derrida arrive at this repetition of Heidegger's thought; what role does Husserl's transcendental attitude play in this; and where does this result stand in relation to the deconstruction of Husserl's phenomenology that Derrida undertook in *Speech*? After these points have been examined, the problem of history will again be taken up, in the context provided by Derrida's first essays on Foucault and Levinas, which notably take history, arguably even ultimately Heidegger's construal of history, as their central theme.

* * *

Let me, then, step back and begin by further comparing Husserl and Saussure. The crux of the issue has to do with the terms on which Saussure is able to establish a science of language, a regional linguistics, in the first place. These must be held firmly in mind, along with how they comport with *Husserl's* understanding of language (and the circumstances under which an appeal to his transcendental attitude may be made), if Derrida's own intentions in *Of Grammatology*'s first half, as well as the problems these intentions face, are to be grasped.

To start from Saussure's standpoint, two related issues need to be set out in order to see how his analysis relates to Husserl's, as well as what sort of starting point this provides to Derrida. The first point is that in the *Course in General Linguistics* Saussure proceeds on a wholly empirical basis. He starts from the mundane, factual situation of actual empirical *communication,* of a speaker addressing an interlocutor and being responded to, in turn, in one of the so-called "natural languages." Unlike Husserl, Saussure does not set aside the communicative situation, nor does he isolate a work of discourse or language that might go beyond this empirical setting entirely—toward a meaning *(Bedeutung)* identical across different languages, in particular—and thus no aspect of Saussure's treatment lets the factuality of a specific empirical language be wholly factored out, as in Husserl's.

Saussure sets out the basic orientation of his science near the outset of the *Course,* in his chapter 3, entitled "The Object of Linguistics." Section 2 of this chapter, "Place of Language in the Facts of Speech," makes Saussure's standpoint in respect to these matters especially plain. Here Saussure ultimately arrives at his famous distinction between *langue* and *parole,* thus defining language as a science of (nonhistorical) linguistics will study it (perhaps the contribution for which his work remains best known even today).[11] With the establishment of language as an autonomous object of study, Saussure's resolutely empiricist approach also comes into view.

In section 2, in order to bring his object of study forward, Saussure sketches what he calls the "speaking-circuit" (Saussure 1966, 11). He first isolates *langue* from *parole* in the context this circuit supplies, and this path is meant to represent *communication empirically.* Saussure sketches this circuit by tracing the path (a) of a thought (or a concept) first being translated into a sign by one interlocutor; (b) the moment of audition and the retrieval back from sign to concept on the part of a second interlocutor; and (c) finally closing off this circuit by way of a response from the second interlocutor to the first, which traces the whole first path in reverse. This circuit, which may be usefully contrasted with Husserl's circuit of expression set out in my chapter 5, represents the broadest setting in which the work of language may be found; it covers language, speech, and an array of other features (thought, sound waves, vocal chords, the ears, etc.) studied by a variety of empirical disciplines, including physics, psychology, and the sciences of audition and phonation (Saussure 1966, 12).

Language, as linguistics will hereafter study it, is isolated by Saussure initially within this speaking-circuit, and the defining features of language that allow it to be isolated are its being a "social" or "collective" rather than an "individual" possession, and a "passive" rather than "executive" component within this total set of communicative facts (Saussure 1966, 11, 12). Language comes forth here as a reservoir, a "storehouse," of common preexisting conventions, as a collective or "social entity," drawn on by the speaker and hearer alike. It provides a preexisting stock of associations, as well as a preexisting set of codes or syntagma—a stock and a set which must already be in place in order for this same circle, this empirical circuit of communication, to operate. Language is speech's precondition, its arrangement or establishment not being at the speaker's disposal but rather being given prior to the speech situation—speech, in turn, being determined as an "executive," active, "individual" function corresponding to the moment when the speech act is initiated through translation of the thought (or concept) into its sign, a moment here said to originate in the mind or brain of the speaker.[12]

Language for Saussure thus emerges as a discrete object of study within this wholly empirical communicative circuit, as itself entirely factual. Correspondingly, for Saussure, the linguistics which studies it stands on the same footing as a number of other regional disciplines, including physics and psychology. The full significance of Saussure's empiricism for all that follows, however, really comes into view only with the other point that needs to be stressed here, one which has in part already started to emerge: namely, the full relation between *langue* and *parole* within this analysis.

After all, in starting with the speech act within the communicative situation, from a moment when a concept or thought originating with one speaker begins to make its way to the comprehension of another, Saussure might appear to be not all that far from Husserl, who, as I have pointed out, indeed sees the work of language as subordinate to speech.[13] Not only, however, does Saussure understand speech in a wholly empirical manner and see its function as purely communicative, but in so doing, Saussure, in contrast to Husserl, puts *parole* and *langue* on one and the same footing, one and the same plane, separating them out oppositionally, not hierarchically.

This proves to be a subtler point than it may seem at first. Husserl, as we noted repeatedly, while doubtless recognizing some role for the signs of conventional language (a matter to which I will come later), *subordinated* these signs (and ultimately all real language) to the acts of meaning which animated them, which made even their conventional bodies (what Saussure would call their signifiers) into spiritual flesh—on which condition alone they were finally really to be taken as *signs*. In turn, though the priority assigned by Saussure here to *language (langue)* in the work of signification obviously checks this course—signitive meaning clearly depends on *langue*—it would also be wrong to say that Saussure's linguistics goes wholly in the other direction and performs the opposite subordination to Husserl's: of the speech act and "logical meanings" *(Bedeutungen) to* empirical language.

Though it is too often overlooked, Saussure departs from a thinker like Husserl not because he affirms the contrary—the subordination of all thought and meaning to signs, embracing a nascent philosophical nominalism and linguistic relativism—but, rather, as his opening discussion shows (which leaves room for a further provenance of thought belonging to psychology and other disciplines), because Saussure *takes no stance at all* on any matters within the philosophy of language. His linguistics, his founding formulations, are and must be entirely agnostic about all such "ultimate" claims.[14] Saussure, in isolating language as we have just witnessed him, proceeds *differentially*—simply by placing the two empirical matrices of communicative speech and empirical languages over against one another and isolating their relative functions. In so doing, he implies nothing at all about which may ultimately be *philosophically* prior, signification or thought, whether there may be logical or even psychological meanings with a universality of their own, whether the laws of logic must be taken as objectively valid or merely anthropologically operationally necessary, and so forth. Indeed, were it incumbent upon Saussure to resolve such fundamental issues in the philosophy of language in order to get his linguistic science off the ground, this science could never arrive at the autonomy which Saussure constructs for it, nor could Saussure or any linguist remain within the confines of an empirical discipline.[15]

Saussure's empiricism, in this sense, goes all the way down: at no moment does Saussure speak authoritatively about any first principles. He delineates an autonomous field for the *empirical* study of language by op-posing this to an equally *empirical* act of communicative speech, and in doing so, he is agnostic about all philosophical issues pertaining to lan-guage (and discourse), especially those which most interested Husserl: namely, that aspect of speech (of what Saussure calls *parole*) which Husserl believes points beyond all empirical culture, any determined historical language or merely factual speech act—though interestingly enough, Husserl in his own way may be said to harbor a different kind of agnosti-cism about the causal or real relations underlying all of these, an issue which will concern me later.[16]

Saussure, then, cannot and does not take a position on any ques-tions in the philosophy of language; he treats both *langue* and *parole* from the first simply on an empirical basis, distinguishing them from one another as the collective to the individual, the passive to the active, the preexisting to the new. And with the actual parameters of Saussure's own project now before us, the precise ambitions, as well as the pitfalls, of Der-rida's treatment may now be brought out. For the true importance of all these stipulations, of what Saussure does or does not do, becomes fully clear only by turning to Derrida's own remarks.

Let me start from what is in many ways the climax of the first half of *Of Grammatology* and of Derrida's treatment of Saussure, and broaden out my discussion from there. Derrida is about to embark on the last of three sections ("La brisure," or "The Hinge") that comprise the chapter of *Of Grammatology* specifically devoted to the treatment of Saussure. At the end of the previous section (whose orthography prevents me from citing its title here), in preparing for this transition, as one part of a two-pronged discussion, Derrida focuses on Saussure's claim that the signifier is not a real sound, but a "psychic image." Derrida writes, in a broader context that I will soon restore:

> Here the Husserlian correction is indispensable and transforms even the premises of the debate . . . The psychic image of which Saussure speaks must not be an internal reality copying an external one. Husserl, who crit-icizes this concept of portrait in *Ideen* I shows also in the *Krisis* how phe-nomenology should overcome the naturalist opposition—whereby psy-chology and the other sciences of man survive—between "internal" and "external" experience. It is therefore indispensable to preserve the dis-tinction between the appearing sound and the appearing of the sound, in order to escape the worst and the most prevalent of all confusions. (*G* 64)

I start by focusing on this moment because it is perhaps the most concrete instance of the numerous appeals to Husserl's transcendental phenome-nology that Derrida will make in the course of his discussion in *Of Gram-*

matology's first half. Derrida's relation to *Heidegger,* the theme my first section in this chapter raised, depends on Derrida's employment of *Husserl*—in this instance and in related ones in his discussion of Saussure—and only after following this out can where Derrida stands in respect to Heidegger's central notions be clarified and that phase of my discussion be rejoined.

What should immediately be clear in the passage just cited, given my review of the opening sections of Saussure's *Course,* is that Derrida here introduces a set of stipulations, or corrections, that no linguist, including Saussure himself, could accept. Derrida, at this moment, is arguing that Husserl's categories from *Ideas I* and the *Crisis* ought to be called on in order to rigorously think the *phone,* the phonic signifier, which Saussure calls the "sound image," the psychic image of sound.[17] And so advocating, Derrida also makes reference to the Husserlian distinction between "hyle and morphe" (the "Husserlian correction" of Saussure, to which Derrida here claims to subscribe, in part consists in affirming the "real [*reell* and not *real*] component of lived experience, the hyle/morphe structure [which] is not a reality [*Realität*]" [*G* 64]).

These moments, however, including "hyle/morphe," all function within the correlation noesis-noema, and the perspective Derrida invokes here belongs entirely to functioning transcendental consciousness; it implies all of Husserl's reductions—the eidetic, phenomenological, and transcendental—and, to this degree, even implies that entire relation to language and meaning in Husserl which we have already seen accompanying these. Indeed, Derrida admits here that the sciences of man "live off" that opposition that Husserl alone, through his transcendental perspective, would have "overcome," and in whose overcoming Derrida now wishes to follow him (namely, that "between 'internal' and 'external' experience" [*DG* 94/ *G* 64]). Derrida thus brings in concerns avowedly foreign, even antithetical, to Saussure's own perspective at this moment—and it should be no wonder, then, to recur to a point my first chapter started to raise, that so few of Derrida's readers have really been able to follow him here in these later but crucial stages of the first half of *Of Grammatology.*

More specifically yet, Derrida wants to say that this signifying substance, which for Saussure was but "the psychic imprint of the sound, the impression that it makes on our senses" (*G* 63), should be seen by way of the reductions, through the perspective of *Ideas I,* as a pure intentional object, rather than as an empirical, anthropological phenomenon, as a feature of our sensory apparatus or our actual psyche. The appeal to hyle/morphe will thus allow for an absolute differentiation between the "sound appearing" and any reality, according to Derrida, including the real (psychological) event of the appearing of the sound. What is once again at issue, then (with certain important differences that I will bring forward)—Derrida being concerned with a phonic signifier purified of all anthropological and even empirical basis—is indeed something very close to that phone, that phoneme, the voice, as it arose within phenomenological interiority in chapter 6 of *Speech*.

Derrida himself, in fact, immediately goes on to make clear that what interests him is the *"essence* of the phone" (my emphasis)—the essential possibility of this sort of signifier, of its givenness and constitution within transcendental consciousness—and he goes on to state that this "essence . . . cannot be read directly and primarily in the text of *a mundane science*" (adding "a psycho-physio-phonetics," which I assume summarizes all possible mundane sciences that might be in question [*G* 64–65]). Once again, Derrida makes clear, no regional science by definition could have access to the perspective which Derrida wishes to introduce into Saussure's project. Thus, were Derrida's own stipulations to be met here, by bringing forward the phonic signifier in its transcendental phenomenological givenness, any regional science of linguistics would in fact be impossible—an outcome not emphasized by the style of Derrida's presentation at this moment, and which has rarely been recognized by his readers, but which is in fact consonant with Derrida's overall project in this part of *Of Grammatology*, of both setting out *and* questioning the possibility of a "grammatology," of any sort of empirical science of writing taken in its utmost generality.[18]

The divide between Derrida and Saussure at this moment, however, is not only one between an appeal to a lived transcendental experience and a science for which such recourse is by definition impossible; and seeing that this divide goes even further will prove key for fully comprehending the gulf that separates Derrida from Saussure, as well as for grasping where Derrida himself stands. In part confirming the argument just made, Derrida goes on to announce that it is in "the temporalization of a lived experience which is neither in the world nor in another world . . . that differences appear among the elements or rather produce them, make them emerge as such, and constitute the texts, the chains, and the systems of traces" (*G* 65). This citation lets us begin to see not only that it is within constituting temporal consciousness, absolute consciousness, that Derrida's analysis proceeds—indeed, breaking with Saussure's or any possible regional investigation—but that his analysis, Derrida's perspective, must also override the distinction which we have just seen Saussure draw between *langue* and *parole*. As Derrida's talk here of "*texts* . . . chains, and . . . *systems* of traces" witnesses, Derrida has in fact melded these two standpoints together.

At the moment that the Husserlian correction proves necessary for grasping the phone and the phonic signifier as such, not only, as attested here, is the *givenness* of language, what permits its signifiers to be *constituted,* Derrida's central (transcendental) question (in a way obviously impossible for Saussure himself), but the problem of the constitution of the signifying medium is broached within the context of speech, as a matter of the *givenness* of language (as a system of signs, *langue*), within language in use *(parole),* as a problem of the signifier within language and within the speech act in effect taken together—and in this fashion it is more in accord with Husserl's stipulations than Saussure's own. In asking about the difference between sound-*appearing* and any real sound or real event, including the appearing of the sound in the individual mind or brain, Derrida broaches the question of the givenness of these linguistic entities (these traces and differences) by asking about them at once as they are already at work in the speech act, as well as in the linguistic system—as text (utterance or inscription), as well as a static system of differential correlations.

Indeed—and this is also a point too often overlooked in discussions of *Of Grammatology,* though again it is part of what Derrida explicitly intends by raising the issue of a grammatology—Derrida throughout the final two sections of his chapter devoted to Saussure proceeds on both of these planes at once. This dual perspective, in fact, forms a large part of what raising the question of empirical writing at the outset of his examination of the *Course* allows Derrida to do. Saussure, at a certain point, has excluded writing from his consideration, and Derrida, investigating this exclusion, is able to pose his inquiry as one asking about a difference between certain *kinds of speech acts* (namely, *acts of inscription* as opposed to those of *vocalization*) as well as about the identity of certain sorts of signifiers over against others within language generally: as to what permits a system of purportedly visual signs and another of purportedly aural ones (phonemes and graphemes) to be mapped on to one another and to a single set of signifieds within language itself—a distinction whose demise or at least transformation we have in fact been witnessing in the passages I have just been citing.[19]

Treating both of these questions together, as we shall soon witness, ultimately permits Derrida in these final sections of his second chapter to think a more radical and a more absolute passivity (and difference) at the origin of both speech and language: at once a radical passivity as the source of what Saussure presumed to be the activity of the one *(parole),* as well as the passivity of the other *(langue).* What is critical to see in more detail right now, however, is how this line of questioning, from first to last, remains consonant above all not with Saussure's language analysis, but with

Husserl's—insofar as only Husserl traces the work of speech *and* language back to a single source, a single animating intentionality.

The coincidence at issue here—between a perspective pertaining to language in its systematicity and one pertaining to its intentional employment—first becomes fully explicit in *Of Grammatology*, notably enough, at a crucial moment earlier in Derrida's presentation in this same chapter. In the passages that I have just been discussing, to which I shall shortly return, the Derridean themes ultimately in question are those of "archi-writing" and "archi-trace"; they are first introduced, in turn, in the context of Derrida's discussion of Hjelmslev (the notion of archi-writing, in particular, makes its first appearance here in *Of Grammatology*, I believe), and at this crucial moment, already taken up here in a provisional way, Derrida also makes plain that what is in question for him in this issue of writing, in distinction from any possible linguistics, along with the structures of the conventional system of language, is something also at work in the act of signification as such.

Despite Derrida's agreement with Hjelmslev concerning the status of empirical writing within language (both being opposed to Saussure), Derrida here stipulates that the concern for signs at work, for the "sign-function," pushes his own perspective beyond Hjelmslev's, making way for the invocation of a certain notion of experience, in turn—an experience beyond the compass of Hjelmslev's concerns, proper to no region, that of transcendental experience solely—and that this finally opens the door to Derrida's talk of "archi-writing." "However original and irreducible . . . might be" Hjelmslev's glossematics (which, unlike Saussure's linguistics, is wholly indifferent to the distinction between writing and speech), Hjelmslev's work, Derrida argues, still ignores the "movement of the *sign-function* linking a content to an expression" (*G*60/*DG*88). The movement of the sign-function, the work which thus allows signs to signify, to purport to speak about something other than themselves, "linking a content to an expression," "could not have a place in Hjelmslev's system" according to Derrida, and, correspondingly, Hjelmslev's thought remains "derivative" in respect to what Derrida calls "archi-writing" (*G*60/*DG*88).

Furthermore, Derrida, after announcing that he, unlike Hjelmslev, investigates not writing, but archi-writing, and does so insofar as he, but not Hjelmslev, asks about the sign-function, the moment when a conventional sign first becomes articulated on the world, next moves the focus to the role that "experience" must play in his analysis as opposed to Hjelmslev's. In line with the restoration of those conditions under which Husserl's transcendental perspective may be thought to function—Derrida here having just given priority (or at least equal standing) to the "movement of the sign-function," to *language in use*—"to escape 'empiricism' and the 'naïve' critiques of experience at the same time," Derrida will stipulate, an appeal to "experience" cannot be avoided (though this concept must ultimately be employed "under erasure"). The notion of experience nevertheless remains necessary to archi-writing, to "experience as archi-writing" (*G* 61/*DG* 89), Derrida goes on to specify—this thought of archi-writing thus proving to be a type or *version of experience*. Such "experience as archi-writing" would be impossible, finally, not if access were barred to any "factual or regional experience"—whose employment, Derrida maintains, Hjelmslev rightfully wished to avoid—but absent access to a transcendental experience which Derrida himself directly identifies with Husserl. "The parenthesizing of regions of experience must discover a field of transcendental experience," Derrida thus goes on to declare, in response to Hjelmslev's presumed objections and having just set out this notion of archi-writing for the first time.

Derrida, here first having evinced the sign-function, which is unthinkable apart from a moment of language in use, next brings in the notion of experience, transcendental experience as Husserl has taught us to understand it. Without an appeal to transcendental experience, the central thought, archi-writing, at which Derrida aims would be impossible (Derrida having already explicitly stipulated that "this theme could not have a place in Hjelmslev's system"), and Derrida will even go so far here—in light of this association of archi-writing with Husserl's own transcendental experience, the dependence of one on the other—to speak of his own text, which brings forth this dependence, as an "ultra-transcendental text," employing the same term he used in *Speech*'s introduction, again to indicate that same singular bridging and overflowing of notions pertaining to language and writing, on the one hand, and Husserl's transcendental perspective on the other, that he brought forward there.

The core of Derrida's concerns in this section of *Of Grammatology*, indeed in its entire first part, thus emerges here. All of Derrida's analyses in these pages focus on the notions of archi-trace, archi-writing (and related ones), and all involve transcendental experience, as well as language-related themes. Derrida's signature terms in *Of Grammatology*, then, all prove to be ultra-transcendental in the sense Derrida has just brought forward. Uniquely combining considerations only discoverable within a transcendental-phenomenological standpoint with topics pertaining to language, linguistics and signs (e.g., archi-*writing*), they designate what concerns not just language, or even speech, but the *givenness* of these, their appearing or constitution within some sort of modified transcendental perspective, and they all take shape within a context, as we have just witnessed, that asks about the sign simultaneously within the system of language and the speech act, as the sign-*function* (the *movement* of the sign in use) and as found in the repository of language at once.

Having just revisited the same portion of *Of Grammatology* that already proved crucial in my chapter 1, the full scope of the problems that I began to lay out there can now be seen. Derrida's own perspective, it should now be evident, clashes with that of Saussure, of Hjelmslev, of all possible linguistics, and does so in particular on two key points. Derrida depends on the notion of experience, of a nonregional transcendental experience, which no linguistics could avow, and in line with this, he approaches the issue of the sign along with that of movement of the sign-function (pertaining finally to signs in use)—both of these gestures by his own avowal being deeply at odds with the concerns of Hjelmslev as well as Saussure. Grammatology, the interrogation "of grammatology," thus in the end represents the deconstruction of all linguistics as a working field, the dismantling of its terms and reference points; these are swept away just as they were in Husserl, and again, it should be no surprise, accordingly, that Derrida's commentators have so often failed to follow him in these outcomes, given how far removed from Saussure's perspective (and that of linguistics generally) are the concerns that occupy him here.

Granting once and for all, then, that Derrida's own aims will never emerge directly from Saussure's, Hjelmslev's, or those of any linguistics— that his model of language and his appeal to experience, themselves intertwined, can never be made to fully dovetail with Saussure's own—what Derrida himself aims to accomplish, and where all this stands in respect to Heidegger as well as Husserl, must now be investigated. Having seen the deep gulf that exists between Derrida's intentions and those of any linguistics in *Of Grammatology*—the passage through the inside of Saussure's text failing to yield solid ground for that transcendental standpoint so crucial to Derrida's own project—the work this passage is nevertheless meant to do in a Derridean context, the thought at which he himself aims, may now start to come forward.

After all, the passage through Saussure's *Course,* through a regional structural linguistics, despite all these caveats, does retain a specific importance for Derrida's own enterprise. The stage on which Derrida's own intentions now unfold will no longer be limited to the history and undertaking of philosophy; instead, it will henceforth also include (in some fashion, in a way yet to be fully specified, for now nominally) a set of supposedly empirical investigations or reference points, thanks to his deployment of linguistics, his detour through it. In *Of Grammatology,* that is, the reference to Saussure and empirical language permits Derrida's own project to take new, more radical positions and to proceed in a vicinity closer to Heidegger's, under some of his rubrics, even while continuing to differ with him in certain key respects—and this new stance of Derrida's, specific to *Of Grammatology*, must now be investigated, at first still within the closing arguments of the second section of *Of Grammatology*'s second chapter.

* * *

Let me begin to restore the context, then, of where I first picked up the thread of Derrida's discussion, for this will eventually let the broadest horizons of Derrida's own ambitions come into view. Derrida had been setting forth a two-pronged argument where I earlier cited him, one prong of which has already been effectively discussed. Having posed the questions: "How does that necessity [the "necessity" which Derrida has just "admitted of going through the concept of the archi-trace"] direct us from the interior of the linguistic system? How does the path that leads from Hjelmslev to Saussure forbid us to avoid the originary trace?" Derrida in response (having conceded that his own concerns originally stem from a source other than linguistics) presents the dual set of themes that will concern him in what follows, including most of the final section of chapter 2 of *Of Grammatology*. To the question of where in linguistics the need for the notion of an "originary trace" makes itself felt, Derrida replies: "In that its passage through *form* is a passage through the *imprint*," adding: "And the meaning of *différance* in general, would be more accessible to us if the unity of that double passage appeared more clearly" (*G* 62).

Derrida here furnishes two sets of concerns, two themes— *"form"* and the *"imprint"*—which, though related, he begins by treating separately. The second one, the "imprint"—the impression made or taken by the aural or graphic signifier—has primarily been under discussion up until now, being Derrida's focus in the passage that I first examined. The imprint, the "being imprinted of the imprint," as we have seen, requires the radical differentiation of the signifier—in this case at first, the "sound-appearing"—from both its (psychic) appearance and the reality of sound itself, and Derrida's analysis consequently entails having continuing recourse to Husserl's standpoint in the way I have already set out. The constitution of the signifiers of language in use, language taken as both a text and a system of traces (thus in their transcendental-phenomenological givenness), turns out to be the object of Derrida's concerns—and apart from Husserl's unique constitutive perspective, neither the phonic nor the graphic would be able to come forward and be rigorously thought as signifying media, in Derrida's eyes.

In turn, while granting all this, and admitting Derrida's unexpectedly profound reliance on Husserl, in taking up the prong that has yet to be addressed, it must also be recognized that none of this cancels the fact that Derrida in these pages is also interested in displacing Husserl's standpoint, nor does it cancel Derrida's intention to address a problem inherent in some way to both phenomenology and structural linguistics in setting out these singular analyses. Derrida does mean to displace Husserl's own perspective (a movement that indeed brings him within the vicinity of Heidegger, closer to Heidegger here in *Of Grammatology* than we have encountered Derrida so far), and this issue of *form,* the second of these two prongs, best introduces us to this phase of Derrida's ambitions.

To grasp the displacement Derrida enacts through the notion of form, a problem pertaining to both Husserl's approach and structural linguistics must first be brought forward, however. Indeed, despite all the differences between them, a problem common, or at least contiguous, to both phenomenology and linguistics arguably exists, though the solution to this problem could never be shared by them, or even be found in either one alone, given all that ultimately divides these approaches. A problem exists, that is, inherent in each, which Derrida, by going beyond them both—by fashioning his "ultra-transcendental text," taking up this ultra-transcendental perspective—can be seen to address, with his second prong in particular (though his solution is one neither linguistics nor phenomenology could acknowledge as such). This problem is most readily identified as that of the word in the case of phenomenology, or that of the actual entity comprising the units of language for linguistics—put otherwise, the ultimate unit of signification. The question of what comprises the actual building blocks of a language gives difficulties to both approaches, though of course their treatments focused on the word and on the sign, respectively, are in many ways opposed.

Let us start from the Husserlian context, where this problem overall is in certain respects easier to grasp. As Dorion Cairns's work began to let us see in my last chapter, for Husserl (and Cairns) words are the primary entities, the fundamental units, of language. These make up the preexistent stock of conventional linguistic signs in a phenomenological context, and they finally have the status of what Cairns called "individual idealities." As found in German or English, let us say, the words *Löwe* and "lion" (which somehow seem to be the standard examples) are themselves ideal, not real, sorts of beings, and in this they resemble a "law" of logic *(modus tolens),* or an essence, such as "straightness." In contrast to the last two cases, however, words are not universals; they are not in principle accessible to all. Words are thus ideal *individuals*—idealities, nevertheless in some way having a *history* of their own, as well as related to history, more broadly speaking. And Cairns, accordingly, ends his piece by raising the problem of how these individuals are ultimately to be conceived when viewed over time: how can a word in a given language be understood as the same word even as its pronunciation or orthography changes, and to what sorts of constitutive achievements, presumably transcendental-historical ones, does this possibility answer (Cairns 1941, 460)?[20]

A similar problem, at least to the extent that it also concerns the ultimate units of language, has long haunted structural linguistics, although here it appears entirely within a *synchronic* perspective. Saussure clearly takes language to be composed of signs—defined as the unity of signifier and signified—yet it remains an open question (and one that was much discussed as the *Course* came to be more widely disseminated) whether and how this unit, the sign, may in truth be identified, especially once all the more usual, merely conventional descriptions of language are left behind. Taken from a purely synchronic point of view, without the aid of dictionaries, and indeed without the outline provided by the notion of the word, in an analysis beginning from the linguistic resources presumed to be at the disposal of any given set of speakers at any given moment, the question arises of how the real units of language can actually be identified, what in truth they may turn out to be—which parts of sentences or utterances genuinely are the discrete *signs* that linguistics studies and language supplies.[21]

This issue goes beyond the one that we have just found Derrida addressing, it should be noted: namely, the status of the *signifier,* in what sort of medium the signifier (and hence the sign) may *appear* and be *given* as the same. The question looms, beyond this, of what in truth are the unities of signified and signifier taken together, their ultimate ontological status and identity—an especially urgent question for Saussure's type of linguistics, since the *combination* of signifier and signified, the total sign alone, is for it the only really positive fact of language, the signifiers as well as the signifieds, as systems of differences, ultimately being rooted in this synthesis or combination. But this raises such questions, then, as what in truth is the smallest significant unit here? Is the pluralizing "s" in English itself a sign, for example, or only part of one; and is an "s" found in the middle of the word, then, only a homonym of it, or no? More broadly, how are such units to be recognized within the stream of spoken discourse, which, according to Saussure, presents itself as continuous in a way that the written does not; and finally, do these least linguistic units, whatever they may be, have any relation at all to what we call the word?

Problems with the ultimate unities belonging to language—in the one case, the historical unity of the word prior to its use in speech; in the other, the systematic identity of the sign as posited in the current repository of language—are genuine difficulties for both approaches, even though the form this problem takes differs strikingly in each case. Accordingly, Derrida, in setting out his "double passage" above, and in particular isolating this issue of form, may be seen as offering, broadly speaking, a response to this set of difficulties taken as a whole—first and foremost as these issues arise in structural linguistics, but also, as we shall see, with implications for this issue in Husserl. Furthermore, Derrida will be able to address both in some fashion, insofar as his response pertains primarily to the *historical* presuppositions of the one and the *synchronic* presuppositions of the other.[22]

To further cash out the issue of *form,* then—the other prong yet to be reviewed, in which Derrida's rejoinder to these difficulties starts to become plain—Derrida, taking *form* up in tandem with the *imprint* here, first addresses it in respect to the formal identity of the *signifier* as such, with an eye to the "reduction of phonic substance" to a single set of repeatedly identifiable traits, which would be discoverable within the sign at work in both speech and language. Derrida goes on to make clear, however, that the work of the "pure trace," or "archi-trace," which he takes to be responsible for this form, goes beyond this. This pure trace and its work, Derrida stipulates, drawing on that ultra-transcendental perspective from which his discussion has already been shown to proceed, "is not . . . a constituted difference, but . . . the pure movement which produces difference"; and "by rights," he continues, it is "anterior to all that one calls sign (signified/signifier, content/expression, etc.)," thus "permit[ting] the articulation of signs among themselves within the same abstract order—a phonic or graphic text, for example—or between two orders of expression" (*G* 62).

Ultimately in question, then, in this notion of the archi-trace is the possibility of the discrete "articulation of signs among themselves," what lets a chain of signs form "a phonic or graphic text." What Derrida calls archi-trace or archi-writing thus makes possible—again, at once within speech and language—the singular identity, the "forms" of the signs themselves within, and across, the different orders of expression; it is a work or movement of pure difference within these individual chains, these discrete texts, allowing them to take shape among themselves as texts, as well as on the interior of language across its different signifying media. Operating at the heart of both speech and language (this modified transcendental perspective also remaining in place), the archi-trace, this constituting movement of difference, consequently is responsible for linguistic form generally—for "the formation of form," as Derrida puts it—for the identity of the *sign* as such, and for all forms of it discoverable in language, spoken as well as written. Derrida thus ends up by declaring that it "permits the articulation of speech and writing in the colloquial sense" and that "language" itself must already be "in that sense [of the archi-trace] a writing," in order that any of these "derived notations" be possible.

This identification of the work of the archi-trace with the forms comprising language as such lets further light be shed on Derrida's ultimate intentions here. Derrida summarizes this phase of his discussion, this prong, by declaring: "*Différance* is therefore the formation of form" (*G* 63), and *différance,* which had indeed been introduced in the passage cited above (for the first time within Derrida's actual discussion of Saussure's text), emerges here within an attempt to account for the identities comprising language: as a movement of pure differentiation, the *work* of a trace both "original" and "pure," engaged in a "constitutive" labor which also makes possible the forms found within discourse. *Différance* itself, moreover, thus stands close to that (ultra-) transcendental *life* encountered in *Speech.* A kind of work, or movement, an "economic" concept, as we have already seen Derrida state, *différance* incorporates the activity or movement of something like a transcendental subjectivity, a labor of constitution, yet now at the heart of language, giving shape to all the entities of which it is ultimately composed.

Derrida here responds to the perplexity at the root of linguistics, then, by ultimately appealing to *différance* and its work. To grasp in full, however, what sort of answer this is, what Derrida comprehensively intends at this moment, as well as to see in what way this response relates to Husserl, it is necessary to review the preparation Derrida had done leading up to this key point in his discussion—in particular, at the beginning of the present section of chapter 2, whose end we have just been examining. Derrida's answer, after all, while clearly aimed at a conundrum at the heart of linguistics, is not primarily directed at this science as such, nor wholly coincident with its own discourse. Derrida here again concedes, in fact, that the focus of his attention could never emerge within the "positive sciences of signification," which "may only describe the *work* and *fact* of *différance*," not this operation itself (*G* 63; his emphasis). By contrast, Derrida's own emphasis falls on the operation of *différance,* the *constitutive movement* of the pure trace, and his discourse thus sheds light above all on the kind of *being* that accrues to language, the sign, and these forms: the ontological status of all that relates to language—without which the ultimate disposition of these forms within linguistics may not be thought, at least not in Derrida's eyes (though, again, not itself being a concern linguistics on its own can broach). The question to which Derrida provides an answer, first and foremost, is what type of entity is Saussure's sign, what sort of thing is this total fusion of signifier and signified, his "thought-sound." Derrida's focus is on the unique *Seinsmodus,* the "mode of Being" (to use a Husserlian term), or the *Seinsinn* (the sense of being) of the

"beings" found in speech and language (the media of inscription and vocalization, the signifying and signified face combined in the formal unity
of the sign), which may well be without parallel in many respects and, indeed, finally exhibit a mode of existence unlike any other. In light of this
problem, Derrida introduces this differential, constituting operation he
dubs "*différance,*" and this ontological aspect of his argument, its most profound dimension, must be plumbed more deeply if what Derrida lays out
at this moment is to be fully grasped.

To bring out further this side of Derrida's discussion, it is necessary
to briefly turn back to the beginning of this section, to the beginning of
this development, a detour which will eventually lead us forward to Derrida's third section ("The Hinge," the concluding section of chapter 2 of
Of Grammatology, the chapter specifically devoted to the *Course*). Prior to
the outset of section 2, in section 1, which I will otherwise not treat, Derrida had initially focused on Saussure's *exclusion* of writing, and thanks to
this, as I indicated, Derrida raised the questions of both the status of
speech acts (vocalized and inscribed) and the system of signs within language, at first within Saussure's own linguistics.

In turn, at the outset of section 2, having simultaneously situated
himself at the origin of both issues, of the difference between voice and
writing within speech acts and within language (and to this degree, as
well, already implicitly situating himself within Husserl's transcendental
perspective), Derrida provisionally raises the problem of writing in respect to a moment of repetition potentially inherent in both moments—
a kind of *becoming or repetition,* integral to the work of discourse, as well as
the systematicity of language, which Derrida will ultimately claim is responsible for the unities to be found in them both, and which ultimately
promises to displace Husserl's transcendental perspective, along with radically resituating Saussure's own project in the ways that I have begun to
describe.[23]

Turning back to this layer of Derrida's text, as we shall soon see, a
tension latent in Derrida's own presentation will also come forward. The
issue is a nice one, insofar as what Derrida starts to lay out here indeed
comes to fruition in the passages that I have just examined; yet Derrida's
starting point in Saussure, though necessary to understanding this and all
that follows, can and has obscured the full scope of Derrida's intentions.
This tension can only be brought forward gradually, however, and it suf-
fices at the moment to see that Derrida starts to derive these operations
(in particular that of the trace, which Derrida's discussion of the "formation of form" finally fleshes out) for the first time at the outset of section
2 from Saussure's own well-known claims concerning the "arbitrariness of
the sign."[24]

Derrida picks up on this claim of Saussure's concerning the sign's arbitrariness to introduce this notion of writing ("when he is not expressly dealing with writing . . . Saussure opens the field of a general grammatology" [G 43]), and it indeed leads Derrida almost immediately here to speak of the "instituted trace" (G 46). This talk of the trace will prove especially critical here since, among other things, the force of Derrida's displacement of Husserl finally makes itself felt with this notion, and the opening for this conception, specifically in regard to this aspect of "*institution*," stems, as Derrida initially points out, directly from the sign's *arbitrariness* ("the very idea of institution—hence of the arbitrariness of the sign," as Derrida puts it in passing [G 44]).

Saussure's work (opening the field of a general grammatology, when it is least aware of it) thus lets Derrida at the outset of section 2 introduce the trace on account of this notion of the sign's arbitrariness. In part for this reason, however, what is difficult to grasp at the moment that the trace first comes forward (the reference to Peirce not ultimately helping either, at least not in this respect) is that what interests Derrida even now in speaking of the trace's "institution" (along with what he calls the "becoming sign of the symbol," "the immotivation of the sign," which all designate the same moment and finally lead him to speak of the "immotivated trace" [G 51]) is itself a *movement,* one that in fact already occurs *within* acts of speech, within language (within both inscriptions and vocalizations, along with the linguistic signs that appear in them).

The problem specifically arises that in speaking of the instituted trace, the border between nature and culture, between language and its other, is to be included—the instituted trace initially being unthinkable without this difference and having important implications for it (which is largely why I have turned to this moment of Derrida's discussion here). "Let us . . . persist in using this opposition of nature and institution, of *physis* and *nomos*" (G 44), Derrida has stipulated, starting to lay out his thought of the trace. Nevertheless, though the trace's movement entails the difference between nature and culture, the border between them, Derrida also insists that its actual operation—its institution, its becoming unmotivated, which ultimately lets the sign go to work as a sign—takes place, and does so repeatedly, *within* a world and meaning already under way, and even in some sense within a language already given (as well as within something like Husserl's transcendental attitude, in the ways that we have already discussed). In question here, finally, is the very same issue that we have just seen Derrida treat: the formation of form, the emergence of those entities of which language is composed with the singular sorts of formal identities belonging to them; and while the shaping of these entities comprising language, responsible for their unique ontological and transcendental status, crucially comprehends a moment of a passage from the natural to the cultural, from the symbol to the sign, across the border between nature and culture that it appears to secure, it turns out itself to be an originary movement, a radical condition, occurring within a world (a conventionalized nature) already there, a work going on in its midst, and thus never takes place for a first time, nor simply once and for all.

Derrida himself ultimately emphasizes this, though due to his starting point in a science of language somehow already given and a supposedly recognizable system of signs, the force of this outcome is easy to miss. Nevertheless, at the conclusion of this phase of his discussion (upon which follows his treatment of Hjelmslev and archi-writing, here already reviewed), "the immotivation of the trace," Derrida now tells us, is "an operation," "not a state," "an active movement," "not . . . [a] given structure" (*G* 51). The trace, the instituted trace, characteristic of both speech and language, permitting signs to go to work as signs, thus proves to be the origin of this system (eventually including, in Derrida's eyes, even the signifieds and the things themselves); yet it is not itself a structure, not something there in its own right, but always a kind of *work within what it constitutes.* The trace thus everywhere *assumes* what one might call the "vertical" functioning of all these *already constituted systems*—of signifiers, language, meaning, thought, things, world, and finally even transcendental subjectivity—even as its own movement is ultimately the operation *generative of them all,* and thus itself represents an instance of what Derrida elsewhere calls an *inscribed origin.* Its work is indeed that of a genesis *of* structure *within* structure: a movement, a genesis—in fact, always referring back to a prior instance of its own occurrence, and consequently, according to Derrida, a sequencing, an *enchainement,* which always exists in a condition of following upon an earlier occurrence of itself, coming after an earlier result of its own work, yet which, in so doing, follows on nothing at all, never itself takes place (having already given way to what it gives rise to as it is in the process of taking itself up again). This is why Derrida speaks here of a *trace,* "of the *movement* of the *trace,*" which "produces itself *as self-occultation,*" and not an entity of any sort (*G* 47; my emphasis).[25]

The ultimate status of these signs themselves, these forms as such, we can now see more clearly, lies beyond any linguistic science; it is rooted in the work of the trace—the trace whose own mode of Being, whose own way of appearing, according to Derrida, must be thought in the form of *self-occultation.* This work of *différance* and this movement of the trace never take place once and for all; these unique formal identities appropriate to language always point back to the workings of inscribed origins without which they could never appear, yet which they themselves must finally call on again and again, even as these origins themselves never cease to remain occluded, or self-occluding, in distinctive ways. And here, then, at these earlier phases of Derrida's discussion, with his talk of the instituted trace, by dint of which he sets forth language and its signs as standing at the crossing between nature and culture, we find that this crossing is an event—indeed, not even an event, but a singular kind of repetition, one that never happens once and for all; and that only on this condition may the singular *ontological* status of language and the work that makes it possible, the kind of being accruing to these forms, and the formation forming them, be thought.

This is also why—to return to the point my discussion had reached earlier, and jump a step ahead—it seems to me that Derrida's formulations concerning the trace in section 3 of chapter 2, his final section on Saussure, following the passage previously examined, should be taken as his genuinely definitive ones. These earlier formulations, though suggestive, even necessary, do tend to conceal the full scope of this problematic, making it appear as if this difference, this instituted character of language, is something that happens only once—or at the very least is something visibly born as a property, as a readily perceivable mark (the mark of the mark itself) within the ongoing work of what we already believe to be language and signs. By contrast, more telling as to Derrida's own aims as well as his displacement of Husserl (and with that, where Derrida finally stands toward *Heidegger* as well) are Derrida's remarks in section 3, which directly stem from his work at the end of section 2. This discussion gives a clearer view of the singular, ontological functioning of what Derrida calls the trace, indeed of all his signature terms—how they themselves do, or do not, "appear" in the world, along with the unique type of (linguistic or signitive) being whose appearance they allow.

* * *

Section 3 of chapter 2 is entitled "The Hinge" ("La brisure"). In it, Derrida expands on the work at the end of his last section—his treatment of form and imprint already discussed—in order to bring forward what ends up as the most comprehensive version of his own standpoint to be found in the first half of *Of Grammatology,* a viewpoint which also proves to embody a greater radicality than any so far seen here, thus letting me establish Derrida's ultimate relation at this moment to both Husserl and Heidegger. Derrida starts section 3, it should be noted, by drawing on both aspects of the account he has just given, both form and the imprint, though the problem of form alone will occupy us at first (picking up where our discussion at the end of two left off), in order to sketch some of the radical implications this entails specifically for Derrida's relation to Husserl. The latter factor, the imprint, will be taken up later, and at that moment, the ultimate relation of Derrida's stance here, his thought of the trace, to Heidegger will be set out.

Derrida starts his third section of chapter 2 by returning again to this notion of the trace and offering a somewhat different, or at least more definitive, view of what "authorizes" him to employ such language. His talk of the trace, Derrida now stipulates, refers not so much to that *enchainement,* that reference to a previous instance of itself, upon which his stress had earlier fallen, but to the notion of an "absolute past," a prior instance with no mode of being other than simply being prior—and this determination of the trace by way of a linkage to an absolute past is finally the most telling overall, in my view, in respect to Derrida's own intentions in the first half of *Of Grammatology* (*G* 66/*DG* 97).[26]

More specifically, Derrida focuses on a certain "passivity" at work in speech, a passivity which stems from a relation to an absolute past. "Speech is originally passive," he writes, "but in a sense of passivity that all intramundane metaphor would only betray." "This passivity," he continues, "is thus the relation to a past, to an always already there, that no reactivation of the origin would know how to fully master and to reveal to presence." A passivity at work in speech (and language, that all intramundane metaphor would betray) refers us back to an absolute past, to a past that in principle can never be fully present. "This impossibility of reanimating absolutely the evidence of an originary present," Derrida continues, "returns us to an absolute past . . . which *authorizes us to call trace* all that does not let itself be resumed in the simplicity of a present" (*DG* 97/*G* 66; my emphasis).

This account of the trace starts to bring more clearly into view the status of the trace itself, even the instituted trace—the difference between nature and culture in the end being joined on the basis of something "older" than them both, this absolute past—and also sets out more clearly the relation of the trace to speech and language generally. Derrida's most complete thought of the trace, and with that the ontology at the root of language and its operation, starts to come forward here: one whose reference points turn out to be an *absolute past* on the one hand (what can never be resumed in the simplicity of a present), and a *radical passivity* relating to language and speech on the other. Indeed, it is worth noting, before proceeding further, that "*speech,*" the work of signs within discourse, in particular is said to establish this passivity now located at the heart of the trace. Speech provides the entry point for Derrida's discussion at the start of this final section, and this will remain the case throughout the stretch of text that interests me. "It is, then, in a certain 'unheard' sense that speech is in the world," Derrida will announce a few pages later, resuming this topic that he breaks off here (*G* 67/*DG* 98).

At the beginning of section 3, then (as was the case at the end of section 2 from whose analysis I first set out), Derrida's viewpoint clearly takes in both speech and language at once, signs at work in speech (something also implied, by the way, by Derrida's now treating the questions of the imprint and of form as one). The singular ontological forms that make signs available in use (speech) and language taken together are now seen to be owed to an absolute past, the functioning of a trace, without which their unique formal identities could never stabilize even in passing. So, too, Derrida has already emphasized that this "passivity" pertaining to speech and language, and intrinsic to the trace and its work, is one that no "intramundane metaphor" can identify or portray, and Derrida's continuing proximity to Husserl and to Husserl's transcendental attitude is thus clearly at work here—since barring this, the inadequacy of the intramundane could never be established, or even arise as a question.

Nevertheless, at the same time—and this is what I wish to stress above all, Derrida's final, most definite version of the trace and its work having started to come into view—even while continuing to rely in some fashion on Husserl's perspective (in line with that singular "logic" of departure which we have already mapped), Derrida at this juncture most strikingly also puts considerable distance between himself and Husserl, thanks to these issues relating to language and its singular ontology. Derrida takes a stance toward Husserl of a radicality not seen here before, in setting out the work of the trace—first of all, with reference to themes stemming from Husserl's last writings—and seeing how this is so, both the trace's status as Derrida envisions it at this moment, along with what it entails for his relation to Husserl, can be further brought forward.

Here, indeed, the importance of the problem raised earlier concerning the dispensation of the word in Husserl's late thought makes itself felt. The trace now lies at the basis of those forms comprising language (the work of the trace standing behind the signs or words, the forms of language as these appear within speech), and this novel construal of the operation of language and discourse, in the first instance, poses a challenge, presents a departure, in particular in respect to Husserl's late transcendental-historical program. Derrida at the start of section 3, in setting out this work of the trace, indeed revisits those issues that we saw emerge in the "Introduction," but now arrives at a very different set of results.

The possibility of a *"reactivation of the origin,"* as well as of *"reanimating the evidence of an originary presence"* (*DG* 97 / *G* 66; my emphasis), in respect to the operation at work in signs in speech, and in the forms of language, has just been raised. And Derrida has *denied* that such reactivation and reanimation are finally fully possible on account of the trace and its work, due to this radical passivity implied in speech and language: in particular, thanks to the relation of these forms to an absolute past. The trace, it here becomes clear, in addition to everything else, is meant to contest those assumptions in regard to the ideality of the word, as well as the recovery of (transcendental) history generally, that Husserl's late project entails. Such "idealities" of language even now understood in a manner not so different from Husserl's own (still subject to their activation in speech, and only appearing in their own right within it) nevertheless are here found to be never fully subject to that recovery in present evidence, never finally open to total reanimation, to the extent that they entail the trace's operation. The full retrieval of the "words," the "thought-sounds," composing even a "pure, transcendental language," thus becomes impossible at the moment the trace's work comes forward—bringing the force of an absolute past to bear—and with these considerations, Derrida indeed finally definitively departs from that construal of language, speech, and writing with which he first engaged in the "Introduction," as well as from that entire transcendental history of truth which depends on this construal, at least to this extent.[27]

If the trace as Derrida thinks it here breaks with the work of any transcendental history, the implications of this work go even further for Husserl's own thought, as Derrida himself next brings forward, graphing the *temporal schema* implied by the work of the trace in both speech and language. The framework of the living present *(lebendige Gegenwart),* though riven by protention and retention and even perhaps complicated dialectically, Derrida now states, remains the product of a "metaphysical," linearist, and ultimately "vulgar" construal of time. Renouncing what appears to be his own earlier position ("it is not a matter of complicating the structure of time while conserving its homogeneity, and its fundamental successivity, by demonstrating for example that the past present and future constitute originarily, by dividing it, the form of the living present" [*G* 67/*DG* 97–98]), Derrida insists that the trace, contesting all ultimate reactivation and reanimation, has more drastic implications for the work of (constituting) time than even a "dialectical" model would allow.

Derrida, accordingly, next maps a temporality demanded by the thought of the trace, as at work in the constitution of linguistic form, *which will never be able to be mapped on Husserl's own.* The temporality of the trace instead parallels the workings of "Freud's *Nachtraglichkeit.*" Its reference to an "absolute past " demands that an essentially foreign term, an "X," be thought to have taken hold, Derrida asserts, between what are otherwise apparently *continuous, successive* nows: stipulated as "now-s" "A," "B," and "C," themselves successive moments of past, present, and future. Though nowhere present within the line of time itself, never having appeared among these protentions and retentions in its own right, a "moment" of "time," an "X," must nevertheless be thought to have already been at work within temporalization (among the nevertheless continuous sequence of now's A, B, and C), according to Derrida. This "X" makes itself known only as "always already there," as always already past, as always already come and gone, through *an essentially delayed contribution* to what is present: investing the becoming-present specific to the forms of language, making possible their unique mode of being, their singular ontological character.

An "absolute past," a "dead time," as Derrida will also later call it—a radical nonpresence finally of *spatiality* as well as temporality, Derrida will go on to make plain—is required by this work of language, by its dependence on the trace, implied by this archi-constitution of its forms, and this total thought represents a greater departure from Husserl on the part of Derrida than any we have so far witnessed. The introduction of these novel linguistic concerns, no matter how volatilized or transformed, no matter how removed from linguistics as such, nevertheless lets Derrida operate a subtle displacement of the very center of gravity of Husserl's project. Derrida now calls into question even Husserl's absolute temporality—the core of his transcendental standpoint, as well as that model of constituting time upon which Husserl's late history also deeply depended, and he does so in a way that seems to me to go beyond, to be more radical, than any of Derrida's other treatments of these matters, of this theme of temporality, including that in chapter 5 of *Speech*. A trace, bringing with it an absolute past, and breaking with the very model underlying Husserl's own depiction of temporality, must now be affirmed to be at work even in transcendental discourse and language themselves.

Even now, however, it must still be stressed that the trace "itself," like all of Derrida's other key terms, is not thinkable wholly without reference to Husserl's transcendental perspective. The trace as Derrida presents it throughout this chapter continues to designate *an inscribed origin,* functioning in the midst of what it constitutes—and only Husserl's transcendental, bringing forward a foundation itself already functioning in medias res (as reviewed in my chapter 4) can make conceivable in the first place how an origin of this type, this apparently nonoriginary style of origin, might be envisioned, no less taken as authoritative.

Nevertheless, thanks to the introduction of these themes pertaining to language, thanks to the thought of the trace and an absolute past which they necessitate, Derrida introduces schemas (arguably still ultra- or quasi-transcendental) that are importantly different from Husserl's at the heart of constituting temporality, as well as different from Husserl's versions of history and language. And having seen that Derrida has thus moved away from Husserl's standpoint in some more definitive fashion than we have so far witnessed, to make clear the full extent of this departure, which will also eventually let us see Derrida's relation to *Heidegger's* work, I now want to take up a second, even broader set of considerations at work at the outset of section 3.

Not only language and its forms are at issue here, after all, but also speech, *parole*. Derrida's discussion is finally aimed at the question of speech, and what I have so far treated is in fact a long parenthesis opened by Derrida within a broader examination devoted to this theme. Shifting focus, then, to this thematic, the one most concretely occupying Derrida himself, the question pertaining to the being-imprinted of the *signifier* that I began by discussing will also return here. In fact, both speech (logos) and the medium of the signifier (the *phone,* as well as the *graphe*) are in question here, along with language *(die Sprache)* and its forms, and this will eventually let Derrida's relation to Heidegger come into view.

Before turning to Heidegger, however, where Derrida finally stands in respect to Husserl vis-à-vis speech itself in this one last instance must be made clearer. Taking up this thematic of speech, of *parole,* linking it to the trace and a radical passivity, Derrida, here at the outset of section 3, is still concerned, perhaps unexpectedly, with those issues relating to the voice, even the phenomenological voice, that we already encountered in *Speech.* Derrida has already stated that no "intramundane metaphor" can capture the passivity that relates to speech, and after his treatment of the trace's temporal diagram, resuming this aspect of his discussion, Derrida announces it is "in a certain unheard sense that speech [*parole*] is in the world" ("rooted in that passivity which metaphysics calls sensibility in general," he continues [*G* 67]). With his insistence on an "unheard" sense of speech, standing apart from all "intramundane metaphor," Derrida clearly intends to differentiate the *medium* of speech, the *signifying* medium of discourse (of the voice and also eventually the grapheme)—this "sensibility" bearing reference to a radical "passivity"—from any finite worldly sensory field, any real human sense or sensibility (sound/hearing, seeing/light, etc.), bringing us back to Derrida's own focus on the phenomenological voice in *Speech.* Derrida here is still drawing directly on those considerations I began this part of my chapter by discussing—concerning the difference of the sound-appearing from the appearance of the sound, as well as the necessity to invoke the framework of hyle/morphe, considerations which he ended up summarizing under the heading of the "being imprinted of the imprint" (*G* 63)—and he has kicked off this phase of his discussion by declaring: "that the imprint is *irreducible* means that speech is originally passive in a sense of passivity that all intramundane metaphor would only betray" (*G* 66; my emphasis).

A form of *sensibility* is thus in question here: a voice, a signifying medium at work in discourse, which is still never simply to be found in the world, never to be heard apart from Husserl's transcendental perspective. Derrida, in fact, goes on to invoke a remark of Maine de Birain, who spoke of "speech," *la parole voyelle* (the "vocalic word"), as "wish sensibilized." The voice, this signifying medium, is thus a matter not of any real sound or any real psychic image, nor any actual empirical language, but a matter, first and foremost, as Derrida says, of will, *vouloir*—wish-, will-, sensibilized—a remark which directly hearkens back to the role played by *Geist* in *Speech*, and to Derrida's translation of *bedeuten* as *vouloir*-dire (*wanting*-to-say). At the same time, however, though invoking these same reference points, Derrida goes further here than we have seen him go before in distancing himself from Husserl in respect to these issues, in line with all that I have so far brought forward. He separates himself by certain decisive nuances from any position in respect to speech, voice, and signification interior to Husserl's thought, and this may be seen especially in what Derrida goes on to assert after having laid out this unique status of this voice. In a statement which virtually summarizes his entire standpoint in this portion of *Of Grammatology*, Derrida declares, on the basis of the concerns that we have just seen him bring forward, that "the *logos* itself" (and thus speech or *parole* as Husserl understands it) "would be imprinted," and that "this imprint would be the scriptural resource of language" (*DG* 99/ *G* 68).

Derrida's claim at this moment clearly invokes what I have repeatedly brought forward: namely, that the units of language, its sounds or words, its signs and signifiers, are in question only insofar as they appear in speech, and insofar as Derrida employs the perspectives of language and speech simultaneously, both of which have been implicitly submitted to Husserl's transcendental perspective. The logos, Derrida further insists here—discourse even within Husserl's transcendental stipulations—would itself be a "writing," the "scriptural resource" of language. The forms of language, all its identities—signs, signifiers, and signified—would consequently be traceable back to a *parole*, this work of speech and the logos, upon which Derrida still claims they depend for their own identity and possibility. At the same time, however, such a dependence on *parole*, on the logos, by language in its totality will only be affirmed here (and with this returns the role of the trace) insofar as the logos itself is already being thought not as speech, not as voice—but thanks to the trace and its work (in respect now to its contribution not only to the form but also to the *"imprint"*)—as a primary, an ur-, or archi-, writing. The logos as such—still largely in the sense Husserl intends it, with a vector toward the phenomenological voice—in the first instance would be an imprint, due to the radical passivity entailed by the trace and a relation to an absolute past, and only on this condition would it be that from which stem the forms of language and signification, itself thus coming to stand as the first imprint, in turn. This is what I understand Derrida to intend by calling the logos, in an odd turn of phrase, the "scriptural resource" of language (compare G. Spivak's translation).

Again, thanks to the added weight of the Saussurean thematics of language (no matter how far deflected), to this work of the trace and an absolute past, Derrida, while remaining even now in closer proximity to Husserl in respect to speech and the voice (the signifying medium generally) than is often believed—indeed, still with reference to something like the phenomenological voice itself—here primarily in respect to speech, rather than language, departs from Husserl's teaching taking the logos itself, with all its originary and transcendental force, as a kind of writing. So, too, this construal of the logos does call into question the distinction between the transcendental and the mundane, as many have noted, though perhaps in a manner not previously fully gleaned. All intramundane metaphors may fail here in the face of the status of the signifying medium as wish-sensibilized; and it continues to be the case that no worldly parallel nor science can ever tell us anything about the voice. Nevertheless, at this moment, the line between the mundane and the transcendental becomes irremediably blurred, thanks to this character of passivity and the pastness of an absolute past, on which account the logos may be viewed as a form of writing, an imprint, an archi-writing, even prior to any considerations pertaining to a constituted language or a regional science. The *parole*, the logos itself, indeed what we have come to recognize as the phenomenological voice, in *Of Grammatology* entail not only difference in self-relation, as in *Speech*, but also now radical passivity—thus that dead time, a radical otherness and absence, definitively breaking with Husserl's models, albeit in favor of something only even now conceivable thanks to them. On account of this dead time, this absolute past, and finally also of the linguistic thematic (even though one no longer recognizable by linguistics itself), the rights of Husserl's (transcendental) subject have indeed been radically uprooted—re-rooted in a zone of functioning deeply foreign to Husserl and his aims.[28]

Last, this departure has implications not only for Derrida's relation to Husserl, but also his relation to Heidegger. Having seen where Derrida ultimately comes out in respect to Husserl, where he stands toward Heidegger, thanks to this, also starts to be clear as well. The logos as such, transcendental-phenomenological ex-pressivity (if I may put it this way, referring back to the discussion of Husserl's circuit of expression in my previous chapter), in some fashion, even now is central to Derrida's text, and Derrida has always seen this as the closest thing within a Husserlian context to Heidegger's talk of Being, of the Being of the beings, as I have previously begun to show. Ultimately responsible for the objectivity of the object, the movement of the logos through this transcendental circuit, entails the transmission or coordination of a certain inside and outside, of a noematic sense delivering the object itself in person over to its preservation in conceptual or theoretical meanings—and later, in Husserl's last works, this logos ultimately takes the form of a passage of absolute truth, an infinite transcendental history, regathering and reweaving itself across a pure tradition.

Husserl's logos for Derrida thus answers to Heidegger's thought of Being; and moreover, since this logos, as we have just seen, stands as the writing-resource of language—the logos, this *legein* (this gathering), thus finding itself in some way also at the heart of language *(die Sprache)*—Derrida's overall outcome here in the end closely parallels Heidegger's own thought. This coordination of the logos, the *legein*—now as imprint or trace-giving language, *die Sprache*—along with its contribution to objectivity parallel to that of Being, indeed sketches a matrix mapping Heidegger's thought in all its pertinent dimensions. And consequently, Derrida, here in *Of Grammatology,* with something like the phenomenological voice now thought as work of the trace, is not only displacing Husserl, thinking the logos as ur-imprinting, but is engaged in a gesture answering to Heidegger's—bringing together something like Being's work with a set of reference points pertaining to language, signification, and meaning.

How closely Derrida parallels Heidegger's thought here in section 3, with this claim about the logos as imprint, and with this notion of the trace more generally, may be grasped even more readily if we pick up a slightly later portion of Derrida's discussion of the trace that further fleshes out what is going on here. Jumping off, as it happens, from the potential relation of the trace to the field of biology, Derrida, in this same section of *Of Grammatology,* drawing on this thematic of passivity and the past, will now invoke "memory" as an "archi-phenomenon." Memory, thanks to the thought of the trace, may be taken as "prior to the opposition of nature and culture, animality and humanity," and as "belong[ing] to the very movement of signification," states Derrida *(DG* 103/*G* 70).

Memory itself is already a central Heideggerean concern, of course, and indeed with very much the profile it has here: memory as itself first, as archi-memory, or archi-phenomenon. Derrida's relation in this chapter to a set of well-known Heideggerean themes becomes clearer still, however, as he continues. Having named as "archi-writing" that work of the imprint or trace that has just come forward here ("archi-writing . . . at first the possibility of the speech, *parole,* then, the *graphe* in a narrow sense"), and having identified this archi-writing with the trace (the logos as archi-writing being identified with memory as an archi-phenomenon of the trace), on this basis, Derrida specifies, "this trace [as archi-writing] is the opening of the first exteriority, the enigmatic relation of a living to its other, of an inside to an outside: spacing." "The outside," Derrida continues, "which we believe we know as the most familiar thing in the world, as familiarity itself, would not appear without the grammé, without *différance* as temporalization, without the nonpresence of the other" (*G*70/*DG*103).

The trace, then, thought at work within the very movement of signification, designating "the enigmatic relation of a living being to its other" (and also recalling, then, *Speech*'s life), thus holds a place, performs a work, clearly parallel to that of Heidegger's Being. According to Derrida here, it stands at the root of the appearance of the outside *as* outside, even as it radically differs from the terms of this appearance. It provides the originary possibility of an articulation of an inside on an outside, here holding sway through the movement and work of signification and language, as well as what we call the world, even as it never appears within these as such.

So, too, further exhibiting this closeness now to Heidegger, in light of this work, Derrida will go on to denounce, eventually under the heading of "onto-theology," a "metaphysics whose entire history was compelled to strive toward the reduction of the trace" (*G*71/*DG*104). "Metaphysics," here being defined as such, would on the rebound seek to close off the trace, either by excluding the provenance of speech and language entirely from thought, objectivity, and Being, or by reducing these to self-present entities. Metaphysics would be defined by this attempt to reduce the trace, and its vocation would be especially clear in that "infinitist metaphysics" of a Spinoza or a Hegel, whose recourse to a positive infinity of some sort is a direct correlate of the trace's absolute past—the invocation of the one (positive infinity) being an attempt to exhaust the resources of the other (the past of the trace), these attempts thus being the most extreme examples of metaphysics' logocentrism (*G*71/*DG*104).

After having set out this irreducible passivity of speech and this invocation of the logos as imprint, and filling out this notion of the trace, Derrida, in bringing forward his own thought, indeed moves along Heideggerean pathways. He sees in the trace a moment much like Heidegger's ontico-ontological difference, and determines metaphysics as an epoch by way of its attempt to exhaust or repress its work (an attempt that is itself the originary possibility of the trace coming forward as trace, coming forward "as such"). At the same time, even as Derrida now patently draws near to Heideggerean themes and considerations, he is also, thanks in part to the Husserlian displacement, still able to subtly displace certain key aspects of Heidegger's own enterprise, thanks to this stress on the logos as such. After all, to recur to the points raised at the outset, not only do the integrity of the word (*Wort* or *Urwort*) and the self-presence of the voice (the *phone*) here come into doubt—shown tied to the work of the trace and a certain radical nonpresence (assuming these were critical issues in Heidegger to begin with)—but insofar as a certain transcendental *parole,* a transcendental ex-pressivity, parallels the work of Being, for Derrida, Being (or its analogue) no longer gathers itself *(legein)* once and for all, and especially not into *die Sprache:* into the historical language of a people or nation, through a destiny or sending, ready to be mined again and again.[29] Just that priority which Husserl gave to discourse in its living intentionality, apart from all actual languages, which here has been traced back to the phenomenological voice, even as now undone by Derrida (seen as rooted in an absolute past and passivity, which thus betoken a being-imprinted of the transcendental logos itself), nevertheless yields a very different schema of the giving of Being, language and its gathering, than any in Heidegger—an arguably more "universal" or, perhaps better, more "formal" schema, centered on the *structures* of signification (sign/ signifier) and the movement of discourse through various levels of sense (including logical ones), rather than any of language's historical dimensions or its inheritance.

Derrida's retention of the Husserlian framework, which I have stressed here all along—his preservation of the outline of Husserl's version of language, speech, meaning, and the object, even as he calls these into doubt in other ways—is, in the end, what permits Derrida in *Of Grammatology* to move away from a seemingly monolithic and empiricist or historicist model of the relations that Heidegger claimed to hold among Being, language, and logos (a model which Derrida will later claim also stands in too-close proximity to the notion of *Geist*). For along with this seeming universalization, formalization, or sublimation of content, Derrida correspondingly finds himself able to maintain (and this is only an apparent paradox) that there will never have been one single sending of Being, one instantiation of *différance* or the trace, certainly not one unique to a given language or peoples (Greeks or German). Indeed, he maintains this again by continuing to give a certain priority to Husserl's models—ultimately combined, straightforwardly or no, with these themes taken from structural linguistics—and does so by paying attention to the givenness of the signifying media (the *phone* and the *graphe*), to language as a system of formal identities ever again fashioned in the work of speech, and by situating the trace and its work (as imprint within transcendental *parole*) as a scriptural resource upon which all language draws. Derrida sets out a problematic with important parallels to Heidegger's in the form of the trace and its work, but here across repeated acts of language, various acts of speech, diverse inscriptions and texts (both oral and graphic)—with no anchor or center, either in any actual history or language—thus already leading Derrida here to a kind of proto-dissemination of Heideg-gerean thought.

Derrida's present discussion of the trace in *Of Grammatology* itself represents an instance of such a displacement, or decentering, or dissem-ination, of Heidegger. The account just commented on, starting from the trace's relation to biology and memory as archi-phenomenon, is but one of many usages of the trace that Derrida brings forward in the concluding pages of section 3. Already anticipating his best-known single short essay, "Différance," in the second half of section 3, Derrida goes about assem-bling an array of names, a sheaf of discourses, a range of sites through which his own core concerns become visible, all able to be seen as substi-tuting for Heidegger's own ur-term of Being, or the ontico-ontological. Not only does Derrida put together such an overlapping nexus of terms, words, signifiers (trace, *différance*, archi-writing, spacing, etc.—all substi-tuting for Heidegger's single one); but in regard to the trace itself (to which notion Derrida seems to give a kind of privilege), perhaps most im-portant, he invokes a sheaf of references drawn from a number of differ-ent discourses and regions of knowledge in order to justify this choice and set forth its work (the trace "makes reference to a number of contempo-raneous discourses," Derrida states—those of Levinas, Nietzsche, Freud, biology, linguistics, cybernetics [*DG* 102/*G* 70]). The thought of the trace is thus itself always in motion, engaged in overlapping systems of traces, and this would not be possible were the trace not encountered preemi-nently, though never once and for all, by way of this route that passes through Husserl, and embodying an initial formalization (and a very dif-ferent model of language and discourse than Heidegger's), even as Der-rida doubtless finally also moves closer to Heidegger's aims—more radi-cally breaking with Husserl's own transcendental perspective, as well as his actual notions of the logos, the *phone*, the signifying medium, and the work of speech and meaning generally.

* * *

This brings me to the last major theme that I want to confront in this work, one which will indeed take me away from *Of Grammatology* itself. Derrida may well have taken up the trace in light of its ability to communicate with a number of current initiatives, and its work thus parallels as well as con-tests that of Heidegger's thought, even as it does not wholly leave Husserl's behind, or depart from it in the manner many may have expected. My original concern with Derrida's relation to Heidegger did not primarily focus, however, on the thematics of language (or even Being and tran-scendentality), but rather on that of history. Where Derrida's displace-ment from Husserl and his drawing nearer to Heidegger stands in relation to history and historicality was to be discovered; and while this proto-dissemination indicates that Derrida has indeed put some distance between himself and Heidegger, Derrida's own relation to history in its positivity has yet to come into view. This is the outstanding piece of business that remains to be discussed.

One possible way to investigate this question, of course, leads through Derrida's discussion of Rousseau in the second half of *Of Grammatology*. Derrida's treatment of Rousseau—whose thought Derrida deems the culmination of the metaphysics of presence in the form of self-presence, and on whose site Derrida undertakes the deconstruction of what he calls "the greatest totality," including the deconstruction of the distinction between nature and culture through the so-called "catastrophe of supplementarity" (*G* 259)—clearly has Derrida's stance toward history and historicity as one of its features. Following out the second half of *Of Grammatology* would take too long, however, and would take me too far away from the authors I have treated so far (if not my actual themes). Moreover, as has been repeatedly noted elsewhere in the literature, Derrida's work on Rousseau, and indeed all of *Of Grammatology*, is marked by a distancing from the term "history"—a sort of withdrawal or disappearance of this concept—which makes it difficult within the confines of *Of Grammatology* itself to satisfactorily articulate where Derrida stands in this regard. Derrida may talk at the outset of *Of Grammatology* of history and epochs; nearly from the first, however, such broad accompanying caveats as Derrida's "history, if there is any history" are to be found—and these marks of reserve or even skepticism only seem to grow as *Of Grammatology* continues.[30]

This difficulty of knowing where Derrida stands toward history in *Of Grammatology* (at the precise moment of deconstruction's advent) has long been taken note of in the literature, and his ultimate relation to these themes remains one of the most vexed issues in Derrida studies even today. These difficulties are further compounded by the fact, already evident here, that as history recedes from Derrida's thought, this clearly occurs not in favor of some supra-historical or eternal transcendent, but in the name of something that somehow purports to be more "history"—more radically historical, more engaged in history—than history itself, even as it no longer travels under this title.[31] Not only why Derrida feels such dissatisfaction with this term, then, but also why he still continues to use it—why, unlike in so many other cases (as that of "origin," "Being," "speech") he continues to have recourse to it, leading to such odd assertions as that history should somehow fail to be history, or that there could be another (non-) history more historical than history to date—what all this means for Derrida's own thought are questions without answers even at present,

and for these reasons it is worthwhile taking another route to these problems, a route that a developmental perspective alone can provide.

After all, one final link in the chain forming Derrida's development
here remains to be explored: namely, how Derrida's relation to *Husserl's*
late history came to be transformed in the wake of the "Introduction."
When this topic was last examined, Derrida, turning away from his prior
position in *Le problème*, had largely realigned himself with Husserl's late
philosophy of history in the "Introduction," even as he had begun to
probe some of its key articulations. Thus, while the transformation, or even
transgression, that Husserl's late standpoint on language and writing undergoes (along with that of Husserl's views on signification, speech, and
the voice more generally) have all now been mapped, this last piece of the
puzzle, what becomes of Husserl's late history project, and where Derrida
finally stands toward it, has yet to be set out. The problematics of the trace
and the absolute past just discussed clearly indicate movement on this
topic. But what this may be—the fate of this final thread of Derrida's development, one able to shed definitive light on where Derrida arrives in
respect to history overall—still has not been made clear. This issue of the
role of Husserl's late history—itself a "history of essences," and thus an
"essential history"—in Derrida's first mature thought, at the advent of deconstruction, is the last issue, then, that *Essential History* will address.

This particular phase of Derrida's development, namely, Derrida's
changing relation to Husserlian history, is observable in the essays he published between the "Introduction" and the first appearance of *Of Grammatology* in 1965—and this is another sign of its importance for Derrida's
mature thought. Derrida published two large-scale essays during this
period, in which he defined his relation to contemporary thinkers of magnitude comparable to his own—his 1964 essay on Emmanuel Levinas
("Violence and Metaphysics") and his 1963 essay on Foucault ("Cogito
and the History of Madness")—and this strand of Derrida's development
takes shape in them both. Both of these essays have history as their central theme, and both show Derrida making a transition between a hesitant
allegiance to Husserl's late history in the "Introduction" and that disappearance of history as a sign under which his own work travels in his first
deconstructive writings.

"Violence and Metaphysics," taken together with "Cogito," in fact
constitutes a single unique phase in Derrida's thought, though this has
too often been overlooked in previous discussions of these works.[32] In both
essays, concerns very close to Derrida's mature thought are already coming to the fore, a kind of proto-deconstruction indeed already appears,
yet in both Derrida still actively embraces history, and his own labor, his
own thought, takes place under its rubric.[33] Already aiming in these works

to affirm an excess, a madness, on the one hand, or an exteriority or alterity, on the other—associated with Foucault's or Levinas's work, respectively—Derrida's embrace of history is not meant simply to affirm Husserl's late thought by any means. Yet both essays also stand closer in time to the "Introduction" than *Of Grammatology* does, and Derrida's continuing, though often concealed or sedimented, proximity to Husserlian history is also visible in them. Derrida is thus already on a path that takes him closer to Heidegger, and in this sense toward the more radical break with Husserl that we have witnessed at the start of *Of Grammatology;* nevertheless, as we shall see, underlying these works are certain aspects of Husserl's, not Heidegger's, views on history, and this fact will play no small role at the moment Derrida comes to abandon history as an explicit theme.

The first thing to be established, however, is that the theme of history does play a decisive role in these transitional works, a role not to be found in either the "Introduction" or *Of Grammatology,* and having one foot in the past of Derrida's thought, another in its future. To start with "Violence and Metaphysics," the work closest to *Of Grammatology* in time, the importance Derrida assigned to history in "Violence's" original conception, its centrality as regards the rest of Derrida's concerns there, can perhaps be seen most readily in the central section of "Violence" entitled "Of the Original Polemic."

"Of the Original Polemic" stands as the focus, the pivot, of Derrida's essay on Levinas. It is the first of three titled sections comprising part 3 of "Violence," and this part is itself nearly twice as long as the two parts that come before it (and is the part in which Derrida explicitly sets out the questions he wants to put to Levinas's project).[34] Derrida's own standpoint, correspondingly, comes forward in this part as well; and near the end of this section, he makes the following declaration in which history's importance to his own work at this stage becomes clear: "*Within history,* which the philosopher cannot escape, because it is not history in the sense given it by Levinas (totality), but is the history of the departures from totality . . . History is not the totality transcended by eschatology, metaphysics, or speech. It is transcendence itself" ("VM" 117/"VEM" 173).

This and other similar passages make plain that Derrida, despite the caveat he later added, understands his own position in "Violence and Metaphysics" to be a defense of history.[35] Derrida, at this phase of his thinking, quite self-consciously sees himself as responsible to history, to "the history the philosopher cannot escape," and in engaging in a thought of "history" as "transcendence"—his position here having obvious links, above all, to Heidegger's. Derrida at this moment intends for his own work to travel under the name of history, though what he actually has in mind here, the concrete significance of these claims, which alone can let the import of this passage for Derrida's development be determined, has not yet been made clear.

Derrida's intention in these declarations must be better grasped, then, and to do so it is necessary to step back a bit and briefly survey the beginning of Derrida's argument, before turning to similar considerations that also may be found in "Cogito." Derrida had started off this section—or rather this subsection of a section, B of "Of the Original Polemic," to which I will here confine myself—by engaging in a twofold critique of Levinas's intention in *Totality and Infinity*. Derrida had raised a double-sided objection to Levinas's intention (as Derrida understands this) to think an exteriority, a "true," "nonspatial" "exteriority" (of the face), which in its immediacy would also break with the economy of inside/outside and with all metaphors of spatiality and light.[36]

Against Levinas's work so construed, Derrida insists, on the one hand (in agreement with Levinas himself, as he points out), that thought and speech are not finally separable. (Derrida here speaks of "modern philosophies which no longer seek to distinguish between thought and language" ["VM" 114], and he even goes so far as to suggest, interestingly enough, that the radical transcendent exteriority that interests Levinas would be easier to maintain if Levinas went a more "classical" route and separated once and for all the object, and the thought of it, from discourse about it ["VM" 115].) The moment of expression, of discourse generally, Derrida thus posits, along with Levinas himself, is not to be avoided.

On the other hand, Derrida asserts that these oppositions—inside/outside, light/night, etc.—which Levinas claims his own discourse of the face dispenses with are themselves *unavoidable*. They are not accidental features of a given language, but inherent in the logos as such. Thus, once the necessity to speak at all is accepted, so must the necessity to employ them. All language entails these oppositions; they are features of "conceptuality itself," Derrida insists, and it is impossible ever to leave them behind entirely ("VM" 113/"VEM" 166).[37]

At this moment, the "polemic" in Derrida's title, what this "original polemic" indicates, can be made clearer, noting the exception Derrida takes to Levinas's argument. Moreover, where Derrida stands in respect to history in "Violence and Metaphysics" more generally can also start to emerge.

"Polemic" simply as a term, after all, suggests a certain intersection of history and language (since its root, *polemos*, means "war," and thus refers to history, while its more common meaning as a rhetorical performance refers to language). And thanks to the criticism just reviewed, finally running against the grain of Levinas's presentation, the necessity for such polemic, *polemos*, in both senses of this term is being asserted by

Derrida. Thought, a thought of radical exteriority or alterity, will have to engage in polemic in a rhetorical sense, Derrida claims, in the face of language's visual and spatial distinctions (a use or "using . . . up" of "language," even a usury or a usurpation, will be required! ["VM" 112–13]). At the same time, this rhetorical or discursive polemic, taking into account and making itself responsible for such rootedness in language, for the dominion of a certain spatial disposition of the logos prior to any actual given experience or instance of speech—thus honoring a kind of ur-situatedness of all discourse—would also itself be history, be an act of war, a historical or historial contestation on the part of thought both within and against language.

Derrida thus affirms, against Levinas, the need for a *war* of thought within *language* to bring something like radical exteriority forward—at first glance his stance, again, thus appearing very close to Heidegger's (leaving aside, for the moment, the overall reconciliation between Heidegger and Levinas at which Derrida arrives at the end of this essay, upon which I will comment later). Derrida's concerns, in fact, are near to those that have already been examined in *Of Grammatology* (where Derrida's proximity to Heidegger already has proved greatest); and upon seeing this more clearly, seeing the sort of proto-deconstructive stance in which Derrida is already engaged at this moment, what Derrida's later writings continue to owe to his affirmation of history in "Violence," even when history ceases to be a rubric that he actively embraces in these later works, can also come into view.

At this moment, in fact, the grounds for Derrida eventually believing that his own thought and its objects partake in a surpassing historicity, even when he himself ceases to refer to history, become clear. Derrida, as noted, will always believe his work has a unique relation to history (is somehow more historical than history itself), and to see why this is so, it must be seen why, at this moment in "Violence," Derrida believes Levinas cannot go the route Levinas is attempting to take in *Totality and Infinity*— why Derrida believes it impossible to do without the intermediation of light to think and speak of an original *nonspatial exteriority*, as well as under what conditions *Derrida* himself would be willing to follow Levinas in speaking of the "face" as originary. Derrida writes here:

> The significations which radiate starting from Inside-Outside, from Light-Night, etc. do not inhabit solely the words proscribed [by Levinas]. They are lodged in . . . conceptuality itself. This is on account of the fact that they do not signify an immersion in space. The structure Inside-Outside, or Day-Night has no sense in a pure space abandoned to itself and disoriented. It surges starting from a zero-point, from an origin,

from an orient which are neither inside nor outside space. This orient [*Cet orient*] of the look is also that of speech [*parole*]. One can then call it Face [*Visage*]. But it can no longer be hoped, starting from there to separate language from space, to disrobe speech from light. (Derrida 1964b, 429)

The functioning of these terms, the necessity and unavoidability to rely on the oppositions "Inside-Outside," "Light-Night," derives from an original *situatedness,* "itself neither in space nor outside of space." Derrida insists that the distinctions pertaining to space, these metaphors relating to light, which Levinas wanted to avoid, belong to language *not* accidentally but necessarily (they are not confined to "the proscribed words," but "to conceptuality itself"), and this is so *because* these distinctions and oppositions, this spatialization or phenomenalization of light/night, inside/outside, *do not* concern a pure space, "a space disoriented and abandoned to itself" (a geometrical space), but rather emerge from an always oriented space, an always situated origin, in which discourse and space have already come together.[38]

The rights of a certain stage of appearing, an originary phenomenologization, are thus being insisted on by Derrida at this moment, against Levinas as he understands him. Not space in general, but an original (transcendental-phenomenological) stage of appearing dictates that an originary *spatialization,* taking in things and discourse about them both at once, be recognized; and this situatedness in which the logos and the phenomena already have become intertwined is what Derrida believes Levinas's work threatens to overlook.

Derrida's own thought here is thus much closer to Husserl and Heidegger than to Levinas at this moment (something a reading of the two sections of part 3 that follow would amply confirm);[39] and Derrida concludes this passage, accordingly, by insisting that the face as an origin may be admitted only if these conditions are recognized ("this orient . . . is also that of speech [*parole*]. One can then call it Face. But it can no longer be hoped . . . to separate language from space" [Derrida 1964b, 429]).

Derrida, at this epoch, then—swerving away from Levinas even as he intends to finally parallel and affirm his concerns—was already in the course of conceiving of a deferred style of origin, of that displaced transcendental functioning that we witnessed come forward in *Of Grammatology* under the heading of the trace, archi-writing, and *différance.* Derrida here, in remarks he added later, also speaks of *"an inscribed origin,"* "an included origin," anticipating the central thought of *Of Grammatology;* and correspondingly, why Derrida will be able to maintain that his deconstruction of the origin is more historical than history itself in *Of Grammatology* can also be seen.[40]

This "origin," that is, this situatedness in space, which keeps such spatialization from pertaining to any pure disoriented space, is itself nothing spatial after all (it is "neither in space nor outside it"). It will, however, always and already have been given over to this movement of phenomenologization, spatialization, which it enjoins upon everything else—and thus have been given over to a kind of originary dissimulation, which is indeed why Derrida will come to call it a trace. This situated or inscribed origin of space always dissimulates itself by always and already being given over to that spatialization of both space and language that it makes possible; but on this account, too, Derrida can maintain that this origin itself knows an unparalleled historicity, with which it opens all history. Always on the way to losing itself in discourse, language, and the concept, this inscribed origin embodies a radical historicity—it being nothing in itself, apart from this movement of self-dissimulation—and it thus prescribes history in the sense that Derrida has already been seen to insist on it here: "history" as "transcendence," as what "the philosopher cannot escape," since it is history "not as totality but the departure from totality."

On these grounds, then, due to the relation to history he exposes here, Derrida will always claim that the operations of his signature terms—the inscribed origin, the trace, *différance*, archi-writing—necessitate a radical historicity. All these notions have this self-dissimulating character, all manifest themselves through a certain nonappearance, and open totality by eluding it; and thus Derrida always believes them historical through and through (once the caveat "if there were any history" has been added).

Alternatively, having seen why Derrida always maintains that his own thought bears the traces of a historicity greater than what is usually called history, why Derrida wished to move away from history, to abandon it as a notion, also can and must come into view.[41] As I will later show, the seeds of Derrida's removal from history can indeed be discerned in "Violence and Metaphysics"; to answer this question right now, however, I want to turn to the other work comprising this crucial stage of Derrida's thought, "Cogito and the History of Madness," and to the light it is able to shed on these matters.

What especially needs to be recognized here, first off, is the extraordinary closeness of Derrida's ultimate position in "Cogito" to that just examined in "Violence," again something too often overlooked by commentators. Both essays follow almost exactly the same path, share a common set of reference points, and embody a nearly identical formation. Both begin with Derrida aligning his intentions with those of the author in question (who himself aims to break with philosophy or thought as known hitherto—through a history of madness or an archaeology of silence on the part of Foucault; through a radical ethical alterity or an immediate metaphysical exteriority in the case of Levinas), only to have Derrida, as we have already witnessed in Levinas's case, question the *articulation* of these intentions, the grounds on which they may come to *expression*. In both essays, Derrida thus delays the arrival of such otherness (itself otherwise of such very different sorts) in order that he himself may reembrace it, after a passage *through* philosophical discourse, *after* the rights of a certain transcendental-phenomenological phase of appearing have been acknowledged, thus arriving at a (different, more transcendental-phenomenological) thought of alterity, of difference, seemingly reconciled with Foucault's or Levinas's, and finally proceeding under its heading—Derrida himself in the end affirming madness or excess in the one case, and the other as a positive infinity in the other case.

The moment in "Cogito" in which Derrida insists on the rights of the logos, analogous to the one just reviewed, will be my focus shortly. Right now, however, I want to tease out further the outcome that Derrida arrives at here, and the fact that when it comes to history, these two essays, "Violence" and "Cogito," bring forward essentially the same matrix. More specifically, near the end of "Cogito," in a passage that has at times received the attention it so richly deserves, Derrida comes to a rather impassioned set of conclusions in which this proximity to his position in "Violence" is especially clear.[42] Having invoked the Cartesian cogito—already identified, at least in some respects, with hyperbole, excess, madness, despite Derrida's admittedly quite orthodox reading of Descartes—and having brought in the "Augustinian" and indeed the "Husserlian" cogitos as well, Derrida goes on to make the following statement, which is almost a profession of "belief."

> I believe that historicity in general would be impossible without a history of philosophy, and I believe that the latter would be impossible if we possessed only hyperbole, on the one hand, or only determined finite historical structures, finite *Weltanschauungen,* on the other. The historicity proper to philosophy is located . . . between the hyperbole and the finite structure, between that which exceeds totality and the closed totality, in the difference between history and historicity, that is in the place where, or rather at the moment when, the Cogito and all that it symbolizes here (madness, derangement, hyperbole, etc.) pronounce and reassure themselves then to fall, necessarily forgetting themselves until their reactivation, their reawakening in another statement of the excess which also later will become another decline and another crisis. ("CHM" 60)

Here, then, Derrida sets out what is in effect the same formation, the same matrix, that has just come forward in "Violence." History as presented here is also opened and shaped by a radical historicity, *a historicity proper to the movement of thought.* To be sure, thought is now identified explicitly with the *philosophy* (and its history), but only insofar as philosophy itself is taken to aim at "hyperbole," "excess," and "madness." Accordingly, the "origin" or engine of history (the possibility of "historicity in general") is again located by Derrida in the movement of a self-dissimulating excess, specific to the project of philosophy and to that at which it aims: an excess, an origin, intrinsically situated, indeed "inscribed," between itself and its own concealment, wavering between "hyperbole" and "the finite structure," "between what exceeds totality and the closed totality." "The cogito" and all that it represents ("madness, hyperbole, excess") thus exceed all history and structure, according to Derrida, as was the case with Derrida's talk of the origin and its transcendence in "Violence."

Here too, however, the matter is still more complex, since once again the moments of expression and of appearance play a crucial role. Hyperbole, madness, and excess must "speak themselves" *(se disent)* in and against the grain of language, "pronounce themselves" in a movement intrinsic at once to their appearance as well as to their disappearance and forgetting (in a "rhythm," Derrida is about to say, which "is the movement of temporalization itself" and what "unites it to movement of the logos" ["CHM" 61]). To "pronounce themselves" is thus also to "reassure themselves," to "fall," "losing sight of themselves," only "to await another *statement* of [this] excess," which will also "later become another decline and another crisis," according to a schema of radical, originary historicity (my emphasis).

The same mobile structure, the same generative matrix is thus at work here as it was in "Violence": namely, that of an origin which opens history by dint of losing itself within it. Of course, here Derrida presents this movement, the opening of history as such, in a less triumphalist tone than he does in "Violence"; it is set out as an oscillation between historicity (of thought and philosophy) and history (in general—as finitude, a contrast to "Violence" which we will soon address). It is indeed presented as a fall: a falling away into work, speech, the labor of recuperation. Nevertheless, history here is thought as the product of an origin which exceeds it—while relating to it, opening it, inseparable from it—an origin engaged in repeated self-dissimulation, a recurrent expression and concealment of "itself," thus conceived as a rhythmed alternation of excess and finitude, which entails its own radical historicity.[43]

Both "Violence" and "Cogito" significantly overlap, then, and taken together they indeed represent a key transitional stage in the development of Derrida's thinking. In both works, an inscribed origin, a self-dissimulating movement anticipating the trace and many of Derrida's other signature terms, is already emerging. At this stage, however, in contrast to his later work, Derrida clearly sets this origin forth in the name of history, himself affirming *both* the history and historicity of this formation. Why Derrida, then, decided to abandon this term, at least the privileging of *history as such* still visible here, and on what grounds he thought himself able to do so, must now be addressed. This too becomes comprehensible, however, thanks to the identication of an inscribed origin at work in both "Violence" and "Cogito," and the reasons for it are best explored at the point where they become especially visible in "Cogito."

What "Cogito" makes particularly plain, being the work closest to the "Introduction" in time, is how much this entire conception of history and historicity, in "Violence" and "Cogito" alike, still owes to Husserl—and it is thanks to this indebtedness that Derrida will finally come to distance himself from history, and even this history, altogether. Derrida's embrace of history at this stage already represents a singular middle way between Heidegger and Husserl, an adaptation of Husserl in a Heideggerean direction, as I am about to make clear. Because this is so, because of this continuing reliance on Husserl, Derrida will finally decide to abandon history as the rubric under which he conducts his own thought (though this is also why, as will become evident later, even as Derrida makes this break, Husserl's late view of history still plays a decisive, though different, role in his thought). Indeed, only if Derrida's dependence on Husserl's late history in "Violence" and "Cogito" is recognized (though in both works Derrida is already on his way to *Of Grammatology*, already moving closer to Heidegger, and both works already affirm an alterity or excess clearly foreign to Husserl's own intentions) may the rationale behind the schema of Derrida's development at this moment, otherwise so puzzling, be grasped: namely, how one and the same movement that takes Derrida away from Husserl *toward* Heidegger can also terminate in Derrida's abandoning history, leaving history behind as a theme in the way that has been sketched here.

Once inserted into a developmental context, how much Derrida's position in the Foucault essay still owes to Husserl (which reliance lies at the bottom of this conundrum), how deeply "Cogito" itself is indebted to various aspects of Husserl's philosophy, can be readily seen. Throughout this essay Derrida explicitly and repeatedly rejects that historicism to which he suggests Foucault draws near. Derrida makes the rejection of all and any historicism the explicit precondition of his own reading of Descartes, and he also draws from time to time on these same arguments, Husserl's anti-historicist and anti-relativist claims that I discussed in my first chapter, to otherwise admonish or chastise Foucault.[44]

Derrida's reliance on Husserl in "Cogito" goes beyond such boundary markers, however, to the very heart of his aims in this essay. Descartes's cogito, after all, is clearly a stand-in for Husserl's. The defense of the one (Descartes's) is wholly a defense of the other (Husserl's), and in line with this, the real issue between Derrida and Foucault, viewed in the context of Derrida's thought, will turn out to be the same one that arose between Derrida and Levinas: namely, whether a certain legacy of transcendental phenomenology is to be retained (perhaps here an even more obviously Husserlian one), even as some form of break with philosophy of the sort that both Foucault and Levinas (differently) envision is affirmed. Thus, prior to the reading of Descartes's "First Meditation," before this is even broached, "Cogito" turns to the question of whether the rights of the transcendental-phenomenological logos must first be respected, or may be dispensed with entirely in favor of what is in Foucault's case—as in Levinas's—in effect a certain empiricism: an empiricism of radical *historical discontinuity*, or epochal difference, in the case of Foucault (answering to that of radical ethical alterity, or metaphysical exteriority, in Levinas).[45]

Early in "Cogito," Derrida focuses on the place given by Foucault in *Histoire de la folie* to what Foucault, and Derrida following him, calls "the decision": a radical splitting-off or separation of reason from unreason, of madness from thought. Though Derrida makes clear that he has more sympathy with the project of graphing the moment of such a decision than he has with other versions of Foucault's enterprise that *Histoire* presents (namely, Foucault's attempt to write "an archaeology" of "madness itself"— thus "an archaeo*logy* of silence," an attempt riddled from the first by impossibility, in Derrida's eyes), nevertheless, Derrida argues against Foucault's resolve to identify this decision, this dissension, uniquely with a specific historical moment, namely that of modernity.

Derrida, that is, contests Foucault's claim that the decision (or "dissension" as Derrida prefers to call it) took place once and for all as an event inaugurating modernity or "the classical age," to use Foucault's term. Yet Derrida at this moment, and this is the key point, will not appeal to some abstract reason, some ahistorical capacity of thought that Foucault has ignored, in order to do so. Rather, Derrida will here insist, and the emphasis is his, that "a doctrine of *tradition*, of the tradition of the logos "must be thought: a thought of the logos as *tradition* is "the prerequisite implied by Foucault's enterprise" ("CHM" 41), and one that Foucault himself has ignored.

This is an obvious reference back to Husserl's late thought—Derrida invoking a *tradition* of the logos as such as what Foucault has insufficiently taken into account. The logos itself, whose dehiscence or decision Foucault wishes to graph in *real history*, already knows a traditionality, a historicity of its own, Derrida insists. In fact, Derrida had already alluded to this conception of an intrinsically historical logos earlier, and there, too, this linkage between talk of reason as a *tradition* and Derrida's recent work on the late Husserl (and thus to Derrida's own recent affirmation of an intrinsic history and historicity of the logos) becomes plain.[46] In introducing this theme, pointing out Foucault's identification of the decision with a given historical period, Derrida had insisted that "it would be necessary to exhume the virgin and unitary ground upon which the decisive act . . . took root." "This common root," Derrida continues, is itself a "*logos*," "a *logos* . . . a reason; an already historical reason certainly, but a reason much less determined than in its so-called classical form" ("CHM" 39).

In Derrida's own words, the crux of his questioning of Foucault's work in "Cogito" thus concerns "an already historical reason," "much less determined" than Foucault's: a logos whose resources are deeper than Foucault's own, yet which are themselves nevertheless still historical. Such a specifically historical logos, able to combine history and reason, in turn hearkens back to Husserl's—thus making clear that a reliance on the Husserlian logos, a certain adaptation of Husserl's late thought, is central to Derrida's arguments in "Cogito" and to "Violence" as well, as it can now be seen (though this is perhaps initially less obvious in the latter instance).[47] In Levinas's case, Derrida nevertheless appeals to something he deems *conceptuality itself;* claiming that no discourse could avoid an originary, though situated, phenomeno-logization that assigns it to history by dint of having one foot beyond it. Here, correspondingly, Derrida invokes the rights of an *undifferentiated,* undetermined historical *reason,* never exhausted by any actual finite history (in fact, entailing this same "ur-situatedness").[48] In both instances, the Husserlian logos in its last, most fleshed-out form as a logos at work *across* all finite history and empirical language, yet never itself wholly removed from language and history as such, proves critical to Derrida's own stance.

Thus brought together, and taken from a developmental perspective, Derrida's standpoint toward Foucault and Levinas, more broadly still, lets us identify Derrida as being in the process of adapting this historical logos taken from Husserl and moving it in a Heideggerean direction, even as he in part continues to affirm the Husserlian evidences. Derrida's displacement of the project of both authors, his own singular affirmation of history and historicity at this stage, indeed remains indebted to Husserl's late thought, though by affirming Foucault's madness, or Levinas's alterity, Derrida has also begun his departure from it, in a direction that my treatment of *Of Grammatology* has already made plain.

Consequently, with this, the deepest grounds for Derrida's own eventual abandonment of history come into view, grounds which have their roots finally in Derrida's own work, in his experiences here, before all other considerations. Derrida came to distance himself from this talk, to cease to affirm his own work in history's name, doubtless with a number of motives in mind; his own thought at this key transitional stage, however, proves to be the most decisive factor here, the sine qua non.[49]

After all, perhaps the single most extraordinary feature of Derrida's stance in these two essays taken as a whole is its ability to contest projects, those of Foucault and Levinas, which, on their face, themselves appear to arrive at such radically opposed results. Taken in the crudest possible fashion, in "Cogito" Derrida takes a stance *against* Foucault's *historicism,* against the reduction of philosophy's work to closed structures and finite historical totalities. By contrast, in "Violence" Derrida takes a stance against what at first glance appears to be the diametrically opposed position: against *transcendence,* against metaphysical excess, against an exteriority that would leave *history* behind. In the one case, Derrida seems to stand *against* history in the *name* of what exceeds it; in the other he *affirms* history, *against* what exceeds it. In both, however, the *same* matrix of thought, the same notion of a radical history and historicity, nevertheless provides the platform for Derrida's self-positioning.

But this makes plain, perhaps as nothing else can, that Derrida himself at this phase practiced that very neutralization of history he will later come to denounce. Though Derrida's manifest position in each text is against stances diametrically opposed, in each Derrida asserts a kind of archi-history or historicity that is only conceivable thanks to the Husserlian logos, returning the discourses of Levinas and Foucault to the same source, the same root. On these grounds, Derrida himself must have come to believe that *even his own talk of history* was not finally viable—that even in his own case, the recuperation of this notion at the hands of the logos, even in the modified form that Derrida presents it here, cannot but occur.

Derrida himself had practiced such recuperation; but this is also why even at the moment Derrida decides to break with this conception, to further radicalize his stance, continuing a trajectory on which he already finds himself, Husserl's version of history will nevertheless still play a decisive, albeit different role: now informing what Derrida's thought needs to turn against. Derrida will never cease to believe that it is impossible for any history, as well as empiricism of any sort, to escape the resources of this logos: he will never cease to affirm the authority of this logos as it has come forward at this stage. Consequently, even at the moment of departing from this formation, and coming to abandon history as an explicit theme, this formation proves to be determinative. Derrida's conviction that the logos has always opened, and now *mastered* or *dominated* history as we know it (and thus history must be rejected as a working concept), continues to rest on these evidences that have just come forward.

And thus, one last time, in line with that model we have already seen to be his, Derrida will assume the validity of that formation he targets, he will first take as legitimate what he ultimately aims to deconstruct. He will continue to affirm the rights of this most extreme form of the history and historicity of the logos, even as he becomes convinced that it necessitates a final reappropriation of presence, a final suppression of difference, in order to launch a still more radical departure, to overcome history, to outdo history (even this modified history of the inscribed origin), and thus cease to have his thought function in its name.[50] Showing concretely how this occurs is the last task *Essential History* will pursue.

To grasp this last point more completely, to see the new yet still decisive role played by Husserl's construal of the logos and its historicity at the very moment Derrida decides he wishes to depart from this formation, let me turn to the conclusion of "Violence and Metaphysics." Though embodying with "Cogito" a single phase and formation, "Violence" is also itself, as I already noted, a deeply transitional work, and its conclusion, in particular, with its final reconciliation of Heidegger and Levinas not yet discussed here, anticipates Derrida's later thought in ways already widely recognized in the literature.[51]

Indeed, this rapprochement of Levinas and Heidegger is clearly important for all of Derrida's future work on these issues—on history, but also on politics and ethics, whose concerns are sometimes thought to occupy, or take place within, the historical field. Derrida, as is well known, will invoke Levinasian concepts more and more, even while retaining a Heideggerean dimension to his thought—continuing to see these concepts as "reconciled with a Heideggerean intention," as he puts it in *Of Grammatology*—and Derrida, at the end of "Violence," is thus offering the first version of that reconciliation between Heidegger and Levinas which will later become almost a trademark of his work.

At the close of "Violence," Derrida reprises the issue of "history" and all that pertains to it in a way that indeed tracks his future thought. Derrida tells us here that both Heidegger and Levinas "question the entire philosophical 'adventure'" and put a certain "eschatology" in its stead. And in offering "to conjecture about . . . the proximity of [these] two 'eschatologies'" (Heidegger's and Levinas's), Derrida at this moment proposes a schema whereby history or something like it will be radically rethought— albeit *rethought in the direction of its radical disappearance* (*VM* 149).

Here emerges, *in nuce*, Derrida's future thought of history, ethics, and politics, insofar as it depends on a certain rapprochement with Levinas. For Heidegger and Levinas would be able to be reconciled, according to Derrida, insofar as each thinks a radical, nonontic, difference; and thus twinning or doubling Levinas's and Heidegger's outlooks, the thought provided by taking both together, in turn, would open "a history," "an adventure" ("VM" 149), envisioned by neither—an adventure without reserve, as yet unthought, not reducible to any eschatology (including that of either thinker), and hence no longer properly described as history at all.[52]

More specifically, Levinas's God, according to Derrida, first of all must be understood apart from all ontic predetermination, as that "which cannot be anticipated on the basis of the dimension of the divine" and as a "nonconcept" ("VM" 149). And Heidegger's ontico-ontological horizon, in turn, according to Derrida, would have been opened by this God, "by means of what Heidegger [himself, though not Derrida] called meta-physics and onto-theology" ("VM" 149). God, or positive infinity, in Levinas's sense, that is, would be the "opening of the horizon," yet "not in the horizon" ("VM" 149)—thus opening the ontological horizon by having already broken with it, by having already escaped or been subtracted from it. Moreover, this has the further consequence that the difference so opened by this escape, what Heidegger called Being, correspondingly would never simply have indicated "the homogeneous identity of the concept," and the "asphyxiation of the same" in the fashion that Levinas himself presents it ("VM" 149).

Instead, the two unique "nonconcepts," the sole two notions to escape the ontic—the ontic-nonontic of Levinasian infinite alterity (God) and the ontological nonontic of the ontico-ontological difference (Heidegger's Being)—would themselves have, according to Derrida, a surprising proximity, a relation, a proximity that finally demands a different version of *something like* history. Indeed, "the beyond history of [Levinasian] eschatology, " Derrida concludes, rather than indicating a radical leavetaking from history, as Levinas himself would have it, instead signals "a transition to a more profound history": to "History itself," "the history of Being"—"a history," however, "which unable any longer to be itself in any *original or final presence would have to change its name*" ("VM" 149; my emphasis).

Derrida at the end of "Violence" thus offers a version of that singular synthesis between these two thinkers that proves so important in his later work: he sketches a "two-handed history" that is no longer properly history at all, no longer able to be identified with a version of history or of eschatology proposed by either thinker—and thus one which "would have to change its name." So too, Derrida envisions in the place of this history something like an "adventure"—an adventure more radical than either Levinasian or Heideggerean eschatology, precisely by dint of bringing these two thinkers together and its implication in such multiple and otherwise heterogeneous reference points.

Derrida's conclusion here clearly anticipates his mature work, although the explicit emphasis on justice so evident later is absent here. At the same time, it is equally crucial to see, along with this anticipation, the role that Husserl's late history continues to play in all this, how its conclusions remain decisive here, and thus potentially so for at least certain aspects of all of Derrida's subsequent treatments of these themes.

For Derrida's talk of Levinas's God, or positive infinity, as an infinity able to open a horizon by breaking with it (and indeed a horizon in some way still affiliated with transcendental phenomenology) is clearly indebted to the work of the infinite Idea in the "Introduction," on whose basis alone, I would suggest, the capacity of infinity to open a horizon of any sort becomes conceivable (though the reappropriation of history by this Idea is what Derrida first and foremost directly wishes to contest at this moment). Moreover, and more centrally, this entire reconciliation of Heidegger and Levinas, Derrida's rethinking of these twin eschatologies, has been prepared by a discussion of the *concept,* which interprets it along the lines I have earlier brought out, as at once situated and nonspecific, as "ursituated," and thus is an understanding that only Husserl's notion of a historical, yet nonfinite reason can deliver.

More narrowly yet, Derrida sets out the *differences* between these two thinkers, the conflict between Heidegger's and Levinas's stances, by presenting these differences as symmetrical thanks to the role the concept plays in both cases. Heidegger's Being, Derrida insists against Levinas, rather than being "the primum cognitum" (the first known) would be the "*first dissimulated*" (by the *concept* of the ontic; "VM" 149). At the same time, it would also be the "*first dissimulating*" (of Levinas's infinite other; "VM" 149). These potential criticisms, the differences between Heidegger and Levinas, thus become balanced out, ameliorated by Derrida, around a work of dissimulation performed by *their conceptualization.* "For Levinas, as for Heidegger," Derrida writes, "dissimulation would be a *conceptual* gesture; but for Levinas the concept is on the plane of Being [i.e., Heidegger's talk of Being dissimulates Levinasian alterity]; for Heidegger, it is on the plane of ontic determination [i.e., ontic concepts dissimulate the ontico-ontological difference]" ("VM" 149).

Yet this equivalence can only be reached, and this is the critical point, if conceptualization itself has been understood in the singular fashion just set out here, Derrida still drawing on Husserl's late views. Derrida has just now emphasized, after all (as he does repeatedly throughout "Violence"), that "the anhistoricity of meaning at its origin is what profoundly separates Levinas from Heidegger" ("VM" 148). Heidegger affirms the *historicity* of meaning, all meaning, including his own, in a way that Levinas does not (this also being what was specifically at issue in Derrida's insistence on a need for an "original polemic" discussed above). This historicity of the concept and its meaning must already be reconciled with *a Husserlian intention,* then, if the work the concept does in dissimulating infinite alterity in Levinas and Being in Heidegger is to be considered equivalent. This notion of the concept Derrida calls on here, this logos, must already have been withdrawn from Heidegger's own views on conceptuality, it must already inhabit a zone at once historical (able to be reconciled with Heidegger's concerns) but not finite, in this sense anhistorical (and thus commensurate with Levinas)—at once a tradition, but a tradition of reason—if it is to unite in a single treatment, and join in one and the same construal, both the dissimulation of Levinasian infinite alterity and of Heidegger's ontico-ontological difference. Only if the work of conceptualization has been so displaced may the dissimulation of Being (which Heidegger took to be historical and finite, through and through) and the eclipse of alterity (which Levinas took to be *performed by* history, a finite history over against an infinite otherness—and which he accordingly presents as not itself in any way historical) thereby be reconciled.

This assumption as to the concept's functioning in a Husserlian vein, moreover, extends to the *rapprochement* of the two that Derrida has just brought about: only if Husserl's model of history, not Heidegger's, nor Levinas's, is implicitly the one in question here can Levinasian "positive infinity" also be thought as the "other name of Being," as Derrida puts it here ("VM" 149). Only if history itself is in some sense already *infinite,* and thus already coincident with the infinite work of history as uniquely prescribed by the historicity of the logos (a notion of history which Heidegger at least would never endorse)—and thus open to the play of the *infinite* and Heideggerean *history* at once—can these two opposed eschatologies, that of ethical alterity and of Being in its difference from beings, both be affirmed in this fashion.

Hence Derrida, even at the moment when he first intends most explicitly *to break with them,* continues to draw on Husserl's view of history, conceptuality, and the logos. Derrida's departure (now more radical than Levinas's and Heidegger's, rather than Heidegger's and Tran Duc Thao's), his launching of an adventure beyond all transcendental history, even now depends on some sort of endorsement of Husserl's views, an appropriation of his model of reason. According to a schema we now know to be unique to Derrida from the first, Husserlian history and historicity—this transfinite history of a quasi-historical logos—above all stands as the *target* of Derrida's break, the theme of his departure, or deconstruction. This version of history is Derrida's target first of all (that *from which* he wishes to takes his leave), now by doubling, or otherwise multiplying his reference points.

Yet, in allowing Levinas's and Heidegger's thought to be folded into each other in this way, Husserl's history and its corresponding view of conceptuality at the same time serve as a *springboard* for this break. Derrida wants to depart from this logos and its history, and he also wants to break with those versions of history and eschatology specific to Levinas and Heidegger. Nevertheless, in accord with the most longstanding schema of his thought, Husserl's late historical logos will also turn out to be the *means* for this departure, its self-evidences in some fashion in fact endorsed, and thus will now be incorporated into this movement at a yet deeper level, as something close to the "sublated" to Derrida's "sublating"—perhaps finally hardly recognizable as such, yet still providing a decisive resource upon which Derrida draws.

With such considerations, my discussion comes full circle. I began by speaking of a future of thought for which Derrida's work gave hope, thanks to forging a middle way between Heidegger and Husserl—without necessarily precluding a more radical questioning of them both. And here again, for one last time, the surprising tendency toward *such a middle way* in Derrida's program, so often seen here, comes to the fore—a tendency that already ought to be visible simply by dint of Derrida wanting to bring Levinas and Heidegger together. A specifically modern, infinite reason would have been grafted onto the Heideggerean schema by Derrida, it now becomes apparent (even as Derrida aims to call a version of this infinity into doubt, along with Heidegger's own reassurances about finite history)—Derrida's rapprochement of Levinas and Heidegger operating on these terms alone.

Derrida is indeed able to forge a new mode of thought—an offshoot, or new branch, of the path opened by Heidegger—in part by dint of his engagement with Husserl and Husserl's late history. On this account, moreover, I would suggest that Derrida's initiative is in many ways more attractive than Heidegger's own, especially when viewed from the perspective of modern knowledge and its claims. Derrida's project at the point to which we have come (in *Of Grammatology, Speech and Phenomena,* and the transitional work immediately preceding it, and also, I would suggest, thereafter) is finally less relativist, less historicist, less allergic to modernity and the rights of the current *episteme* than Heidegger—and by this same token, Derrida is able to foster a radicality, still of a Heideggerean stripe, which arguably goes further than Heidegger himself in important ways when it comes to both history and language.

By 1967, Derrida's project had thus opened a highly enticing prospect for thought (holding in abeyance, of course, the issues already discussed concerning this project's ultimate, total validity). Whether these strengths, however, in addition to everything else, finally also let it pave the way to a more viable political or ethical outlook, an issue that has become ever more pressing for Derrida and his readers in recent years, cannot be answered here. It is possible, however, on the basis of what has been brought forth in this book, to signal the direction from which such an interrogation might come.

Indeed, whether these new vistas Derrida opened for thought— built on the phenomenological logos and offering a way beyond the opposition between timeless truth and historicism, transcendence and immanence—can be meaningfully translated into the sphere of action is the question that someday must be confronted. What finally makes Derrida's work so intellectually promising, the astonishing transformation of certain Husserlian themes and strands—to whose setting out this entire present work has been dedicated—is itself what ultimately motivates the question as to how deconstruction precomprehends and thematizes the political in the end. Derrida, as we have seen, delays or reroutes all standard empiricism and facticity in his thought, deploying Husserl's own sophisticated and pliant construal of rationality, even as this rationality is what Derrida wants to and does contest above all. Accordingly, given what might be called the trace of Husserl's last history writings in Derrida's mature thought (and a similar case, by the way, could be made for the role of Hegel), where and how thought's relation to praxis in the first place has been determined, where and how a theoretical vocation, albeit one on the way to being deconstructed, has been positioned initially in respect to the political and social strata—strata from which some might believe it never truly manages to free itself in the first place—indeed must be investigated as a question.[53]

No one may deny (and I certainly do not want to) that Derrida himself, at least, has earned a right to take his chances in this way—to mount what interventions he may, according to his lights. Nor, indicating this question, has real justice obviously been done to these problems and Derrida's positions here, the investigation of which doubtless remain tasks for future work. The concrete rethinking of the tradition of political philosophy Derrida has undertaken in the last ten or fifteen years (in his commentaries on Aristotle, Marx, Kant, Schmitt, and Benjamin—to mention the most notable) must be confronted individually, and perhaps contrasted with possible alternative interpretations of these works (as has started to be done here in the case of Husserl, Heidegger, and Saussure), in order for any genuine confrontation with Derrida's late political thought to take place.

Essential History can draw no conclusions about what such interpretive work might finally reveal. What it has aimed to establish in respect to these matters, as well as most other critical issues pertaining to Derrida's thought, is that one important precondition (though of course not the only one) for responsibly engaging in such work is an awareness of Derrida's formative fifteen-year engagement with Husserl. Everything Derrida will subsequently do and think demands taking his prolonged passage through Husserlian phenomenology into account, and correspondingly also requires some kind of acquaintance with Husserl's thought.[54] Without this, without an appreciation of Husserl's claims, and Derrida's aims in respect to these claims, Derrida's intentions will never be fully understood, including his claims concerning the essence, or ultimate status, of history and politics—nor will it be possible to meaningfully inquire into the *validity* of these claims, as well as Derrida's other intentions, to ask whether Derrida's thought *achieves* all that it sets out to accomplish—a kind of questioning that seems to me unavoidable if Derrida studies are to have a future in any way as vibrant as their past.

Indeed, at a time when that deep obscurity to which we are fated in both intellectual and political matters becomes ever more plain, when the absence of solid reference points for both praxis and thought, action and intellection, becomes ever more evident in proportion to their need, this much should be clear. It is more urgent than ever to get to the heart of this surpassingly difficult work, to get some kind of fundamental clarity about Derrida's positions—which, along with a handful of others, continue to point toward the future of thought, as well as to define a period of breathtaking intellectual achievement, now sadly rapidly coming to a close. In this respect, too, the study of Derrida's development, and all of his texts, will long remain matters of essential history.

Notes

Introduction

1. I am of course aware that since the late 1980s, with what is now sometimes called the "turn to religion," Derrida's interests and those of many of his commentators have shifted away from a focus either on language or broader philosophical concerns and toward one on ethics and politics, and along with this, that Derrida has apparently reconstrued what he himself understands by "deconstruction," perhaps most notably in the essay "The Force of Law," first delivered at a 1989 conference entitled "Deconstruction and the Possibility of Justice." On this later construal, which is central to a recent major book on Derrida and Husserl authored by Len Lawlor (*Derrida and Husserl: The Basic Problem of Phenomenology* [2002], a work which treats many of the same texts studied here, and about which more will be said below), deconstruction, according to Derrida, would have a vector, an ultimate orientation, toward justice as what is "not deconstructible" (Derrida 2002, 243), a vector brought forward through "an experience of aporia" or an "experience of the impossible" (Derrida 2002, 244). Justice, unable to be directly experienced or addressed in itself (a startling claim, by the way, should it turn out to be true), would be the value ultimately orienting Derrida's own undertaking, and this value would only be available through an experience of the impossible, through an aporetic engagement. This rethinking on Derrida's part of the work of deconstruction, in effect, presents a more encompassing view of the norms, values, and motives orienting even his earlier work, and it should by no means be neglected or fail to be given its due. At the same time, it seems to me that only if one has first successfully grasped this earlier work in its own right can Derrida's statements about deconstruction's relation to justice be evaluated or even fully understood. Certainly, it is odd to orient a study largely, though not wholly, devoted to Derrida's first writings, those writings between 1954 and 1967, as is Lawlor's, by these statements made in 1989. For these first works continue to define Derrida's thought, both for the majority of readers and for Derrida himself, to the degree that he draws on them constantly in the later phases of his thinking (not to mention the fact that why, or in what way, a reading of Saussure or Plato on writing, or Husserl on the sign, might be an act of justice may only be seen if what these readings did or claimed to do has already been grasped on its own terms). What I am undertaking to do in this book, then, is to clarify what Derrida accomplished in these first works, something which, I argue, has still not been satisfactorily achieved—to introduce a new way of looking at Derrida's writing and develop-

ment, and to do so, moreover, in part by showing that what Lawlor as well as many others take to be the standard versions of deconstruction (see Lawlor 2002, 2n6), upon which most commentators still depend at decisive junctures, themselves have not been adequate.

2. "What has been seen—both positively and negatively—as revolutionary about Derrida's work for philosophy and literary studies is the particular way he attends to language" (*Norton* 2001, 1815).

3. The proximity of early new historicism, as it came to be known, to Derrida is especially noteworthy. A new historicist as paradigmatic as Stephen Greenblatt, an anti-theorist as stalwart as Walter Benn Michaels, both appeal to Derrida in their early works (e.g., Greenblatt 1989, 8; Michaels 1987, 28n43).

4. I provisionally include under this heading some other of Derrida's best critics, such as John Llewellyn, John Caputo, or John Sallis, though I will later further differentiate their projects, which indeed cannot be confined to this characterization. How widespread the dependence on Gasché's formulation of deconstruction as a quasi-transcendental project remains is telling (e.g., Caputo and Scanlon 2002, 3–4), however, and even Lawlor, whose work stakes much on offering a novel view of these matters, has recourse to this version of Derrida's project at decisive points (e.g., when glossing *différance,* Lawlor 2002, 203).

5. Of course, since the 1990s, in part thanks to the controversy concerning Derrida as a reader of Husserl (see Evans 1991; Lawlor 1994; McKenna and Evans 1995), the importance of Husserl to Derrida's thought has become more and more widely known, in both philosophical circles and more recent literary criticism (e.g., Hobson). This controversy, in which I played a small role (Kates 1993, 1998), is in fact a proximate cause of the present work—Claude Evans's book, whatever its other drawbacks, and in particular our correspondence (now published, Kates 1998), having waked me from my dogmatic Derridean slumber. Thus, one of my primary goals in tracing Derrida's development in the present work is to offer an account of Derrida's encounter with Husserl that makes a case for him as a responsible reader of Husserl's work and answers the charges against his work brought by readers like Willard, Hopkins, Mohanty, Evans, and others. This endeavor, whose outlines I first sketched in print in my "Derrida, Husserl and the Commentators: Introducing a Developmental Approach" (Kates 2003), seems to me something Len Lawlor's most recent book on Derrida and Husserl, whatever its other merits, has been unable to accomplish. Lawlor does not make the case for Derrida's actual interpretations of Husserl in such a fashion as to convince anyone not already convinced, as he does not answer, or really even take notice of, the sometimes substantial objections raised to Derrida's readings by informed Husserlians.

6. Derrida himself in "Time of a Thesis" describing his "three works published in 1967" takes note of a radical innovation that characterizes them all: "During the years that followed, from about 1963–1968, I tried to work out . . . a sort of strategic device, opening onto its own abyss, an unclosed, unencloseable, not wholly formalizable ensemble of rules for reading, writing, and interpretation" ("TT" 40). The present work, it would be fair to say, starts from this moment Derrida describes and investigates how and why he came to such an invention. It in-

vestigates what prompted Derrida to become dissatisfied with the current norms of "reading, writing, and interpretation," and what the implications of this are for his own interpreters—innovations in these areas, especially of the type described here, by no means being ones to be taken lightly.

7. Lawlor's recent book, in particular, occupies a rather odd position when it comes to these claims, to the assumption of a deep continuity of positions in all of Derrida's work. For Lawlor has perhaps shown more (or at least as much) awareness of the possibility of development in Derrida's thought as any other critic (Rudolf Bernet and Françoise Dastur being two others who deserve special notice in this regard—Bernet 1989; Dastur 1994), including Marrati-Guénoun, whose *La genèse et la trace* (1998) remains the finest book-length work on Derrida's engagement with phenomenology to date, despite largely omitting this dimension. (Bennington also concurs in this judgment concerning Derrida's corpus; see Bennington 2000, 5.) Lawlor often speaks of turning points in Derrida's thought—noting a deepening understanding of Heidegger's work on Derrida's part after *Le problème* (Lawlor 2002, 48), declaring "Violence and Metaphysics" to have "an unrivaled privilege in regard to the general development of Derrida's thought" (Lawlor 2002, 146), and recognizing a substantial difference in the work of the 1980s and 1990s from what comes before (Lawlor 2002, 212). Nevertheless, these historical nuances too often fail to enter concretely into Lawlor's actual exposition of Derridean themes, his presentation of Derrida's own arguments or interpretations. This is nowhere more evident than in the premise organizing Lawlor's work: namely that a single problem, that of genesis, underlies the totality of Derrida's encounter with Husserl, and indeed his thought as a whole, including the work of the 1980s and 1990s. "The basic problem of Derrida's philosophy is the problem of genesis" (Lawlor 2002, 21), Lawlor declares, and this problem carries over into his work on Derrida's treatment of language and the sign in *Speech and Phenomena* (Lawlor 2002, 23), as well as into Derrida's later writings ("We must [now] say that Derrida conceives genesis . . . not in terms of the question but in terms of the promise"; Lawlor 2002, 211). This characterization of Derrida's thought, however, as I will show, omits crucial differences in Derrida's philosophical concerns and in his relation to both Husserl and Heidegger even simply from the 1954 *Le problème* to the 1962 "Introduction," differences of which Derrida himself has given important indications (see *LPG* 264n12/*PG* 164n12). And it is perhaps in part because Lawlor, conceptually speaking, paints Derrida's enterprise with such a broad brush that, as mentioned above, he finds himself unable to respond to the concrete criticisms of Derrida made by so many North American Husserlians.

8. The schema most often invoked to explain the hermeneutics of deconstruction, how it functions as commentary, namely that of double reading, as I argued as long ago as 1993 (see Kates 1993, 321), is not in fact genuinely Derridean, nor in any case does it successfully accomplish what it sets out to do: chart the highly complex relation of Derrida's work and thought to those he reads. After all, if two readings really were distinguishable in Derrida's work—one which recognizes the so-called dominant interpretation and prevailing norms and another reading that is more transgressive and more inventive—how would the first be able to justify the second, and why would the latter not simply appear as an un-

motivated addition or invention in respect to the former? Only if these two aspects are seamlessly combined in a single reading, only if Derrida's work focuses on a unitary "hold" of the sort that he specifies in the introduction to *Speech* as "neither simply operative nor directly thematic, in a place neither central nor peripheral" (*SP* 16/*VP* 16)—clearly largely uncharted territory for reading (see, however, Michael Nass whose 2003 work seems motivated by some of these same concerns)—does Derrida's own work as a thinker stand a chance of being ultimately persuasive. (Geoff Bennington's ongoing insistence on something recalcitrant to commentary or categorization in all of Derrida's work, it should be noted, in its own way at least comes close to identifying this difficulty, albeit in a celebratory mode that I find rather puzzling, given that he himself is one of Derrida's commentators. See, most recently, Bennington 2000.)

9. As is well known, nearly all the trailblazing works in fields allied with literature, as well as history, in the 1980s—in gender studies, queer theory, postcolonialism, race theory, cultural studies—explicitly drew on Derrida's earliest deconstructive works in order to find their own footing. Eve Sedgwick, Judith Butler, Gayatri Spivak, Homi Bhabha, Henry Louis Gates, and Houston Baker, to name but a few of the leading exponents of these approaches, all took over central theses from Derrida's 1967 (and 1973) works and drew on what Derrida had accomplished when they gave definitive shape to their own thought (see Sedgwick, *Epistemology of the Closet*, 92; Butler, *Gender Trouble*, 32–34; Bhabha, *The Location of Culture*, 110, 115, 116; Baker, *Blues, Ideology, and Afro-American Literature*, 123). My point here is by no means to denegate these significant achievements, but rather to ask about the possibility of future equivalent ones and whence they might stem.

10. I have in mind here Derrida's engagement with Husserl's late historical thought in his 1962 "Introduction"—Husserl's work on geometry indeed purporting to give a novel "history" of geometry's objects, which Husserl believed in part to be types of essences. I comment on this phase of Husserl's work and Derrida's engagement with it in chapter 3.

11. I should mention, by way of anticipation, that Lawlor, though he comments on this same passage central to my own account, seems not to have grasped its consequences for Derrida's thought in their specificity. Lawlor treats Derrida, along with Husserl, Heidegger, Merleau-Ponty, and even Levinas, as roughly all engaged in the same enterprise (see Lawlor 2002, 1–2), and he does not seem to see the deep methodological differences that divide them: those that separate Husserl from Heidegger or Merleau-Ponty especially. Consequently, he does not grasp that the unique position of Derrida in this tradition to some extent stems from allying himself *intra-philosophically* with Husserl, siding with Husserl on all the most important points—those concerning the status of essences and the authority of the reductions—thus rejecting all intra-philosophical empiricism, and only from there launching his engagement with what purports to exceed philosophy's purview altogether (cf. Lawlor 2002, 83, 66).

12. Lawlor also points out the importance of Fink for Derrida's early thought and his orientation toward phenomenology. Yet he never makes clear, to the extent that I follow him, how in *Derrida's own work* the problem of Husserl's transcendental-phenomenological reduction relates to the problem of genesis or,

more important, where Derrida himself stands on these questions that are defining ones for any phenomenology (see Lawlor 2002, 21–23). This is a symptom of a larger problem with Lawlor's treatment, which is visible in the very organization of his book and in his rather surprising claim that deconstruction is to be understood as a form of criticism or critique (Lawlor 2002, 3, 24). Lawlor's chapters are organized such that he begins with a discussion of a prominent phenomenological commentator (or, in the case of Hyppolite, a Hegelian one), only subsequently turning to Derrida's own texts. Since, however, all Derrida's texts are taken to be criticisms of phenomenology, the positive contribution of Husserl's thought to Derrida's own is never broached by Lawlor, nor is the delicate issue faced of how Derrida may simultaneously maintain this positive contribution even as he claims to go beyond it: how he may retain the Husserlian evidences and starting points (and thus not lapse into skepticism), yet also ultimately delimit Husserl's enterprise as a whole. The actual import of these issues in phenomenology for Derrida's own thought is thus never really cashed out: the segregation of the one phase of Lawlor's discussion from the other makes visible the distance that almost everywhere separates Lawlor's commentary on Derrida from the concrete phenomenological and philosophical problematics which introduce these discussions—all this, despite the unarguable contribution Lawlor's work has made (his latest writings as well as his earlier), thanks to the important historical considerations that Lawlor does bring to bear.

Chapter 1

1. Again, I am aware that Derrida has since reconceived what he understands by deconstruction in tandem with his so-called turn to religion. Derrida has done this, however, on the basis of his earlier work, to which he constantly makes reference; and if we are ever to get straight about where Derrida stands now, and what this really represents, it will be necessary to arrive at an independent evaluation of his earlier positions of the sort I am undertaking here. (Again, my stance may be contrasted with Lawlor's most recent work, which attempts to explicate Derrida's earlier thought in a framework made possible only by his most recent writings.)

2. A. J. Cascardi, in an especially influential essay, argued that deconstruction, while differing from traditional skepticism, arrives at an even more skeptical result than it. Deconstruction affirms "radical doubt (madness)"; in "contrast . . . [to] the Wittgensteinian response [where] . . . reason . . . remains the stable anchor, the pivot around which doubt and knowledge turn" (Cascardi 1984, 11; cf. Wilmore 1987). This interpretation of deconstruction as a new, more radical skepticism, often language-based, has been particularly widespread, well beyond Cascardi's and Wilmore's construal, for reasons this chapter eventually brings forward. It remains the most prevalent one even today, extending from "popularizers" of deconstruction like Christopher Norris and Jonathan Culler to more "specialized" recent critics like Robert Bernasconi, Simon Critchley, and Ewa Ziarek. For most of these critics a more radical skepticism is not the only thing that de-

construction aims to accomplish, but for all of them this plays an important role. In my "Deconstruction and Skepticism: The First Wave" (Kates 2002), I have discussed these issues at greater length, and I am reprising part of that argument here.

3. Culler's claim comes in the course of comparing deconstruction's skepticism with that of a more traditional skeptic, David Hume; and Culler claims that deconstruction's undecidability, "this double procedure of systematically employing the concepts or premises one is undermining puts the critic in a position not of skeptical detachment but of unwarrantable involvement." Culler then appeals to Nietzsche to offer a more radically skeptical deconstructive treatment of cause than Hume's (Culler 1982, 88; cf. Bennington 1994, 14).

4. Derrida's earliest statement of such commitment remains the opening of his 1964 essay "Violence and Metaphysics," where he identifies himself with the "community . . . of those who are still called philosophers," even if he stipulates that such a community, a "community of the question," "may even be" founded on "questions [that] are not philosophical" simply ("VM" 79; cf. 80, where Derrida also speaks of "an unbreachable responsibility" and those who "look into the possibility of philosophy" and "act in remembrance of philosophy"). A number of more recent American interpreters, perhaps John Caputo foremost among them, have insisted that Derrida *decides* on undecidability for the sake of a renewed and more encompassing responsibility (Caputo 1993); few, if any, however, have raised the question of whether Derrida, or deconstruction in its most canonical form, in fact wholly succeeds at this.

5. Rorty seems to prefer "recontextualization" (e.g., Rorty 1989, 134; 1998, 311n7), though the point remains the same. Since Rorty believes, as he repeatedly indicates, that one can only argue in a "language game" whose "rules" one accepts, Derrida cannot in any way be offering arguments against the philosophers he reads, according to Rorty, or exposing problems with their work, but must rather be "recontextualizing" them: making "suggestions" for new ways of viewing their work (Rorty 1991, 125), offering novel descriptions of what they were saying which lack the pragmatic conditions for the sort of semantic stabilization that would allow these suggestions to be deemed right or wrong, to be assigned truth values of any sort. Derrida aims at "autonomy" (Rorty 1989, 137), not truth, Rorty claims, and Rorty frames Derrida's project, as well as his own, in these terms—as redescriptions, or recontextualizations of those that he and Derrida comment on. I will return to Rorty's singular claims concerning the status of Derrida's arguments, as well as his own, and treat them at greater length in the final section of this chapter. (For Derrida, see Rorty 1977, 697; 1982, 93; 1991, 93, 120; 1998, 10, 313. Rorty explicitly avows that his own work functions in this way at *Contingency, Irony, and Solidarity* 8; this is what he appears to designate by talk of "ironist theorizing," and Rorty implies this sort of self-understanding and that his own positions have no truth values on numerous other occasions: e.g., Rorty 1982, 107; 1991, 105, 121; 1989, 125; 1998, 319–20.)

6. Thus Gasché at a central point in his argument in "Deconstruction as Criticism" emphasized the need for both reversal and reinscription to be taken into account: "What does . . . deconstruction consist of, what does it accomplish,

and to what effect is it being carried out . . . Two movements are . . . characteristic
of deconstruction: a *reversal* of the traditional hierarchy . . . and a *reinscription* of
the newly privileged turn" (Gasché 1994a, 38).

7. The discussion of *Of Grammatology* about to be set out, it should be noted,
is only provisional. In the final chapter of *Essential History,* I will bring forward an
interpretation of these same sections of *Of Grammatology* focused on the trace. This
interpretation treats these sections in far greater detail, with the aim of clarifying
once and for all the actual object or topic of Derrida's discussion here (whether it
is language, infrastructures, alterity, etc.), something only possible after Derrida's
development and the problems that gave rise to it have been set out. In what follows, then, Derrida's text and the broader schemas of deconstruction offered by
Derrida himself (reversal and reinscription) as well as his commentators (quasi-
transcendentals) are all being approached together, and my sole concern is to
show that these indeed apply, that this portion of *Of Grammatology* may well be
viewed in this way, with an eye to eventually setting out a problem with the "architecture," if one will, of Derrida's thinking. In chapter 6 an entirely new view of this
text is intended, one that in part assumes I am right about the issue brought forward here.

8. Rorty seems to have started out believing that Derrida, as opposed to Heidegger, perhaps uniquely avoided this dilemma (Rorty 1977, 677). By the time of
"Philosophy as a Kind of Writing," a good and a bad side of deconstruction, a de-
constructivist and constructivist side, had emerged (Rorty 1982, 99); this opposition then morphed into this dilemma here, as well as in "Is Derrida a Transcendental Philosopher" (Rorty 1991, 125), surfacing also as a "a self-referential"
problem in *Contingency, Irony, and Solidarity* (1989, 125). It plays a lesser, though
still visible, role in Rorty's later work, as a more concrete problem coordinated
with it comes to the fore. The latter I examine on pages 23–31 in this chapter.

9. "The system of language associated with the phonetic-alphabetic writing is
that within which logocentric metaphysics, determining the sense of being as
presence, has been produced" (*G* 43).

10. As will become clearer when the development of Derrida's methodology
is explored in my chapter on *Le problème,* the notion of the supplement that Derrida brings forward in the second half of *Of Grammatology* is clearly meant to address my and Rorty's concern: to thematize how something added on after—here
entailing a mode of thinking already called into question—can nevertheless bring
us before what is most original or oldest, an *arche,* albeit one understood *sous ra-
ture.* Nevertheless, since this logic of the supplement is itself brought forward
through the very sort of operation it is supposed to justify (through a supplementary *reading* of "supplement" in Rousseau), and thus presumes the validity it appears to establish (it really being more of a description of the problem than its resolution, as Derrida undoubtedly knows), I doubt that this conception would do
much to assuage Rorty's doubts. At a minimum, this implication of the supplement in its own functioning has been a further cause of what I have already described: the disappearance in the literature of Derrida's transcendental concerns
as they actually manifest themselves in his text.

11. David Wood in an early essay, it is worth noting, offered a similar mapping

of deconstruction in order to define a problem with it, yet he ended specifying one almost precisely the opposite of mine and Rorty's here. For Wood the issue was how Derrida, or anyone, could ever stop doing metaphysics or philosophy, not start (Wood 1980, 231). And thus Wood, I believe, underestimates the inherently skeptical force of these opening considerations, though his conclusions have kept Wood's work afterward in closer contact with philosophy than many of Derrida's other readers, even while Wood's own stated qualms about deconstruction have fallen away, as far as I can tell.

12. "Even if those relations are . . . relations of pure idealities and 'truths,' they do not therein give rise any less to some singular placings in perspective, some multiple interconnections of sense, and therefore some mediate and potential aims." The context of Derrida's remark is the famous comparison between Husserl and Joyce. Derrida's point is that any insight, even one capable of genuinely founding a true body of knowledge such as geometry, must necessarily be open to equivocity and sedimentation, and thus lack total transparency, at the moment of its inauguration, as long it remains within history, even the sort of transcendental history that Husserl describes. My chapter 3 offers an extended commentary on Derrida's discussion of these matters in the key section 7 of the "Introduction," one whose nuances still seem to elude many of Derrida's readers.

13. On the unlikeliness of the role that authors like Schnadelbach and Werner Flach are assigned to play in *Tain,* see Robert Bernasconi's review (Bernasconi 1988a, 225). Bernasconi brings forward concerns akin to those I am about to set out (Bernasconi 1988a, 228). He does this, however, in the name of an alternative way of viewing deconstruction that he himself has articulated; he believes that the critic must each time approach deconstruction by way of Derrida's own "double readings" of the philosophers that Derrida comments on (Bernasconi 1988a, 228). Elsewhere, I have argued that this account of deconstruction in terms of "double reading" is neither coherent in its own right nor authentically Derridean (Kates 1993, 321). And while this issue of the hermeneutics of deconstruction receives further elaboration in my chapter 2, let me simply add here that Bernasconi's approach, though undoubtedly fruitful in many ways, and having yielded some of the best individual work on Derrida to date, confines Derrida's project wholly to one in the *history* of philosophy—it makes of deconstruction solely a new way of doing philosophical commentary in a historical register. Understood as double reading, deconstruction is but a new phase in the historical interpretation of philosophical texts—a little more inventive but no different in kind than the work that someone like Bernasconi or I myself might undertake. This limitation, to be sure, is the source of much that is strongest in Bernasconi's own practice (and many of those who follow this path), due to the kind of sound scholarship that this work exhibits and that Bernasconi here enjoins (Bernasconi sides with Gasché at the end of his review in rightfully imploring more such scholarship). Nevertheless, this approach seriously downplays the scope of Derrida's own ambitions. As far back as 1954 Derrida had refused to limit his intervention to the history of philosophy, apparently ending up dissatisfied with *Le problème* for falling within these bounds (*LPG* 1n1/*PG* xvii n1). And it remains to Gasché's

credit (along with Rorty's) to have attempted to cash Derrida's ambitions out in their own right, to approach this work argumentatively and in principle, beyond an episode in the history of philosophy, despite whatever other pitfalls they may have encountered.

14. Gasché has just invoked a discussion of Aristotle's in the *Metaphysics* to motivate the turn his argument is in the course of taking here. Without entering into an interpretation of Aristotle's own remarks (which I read rather differently), suffice it to note that: (a) as Gasché would readily concede, Aristotle himself would never agree to the sort of abandonment of philosophical norms that Gasché at this moment embraces (Aristotle arguably having been their originary institutor); and (b) as I make plain in note 16, this problem is one that does not just surface here but affects Gasché's argument in *Tain* at a number of decisive points.

15. It should also be noted that this problem has left its mark even more deeply on those skeptical readers whom Gasché tried to answer. For none of these commentators believed that such skepticism was the sole thing that deconstruction intended. Neither Culler nor Norris, to confine ourselves to them, believed deconstruction aimed at skepticism alone (see Culler 1982, 85–86; Norris 1987, 86); rather, having grasped this first phase of reversal, they could not successfully conceive how it could ever accomplish anything else; they could give no coherent account of where Derrida went from there, even though they were aware he did go beyond even radical skepticism.

16. We have already begun to see Gasché do the former; places in *Tain* where Gasché does the latter tend to cluster at the end of *Tain,* in the course of Gasché's individual treatment of the infrastructures. (See Gasché 1986, 206, 208 on the supplement; 214, 215 on iterability; 223 on the mark; and especially see 236, where Gasché appears to be forced to arrive at exactly the opposite conclusion that his discussion of Schnadelbach earlier set out and now declares that "from [Derrida's] perspective the elements of the aporias of reflection evade all final solution.")

17. As far back as 1954, Derrida had already proclaimed that the apriori with which he worked had led "to quitting the plane of classical philosophy" altogether (*à quitter le plan de philosophie classique; LPG* 102/ *PG* 48). Derrida's construal of the transcendental and the apriori thus differs from Kant's, and is meant to withstand the criticism that Rorty here (perhaps rightfully) makes of Gasché's and Bennington's treatment of the transcendental as succumbing to illicit substantialist commitments. At the same time, even if not identifiable with Kant's treatment, the status of the concept in Derrida's thought and of the apriori generally, as well as whether Derrida may be said to have made the linguistic turn in the form that it is most usually recognized, are important issues—issues still largely unexplored in the literature, and which my final two chapters, particularly the last, investigate in some detail. Here I am establishing the overall philosophical context in which Derrida arrived at these decisions.

18. See also the three essays in Rorty's *Philosophical Papers II* (1991, especially 106, 110n4, and 126).

19. That Rorty's interest is really in a linguistic starting point for philosophy rather than some other—as opposed to the issue of transcendental arguments per

se—is further confirmed by his admission earlier that he is willing to admit transcendental arguments as long as they are linguistically based (Rorty 1998, 331n6; cf. Rorty 1991, 112).

20. Even while Bennington does much good work in this section, it should be noted that his understanding of the notion of the transcendental itself is somewhat shaky, whether taken in a Kantian context or some other. At times Bennington seems to confuse the "transcendental" with "transcendence" (Bennington 1993, 277), though these are virtually opposite philosophical notions in a modern context. And thus while Bennington comes up with this important formulation of the work of deconstruction, he sometimes falters when it comes to giving concrete accounts of Derrida's individual texts.

21. A little bit earlier in this essay Rorty explicitly avows "being nominalist and historicist," defends "Dewey . . . conducting empirical inquiries," and asserts that "his [Dewey's] historicosociological tale . . . suggests that we might now be in a position to escape from the philosophical tradition" (Rorty 1998, 334–35). This is in line with the role that the application of Kuhn to the history of philosophy has always played for Rorty—an application that seems to me un-Kuhnian and to be prima facie the least convincing stand of all those Rorty takes in these debates (Rorty 1977, 679; 1982, 104; 1991, 88n6; 1998, 359n14).

22. Rorty explicitly refuses to admit my claim, on at least one occasion, it should be noted: he denies that he has any interest in "the nature and function of philosophy" (Rorty 1998, 317), in pursuing debates in what he sometimes calls metaphilosophy. Yet not only do his own views on this seem to have altered somewhat over time (see Rorty 1977, 681; 1991, 86n3, 93n14), but more centrally perhaps, Rorty discusses nothing else, and even his apparent philosophical assertions, his critique of the concept, his advocacy of nominalism (and so on), do not pertain to philosophical inquiry, normal philosophical discussion as Rorty himself defines it, but rather are made in the service of motivating Rorty's own claims that philosophy be abandoned and are thus metaphilosophical through and through— as our discussion of Rorty's recontextualizations just below will further clarify.

23. Rorty makes this distinction between "inferential connections between sentences, the connections that give the words used in these sentences their meaning" and all other usages of words, which are properly meaningless, lacking the pragmatic consensus that would establish these connections, most clearly in the essay first cited, "Deconstruction and Circumvention" (Rorty 1991, 97), though it is a leitmotif of almost all his discussions of Derrida (Rorty 1982, 98; 1991, 126; 1989, 135; 1998, 314).

24. I take Rorty himself to be conceding something like this when he speaks of philosophy "now surviv[ing] largely in the form of self-parody" (Rorty 1989, 105) and in his repeated remarks about "ironist theorizing," which is "the only solution to the self-referential problem which such theorizing encounters" (Rorty 1989, 125).

25. Derrida's relation to Hegel is certainly an important one, and I comment on it further below. It is perhaps time to face the fact, however, that if the price of admission to deconstruction, to Derrida's project, is the affirmation of the literal truth of Hegel's system, then that price is just too high. The traditional criticisms

of Hegel, centering on the role of nature and the knowledge of nature in his program, seem to me as convincing as ever. There are others, relating to the role of the logic and the Kantian concept in Hegel's thought, brought out, most notably, by Thomas Seebohm, that also seem to me important and indeed border on some of Rorty's concerns.

26. Bennington's lack of familiarity with Husserl apart from Derrida's account of him inhibits his argument not only here, but generally. The problem he has in really specifying the transcendental and its relation to transcendence noted above is traceable back to this. See his section "Husserl" (Bennington 1993, 64–84), in particular 68.

27. It is worth noting in this context that Rorty himself has recently seen fit to declare that "truth is, to be sure, an absolute notion" (Rorty 1998, 2), which seems to me to be something of a shift from his earlier position, though here he denies it is a decisive one (cf. Rorty 1982, xxvi, on James).

Chapter 2

1. Again, as previously noted, Len Lawlor's 2002 book furnishes a significant example of a work which ultimately assumes that no real development takes place within Derrida's *philosophical thinking*—that all his texts, at least as far as their relation to phenomenology is concerned, may be viewed by way of a single theme, that of genesis—even as Lawlor himself is fairly sensitive to the specific historical variations that Derrida's thought overall may seem to undergo. In the chapters that follow, especially chapters 3 and 4, I will point out my specific differences from Lawlor: where in Derrida's understanding of Husserl, and in his stance toward related thinkers such as Fink or Cavaillès, Lawlor sees no substantial changes or departures, in contrast to the differences among Derrida's first writings in respect to these and other thinkers, to which I assign considerably more importance.

2. Rorty's claim that Derrida's interchanges with the philosophical tradition take the form of "recontextualizations" rather than arguments (see Rorty 1989, 134, especially), which my last chapter treated, is one attempt to specify the unique hermeneutics of deconstruction. Paul de Man's classic discussion in "The Rhetoric of Blindness" is another. As I have noted, there is a strong line of Derrida interpretation, most extensively thematized by Robert Bernasconi, that sees Derrida as engaged in double readings: starting from a first traditional, or dominant, reading, which is then compounded with a second "parasitic" and more unusual one (Bernasconi 1988a, 228). My primary objection to Bernasconi's suggestion has long been that there cannot be *two* distinct readings discernible in Derrida's text (since the second, the vehicle of Derrida's own insights, would thus be deprived of all its motivation [Kates 1993, 321]). In what follows, I try to offer a substitute that might function more satisfactorily, even while giving its due to the problem Bernasconi's formulation acknowledges, yet does not satisfactorily resolve—namely, how Derrida is to honor both his own aims and those he reads at one and the same time.

3. Some of the most recent work on Derrida, in particular Michael Nass's *Taking on the Tradition* (2003) and Marian Hobson's *Jacques Derrida: Opening Lines* (1998), has begun to confront these issues more directly.

4. Despite the enormous attention given to Derrida's 1967 works, it should be recalled that even today very few commentaries are available that gloss Derrida's actual statements, that even claim to set out the specific arguments he makes page by page, though these arguments are often of an astonishing degree of difficulty and density, and thus cry out for such treatment. As far back as *Jacques Derrida*, Derrida himself had taken note of this lacuna, in the specific case of Bennington's commentary (Derrida 1993, 16). One aim of the present work, accordingly, is to foster and embark on such commentary, with the result, admittedly, of arguing that there are reasons internal to Derrida's own way of working that have impeded this sort of discussion so far.

5. For a rare, recent reflection on the proximity of phenomenology and analytic philosophy from the analytic side, see Michael Dummett, *Origins of Analytical Philosophy* (1993).

6. Besides Rorty, Searle (whom I intend to discuss elsewhere), and Henry Staten, Samuel Wheeler is the critic best versed in analytic philosophy of language who has lately devoted serious attention to Derrida's thought. His various attempts to explicate Derrida for Anglo-American philosophers have recently borne fruit in the form of a book (Wheeler 2000). While I find Wheeler to be a careful thinker in his own right and I find much that is provocative and quite insightful in his work, finally, as should be clear, the main difference between us is that Wheeler sees Derrida primarily as a thinker (or philosopher) of language, while, though I believe this is a critical theme, I argue it finally takes shape in a context provided by a very different set of concerns. Meaning, from a phenomenological perspective, is not primarily a linguistic phenomenon at all, and only after *Husserl's* relation to analytic thought more generally is taken into account, I believe, is the corresponding mapping of Derrida's program on to analytic philosophy able to get at the most decisive issues here.

7. The characterization of the depth of these differences just offered is, of course, an exaggeration, though only a slight one. Yet readers more oriented toward Derrida's thought, as I am about to show, do think Derrida is on to something, for the most part (see Sallis 1992; Lawlor 1994, 2002; Gasché 1994b; Hobson 1998, 7–58; Howells 1998; Marrati-Guénoun 1998, 7–98). Many argumentatively oriented Husserl scholars, in turn, *are* critical of Derrida's Husserl interpretation. (Evans, Hopkins, Willard, and the early White find little persuasive in Derrida's Husserl readings: White 1987, 59; Evans 1991, 184; Willard 1995, 41; Hopkins 1996, 79.) Some scholars in each camp are doubtless harder to place than others. Mohanty has a more nuanced view than Evans (Mohanty 1997, 62–76). Llewellyn sees more difficulties than Lawlor (Llewellyn 1986, 16–31). The most preeminent Husserl scholars other than Mohanty to have weighed in on this issue, Bernet and Seebohm, tend to have the most nuanced views. Bernet, Seebohm, and Mohanty are all acutely aware of the problems Husserl's thought leaves in its wake and are thus much less closed off to assistance, wherever it may come (Seebohm 1995; see also Depp 1987, 241; Hopkins 1985, 212; White 1987, 59). (In this note and others,

and in some of what follows in my text, I present material some of which I already brought forward in a 2003 *Husserl Studies* article devoted to the debate over Derrida's relation to Husserl.)

8. "My aim is . . . with what Derrida . . . takes Husserl to have said" (White 1987, 46; cf. Depp 1987, 226; Evans 1991, xv; Mohanty 1997, 62). Hopkins has a more nuanced view (Hopkins 1985, 193–94, but cf. 204).

9. "I will not . . . be directly concerned with Derrida's various criticisms and his deconstruction of Husserl; however to the extent such criticisms and deconstructions rest on his understanding of Husserl, they would unavoidably be affected by our evaluation of that understanding" (Mohanty 1997, 62; cf. Evans 1991, xv; Depp 1987, 226; White 1987, 46). Again, Hopkins is something of an exception. Even Hopkins's aim, however, is to show that "a lack of warrant characterizes Derrida's account of Husserl's thought" (Hopkins 1985, 194).

10. Modeling his own interpretation on the style he believes to be Derrida's, Gasché states this as follows: "'*Through* (à travers) Husserl's text,' is indeed the way Derrida has characterized his reading of the first *Logical Investigation* in *Speech and Phenomena*. This is a reading that cuts across the text in order to go beyond it" (Gasché 1994b, 3, Gasché's emphasis; cf. Hopkins 1985, 195). Many other commentators work this way as well, though rarely this explicitly (Sallis 1992, 123–24; Hobson 1998, 7, 9; Howells 1998, 7; Lawlor 1998, 185; Marrati-Guénoun 1998, 9; but cf. Marrati-Guénoun 1998, 36n81—her important work, the recent English translation of which came too late to be referred to here, is finally closest to mine in a number of important respects and is treated repeatedly in later chapters).

11. Lawlor, after all, is not simply wrong in the end. Without an understanding of Derrida's aims, the sense of Derrida's assertions concerning Husserl cannot even be gotten straight (the former providing the context for the latter), and understanding the meaning of Derrida's statements about Husserl, of course, is the condition for doing what the first camp wants: judging whether these statements are true. A serious confrontation with Derrida's thought is thus necessary in order to know what Derrida is saying Husserl is saying (especially given the manner in which Derrida's own concerns explicitly exceed Husserl's intentions), even though what the first camp demands also ought not to be omitted. Lawlor's remark was made in the course of an interchange with Claude Evans, who, it should be noted, remained unconvinced. Evans asked how the bite of Derrida's intentions' is to be felt without "starting with Husserl's texts and Derrida's reading of them?" (Evans 1996, 316). Evans calls this the "how do we get there from here" problem, and he put this problem to me first (see Kates 1993; Evans, Kates, and Lawlor 1998, 228; Evans 1996, 316); I hope with this more recent formulation to have responded to some of his questions. Evans's work, despite its shortcomings when it comes to Derrida's thought, was a spur to investigate all these matters more carefully when I first encountered it. Though I had already begun to study these issues extensively, Evans indeed roused me from a certain dogmatic slumber when it came to Derrida and Husserl.

12. Claude Evans himself repeatedly says this: "Both elements are necessary: critical attention to the rigor of Derrida's interpretation of Husserl and an openness to a challenge that might threaten the very sense of Husserl's enterprise"

(Evans 1991, xviii; cf. Evans 1996, 316). Evans believes that these can go on as distinct enterprises, however: some pay attention to rigor, others inquire into this threat (Evans 1996, 316). Such a division of labor is not feasible, as I believe the current state of Derrida/Husserl criticism shows.

13. Here the merits of the double reading school in general, and Robert Bernasconi's work in particular, must be recognized. Their explicit methodology may miss the mark, in my view, but in practice Bernasconi, Sallis, Llewellyn, Caputo, Krell, and Wood (to name but some of these contributors) have come closest to undertaking the sort of readings that I have been describing—honoring both Derrida and his author at once.

14. I am referring here to *Le problème* and Derrida's "Introduction."

15. Perhaps the key example of such sedimentation is Derrida's talk of the "constitution" of ideality, first by way of a subjective "power of repetition" and later on thanks to "writing" as this surfaces in *Speech* (*SP* 58/*VP* 52–53; *SP* 90/*VP* 80). Hopkins, Willard, and other Husserlians take Derrida to be denying ideal objectivity's atemporal (or omnitemporal) status by way of this claim. "For every ideal object there is a point in cosmic time when it does not exist," Willard says Derrida claims (Willard 1995, 38; cf. Hopkins 1995, 85). Derrida has always been aware of ideality's rights and defended them from the first, however. Derrida has always known there is a problem with attributing genesis to ideality in any straightforward way. "It is necessary in order that all genesis, all development, all discourse may have a sense, that this sense would be in some fashion 'already there,' from the first" (*LPG* 9/*PG* xxiii). "The primordial passage to the limit is possible only if guided by an essence which can always be anticipated and then 'recognized,' because a *truth* of pure space is in question. That is why passages to the limit are not to be done arbitrarily or aimlessly" (*IOG* 135, Derrida's emphasis; cf. Depp 1987, 227). This is not the last word on these matters, doubtless. The key point is this. Derrida's 1967 writings take these claims for granted. Some of Derrida's views do change in *Speech* in difficult and surprising ways. Even those changes assume these earlier steps. Derrida denies his work is historicist, relativist, skeptical, even today. And Willard's powerful though idiosyncratic Husserl interpretation, in particular, fails to hit its mark and serves no productive end, attacking Derrida's "historicist/ nominalist interpretation of Husserl" (Willard 1995, 35), due to Willard's neglect of Derrida's organizing aims and those aims' sedimented development.

16. J. N. Mohanty has also drawn attention to something like this phenomenon, noting that Derrida "may be said to read—as Barry Smith, a dear friend complained of to me—the earlier work of Husserl in the light of the later" (Mohanty 1997, 65). Mohanty attributes this to Derrida's belief "in the continuity of Husserl's thought," which is also true, along with the reason offered here concerning Derrida's prolonged prior engagement with Husserl. Mohanty agrees with Derrida about Husserl's corpus's continuity, it should be noted: "insisting as he [Derrida] does, and rightly in my view, on the continuity of Husserl's thought" (Mohanty 1997, 64). That's just one sign of the extraordinary closeness (but also, consequently, distance) between Mohanty's and Derrida's Husserl readings. Mohanty's treatment of Derrida overall is sober, serious, and respectful. On that Mohanty and Mohanty's "dear friend" unfortunately diverge (cf. Derrida 1995, 419–21).

17. This may seem a rather strong conclusion to draw: to claim that *Speech* is in any way flawed; yet it should be emphasized just how great a gap exists between Derrida's discussion of Husserl in *Speech* and that of a majority of responsible Husserlians. I hope the foregoing has made clear that my own aim is in fact to narrow this gap, and I believe that much of importance in Derrida depends on this, to some extent, even the future of Derrida studies as a viable discipline. Only if these problems are really recognized, not avoided or denegated, can solutions be found, and I, at least, have enough confidence in Derrida's acumen as a Husserlian to believe a convincing case can be made for his interpretations.

18. Practically speaking, this initial distance or deviation *from which Derrida's readings begin* is what the advocates of "double reading" ignore, both in their explicit hermeneutics and too often also in their actual interpretation, despite the good work they have done in so many individual instances.

19. Chapter 5 treats *Speech* in great detail, including Derrida's treatment in his first three chapters of Husserl's initial discussion of the sign. There I try to situate this treatment in the context of Derrida's larger argument; nevertheless, to stay with just this instance, Husserl himself, it must be recognized, clearly is not interested in giving an account of semiosis in general at this moment, but indeed readily admits that all he says is provisional and oriented toward his subsequent logical work. And thus to the extent Derrida appears to attack Husserl on the grounds that Husserl has given an inadequate account of linguistic and semiotic functioning, not only is such an attack unpersuasive, but it obscures a key feature that Husserl's and Derrida's approaches ultimately have in common: that neither thinker is finally interested in providing a theory of language, or a philosophy of language, as such, though for quite different reasons. (See Kates 1998 for an earlier attempt at setting out Derrida's real intentions in these very difficult early pages of *Speech*.)

20. Many commentators discuss *Speech* without referring to the earlier writings at all (Evans 1991; Sallis 1992, 103). Those who do examine the early work see *some* differences, doubtless. Underlying unity is asserted (or assumed) almost always (Llewellyn 1986, 22; Gasché 1994b, 3–4; Marrati-Guénoun 1998, 10, 40, 44; Howells 1998, 12; Hobson 1998, 8—Hobson's approach to Derrida's early Husserl writings as instances of "Derridean syntax" assumes this too). Hopkins and Depp are some of the few in their camp to discuss the "Introduction" in depth. Both assume this unity. Depp brings in *Speech* and *Writing and Difference* in the course of a discussion of the "Introduction" without further comment (Depp 1987, 236n25). Hopkins's "Introduction" discussion goes decisively wrong because he just assumes agreement between the "Introduction" and *Speech* at a key point (Hopkins 1995, 84). The unity thesis hinders what remain important achievements by these authors. Lawlor is something of an exception here. It is to Lawlor's credit to have raised the development issue explicitly at all (Lawlor 1992, 109–10; 1996b, 118–21). Lawlor's Derrida interpretations here and in his latest work, as has already been suggested, tend to minimize developmental concerns in practice, however, despite the useful suggestions they sometimes provide (see Lawlor 1992, 25). This will be more concretely documented in the case of Lawlor's latest work in my next two chapters.

21. Some commentators do importantly distinguish among Derrida's Husserl writings. A major distinction between *Speech* in its entirety and Derrida's prior work on Husserl (the "Introduction") is recognized by both Bernet and Dastur. "There is . . . a clear difference in Derrida's reading of Husserl in 1962 and in 1967. In the 'Introduction' phenomenology is not unilaterally seen as a restoration of metaphysics" (Dastur 1994, 121–22n37). It is "very striking that in the present work [the "Introduction"] Derrida still deals with these themes in the context of a transcendental philosophy—albeit one of a new kind" (Bernet 1989, 151–52). Why even Dastur and Bernet are led to downplay the difference both see is discussed below in my next paragraph. J. N. Mohanty is an equally important exception. Mohanty shows an exemplary awareness of *Speech and Phenomena*'s hermeneutic situation (Mohanty 1997, 64–66) and makes a stronger distinction between *Speech* and the "Introduction" than anyone else, arguably. Mohanty has no quarrel with the "Introduction's" Husserl interpretation at all. ("Derrida's understanding . . . in his "Introduction" is in my view as 'Husserlian' as any other . . . Derrida's is a viable interpretation, faithful to the texts, aware of the enormous complexities of Husserl's thinking" [Mohanty 1997, 75].) Yet Mohanty has big differences with *Speech*. Mohanty's comments point toward the possibility that a deep change of perspective on Derrida's part took place between the "Introduction" and *Speech,* a suggestion that Mohanty himself nowhere follows up.

22. Derrida, for whatever reasons, seems reluctant to speak of his thought from a genuinely developmental perspective, at least on the occasions that have so far presented themselves, in the sense that he almost never specifies real obstacles or problems that he had to resolve in order to arrive at his mature thought. Perhaps the most notable example of such reluctance is Derrida's 1990 "Avertissement" for his 1954 *Le problème*—the most prominent instance in which Derrida has had to acknowledge real discontinuity between his earlier and a later work. Even in this instance, however, Derrida never states that he has changed his mind in a significant fashion (or how or why), but instead presents this change in standpoint as a purely lexical matter. "Mais à travers les moments, les configurations, les effets de cette loi, la 'contamination' originaire de l'origine recoit alors un nom philosophique auquel j'ai dú renouncer: la dialectique, une 'dialectique originaire.' Le mot revient avec insistance, page après page" (*LPG* 7; cf., however, *LPG* 264n12, where Derrida does specify an actual change of mind, and a critical one at that, which I discuss below). The role of *Le problème* in Derrida's early corpus—which is that of a stabilizing force, a pole of continuity, in my view, in contrast to the "Introduction," which proves to be an agent of change—is discussed in detail in my chapter 4.

23. The "Introduction" *can,* of course, be understood in some fashion to take up the topics that Derrida lists here. A long note in the "Introduction" goes into the phenomenological discourse problem in great depth (*IOG* 69–70n66). Intuitionism and the living present's privilege are questioned in the "Introduction" insofar as Husserl's intuitionism answers to a teleology (and the functioning of an Idea in a Kantian sense) that this intuitionism (Husserl's principle of principles) cannot account for, such that "phenomenology cannot be reflected in a phenomenology of phenomenology" (*IOG* 141). For related reasons "resting in the simple

maintenance of a living present" is said to be impossible as well (*IOG* 153). None of this should make us overlook the following. Husserl's unthought axiomatic *does not* hold center stage in the "Introduction." Phenomenology's discourse's discussion takes place in a footnote and ends on an ambiguous note. Intuitionism and the living present's privilege are raised as thematic problems only at the "Introduction's" end, on the work's outskirts. They are not its central focus, and even at the end of the "Introduction" Derrida concludes by affirming "a *primordial and pure* consciousness of difference" (*IOG* 153, my emphasis) and by announcing that "difference would be *transcendental*" (*IOG* 153, my emphasis). The opening discussion of my chapter 3 fleshes this point out further, presenting the work of the "Introduction" as it would have looked in context at the time it appeared, rather than in light of Derrida's subsequent achievements.

Chapter 3

1. Rudolf Bernet is first and foremost whom I have in mind here; his important 1989 interpretation of the "Introduction's" section 7 has guided all who followed after him. Bernet's treatment is illuminating, subtle, and careful, and I will refer to it repeatedly, making clear its relation to my own. Bernet, nevertheless, does seem to substantially identify Derrida's treatment of writing in the "Introduction" with that in his later work ("writing makes possible the development of an original sense and also produces the loss of sense . . . thus it is no surprise that Derrida soon began to treat historical events and experiences as particular forms of the universal structure of the written sign or the trace" [Bernet 1989, 144–45]). Bernet seems to assume that the same problematic of writing is in place in 1962 and 1967, even as he recognizes other important differences between the "Introduction" and Derrida's later writings (Bernet 1989, 151–52; cf. Dastur 1994, 121–22n37). Subsequent commentators, with the notable exception of Hopkins, have largely followed Bernet, and I will refer to their readings in what follows as well.

2. Lawlor had also noticed this absence of context (Lawlor 1995, 156n22), and in his 2002 book he attempts to make good on this omission. Since, however, in *Derrida and Husserl* Lawlor, on the one hand, approaches the entirety of the "Introduction" through a discussion of Hyppolite (Hyppolite's work, according to Lawlor, caused Derrida to turn to language as a theme at this period—not anything intrinsic to Derrida's own ongoing engagement with Husserlian phenomenology [Lawlor 2002, 102]), and since, on the other hand, Lawlor is finally interested in finding in the "Introduction" an anticipation of Derrida's notion of *différance* (from this stems the title of his chapter "The Root, That Is Necessarily One, of Every Dilemma" [Lawlor 2002, 88]), Derrida's deepening understanding of Husserl's work, and the shift in orientation toward it I am about to present—in short, Derrida's development—is ignored. This is part and parcel of Lawlor's broader orientation, thanks to which Lawlor denegates many of the historical insights and actual differences in Derrida's thought that he himself often brings forward. For Lawlor sees Derrida as everywhere a *critic* of phenomenology (in his dis-

cussion of the "Introduction" Lawlor presents the material, his actual interpretation of Derrida's text, in the form of four difficulties that Derrida is purported to identify in Husserlian phenomenology, one of which has five objections as its subset [Lawlor 2002, 105 ff.]). This, however, is necessarily to view Derrida in 1962 wholly from the perspective of his mature deconstructive stance; it suppresses the issue of how Derrida came to make his break, or breaks, with Husserl (and finally philosophy), and with that, it wholly short-circuits the question of the positive contribution Husserl's phenomenology makes to Derrida's own thought—what deconstruction must take from phenomenology if it is itself to be valid—the last being the question that perhaps should most concern us here.

3. The classic Husserlian text for such anti-historicism is the concluding section of the 1910 "Philosophy as Rigorous Science" (Husserl 1965, 122–47).

4. David Carr's 1974 work remains the indispensable English-language text on Husserl's history writings. Carr's stance, however, is finally not so sympathetic to Husserl's attempt, something true of many interpreters, but perhaps not the most desirable position for its primary English expositor to hold. Carr, more narrowly, seems influenced by Landgrebe's Heideggerean concerns in respect to whether any treatment of the life-world may be a priori, and this, along with the threat of historicism the late works may bring, are the central problems that orient Carr's treatment of Husserl's late thought. (Landgrebe's own work on this phase of Husserl seems to me to become ever more sympathetic and nuanced in the 1970s [especially Landgrebe 1982, which even refers to the "Introduction" on p. 124]; on the issue of the life-world and the apriori, see Mohanty 1985, 101–20, 139–54, which I take in part to be a response to Carr's concerns.) Besides Ricoeur's far less detailed presentation, to which Derrida himself refers, Gerhard Funke's "Phenomenology and History," though written in a style somewhat off-putting today, makes a strong case for Husserl's late thought, one surprisingly close to Derrida's 1962 interpretation (Funke 1973, 3–101). Finally, Elisabeth Ströker's treatment of these themes, now collected in translation in *The Husserlian Foundations of Science*, though premised on a far greater discontinuity between Husserl's genetic phenomenology and his earlier analyses than any Derrida was ever willing to recognize (Ströker 1997, 215), is compelling reading for anyone concerned with these questions as they pertain to Husserl himself

5. Bernet, perhaps more than any other commentator, is aware of the extreme proximity of Derrida to Husserl in the "Introduction" and the singular character of his intervention; he speaks of "Derrida's almost unqualified defense of Husserl's understanding of history" and of "a polemical confrontation with the relevant literature" (Bernet 1989, 142).

6. Foucault, in his introduction to Canguilhem's *On the Normal and the Pathological*, isolates an "objectivist" strand of "phenomenology," which he explicitly traces back to "Cavaillès, Bachelard and Canguilhem," with clear affiliations with Foucault's own way of working (Foucault 1978, x).

7. Ricoeur made this objection, it should be noted, in the context of treating mainly the work of the *Crisis*, and thus contrasted historicity to the "unity of history" that Husserl's philosophy of history seemed to him to assume.

8. Lawlor, taking up this question of historicity, misses Derrida's point at this

237

NOTES TO PAGES 56-57

moment, in my view. Treating Derrida, again, wholly as a *critic* of Husserl (Lawlor addresses the subject under his first difficulty, "A) The Difficulty of Tradition" [Lawlor 2002, 106]), Lawlor sees Derrida as accusing Husserl of holding to a "paradoxical historicity" (a phrase Derrida himself uses—but not everything called "paradoxical" is disqualified or ultimately unworkable in Derrida's eyes), whose status Lawlor sets forth as follows—"it [such historicity] seems to have broken with all empirical content of real history and yet it seems to be irreducibly connected to history since it is the only means by which real history has continuity" (Lawlor 2002, 110)—which, however, is not really an objection to Husserl's, or Derrida's (identical) views on historicity.

9. Lawlor, to his credit, takes notice on a small scale of Derrida's difference with Merleau-Ponty, though this appears to give Lawlor himself qualms (Lawlor 2002, 111n42). This, I believe, is due to the fact that the position I have just sketched as belonging to Merleau-Ponty, entailing a symbiotic coordination of the empirical and the transcendental, is the one that Lawlor believes that Derrida also holds (see Lawlor 2002, 48n4)—at the very least, nowhere does Lawlor confront head on the questions of the very different versions of phenomenological methodology presented by Husserl, Heidegger, and Merleau-Ponty, respectively, and to which of these Derrida himself subscribes.

10. In sections 2–4, Derrida argues that Husserl's approach to history is legitimate as well. Husserl's apriori is a matter of "history itself," Derrida states near the end of four, and he ends this section declaring that "history gives itself its own apriori" (*IOG* 65; cf. *IOG* 116–17, however).

11. To be sure, this defense of Husserl may redound in part to the protocols of genre: Derrida introducing this work to the French public for the first time would be unlikely to place his criticisms of it front and center. Yet the fact that Derrida chose to translate this work in the first place and introduce it at such extraordinary length—Derrida's "Introduction" is more than four times as long as Husserl's original text—attests that Derrida found something intrinsically valuable and legitimate in this work. Indeed, my final chapter explores Derrida's continuing reliance on these findings even after the "Introduction," in the 1963–64 works on Foucault and Levinas. This reliance is most readily visible in Derrida's claim in "Cogito and the History of Madness" "that historicity in general would be impossible without the history of philosophy" ("CHM" 60)—a statement that can only be understood on the basis of Derrida's work in the "Introduction" and that indeed continues to assume that Husserl's stance in important respects is correct.

12. Lawlor misses this point, and this is perhaps one of the most glaring instances in which his presumption that no deep development takes place in Derrida's thought (his treatment of Derrida's early writings taking shape almost wholly in terms of how they anticipate his later ones, at least when it comes to Derrida's positions and arguments) leads Lawlor to a significant misreading of Derrida's work. Lawlor see Cavaillès, whose work he discusses at some length, as having anticipated some of Derrida's mature views—and this precisely in Cavaillès's own critique of Husserl, Lawlor thus believing that Derrida ends up closer to Cavaillès than to Husserl himself (Lawlor 2002, 66, though see also 60n42). Moreover, in

regard to the point at hand, Lawlor seems not to notice at all the momentous difference in Derrida's stance toward the *Origin* as a whole (along with Cavaillès's critique of it) as manifested between *Le problème* and the "Introduction," simply situating Derrida's turn to *language in* the "Introduction" in the context of his discussion of Husserl's *late history writings* in *Le problème* (Lawlor 2002, 88).

13. Derrida's reliance on Cavaillès in *Le problème* in respect to this charge of empiricism is further visible in the theme of probability—the accusation that Husserl's account of the origin of geometry from the life-world is itself merely probabilistic. "Its modality is probability, not necessity," says Cavaillès of the event by which geometry originates (Cavaillès 1997, 80). Compare Derrida: "It is then, it seems [when having recourse to the life-world], that transcendental analysis deteriorates [*dechoit*] into a surprising interpretation whose poverty reunites in a somewhat derisory fashion all the insufficiencies of an adventurous explicativist hypothesis, of a confused probabilism and a prephilosophical empiricism" (*LPG* 267/*PG* 167).

14. This is why I believe that Rudolf Bernet makes too much of Derrida's demonstration that "a purely phenomenological understanding of phenomenology is an impossibility," as Bernet puts it, glossing this same moment (Bernet 1989, 142). Not only is Derrida's tone far more conciliatory than Bernet gives him credit for (see Bernet 1989, 142, and *IOG* 141), but Bernet neglects the degree to which what brings a phenomenology of phenomenology into doubt in the "Introduction" is itself the Idea of infinity, an Idea in the Kantian sense. Derrida, to be sure, argues that this infinite telos no longer answers to phenomenology's notion of phenomenality; yet he still affirms the rights of infinite absolute truth in a way far different from his 1967 treatment of this theme. Bernet, however, draws a distinction between the "authentic" and the "inauthentic idea" of infinity (Bernet 1989, 150), which, while provocative, I myself cannot find in Derrida and by which Bernet moves Derrida's stance in the "Introduction" closer to his later work. That Bernet has somewhere gone too far is plain, however, it seems to me, when he ties his notion of authentic infinity to the thematics of temporality, claiming, in a reading now almost canonical, that Derrida speaks in favor of a mortality that Husserl neglects. Bernet claims that Derrida will deviate from Husserl in the "Introduction" by showing that "an original presentation of the temporality of . . . knowledge is only possible at the cost of denying our facticity or death" (Bernet 1989, 151). Derrida, however, if he is questioning Husserl's notion of time at all at this point, is doing so in favor of this idea of infinity itself, which is indeed coordinated with a finitude, yet precisely a finitude that is *not* that of the subject's mortality, but is rather indicated here under the heading of "thought." Noting that Husserl needs the indefiniteness of the future to make itself known in the present, Derrida rules out the relation to death: "Death would not be understood as sense, but as a fact extrinsic to the movement of temporalization," he declares—and continues: "The unity of infinity, the condition for that temporalization, must then be *thought* [*pensée*] since it announces itself without appearing and without being contained in a present" (*LOG* 150/*IOG* 137). (The stress here is thus on the difference between any experience, including that of death, relating us to the infinity underlying temporalization and the unique work of *thought* in this regard.) Finally,

Bernet is right, of course, that in the final pages of the "Introduction" where Derrida takes up the question of facticity, of ontology in Heidegger's sense, Derrida propounds themes close to his later writings (Bernet 1989, 151). Even here, however, these are still only to be posed in the aftermath of the affirmation of work of the Infinite Idea, now in the form of the transcendental logos and Husserl's late meditations on God, and Bernet thus seems to me to underestimate in respect to the workings of the infinite to what degree Derrida's thought will undergo a further transformation that brings it yet closer to Heidegger's before Derrida's mature stance in *Speech* and *Of Grammatology* emerges, a transformation indicated most notably by Derrida's later talk of metaphysics' "closure," talk of course wholly absent here (see notably *VP* 115/*SP* 102).

15. Indeed, Derrida now claims that the "dialectical genesis" that Cavaillès failed to find in Husserl—an interplay between an "absolute logic" of the object and a "transcendental logic" of its "creative" apprehension—"is precisely what Husserl describes in the *Origin*" (*IOG* 143). (Contrast this with *LPG* 267: "if ideality is a logical predicate of pre-predicative being, it is produced by a logical *genesis* of which nothing is here said"; my emphasis.) This is what Lawlor neglects in his gloss on Derrida's phrase the "absolute is passage" (Lawlor 1995, 169–70). Lawlor does not seem to understand that what is in question is the workings of the infinite idea of truth, that the absolute as passage is a passage within "*transcendental* history," that this passage is thus unique to a specifically "*transcendental* historicity" (*IOG* 147)—a movement whose interpretation oscillates between being seen as the fulfilled telos of truth, the absolute transcendental logos, God merely expressing itself *through* transcendental history, and as a wholly immanent pole of an ongoing transcendental historicity—the latter thus putting itself, the truth, in danger. Lawlor instead brings in concerns relating to the merely "empirical" ("the absolute of passage means first of all that sense arises out of a series or iterations of singular, factual, empirical events" [Lawlor 1995, 170]), as well as "linguistic iteration" (having wrongly identified "language" and the transcendental "logos" [Lawlor 1995, 168]). In his latest work, while no longer focusing solely on "linguistic iteration," and moving instead toward a reading that focuses on temporalization (Lawlor 2002, 131–32), Lawlor still seems to assume the results of his earlier reading and to reach conclusions largely consonant with it (see Lawlor 2002, 135).

16. The role of history and historicity in Derrida's thought, already unstable, and undergoing alteration in the passage from *Le problème* to the "Introduction," will undergo further transformation from the "Introduction" to the 1967 works. These changes are explored further in chapter 4 and again in chapter 6.

17. Where Derrida's still-unpublished 1957 thesis on the literary object ("TT" 36) fits in here, whether Derrida there treated writing and how, would be worth knowing. An important footnote in section 7 of the "Introduction" (*IOG* 90n93) clearly draws on Derrida's 1957 work in the context of a transcendental theory of the *book*—itself an indication that Derrida's stance toward the written and the graphic undergoes some kind of development after the "Introduction" (cf. Bernet 1989, 146).

18. "Absolute ideality" is the Husserlian term for the mode of being (the *Seinsmodus*) of theoretical or scientific truth. Ideal modes of being are distinguished

from real modes by the absence of spatiotemporal individuation and they thus pertain most obviously to certain classes of meanings—such as essences, as well as the contents of assertions, and even the identities of the objects these assertions are about, none of which idealities are simply to be identified with one another. In the "Introduction," as we shall see, Derrida believes it meaningful to speak of a historical transcendental constitution of ideality and thus of essences, a claim which is notably contested by Mohanty, at least in the sense given it by Derrida (Mohanty 1997, 71–72, but see his remarks on the "Introduction" itself at 75), as well as by Dallas Willard on very different grounds. (Depp and Hopkins are closer to Derrida in this respect, though both also express doubts about his analysis—see notes in the previous chapter for the appropriate references.) The entire question of ideality, and in particular essences and how these do or do not comport with Husserl's later transcendental teaching is a vexed question in Husserl studies generally. Essential knowledge, a priori knowledge, is the type of knowledge proper to philosophy itself, according to Husserl; yet if all objects, including essences, are constituted, are finally subject to the world-establishing powers of transcendental subjectivity, it is hard to see how Husserl is able to ultimately maintain the primacy of his essentialism as well as his transcendental standpoint at once. Both Mohanty and Ströker, as I read them, finally subordinate the former to the latter: they see essences as more of a heuristic device, or provisional moment in Husserl's thought (Mohanty 1964, 60; 1985, 191–213; 1989, 33–35; 1997, 8, 75; Ströker 1993, 70–75). Bernet et al. and even, perhaps strangely, Derrida himself seem to hew more closely to the letter of Husserl's teaching in this regard (Bernet, Kern, and Marbach 1995, 83–87).

19. Bernet is clearly aware of this context (Bernet 1989, 145–46), yet he does not give the stipulations it establishes (which I am about to lay out) enough weight, in my view, and for this reason comes to a very different estimation of where Derrida stands in section 7, in particular with regard to the predicament of Derrida's that I later bring forward. Christina Howells's reading is quite close to Bernet's (Howells 1998, 15–16), while other commentators depart from Bernet to varying degrees. Lawlor's first treatment of this material largely follows Bernet and also does not consider this larger context very much. Lawlor reworked his earlier treatment (Lawlor 1992, 97–98; and 1995, 160–62) to take this context more into account, and in his latest discussion he gives significant attention to section 6, which I am also about to comment on (Lawlor 2002, 110–15). Marian Hobson is to be lauded for the intention she pays to Derrida's early work (Hobson 1998, 51–52), and Marrati-Guénoun starts with a focused, helpful discussion of writing (Marrati-Guénoun 1998, 45–47, 56), but neither stress this larger context and both seem to me to fall short of ultimate clarity about where writing stands in the "Introduction's" section 7.

20. Lawlor in his most recent work, as well as Burt Hopkins in an earlier piece, both register Derrida's insistence that only a transcendental language is in question at this point, and Hopkins also sees the writing at issue in section 7 as continuous with Derrida's treatment here in section 6 (Hopkins 1995, 68; Lawlor 2002, 111–12). Both Hopkins and Lawlor, however, seem to agree that Derrida must somehow have already taken a stance critical of Husserl (thus assimilating Der-

rida's views at this moment with his later work), and Lawlor, rather unexpectedly, immediately goes on to list what he claims are "five objections" on Derrida's part to the Husserlian notion of a transcendental language that Derrida has just set out (Lawlor 2002, 112). In line with the highly tentative and interrogative style that everywhere marks Derrida's treatment of Husserl in the "Introduction"—a style different to my mind from all of Derrida's other writings and one of the prime reasons, no doubt, why the "Introduction" has remained so difficult to interpret— Derrida does go on to raise three, not five (Derrida himself enumerates them) points (not questions) provoked by this talk of transcendental language. All three of these, even point two which stretches Husserl's thinking the furthest and questions it most profoundly, seem to me to finally come down on Husserl's side, however; and in the last point, which is meant to show how Husserl's thought ultimately *successfully* incorporates a tension "between objectivism and the transcendental motif" (*IOG* 83; not succumbs to this tension altogether, as Lawlor seems to believe; Lawlor 2002, 105–6), Derrida in fact ends up siding with Husserl's transcendental, nonobjectivist determination of the sense of earth, drawing a conclusion ("there is then a science *of* space insofar as its starting point is not *in* space" [*IOG* 85, his emphasis]) that Derrida will return to later at a crucial moment in "Violence and Metaphysics," in which he defends a version of Husserl's transcendental opening once more against what he believes to be a too-precipitous charge of objectivism and intuitionism, this time at the hands of Levinas ("VM" 113).

21. Thus, even if a new interpretation of transcendentality turns out to be contemplated on this basis, not only would the scope of Derrida's ambition still be wholly within phenomenology and philosophy, but the *continuity* of this transformation with Husserl's earlier thought, stressed by Derrida himself, should be emphasized. Derrida at most contemplates a transformation of transcendentality at the limit, not a revolution within Husserl's thinking à la Merleau-Ponty. This can be clarified by the singular position that Derrida assigned to the *Origin of Geometry* within the totality of Husserl's corpus from the very first pages of the "Introduction." Having noted that "it is truly necessary to see that this order of dependence [of Husserl's historical writings on his transcendental and logical researches] is not reversed," Derrida goes on to state, nevertheless "by a spiraling movement . . . a bold clearing is brought about within the regional limits of the investigation, which transgresses them toward a new form of radicality" (*LOG* 14/*IOG* 33–34). Only upon the acceptance of the rest of Husserl's program will a new form of (transcendental) radicality thus arrive, one which Derrida seems to suggest may itself be largely in line with Husserl's own intentions (cf. Lawlor 2002, 105–6). I follow up Derrida's claim about the *Origin*'s position in Husserl's corpus in chapter 4, where it helps to establish the chronological relation of the "Introduction" to Derrida's other early published work, "'Genesis and Structure' and Phenomenology."

22. It is worth noting that Derrida, at points, also affirms a dependence in the other direction: if only language within the reductions, conceived from a transcendental-phenomenological perspective, can play any role in the constitution of truth, nevertheless *all* language, Derrida has maintained, already implies an eidetics, and a kind of essentialism. Derrida footnotes André Muralt's 1958 *L'idée*

de la phénoménologie: L'exemplarisme Husserlien for the claim that all language has an implicit eidetics built into it (*IOG* 68n63), and this belief, which Derrida seems never to have subsequently questioned, plays an important role even in his more mature treatment of language. Not only is there good reason to believe that Muralt is incorrect, however (see Bernet, Kern, and Marbach 1995, 172–75, and this is implied by Mohanty's stance on essences generally, see my note 18 above, but also Mohanty 1964, 61, 75), but this issue, in any case, does not centrally pertain to the one before us now, which concerns the transcendental-phenomenological reductions and the constitution of truth within these reductions, including essential truth, not the status of essences more generally, which are presumed to function apart from and prior to the reduction. It is worth noting further, however, that Derrida, following Gaston Berger, I believe (Berger 1972, 22–24, 58–61), has always linked the possibility of essential knowledge (e.g., in logic or geometry) to Husserl's transcendental standpoint much more closely than is common, even in own Husserl's works (see *LPG* 102–3), and this perspective is tied to those objections Derrida raised against Mohanty in 1964 (Derrida 1964a). Derrida and Mohanty (and Ströker) all see Husserl's essentialism as bound up with his transcendentalism; the latter two, however, bite the bullet and concede that this entails some etiolation of Husserl's essence doctrine, something Derrida himself always denied.

23. This last is the matter of some dispute. As early as 1921 in a famous fragment Husserl had spoken of "history as the great fact of absolute Being" (*Erste Philosophie* II 506 [cited by Landgrebe 1974, 111]), and the notion of a facticity or factuality on a transcendental level seems to have entered Husserl's thought more and more, as he gave further attention to history. Some commentators believe this has dire consequences for Husserl's late thought, driving him into that historicism that Carr was worried about (e.g., Bernet, Kern, and Marbach 1995, 234); others seem to deny this (see Lester Embree's introduction to the English translation of Bernet, Kern, and Marbach 1995, xiv), and some arrive at more of a middle position (see Mohanty 1997, 74–75). What is clear is that *Derrida* insists that the a priori character of Husserl's thought may be maintained even in his late historical phase, arguing for this repeatedly throughout the "Introduction." (Though Mohanty points out that the final conclusion to which Derrida comes in the "Introduction" is very close to both his position and Ströker's [Mohanty 1997, 74], Derrida claims to question the *transcendental* reduction as such in the name of a radical facticity, not transcendental facticity, and in this way differs from these interpretations—thus also maintaining the eidetic reduction, and Husserl doctrine of essences, unequivocally up until this point.)

24. What Husserl understands by "constitution" has long been a vexed question. Interpreters such as Walter Biemel and Gaston Berger, whom Derrida cites approvingly, had made clear that constitution differs from creation, certainly creation ex nihilo (see Biemel 1959, 50; *IOG* 27n4; Berger 1972, 79); and though Husserl's late thought for Derrida shifts the balance toward invention or creation over and against discovery, even in 1962, it seems to me, Derrida did not wish to sever the "dialectic" between the two that he had already so eloquently described in his introduction to *Le problème:* "toute innovation est verification, toute création est accomplissement, tout surgissement est tradition" (*LPG* 9).

25. In section 4, Derrida, following Husserl, had already set out a moment within the solitary consciousness of a protogeometer, himself or herself ideal, when this founding insight arises: when a discovery or invention grasping geometry's ideal contents may be said to come to pass—postponing until section 10 the movement of thought by which this idealization takes place (see *IOG* 64, 127).

26. Part of what is implied by my argument here against many portrayals of Derrida's thought is Derrida's surprising affirmation of Husserl's teaching on (transcendental) intersubjectivity; this is visible here in the transcendental roles of both writing and language, as well as in his first work on Levinas and even in the introduction to *Speech* (where Derrida upholds Husserl's account in *Phenomenological Psychology* of an "enworlding self-apperception" on the part of the absolute subject [*SP* 11]). Derrida was clearly familiar with Schutz's famous critique (it appeared in the same volume as Biemel's article to which Derrida refers [see Schutz 1959]), and Derrida's siding with Husserl against Schutz is worth noting in its own right. (I myself have always found Schutz's claims convincing, and even Ströker, who wishes to uphold this phase of Husserl's thought more generally, takes *Cartesian Meditations* 5 to fail, claiming it hails from an earlier phase of Husserl's thought [Ströker 1997, 217–18—I believe something has gone awry, by the way, in the English translation].) More centrally, perhaps, this decision of Derrida's has important consequences for his relation to Levinas, though this continues to be severely underestimated in the literature. Derrida, at least intra-philosophically, affirms Husserl's account of intersubjectivity in a way that Levinas does not; and this is crucial for any thoroughgoing evaluation of the relations between Derrida and Levinas (cf. Lawlor 2002, 115).

27. Lawlor also cites this passage, and to his credit, in his latest work, he makes plain its implications, thus going against the grain of the prevailing interpretation ("the constitutive role of writing does not imply, however, for Derrida, that truth's ontological sense now derives from its factual linguistic incarnations, that truth is now relative in the worst sense of the word" [Lawlor 2002, 117]). At the same time, Lawlor undoes much of the good work he achieves here by (1) making too much, in my view, of the French word *consignation* (perhaps with Derrida's 1995 "Archive Fever" in view), and thanks to the fact that *consignation* quite literally contains the word "*sign*(e)," he manages to assimilate Derrida's doctrine of writing here to that of *Speech* (just the issue in question at the moment); and (2) insisting that Derrida's insistence on the transcendental status of writing finally entails a novel "transcendental sense of death" (Lawlor 2002, 118), which also brings Derrida in 1962 in line with what Lawlor takes to be his later positions, a claim that goes back in some form to Bernet's 1989 article (see note 14 above), and one that to my eyes is dubious generally. (Derrida does, of course, use this phrase here, but by no means in the portentous sense so often given to it, one that comes from reading Derrida's remarks in *Speech* concerning Husserl's analysis of occasional expressions, the first-person pronoun in particular, back into the present context [see *SP* 96; as well as my forthcoming "'A Transcendental Sense of Death'?: Derrida and the Philosophy of Language"].)

28. Bernet, just to be clear, is of course aware of this correlation as well: that only a transcendental or constituting writing, writing as "pure . . . transcendental

possibility of the embodiment," plays a role in truth; and Bernet goes so far as to concede, rightfully, that "Derrida does not present an explicit critique of this separation between constituting and constituted" language (Bernet 1989, 146), as I myself have repeatedly stressed. Bernet, however, insists that "language and writing are always simultaneously and undecidably" *both* transcendental and mundane, constituting and constituted (Bernet 1989, 146–47); and Lawlor, as well as other interpreters, follow him in this (e.g., Lawlor 1995, 161). Right now our main concern is that even if this were right, this first set of stipulations, according to which writing or language has any role in truth, is noticeably absent in Derrida's later work, along with this sort of explicitly "double" perspective on language and writing: no sort of transcendental stipulations are there to be found. Beyond that, however, as will shortly become clear, this claim that Derrida puts constituted and constituting language on the same footing in the "Introduction" is far more problematic than has been suspected. The sentence of Derrida's that Bernet cites I read differently (see below), and this leads Bernet into what I take to be a significant error in respect to the argument of section 7's second half (see note 30 below). More immediately, however, one may ask: if Bernet and those who follow him are correct, why does this not simply return us to Merleau-Ponty's stance in which all inquiry inhabits a nowhere's land at once transcendental and empirical and "in which the most important lesson the reduction teaches us is the impossibility of a complete reduction"? (Merleau-Ponty 1962, xiv). How can we grant genuine authority to Husserl's transcendental doctrines if the language upon which these depend is already at once empirical and mundane in any significant way? In what way these two views of language are to be coordinated such that most of Husserl's claims, as well as Derrida's, do not immediately become invalid—such that the constituted side does not impugn the constituting one—has never been thought through, as far as I can tell, even by Bernet himself. Insofar as Husserl's own doctrines are in question here, the relation of constituting to constituted language thus poses far greater problems than has been recognized, and this also becomes clear in Derrida's own interpretation in the remainder of section 7, as we are about to see.

29. In chapter 4, having established here that Derrida's thought does develop, I reinsert the "Introduction" into the context provided by Derrida's other early works, *Le problème* and "Genesis and Structure," and thereby fashion a picture of Derrida's development as a whole.

30. Even Bernet goes wrong in this respect, as I will show. Howells (1998, 16) follows Bernet in this, affirming unequivocally that such a fall into empiricism, such a disappearance of truth, at factical, sensible writing's hands, really takes place. Marrati-Guénoun (1998, 62) and Hobson (1998, 51) are more careful, though they too come down somewhere in the vicinity of such an affirmation, I believe. Lawlor earlier hews to this interpretation (misconstruing *Leib,* and asserting that there could indeed be destruction of truth, truth itself, including that of geometry, at writing's hands; Lawlor 1995, 162). In Lawlor's latest treatment, he is far clearer about Derrida's rejection of the possibility of the annihilation of truth at the hands of a worldly sign (Lawlor 2002, 120). Nevertheless, once again assimilating Derrida's position in the "Introduction" to that of *Speech,* Lawlor does finally affirm

the disappearance of truth as a radical possibility (Lawlor 2002, 124), here and elsewhere, in the form of the perhaps even more problematic claim that Derrida denies that any constitution (and hence possession) of theoretical (or mathematical) knowledge is really possible in the first place (see Lawlor 2002, 108: "the difficulty of recognizing the starting point implies for Derrida that geometrical truth has never and will never . . . unconceal itself as such").

31. This is clearly the case with Bernet, who sees the ambiguity Derrida is about to specify as "simultaneously and undecidably" pertaining to a language and writing that Bernet believes he is otherwise able to identify as a whole. To be fair to Bernet, Derrida himself does seem to swing back and forth between this stance and the more careful one that he is about to put forward, especially later on in section 7.

32. Again, as noted, there is at times some confusion and hesitancy on Derrida's own part about these matters, and even here, at this moment, apparently intrigued and excited by what he is seeing in Husserl's thought, Derrida has also just made a claim, seeming to me somewhat out of the order of his argument, which appears to ignore these distinctions and if it proved to hold good would most closely approximate his later view, of all his claims in section 7—namely, "if it is by its language that truth would suffer a certain shiftiness [*labilité*], its default [*decheance*] would be less a fall toward language than a degradation at the interior of language" (*LOG* 90/*IOG* 92). Nevertheless, it is necessary to insist on how deeply runs the distinction Derrida has just drawn, insofar as the entire development that has just been reviewed, the identification of ambiguity in writing and language as "movement of incorporability" over against their function as "contingent and factical place," derives from an earlier distinction between an "original spatiotemporality" (to which this "movement of incorporability" here corresponds) and "sensible spatiotemporality" (corresponding to their "contingent and factical" character). Derrida had made this distinction earlier, starting from a "reversal" of Fink, whereby Derrida identified constitutive writing and language with a "freeing" of sense (and truth) from place and time (rather than assigning them a spatiotemporal location), and thus identified constitutive writing and language with a "spatiotemporality that escapes the alternative of the sensible and the intelligible, the empirical and the metempirical" (*IOG* 90). This tantalizing formulation of an original spatiotemporality allied to a "pure tradition and history" immediately leads Derrida to offer his "phenomenology of the written thing" in the form of "the book"; and is thus specifically contrasted at this moment with "sensible spatiotemporality," as well as all factical or mundane inscription, and continues to be so contrasted here: with that sensible spatiotemporality from which the supposed peril to truth at writing's hands is about to emerge. (Derrida had written: "In order that ideal objectivity may be radically independent of *sensible* spatiotemporality . . . it prescribes to communication, then to pure history and tradition, an *original* spatiotemporality" [*LOG* 88/*IOG* 90; my emphasis].)

33. Lawlor in his latest work also distinguishes and reviews these three scenarios that Derrida sets out at the end of section 7 of the "Introduction" (Lawlor 2002, 119–24). Apart from concluding that truth does disappear, in a more inventive manner than is usually the case (not through the physical destruction of

its signs)—a conclusion based on Lawlor's interpretation of *consignation* and his correlative assimilation of Derrida's stance toward the sign in the "Introduction" and *Speech* (Lawlor does not see the difference that I have just emphasized between Derrida's two treatments of Husserl's work on the sign in 1962 and 1967— just the opposite: his analysis in the body of his chapter is premised on the assumption that no such difference exists at all, though cf. Lawlor 2002, 136)—Lawlor's analysis moves immediately from the end of section 7 to Derrida's treatment of the idea in a Kantian sense later on in the "Introduction," though this actually begins in section 10, not eight or nine, a gap which is important to my estimation of Derrida's treatment of writing in the "Introduction" and its difference from his later work, as stressed above (see my chapter 2). The concluding pages of the "Introduction" are some of the most difficult of Derrida's—some of the most difficult in what is already a highly difficult corpus; my comments above (see note 14) aim to point the way toward a possible interpretation. Finally, the issue of a dialectic between Heideggerean ontology and Husserlian phenomenology, for which the end of the "Introduction" is now nearly a locus classicus, is treated at the beginning of my next chapter, where I situate Derrida's other early published writing, "'Genesis and Structure' and Phenomenology," in relation to this present work. As already noted, however, to speak of a dialectic between Husserlian phenomenology and an other, a real, or an "ontological" seems to me an inadequate characterization of Derrida's aims, and while Lawlor seems to me to do a fair job of specifying how Derrida wishes this to be understood at this moment (see Lawlor 2002, 133–35), his further gloss on this in his conclusion, which once more stresses the unlikely direct influence of Hyppolite in order to assimilate, or anticipate, Derrida's discussion here with respect to his later notion of *différance,* seems to me to retract many of the insights Lawlor offers earlier (see Lawlor 2002, 138–40).

34. This includes Bernet. His belief that writing and language are "simultaneously and indecidably" both "constituting and constituted" is bound up with the assertion that "a moment of essential and thus irreducible facticity and materiality . . . affects writing not simply as a sensible body but as spiritual corporeality as well" (Bernet 1989, 147). Bernet, that is, claims it is meaningful within phenomenology for truth to disappear—thanks to "facticity and materiality," thanks to "a burning of books." Bernet affirms scenario two, and for this reason, above all, I believe Bernet's core interpretation of the "Introduction's" section 7 must finally be rejected, though it is in so many other respects careful and insightful.

35. I thus do not finally reject the view of Lawlor, Hobson, Marrati-Guénoun, and so many others who see language and writing in Derrida ultimately as the locus of an interplay of empirical and transcendental concerns, following up the leads of Rodolphe Gasché and Geoff Bennington (even much of Lawlor's most recent work seems to me to hinge on this sort of claim; see Lawlor 2002, 47–48, 66, 86, 109, 177, 180; also Lawlor 1995, 156, 176; Hobson 1998, 51, but see also her arguably more interesting account on 57; Marrati-Guénoun 1998, 61). Where we disagree, above all, is that in my view the difficulty in genuinely thinking this has been deeply underestimated. How one, the empirical, would not simply cancel the other, the transcendental—how writing can be said to be genuinely *constitutive* of truth (a claim that clearly derives from Husserl's thinking), yet also viewed as em-

pirical or worldly (which runs counter and indeed would be disqualifying of Husserl's standpoint)—how writing, in sum, *can* take on both roles is far less obvious than many seem to believe. Moreover, if this question fails to be raised, the specific work of deconstruction is largely missed to various degrees, I am claiming here, as well as leaving unnoticed important nuances in the 1967 works themselves.

36. See note 32 above.

37. As far as I can tell the *Origin*, after raising the theme of writing, almost immediately passes over to the themes of sedimentations and equivocation with which scenario three deals (cf. Husserl 1970a, 360–61). Yet, as I am about to show below, Derrida himself had already invoked the distinction between *Körper* and *Leib* that this new reduction brings forward at the beginning of section 7 (already recognizing its importance for the consistency of Husserl's argument), and thus Derrida's talk of a new reduction here seems to me largely a function of that tentative, exploratory character of much of section 7 in respect to writing and language that I have begun to discuss. This entire thought experiment, after all, all three scenarios that the second half of three discusses, by no means have an obvious correlate in Husserl's own text, in the *Origin* as such. For these same reasons, however, because of the sometimes wavering character of Derrida's thought, it is possible to read Derrida's own intentions at certain junctures in section 7 differently than I have done, though I believe my interpretation hews most closely to the underlying structure of Derrida's own discussion, as well as of Husserl's.

38. Husserl first discusses these matters in his preparatory remarks to his late logical work, *Formal and Transcendental Logic*, where he replays some of the opening considerations in *Logical Investigations* II. In *Formal and Transcendental Logic* §3, more specifically, Husserl asserts that "in speaking we are continuously performing an internal act of meaning which fuses with the words, and as it were, animates [*beseelendes*] them. The effect of this animation [*Beseelung*] is that the words and the entire locution, as it were, embody [*verleiblichen*] a meaning and bear it embodied [*verleiblicht*] in them as their sense" (Husserl 1969, 22). Bernet distinguishes such *Verleiblichung* from *Verkörperung* in his essay on the "Introduction" (Bernet 1989, 147), and even more usefully, in another essay, drawing on Husserl's 1914 lectures on signification (prior to *Formal and Transcendental Logic*), with an eye on *Speech*, Bernet makes clear the dependence that the conventional sign always had for Husserl on the self-consciously willed meaning-conferring act: "the expressive will . . . both bestows meaning on a sign and makes the sign point to its meaning" (Bernet 1988, 8; cf. 10, where he decisively contrasts this view with Heidegger's account of *Rede* and how signs function in it; see also Bernet, Kern, and Marbach 1995, 167–68). Bernet takes almost the opposite tack to Merleau-Ponty's interpretation of the *Verleiblichung* (Merleau-Ponty 1964, 85). And while Bernet and Derrida agree with one another, and disagree with Merleau-Ponty, in seeing no break in Husserl's own doctrine, it is worth noting that Derrida will subsequently move closer to Merleau-Ponty's position, particularly in "Form and Meaning," seemingly more and more impressed by the fusion, the *Verschmelzung*, of meaning and sign, also just cited here, and thus seeing a tighter linkage in Husserl between speech and (conceptual) thought than many other Husserlians, while

still leaving their relations ultimately unresolved. (On "Form and Meaning," see Kates 1998, especially 194, 198.) (The status of the entities comprising *language* as such [roughly words] as ideal individualities to which Dorion Cairns most notably drew attention in his important article [see Cairns 1941] with an eye to these same late works is treated below in the notes and taken up again in chapter 6.)

39. This is an important point too often ignored in the literature on Husserl and Derrida, at least from the side of Derrideans. Husserl, notoriously among twentieth-century philosophers, never made what is sometimes called the linguistic turn. Other phenomenologists, like the early Heidegger and the later Merleau-Ponty, recognize a much closer connection between thought and empirical language, thought and discourse, than Husserl (*Being and Time* §33; Edie 1976, 102–3). So too, Husserl never seems even to have arrived at a definitive statement of his views on these matters, on the status of language and thought, speech and meaning, instead making numerous suggestive remarks scattered throughout his corpus (cf. Merleau-Ponty 1964, 84; Edie 1976, ix). While most who are familiar with Husserl's corpus recognize this, the result has been no clear consensus about where Husserl stood on these matters, how close or far he was at any point from really tying together thought and speech (or writing), language and conceptual meaning.

40. Bernet, as we have already noted, arrives at this conclusion, one in which the sign and significations remain subordinated to those lived acts of meaning that employ them. So too, Mohanty in 1964, on different grounds, and recognizing a tighter correlation than most between such acts and even the idealities Husserl specifically associates with *language* (Mohanty 1964, 62), concludes that all of Husserl's different approaches to language, including that implied by his last writings, "could have been developed only from the phenomenological attitude of the communicating subject" (Mohanty 1964, 66). The ultimate dispensation of these matters, the relation of language, discourse, signification, and thought in Husserl, remain very difficult. Yet it seems to me, it cannot be forgotten that Husserl's is already a theory that posits the subject as a source of meaning generally (in respect to *Sinn*, but also in other ways), and thus I side with both Bernet and Mohanty who, on these grounds too, keep all meaning, including conceptual meaning, as rigorously subordinate to such acts—against those like Edie, Merleau-Ponty, and, more and more, Derrida himself, who seem to see conceptual meanings and language as more closely allied (cf. Mohanty, who argues for this "phenomenological attitude" toward all linguistic matters after explicitly recognizing the primacy of the correlation noeses-noema [Mohanty 1964, 63]).

41. There is a further complication due to the fact that another layer, specific to language, to *langue*, inserts itself here. Not only are the *Körper*, the bodily signs, turned into *Leib* due to such animating acts, but these signs themselves, simply as belonging to a language, are already spiritual or cultural entities, idealities, of a very peculiar kind—theirs is already a "spiritual corporeality" (Husserl 1969, 21) and they are never mere spatiotemporally individuated singulars. In discourse, such cultural entities become enlivened, and they take on their capacity to signify thanks to the intentions of a subject; nevertheless, according to Husserl, an ideality already accrues to them simply as pieces of language, and this is perhaps where

the deepest source of confusion lies. Husserl always maintained his views about signs taking on significance in discourse, in the act of speech (thanks to what is sometimes called speaker's meaning), and in his later work he started to pay further attention to language, yet how these two potential reservoirs of meaning, of signification, ultimately relate to one another Husserl never made clear. Thus, it is possible for James Edie, for example, in his important study *Speaking and Meaning* to pursue a rather different tack than the one so far set out here. In contrast to a "phenomenological view" of meaning giving primacy to the discursive act, Edie, being impressed with this later side of Husserl's project, as well as Husserl's early program for a pure grammar and the tie between language and ideality more generally (Edie 1976, 17, 20–21), sees Husserl's work in quite close proximity to linguistics (both Saussure's and Chomsky's), while taking Merleau-Ponty, by contrast, "almost as an Oxfordian" (Edie 1976, x–xi). (Edie's framework perhaps threatens at times to lose sight of the distinction between (*a*) an intentional, versus (*b*) a linguistically based theory of [conceptual] meaning; and between (a_1) a theory which gives priority to essential or ideal treatments of language-related phenomena versus (b_1) one which maintains an insistence on the realities of the diversity of empirical languages; Husserl can be seen to assert both *a* and a_1, as opposed to John Searle, who would maintain *a* and b_1, and Saussure, who seems to hold *b* and b_1.) Edie sees Husserl as close to linguistics, and to a view of language as a relatively autonomous source of meaning, downplaying others' emphasis on discourse and the speech act. Yet the understanding of Saussure's distinction between *langue* and *parole* common in phenomenology at that time (something I comment on in chapter 6) makes it difficult to know where Edie or anyone finally comes down, and later on in *Speaking and Meaning*, attesting to these difficulties of which he is also well aware, Edie himself acknowledges the primacy that "all phenomenologists" must give to "use" and the "sentence" (Edie 1976, 112). It is important to keep Edie's reflections in mind, however, since, having been influenced by many of the same works in the phenomenological tradition as Derrida (Cairns, Muralt, and even Berger), Edie's stance seems to me relatively close to the one to which Derrida later comes, which emphasizes the tie of ideality to language, even in the context of so-called "static phenomenology," and thus asserts a somewhat similar proximity of Husserl to linguistics. (Edie himself was aware of Derrida's work [Edie 1976, 33], yet appears to have become less taken with Derrida's thought over time [see Edie 1990].)

42. In line with the hesitation that we have already recognized in Derrida's treatment of these themes, Derrida, even after making these further stipulations pertaining to *Leib* at the outset of section 7, goes on to declare it necessary that ideal objectivity "*can* . . . be engraved in the world" (*LOG* 86/*IOG* 89, his emphasis). Yet by way of his discussion of Fink, Derrida will come to say of this "ideal objectivity," now "essentially inform[ing] the body of the word and writing, and depend[ing] on a pure intention of language," that it can be "radically independent of sensible spatio-temporality" (*LOG* 88/*IOG* 90), and from this derive "a phenomenology of the written thing . . . of the book." Derrida thus now comes to renounce any *empirical*, or sensible spatiotemporal, worldliness of this engraving, in favor of an "original spatiotemporality, neither empirical, nor metempirical," that

we have already encountered (*LOG* 88/*IOG* 90), and Derrida cashes this out through the book "as a unity of enchainments of signification"—the book and its affirmation thus preserving Derrida from that straightforward empiricism with which he repeatedly flirts and indeed being another important sign of the distance of Derrida's stance in 1962 from that in 1967, as has already been noted.

43. Compare *IOG* 106–7. Derrida cites Husserl in the "Introduction" on the possibility of "confronting "a tradition empty of meaning": "'Unfortunately . . . this is our situation, and that of the whole modern age'" (*IOG* 107; Husserl 1970a, 366). This appeal to our own situation, this sense of crisis as loss of meaning and with that the historicity of Husserl's own philosophizing about history, is perhaps the best defense overall for Husserl's late work: for his turn to history. Spurred by the singular circumstances in which he finds himself, Husserl's turn to history would not be a fall back into metaphysics—neither the spirit-bound metaphysics of Hegel's philosophy of history or the metaphysics of which Husserl himself claimed no other knowledges or philosophies prior to his own had been shorn—but rather a radical act of self-responsibility and historical authenticity, one which in a number of ways prefigures the radical historicity that Derrida himself eventually imputes to the work of deconstruction, even as he tampers with those values under whose heading Husserl undertakes this task, especially questioning the notion of horizon which plays such a prominent role here and again at the end of the "Introduction." (Cf. Ludwig Landgrebe's 1974 essay, which also ends with a moving defense of Husserl's late thought on account of its historical self-situation, along very different lines.)

44. It is worth emphasizing that even at this moment Derrida maintains a *parallelism* between the transcendental and the empirical planes: Husserl's project "knows the same relativity" "as the *transcendental parallel* to Joyce's" (*IOG* 103, my emphasis). As to Joyce's project, according to Derrida, it is directed, in the sphere of finite language and finite history, toward equivocity as such—toward unavoidable equivocity, to what Derrida is about to call "equivocity itself." Joyce attempted to confront an equivocity irreducible in all finite languages and cultures—to proceed through these by way of their differences and gather them up and thereby in his own way overcome history. Joyce's project, says Derrida, would be "to repeat and take responsibility" "for . . . equivocation itself" (*IOG* 102).

Chapter 4

1. As noted in the list of abbreviations, due to the date that the English translation appeared, all translations of *Le problème* are my own, and the primary references given are to the 1990 French text. I have also supplied the corresponding page numbers for the English translation when possible.

2. The English translation of "Genesis" in *Writing and Difference,* following the original French, assigns a 1964 publication date to the conference volume *Entretiens sur les notions de genèse et de structure* in which "Genesis" first appeared (along with other papers and transcriptions of some of the discussion that originally fol-

lowed these papers' presentations). The only edition of this book that I have ever seen bears a 1965 publication date, however.

3. Husserl's orientation to history started from the history of the ego, of the absolute subject. His genetic phenomenology program, which he announced in *Cartesian Meditations* 4 and which I comment on further below, in any construal of Husserl's corpus bears a close relation to Husserl's late work on history (Carr 1974, 68–75; Ströker 1997, 207, 215). What sort of further transformation Husserl's turn to history represents in his thought is open to question, however, and this is clearly part of what is at stake in Derrida's two different construals of Husserl's later corpus in the "Introduction" and "Genesis."

4. At this moment in his text, Derrida is specifically arguing that Husserl's prior *essential* descriptions of history, limiting this theme to a given region, remain in place and are valid, even as Husserl comes to a new view of the relation between philosophy and history overall. It is worth noting that the dual role Derrida assigns at this moment to the "Introduction's" analysis, as at once novel and not, is part of Derrida's broader answer to a question which had long been a crux in the Husserl literature: namely, how Husserl could legitimately address historical themes within the provenance of phenomenology without violating the tenets of phenomenological *knowledge*—how phenomenology as a science of essences could address a field, history, seemingly composed of singular facts (see Ricoeur 1967, 145 ff.; Carr 1974, 127, 185; Ströker 1997, 207). In the opening section of the "Introduction," and in what follows, Derrida will quite cleverly argue that the overall function of Husserl's *Origin of Geometry,* in particular, is to answer this very question: to give an account of this "new access to history" that the *Crisis* and other history writings of Husserl presupposed but "never made a problem" (*IOG* 29). Derrida wishes to see this new answer emerge within the continuity of the *Origin* with Husserl's earlier works (and thus against the kind of empiricist break Merleau-Ponty wanted to recognize), even while now insisting on the relative novelty of the *Origin* (in contrast to Derrida's own presentation in "Genesis"). Whether Derrida in fact succeeded in this tightrope walk, whose methodology he makes explicit within Husserl's own text under the heading of the *Ruckfrage,* "return inquiry" (*IOG* 50), can only be the purview of a future study. What I believe is clear is that the belief that he had done so, that he had successfully followed Husserl to a new region, or stratum, at once historical and philosophical, historical and transcendental, is presupposed in some form by all that Derrida will subsequently think and write. (Compare Lawlor's most recent treatment, where, if I follow him, he takes this radicality as a feature of Derrida's analysis *opposed to Husserl's own;* Lawlor 2002, 105.)

5. In *Le problème,* at the moment his discussion passes from genetic phenomenology to Husserl's late history, Derrida speaks of Husserl's "philosophy of history, completing [*parachevant*] the system of transcendental phenomenology," and Derrida says he must investigate how this philosophy of history "sanctions at the same time and in the same moment the insurpassable depth and the irreducible insufficiency of the Husserlian philosophy of genesis" (*LPG* 241/*PG* 149).

6. The major shift in "Genesis" from *Le problème* accords with what I argue below to be the major flaw Derrida found in *Le problème* shortly after he wrote it:

namely, *Le problème*'s invocation of a real, a radical existent corresponding to the individual in perception, providing its substratum or ultimate non-constituted core. In "Genesis," as opposed to *Le problème,* Derrida postpones all such talk until the end, and when he does so, what is at stake is a matter of the radical facticity of death, rather than the origin of what Husserl calls hyletic data—Derrida thus already executing in "Genesis" a program for the deferral of the question of (radical) facticity that Derrida also sketches, and in part enacts, at the end of the "Introduction" (*WD* 168; cf. *IOG* 151–52, especially n184). This is the origin of that specific dialectic between Heideggerean ontology and Husserlian phenomenology that has drawn so much attention in the literature. (For Lawlor, in his latest work, it should be noted, "Genesis" unproblematically represents Derrida's stance toward Husserl throughout all his early writings [Lawlor 2002, 24].)

7. Derrida does give a retrospective account in his 1990 "Avertissement" as to what he *now* finds inadequate in this text, aspects of which I comment on further below. This 1990 account has tended to obscure the more pressing issue, at least from a developmental perspective, of what in the *mid-1950s* Derrida found problematic in *Le problème.*

8. The second half of Marrati-Guénoun's 1998 book is the best sustained study of Derrida's relation to Heidegger that we have, being informed by a solid firsthand acquaintance with Heidegger. Despite this, Marrati-Guénoun does not recognize any significant development in Derrida's thought, and begins her discussion of Derrida and Heidegger from the 1980 "Envoi." Besides Marrati-Guénoun (and John Caputo, whom I address in a later note), Rudolf Bernet has recently published a book in French, drawing in part on previously published articles, which is an extended meditation on the relation of Husserl's work and Heidegger's, and where he gives important signposts to how Derrida's concerns would relate to these issues as well (Bernet's chapter in McKenna and Evans's *Derrida and Phenomenology* devoted to a reading of Derrida and focused on *Speech,* is taken up in my next chapter). Similarly Françoise Dastur's contribution to the 1993 Spindel Conference, though not aimed at this theme, in the footnotes especially, has sound insights concerning the relations of Derrida to Heidegger, though she is sometimes too quick to accept Derrida's own self-interpretation on these matters (Dastur 1994, 120), in my view, and she and I disagree significantly about Derrida's relation to Merleau-Ponty.

9. Lawlor also raises this point (Lawlor 2002, 48). Lawlor, however, sees Derrida in *Le problème* as falling prey to a "humanism" which later gives way to a "meta-humanism," rather than the "anti-humanism" of Hyppolite (Lawlor 2002, 141–42)—characterizations which do not, however, seem to me to get to the real heart of the problem, for reasons that will become clear as my exposition continues.

10. Recent Husserl scholars, most notably Donn Welton, but also Thomas Seebohm, have criticized Derrida's Husserl interpretation for its relative lack of familiarity with an important portion of Husserl's corpus, precisely that part which will soon be most in question here: namely, the writings of the 1920s which are concerned, broadly speaking, with genetic phenomenology (Seebohm 1995, 190; Welton 2001, 395). Both Welton and Seebohm are quick to note that much of this

work, some of which is now collected in the *Analysen zur passiven Synthesis,* was simply unavailable in the early 1950s at the time *Le problème* was written and Derrida's Husserl interpretation was being formed (Derrida indicates he did consult Groups A, B, C, and D of the *Nachlass* [*PG* 287]). Welton himself, it should be noted, both in his more recent and in his earlier work, indicates that he thinks many of Derrida's criticisms would be justified, if his own new interpretation of Husserl were not accepted (Welton 1983, 163–64; 2001, 401). Thus, not only is it too soon to say that the core of Derrida's earliest thought here in *Le problème* has simply been superseded, but the questions that animate Derrida's reading, I would insist, are still largely those that lie behind the more specialized treatments of phenomenologists today and motivate their inquiries, even as a new and more complex understanding of these same issues is emerging. Accordingly, a future task here appears (one not undertaken in the present work): Derrida's deepest roots in phenomenology having begun to be established in respect to the state of Husserl and Heidegger studies at an earlier epoch, a more definitive working through of these positions will be necessary that takes into account more current scholarship, the researches of such scholars as Welton, Ströker, Zahavi, Crowell, Hopkins, Steinbock, and others.

11. Part of what makes this juncture, represented by Husserl's genetic phenomenology, so critical as a focus for Heidegger's alternative claims, as well as Derrida's, is an uncertainty as to what genetic phenomenology represents for Husserl himself. As I have noted, some commentators, most notably Donn Welton, following Ludwig Landgrebe's account, have long argued that a rather sizable alternation, indeed a veritable revolution, in Husserl's view takes place at this juncture, though for Welton the *Cartesian Meditations* themselves and the passage that I am about to focus on give an inadequate picture of Husserl's project (Welton 2001, 7, 252; 1983, 173, 179). Welton has the most extreme view of the discontinuity that genetic phenomenology inaugurates in Husserl's thinking; Ströker, though more moderate, is closer to Welton than most (Ströker 1993, 147, 148). Mohanty, and it would appear Bernet, stand at the other end, denying that Husserl's genetic phase represents any significant discontinuity with his earlier thought, a position with which Derrida seems to have always agreed, as Mohanty himself points out (Mohanty 1997, 64). Iso Kern (in Bernet, Kern, and Marbach 1995) gives a very useful introduction to some of the stakes of this distinction, which I discuss further below, as well as some of the problems, scholarly and conceptual, with arriving at a definitive appraisal of where Husserl himself actually stood (Bernet, Kern, and Marbach 1995, 195–204). (Stated most broadly, my response to Welton's work *solely as it speaks to Derrida,* and to Derrida's work with Husserl, not Husserl himself, is that my own attention to Derrida's development may be said to show that Derrida also underwent the discovery of something like an "other Husserl"—a revelation of a Husserl more resistant to the standard criticisms than Derrida had previously believed, thus in important ways opening the door to Derrida's own later work—but this occurred in the "Introduction" and in respect to the history writings in their specificity. This aspect of Derrida's thought, indeed the "Introduction" itself, Welton seems to leave out of account: thus arriving at the "same" Der-

rida, I would suggest, even as he criticizes Derrida for hewing to the "same" Husserl, though Welton's comments on Derrida, to be fair, are finally only made in passing.)

12. Derrida will thus go on to speak here of "the essential and definitive limit of all eidetic phenomenology of genesis . . . which is not genesis itself but solely its phenomenological sense, always already constituted upon the foundations of a world whose ontological structures, themselves produced in the unity of a history, are not put into question or thematized as such" (*LPG* 228/*PG* 139–40; see also *LPG* 237/*PG* 147 for a related result drawn from Husserl's discussion not of active, but passive, genesis).

13. This is commonly agreed on in the literature (see Carr 1974, 68–76; Ströker 1993, 146–47; Bernet, Kern, and Marbach 1995, 200). Ströker, who is close to Welton in this regard, denies this account centered on the transcendental monad is an adequate one, however (Ströker 1993, 161). (Welton not only demotes *Cartesian Meditations* 4, but claims that even *Experience and Judgment* and *Formal and Transcendental Logic* give a misleading view of the deepest significance of Husserl's turn to genetic phenomenology; Welton 1983, 175). Ströker also denies, along similar lines, that Husserl's treatment of intersubjectivity in *Cartesian Meditations* 5 is adequate—the two accounts (*Cartesian Meditations* 4 and 5), however, accord with one another and with the vexed transcendental idealism that Husserl goes on to announce in four, none of which he ever explicitly, publicly renounced, as far as I know. Lawlor does not consider the vexed status of *Cartesian Meditations* 5 in the Husserl literature, and in relation to the whole theme of intersubjectivity more generally. Hence, he does not note to what great extent, for example, Levinas's entire philosophy constitutes a criticism of this analysis, nor how difficult and unexpected is (1) Derrida's defense of this analysis in "Violence and Metaphysics" and (2) Derrida's ongoing rapprochement with Levinas despite this marked divergence. Lawlor may not be alone, of course, in failing to see how difficult is the reconciliation of Derrida's thought with Levinas's that Derrida proposes, but at least as far as the interpretation of the analysis of *Cartesian Meditations* 5 is concerned, it should be clear that Husserl by no means has given an account that places the "other" above the transcendental subject, and that gives priority to language and community over against the absoluteness of the transcendental ego's constituting intentionality (see Lawlor 2002, 4, 135, 161–63, 176, 179).

14. On the notion of horizon, see Husserl's *Experience and Judgment* (1973b, 35–39); for internal horizons, see Husserl 1973b, 112–20. For external horizons and world, see Husserl 1973b, 28–31, 162–67. My overall account has also been influenced by Husserl's discussion of the so-called "life-world" path to the reduction in the second half of the *Crisis* (especially Husserl 1970a, 157–64), which I take to shed important light on Husserl's understanding of these themes. In his *Radical Hermeneutics* John Caputo gives an account of Husserl's thought in its relation to Heidegger and Derrida centering on the role of horizons, which is solid as far as his treatment of horizons themselves is concerned, and which also raises problems close to those that I am about to suggest (see Caputo 1987, 39 ff. for horizons, 55 ff. for problems, especially 57). Caputo, though, seems finally at the opposite pole to the one at which I stand here. Despite the considerable magnitude

of his achievements as a commentator here and elsewhere, he views both Husserl and Heidegger *retrospectively* from the viewpoint of Derrida's mature thought, in fact stressing the *continuity* among all three thinkers, while seeming to believe that Derrida has arrived at the definitive account of these matters. Caputo thus never attends to the development within Derrida's own corpus or that which may take place within the phenomenological tradition. For all his emphasis on "difficulty" and shaking things up (Caputo 1987, 1), Caputo, while recognizing the problems that Husserl's account potentially faces (about which he and I are not far apart), never seems worried about whether *philosophically meaningful alternatives* to Husserl's standpoint really exist, and Derrida's project, in particular, for him is only in need of sufficiently perspicuous presentation or articulation, not validation or justification, as far as I am able to discern. Lawlor, too, it should be noted, comments on *Cartesian Meditations* 4 and Derrida's treatment of it in *Le problème,* which I am also about to discuss. Yet Lawlor seems to draw dire consequences for Husserl's project as a whole from the fact that passive genesis is assigned a role in giving an object "already there," though this is an entirely Husserlian analysis, having the form that I have just rehearsed (Lawlor 2002, 76).

15. In part inspired by the publication of volume 6 of Husserl's collected works in English translation (*Psychological and Transcendental Phenomenology and the Confrontation with Heidegger*), much good work has recently been done on Husserl's relation to Heidegger; these considerations fall beyond the scope of the present work, however—as already noted, in part, since much of this material was not available to Derrida in 1954.

16. See the critique of "Cartesianism" throughout *Being and Time,* especially in its first half (§§ 19–21, 89–101). While I agree with Welton, who believes charges of Cartesianism have become something of a shibboleth and today are as likely to prevent thought as to provoke it (Welton 2001, 401), it does seem to me to remain the case that Heidegger's notion of the ready-to-hand, the primacy given to the hermeneutic over the apophantic and, with these, the toppling of the subject-object relation itself, is a crux to whose depth, at least in the past, much of the rebuttal of Heidegger by Husserlians does not come (see Bernet 1988, 9–10, where, with characteristic precision, Bernet nicely captures the force of this difference in respect to the treatment of signification, focusing on the absence of any account of context in Husserl's treatment). More important for my present concerns, however (and here above all perhaps is where I take leave from Caputo's analysis), as I am about to show, Derrida from the first and always *has sided with Husserl and Husserlians on just these points.* He has always downplayed the overturning of the very model of consciousness (and with that its functioning as an epistemological principle) at the outset of *Being and Time.* This remains true of all Derrida's work, and is most evident in *Of Spirit* and "Geschlecht II," where the issue of Heidegger's hand must be seen first and foremost in light of Heidegger's break with Husserl's phenomenology in these opening sections—and Derrida's decision to initially side with Husserl on just these points—before Derrida's own concerns with Heidegger's supposed phono- and logocentrism can be evaluated.

17. See *Cartesian Meditations* §32 (Husserl 1960, 66–67): "The Ego as substrate of habitualities," where Husserl declares "[I] find myself as the Ego who *is* con-

vinced, who, as the persisting ego is determined by this abiding habitus or state," and that, consequently, "by his own active generating, the ego constitutes himself as identical substrate of Ego properties . . . as a 'fixed and abiding' personal ego."

18. Habit turns out to be correlative to those virtual dispositions and potentialities of the subject with which, and through which, the individual in perception now always finds itself given (though the ultimate relation of habits formed actively and habits functioning passively is left unresolved by Husserl in these brief pages, as far as I can tell). Thus later on in *Cartesian Meditations* 4, discussing the role of habit in passive synthesis, Husserl writes: "When these habitual apperceptions become actually operative, the already given objects formed for the central Ego appear, affect him, and motivate activities. Thanks to the aforesaid passive synthesis the Ego always has an environment of 'objects'" (Husserl 1960, 79/ Husserl 1973a, 113).

19. In discussing the role of habit (in passive syntheses), Husserl goes on to say: "Even that everything affecting me as developed ego is apperceived as an object, as substrate of recognizable predicates, belongs here, since this is an already familiar goal form . . . and this goal-form is understandable in advance as having arisen in a genesis" (Husserl 1960, 79–80/Husserl 1973a, 113). This last remark, concerning the goal-form of the object and "its primal instituting" *(Urstiftung)*, so important for the connection to Husserl's work on history, opens on to the problem of to what extent Husserl at this moment is envisioning genuine genesis, or merely structures (or essences) of genesis as the ultimate object of his genetic phenomenology—whether Husserl is envisioning simply a "dynamic static analysis" (Welton 1983, 173) in respect to"constitutive systems," or instead the "*genesis* of this constitution," of these systems (which itself, in turn, would be subject to an eidetics, to questions of "universal form or type"), as Iso Kern puts it (Bernet, Kern, and Marbach 1995, 201, my emphasis).

20. Husserl himself, in fact, has to recognize something very close to this problem as he is setting out his genetic phenomenology program for the first time here in *Cartesian Meditations* 4. Husserl stipulates, as he bring this phase of his discussion to a close, that the developmental structures of the transcendental ego still represent but one possibility among others within a "maximally universal eidetic phenomenology." Such maximal eidetic universal treatment of the ego has yet to be attained, according to Husserl, however, and with that, "questions of universal genesis and the genetic structure of the ego in his universality" are not yet resolved (Husserl 1960, 76–77). Husserl's own sketch of transcendental egological genesis, accordingly, continues to remain less than "maximally universal," and still refers back to factuality; and this problem, Husserl's difficulties with the ego's pure determination, can also be seen in his repeated invocation in his later writings of such odd conceptions as transcendental normalcy and pathology—notions which seem severed once and for all from any possibility of wholly a priori determination.

21. The problem in part perhaps has to do with the notion of constitutional analysis itself. This model, like everything else in Husserl, was aimed at objectivity, was framed to make apparent the constitution of objects as self-identical by way of a plurality of noemata. At this phase, however, as we have begun to see, what is

now to be the target of transcendental constitutive analyses is the subject and many of its achievements, which themselves are already supposed to do constitutive work in turn (for objects and existents of a nonsubjective sort). And despite the general methodological postulate that for anything to be given, it must be given to some noesis, it is by no means clear whether this avenue in this instance holds out any promise of achieving really substantial results: whether constitutive analyses of what is itself already constituting can be meaningfully envisioned even as a program, and whether this model thus can withstand the pressure exerted by the transformation that its original focus here undergoes. (The most notable instance of a difficulty of this sort, of the recursion of the constitution project onto what is itself supposed to be constituting, remains Alfred Schutz's famous treatment of the inadequacies of Husserl's analysis of the "other" and transcendental intersubjectivity in *Cartesian Meditations* 5. In his 1959 study, Schutz argued that the I and the other must already be given factically together, prior to the possibility of any constitution (and thus of the rights of my consciousness taking hold), if the authentic character of *social* experience is not to be forfeited [especially Schutz 1959, 359].)

22. This is always the defining difference, then, between Derrida and other heterodox phenomenologists: Derrida never questions Husserl's findings intraphenomenologically (with the sole exception perhaps of his discussion of the sign at the start of *Logical Investigations;* see, however, chapter 5, where the scope of the unique style of this questioning, still not finally assimilable to an intraphenomenological criticism, is specified). Derrida thus remains a fairly orthodox Husserlian as far as phenomenology itself is concerned (in comparison with Heidegger, Merleau-Ponty, and even Levinas), and this is what Lawlor fails to note, starting from Derrida as a critic of phenomenology, even if his suggestion that Derrida's criticism takes two forms, an intra- and super-phenomenological one, runs parallel to these two phases of Derrida's treatment owed to his own dialectical stance that I am specifying here (Lawlor 2002, 3). Moreover, it should be noted, though this dialectical strategy in *Le problème anticipates* that of deconstruction, in *Le problème,* of course, all of this still takes place in the name of *philosophy,* and is explicitly aimed at its completion. Dialectic may "supervene" on a structural insufficiency in phenomenology (and thus already gestures in certain respects toward that excess of all philosophy which Derrida later wishes to think); nevertheless, Derrida is here well aware of the philosophical lineage of dialectic, he has recourse to it for the sake of *completing philosophy itself,* and in this way *Le problème*'s strategy also differs from Derrida's later thought, and leaves room for its further development. (See *LPG* 16/*PG* xxviii for the "supervenient" relation of dialectic to phenomenology and an overview of dialectic's role.)

23. "Si l'on ne commence pas par une description des essences *a priori* jamais l'on pourra prétendre à aucune rigueur. L'existence elle-même, dans son surgissement le plus originaire, ne pourra apparaître à un regard philosophique. Aussi, tout reproche adressé à cet essentialisme husserlien au nom d'une originarité empirique ou existentielle ou de quelque moment antérieur de genèse, devra, pour avoir un sens, supposer une eidétique déjà constituée . . . C'est ce qui nous autorise à parler d'une philosophie dialectique comme seule philosophie

possible de la genèse . . . Le sens de la genèse est produit par une genèse mais la genèse n'est accessible dans son être, possible dans son apparition, que si l'on part de l'originalité de son sens. Toute philosophie est condamnée à parcourir en sens inverse l'itinéraire effectif de tout devenir. Toutes les critiques adressées à Husserl (celles, notamment, de Heidegger et de Tran Duc Thao, d'ailleurs très différentes entre elles) tendent à un reversement radical dont on ne voit pas qu'il suppose la problématique définie et résolue par Husserl" (*LPG* 225–26).

24. Lawlor, by contrast, sees Derrida's engagement with Tran Duc Thao as having "provide[d] for Derrida new ways of thinking about phenomenology" (Lawlor 2002, 48), and also uses his writings to motivate the problem with genesis (and many of its implications) that Lawlor identifies as Derrida's (Lawlor 2002, 54). At the same time, Lawlor does register some of these differences of Derrida from other phenomenological critics—he sees Derrida as "upping the ante" on their dialectical criticism (which he identifies with both Tran Duc Thao's position, as well as Cavaillès's; Lawlor 2002, 48), an approach which still puts Derrida on the side of these authors rather than Husserl himself. Lawlor, lastly, does comment on the passage I cite. He argues, however, that what Derrida rejects is Tran Duc Thao's materialism, a claim that seems to me to understate the scope, and stakes, of Derrida's disagreement with him (Lawlor 2002, 55–56).

25. Derrida's loyalty to Husserl's philosophical and phenomenological starting points, so long downplayed in the literature by Husserlians and non-Husserlians alike, has been defended by Derrida himself on a number of occasions. (This stance is still readily visible at least through *Speech* [though thereafter in many places more faintly], most of all in its introduction, where Derrida upholds Husserl's singular doctrine of the mundane ego's "derivation" from the absolute transcendental subject by way of an "enworlding apperception" [*verweltliche Selbstapperzeption*], a doctrine from Husserl's late *Phenomenological Psychology* which very much entails this same set of commitments, and seems, at least to me, somewhat questionable [*SP* 11].) Derrida's most notable defense of Husserl's reductions, and his siding with him in the context of Heidegger's objection, comes in a note late in the "Introduction," to which Dastur also draws attention (Dastur 1994, 120; *IOG* 138n164). Derrida's assertion that "an essential finitude appears in phenomenology" thanks to the eidetic reduction (because the transcendental function thereby would dissimulate itself in a region), thus implying Husserl's treatment of these matters is equivalent to Heidegger's, seems to me, however, to ignore all the critical issues pertaining to philosophical knowledge itself that I have here begun to bring out: that the reduction, and Husserl's transcendental idealism are meant to make possible authoritative philosophical discourse, while Heidegger's analysis of finitude calls into question whether such knowledge is ever really possible, though no other knowledge for Heidegger would be more authoritative.

26. In the passage that I cited at the outset, Derrida raises questions in regard to this portion of Husserl's analyses close to those that I brought forward in my discussion of Heidegger and Husserl: issues related to "an already constituted ontology" which holds back the ego from wholly free and universal reflection on its own genesis, and thus sets "an absolute existential limit" to Husserl's inquiry (*LPG*

228/*PG* 140). Due to Derrida's unique strategy of deferral and delay, the ultimate congruence of these concerns with Heidegger's or Merleau-Ponty's (a congruence which will fall away as early as "Genesis") is not, in my view, a decisive factor, especially given the problems these assertions already encounter even in *Le problème*, upon which I comment further below.

27. Derrida speaks of dialectic, indeed an "infinite dialectic" as the total outcome at which he aims, and as "the idea . . . of philosophy itself" repeatedly in *Le problème* (*PG* 226; cf. 125n44, 32). This dialectic and my description of it hearken back to Geoff Bennington's account of deconstruction that I discussed in my first chapter (Bennington 1993, 278). This further attests to the acuity of Bennington's description; yet, as I discuss below, this version of Derrida's project is also one that will be superseded in certain respects, especially in regard to what it understands by the empirical or the constituted.

28. This intention, of course, is what Rodolphe Gasché first fixed on and made known, eventually most popularly, though perhaps somewhat misleadingly, under the heading of the quasi-transcendental.

29. Derrida's own more radical leave-taking from philosophy will always imply a core acceptance of Husserl's essence doctrine as its springboard. Derrida's interrogations of Foucault and Levinas make this plain with their attack on Foucault's historicism and Levinas's empiricism, which I discuss further below, as do Derrida's remarks in the aftermath of his presentation of "Genesis," which also clearly attest that as late as 1959 Derrida still held these views ("GS" 263–64). Even more centrally, however, Derrida's embrace of Husserl's position underlies that seemingly skeptical model of the unopposable logos—the supposed "metaphysical" character of all discourse that prevents the articulation of any stable outside—whose forebear it clearly is, since without the belief that Husserl is right about meaning and essences, right about philosophy's methodology, that Derrida expresses unabashedly here, Derrida would have no reason to believe that these claims, as it were the tain of Husserl's essence doctrine, were in any way valid.

30. As I previously noted, Lawlor overlooks this crucial footnote; he understands Derrida's treatment of Husserl's history writings at the end of *Le problème* as essentially in line with Derrida's view of them in the "Introduction."

31. Marrati-Guénoun, importantly, recognizes such a demotion as well. "Derrida n'utilisera plus par la suite le concept de genèse," she writes ("Derrida will no longer utilize in what follows the concept of genesis"; Marrati-Guénoun 1998, 144; her emphasis). Her account of why this is so focuses in part on the resources of the *concept* of genesis, rather than Derrida's development (see 144n33), and though she rightfully points out that much of the work done by this notion in *Le problème* (especially as it relates to time and passive synthesis) is taken over by new themes in Derrida, I also think that Derrida's interpretation of time in Husserl undergoes significant alteration between 1954 and 1967 (among other things, passive synthesis in its specificity becoming less of an issue), while she does not.

32. Lawlor, as I have already begun to note, also sees a shift in Derrida that brings him in greater proximity as the works of 1967 approach (Lawlor 2002, 145–46). Since, however, according to Lawlor, this is also accompanied by a wholesale incorporation of Levinas's themes and standpoints ("all of Levinas' questions to

Husserl and Heidegger become Derrida's questions" [Lawlor 2002, 145]), what this incorporation of Heidegger really represents in Derrida's thought remains unclear.

33. Apart from the passage I cite below, Derrida most notably closes out his discussion of part 2 by insisting on the necessity of a "real genesis" (*genèse réelle* [*real*]; *LPG* 173/*PG* 100); this is the result of an argument focused on the role of hyle (noetic, yet nonintentional, sensuous stuff) in *Ideas I* (Husserl 1983, 203 ff.), Derrida making the case that Husserl's account of hyle implies a real transcendent (*LPG* 153, 155, 161), contact with which it cannot, however, account for—an argument that refers back, in turn, to his discussion of time and the role of the real (where "empirical or ontological genesis . . . are essentially implied" [*LPG* 118/*PG* 61]) that I am about to further discuss. Much of this argument, here and throughout *Le problème*, has Husserl's transcendental idealism, his denial that it is meaningful to speak of a real beyond its appearance in consciousness (see Husserl 1960, 83ff.), as its ultimate context and is aimed at preserving the full meaning of *intuition* (e.g., *LPG* 151), interestingly enough, a concern that obviously drops from Derrida's work, along with the disappearance of these other themes.

34. Derrida on Heidegger's *readings* of poets (and fragments of philosophers) in works such as "The *Retrait* of Metaphor" and *Signéponge* is perhaps the finest interpreter of Heidegger's later thought that we have. Derrida somewhere calls Heidegger's notion of the ontico-ontological difference the "most difficult thought," and I am in the midst of arguing that in the course of Derrida's development his understanding of Heidegger's core philosophical concerns grew as well. At the same time, as I indicated above, even Derrida's works on Heidegger in the 1980s, *Of Spirit* and "Geschlecht II," in my view must be seen in the context here set out, as taking the side of Husserl and swerving away from Heidegger's powerful rethinking of phenomenology in the opening pages of *Being and Time*.

35. This is part of a larger problem which Derrida himself points out in his "Avant-propos" (*PG* 32), which I can only touch on here concerning the grafting on to one another of two very different structures of argument—one phenomenological, the other dialectical. What weight dialectic, presumably a dialectic of concepts, has as a form of argument in a context otherwise phenomenological and dedicated to originary evidence is far from clear. Neither Heidegger nor Husserl would have assigned it any value—and this question, of the heterogeneity of the philosophical resources Derrida calls on as early as *Le problème*, clearly foreshadows many of the issues that I have raised pertaining to the methodology of deconstruction. (See Steven Crowell 1996 on this point, who raises an almost identical objection, albeit posed through a reading of Gasché.)

36. Derrida himself is by no means simply unaware of these difficulties. He claims that "the simultaneous or a priori synthetic taking consciousness of this necessary insufficiency and this possible rigor . . . constitutes the idea itself of philosophy as infinite dialectic" (*LPG* 226/*PG* 138). The version of Derrida's own project that he holds at the time of *Le problème* (which Derrida repeatedly invokes under the heading of "dialectic" and "infinite dialectic"; especially *LPG* 125n44, 172/*PG* 66n44, 99) is one in which what calls thought into question, at times at least, is simply the constituted itself, not a previously unheralded or excluded in-

stance (an absolute alterity, which Derrida, in fact, at one moment distances himself from [*LPG* 24]), thus calling for an infinite repetition of this cycle. For all the attraction of this position's austere removal from any conceivable dogma, as I go on to show, in the form Derrida sets it out here (unlike, for example, in the mature writings of Paul de Man), it nevertheless results in a constant instability in Derrida's own discourse and his vision of his own project. The role of dialectic itself wavers insofar as Derrida speaks, at times, as if dialectic is *intrinsic* to that "other" at which Derrida's engagement with Husserl arrives (an option which, with its emphasis on a previously unheralded radical alterity, stands quite close to Derrida's mature writings); yet more usually in *Le problème,* dialectic ends up looking like a mere heuristic device: a movement immanent only to *knowledge,* leaving no ultimate mark or trace on its object as such. In Derrida's subsequent discussion here of passive genesis, to which his treatment of active genesis in part is meant to serve as an introduction, he appears to offer the first more genuinely dialectical account: focusing on a moment in which "the absolute divides itself" in a "unity of intuition which is originally synthetic" (*LPG* 233/*PG* 143). Yet the ability to claim that this self-division of the absolute recurs to a previous facticity, a recognizable ontology, empiricity, and worldliness, and thus to maintain that the outcomes of his treatments of active and passive genesis ultimately coincide, itself ultimately relies on the analysis of time in section 2 that I am about to treat, raising questions as to the ultimate cogency of even this phase of Derrida's discourse.

37. Early on in *Le problème* Derrida speaks of "two vast movements of recoil and advance" as characterizing the relation of Husserl's corpus to genesis (*LPG* 4/*PG* xix). Derrida also notes that such a description is superficial, and though this "recoil and advance" remains determinative for his treatment of the totality of phenomenology proper, Derrida's treatment of genesis, as his introduction lays it out and in what follows, actually asserts more continuity than this statement suggests. Derrida's interpretation of Husserl's corpus overall in fact can be seen to be a reversal of Walter Biemel's famous account of the stages of Husserl's thought (see Biemel 1959). Biemel saw Husserl's work on psychogenesis in the prephenomenological *Philosophy of Arithmetic* as a precursor of Husserl's later work on constitution, and on this basis argued that all of Husserl's work and corpus could be seen as an ongoing engagement with this single topic (namely, constitution). Derrida, here for once perhaps the more literal reader, takes *genesis,* which Husserl in fact spoke of first, as primary and sees the problem of constitution as a subset of this, yet in a way similar to Biemel, he takes all of Husserl's thought to be organized around this earlier, broader theme.

38. Perhaps surprisingly, Derrida takes Brentano's side, relatively speaking, in respect to Husserl's criticism of Brentano's time interpretation (*LPG* 117). This accords, however, with Derrida's early "existentialist" understanding of Heidegger, his concern with Husserl's exclusion of the transcendent, and gives us a further indication of the direction in which Derrida's thought will go, since whatever else may be said of Derrida's treatment of temporality in *Speech,* this facet of his critique has been dropped. Brentano had correlated the movement of time, its inner intentional awareness, to the perception of a real temporal object; and Derrida sides with Brentano in order to argue that a real ontological genesis must be thought

to precede the phenomenological genesis of internal time, and thus to argue against the reduction of lived temporality to its essence, or noemata (an odd distinction between time as intended and time in itself that immediately drops from all of Derrida's subsequent work; for noematic or eidetic temporality, see *LPG* 112, 117, 122, 129, 130).

39. In line with his notion of dialectic, as well as his attempt to identify the other that conditions constitution as the constituted simply, Derrida will claim even here that his thought of the other still bears a "dialectical" relation to absolute temporal consciousness; such a radical real could never be taken up if there were no living constituting temporality, nor could any radical alterity be spoken of meaningfully at all barring such transcendental functioning ("the originary synthesis is precisely that of constituted and constituting, of present and nonpresent, of originary temporality and objective temporality" [*LPG* 123/*PG* 64]). This notion of "syntheses" chaining backward, each indicating a prior anterior genesis, is doubtless why Marrati-Guénoun and others have rightly seen Derrida's analysis as so close to some of his later ones, verging on key notions such as supplement or trace (see Marrati-Guénoun 1998, 21). Nevertheless, the thrust of Derrida's analysis continues to fall on the strange difference between time as noema and time as transcendent, and a further indication of the distance Derrida has yet to travel is to be found in *Le problème* 120n27, where Derrida joins Heidegger, against Husserl, in insisting on "the primordiality of time over space," a key claim, soon abandoned, that holds in check any immediate identification of Derrida's positions here with his later ones.

40. Derrida had already stated that "if the separation between fact and essence appears possible in other ontological regions than that of consciousness," in the case of time (and the region of inquiry proper to it, consciousness itself) the "eidetic reduction" would not be possible; and he concludes this argument by declaring that "phenomenology would no longer entirely master itself. Ontology would *already* be in its place" (*LPG* 117).

41. Derrida will conclude part 2 of *Le problème* claiming that the "empirical and the transcendental" would "resist a rigorous disassociation" (*LPG* 173/*PG* 100), and that the "validity of the eidetic and transcendental reduction would be put into question" (*LPG* 172/*PG* 100). He thus presents all of Husserl's subsequent thought as a (failed) defense against this prior breakdown: as successive attempts to enlarge the sphere of the reductions, attempts that are doomed to fail due to this initial omission of radical genesis.

42. Again Derrida is not simply unaware of these issues. Not only does he want to defend the reduction and Husserl's starting point, the absolute methodological rights of Husserl's philosophy, as I have argued above, but he also wishes to embrace in some form the vulnerable position into which this puts his own argument and the tenuous character of his own standpoint that results from this embrace.

43. Lawlor most notably has drawn extensive attention to the importance of Fink for Derrida (Lawlor 1995, 154 ff., especially n13), and in his latest work, this same 1933 essay by Fink upon which I am about to comment plays a similar, even greater, role than it does here, since through his commentary Lawlor lays out the problem of genesis as such (which he takes to be "the basic problem of phenome-

nology"), and this problem, as already noted, provides the conceptual axis through which Lawlor approaches all of Derrida's writings on Husserl up through 1967, including *Speech* (Lawlor 2002, 14–21). Lawlor provides useful commentary on Fink's text, although issues I have mentioned earlier—the segregation of Lawlor's discussions of Husserl's commentators from his work with Derrida's own texts, his interest in finding anticipations of Derrida's mature views in his earlier writings, as well as his belief that Derrida is first and foremost a *critic* of phenomenology—impede Lawlor from really making concrete what in Derrida is owed to Fink (see Lawlor 2002, 21–23, as well as Kates 2005). Certainly, in respect to the theme of genesis in Derrida's own writings, the connection to the transcendental reduction in its specificity, which is what I emphasize here, is not highlighted by Lawlor (Lawlor 2002, 30–33).

44. It is important to emphasize that in this case, as a number of Fink's articles attest, a problem, or question, related to Husserl's work was already recognized in the literature (by Fink and other Husserlians) and was already the subject of debate. This is why Derrida in taking up this theme, and in a sense attempting to resolve it with his thinking of genesis, should in no way be seen as mounting a still further break with Husserl in *Le problème* beyond the dialectic that we have already witnessed. At the same time, if Derrida does not by any means cast the transcendental reduction as such into doubt, at least no more than it had been already, nevertheless, it should also be stressed that Fink's writings themselves remain entirely in the service of Husserl's philosophy. Fink's own responses to these questions, including his famous article on operative concepts, are all meant to function intra-phenomenologically, and thus he himself never saw the necessity for the kind of radical step that we have already seen Derrida take, although this step in its own way may also be seen as in the service of Husserl's philosophy. Indeed, because both of these things are so—because a problem, or mystery, was already recognized by Husserlians, in response to which in part Derrida also fashioned his own unique beyond—*all* of Derrida's Husserl writings can, and I think *should* be viewed, at least in part, as siding with Husserl, and furthering his transcendental standpoint. They contain an element of restitution for the break that Derrida is also in the course of making, and this continues to be so even in 1967, as we shall see, since the status of language, and its relation to Husserl's core thought, to the reduction, is something that Husserl himself never established definitively.

45. For other accounts of the work of Husserl's transcendental reduction, see Bernet, Kern, and Marbach 1995, 58–77; Seebohm 1989; McKenna 1982; and Sokolowski 1964. Fink's writings, to which many of these works are in part responses (see Seebohm 1989; Sokolowski 1964 [I owe this reference to Frank Hunt]; and Crowell 2001), remain the single most powerful sustained elaboration of this thought and certainly the one that most influenced Derrida. (In addition to the work I comment on here, see McKenna, Harlan, and Winters 1981 for translations of other seminal texts of Fink's, as well as Ludwig Landgrebe's, which shed important, different, collateral light on many of these issues.) This Husserlian theme, Husserl's transcendental attitude, is the one that I believe readers of Derrida most need to appreciate of all that Husserl has to offer and is the issue that perhaps remains even today most poorly understood.

46. Fink's argument here may become confusing, since he also insists that it is by a "transcending passage" that Husserl arrives at the absolute (Fink 1970, 99) and that only by dint of this does Husserl's philosophy perform a transcendental function in the Kantian sense of providing the conditions for all other knowledges (Fink 1970, 100). Such a "transcending passage," as Fink presents it, is nevertheless easily distinguished from recourse to a traditional transcendent, and indeed for Fink, Husserl's account goes beyond even Kant's, insofar as the Kantian viewpoint for Fink remains fixed on an older understanding of the transcendent and the opposition between it and world-immanence: confining philosophical knowledge, on the one hand, simply to the world, to the "ontic" (to the disclosure of an apriori *of* the world), while also remaining fixated on real transcendence, such that the ultimate achievement of philosophy for Kant is to show that access to these sorts of transcendents for us is impossible (Fink 1970, 100).

47. In *Ideas I,* Husserl begins from the epistemological status of consciousness, the indubitability or apodicticity of claims about it, and uses this as a basis for establishing the transcendental character of its functioning—for laying bare the grounds that the intentional life which becomes evident in this consciousness is supposed to supply for everything else. Notoriously, however, this obscured, even if it did not wholly efface, the difference between the psychic (of which the same sort of certainty holds true, yet as a fact of my consciousness, and which ultimately implies a reference to myself as mundane, as just another worldly being, a psychophysical unity) and the transcendental ego as such (whose status is tied to that unique intentionality without which no world or worldly being, including my person, could be given). Though Husserl, of course, already acknowledged this difference (between the transcendental and the mundane, and even its apriori and the eidetic) without granting it an absolute value, the version of the reduction in the *Crisis,* already mentioned, has the virtue of highlighting this difference and emphasizing the unique status of the transcendental reduction as such.

48. In addition to Derrida's claim, already cited, that Husserl's thought "quits the plane of classical philosophy" (for reasons similar to these; *LPG* 102), see *LPG* 85 ff./ *PG* 37–39, where Derrida explicitly compares Husserl's standpoint to Kant's and insists that the difference consists in Husserl's recourse to "an originarily concrete experience."

49. See also Landgrebe's exemplary discussion of this theme of an "absolute experience" (Landgrebe 1981a, 78), and a new notion of the "a priori 'priority'" (Landgrebe 1981a, 80).

50. In the literature, this problem has sometimes been approached, in a way very different from Derrida's, as the problem of the protreptic, of what gives rise to the turn to philosophy, what motivates philosophical inquiry in the first place, thus linking this latest problem in Husserl with classical philosophy, and ultimately with the status of philosophy and political philosophy in Plato's *Republic.* (See the work of Thomas Prufer, in particular the conclusion of "Husserlian Distinctions and Strategies in *The Crisis,*" Prufer 1993, 57; I owe this reference to Frank Hunt.)

51. Mohanty has also identified this problem, drawing his concluding formulation of this "paradox" from the "great Buddhist philosopher Nagarjuna, . . .

[who] said, 'the . . . *samsara* (or the mundane) and *nirvana* (the transcendental) are not different'" (Mohanty 1985, 153).

52. Of course, as I have already noted and as should now be even clearer, Fink, at least in his articles specifically devoted to Husserl's thought, saw these issues as ones for ongoing research within phenomenology, rather than ones that brought Husserl's project as a whole into doubt. In raising these issues, Fink seems more interested in fleshing out the consequences of Husserl's radical change of standpoint within phenomenology, rather than calling into question its operation. This also seems to be the primary thrust of his essay on operative concepts, whose point is to stress the difference between Husserl's transcendental concepts, so-called "transcendentalese," and mundane discourse, for the purpose of giving room for Husserl's transcendental analyses to operate. (Lawlor, along with many other Derrideans, seems not to recognize how far Fink's own intentions stand from offering disqualifying criticisms of Husserl's phenomenology, as when he conflates Fink's discussion of a transcendental *Schein*, intrinsic to the transcendental attitude in its uniqueness, with the problem of operative concepts within phenomenology more generally [Lawlor 2002, 22].) Nevertheless, it finally seems to me an open question to what degree Fink himself saw these problems as soluble.

53. Not only is this so in the introduction to *Speech* to which I have already alluded, where Derrida will insist on that "supplementary nothing that is the transcendental and without which no world would appear" (*VP* 13), but also in the early essays on Foucault and Levinas, which will be examined later, as well as numerous places in *Of Grammatology*, in which Derrida gives Husserl's transcendental attitude the status of a unique, singular, difference distinct from those that may be found in language, the concept, or any other mundane determinable realm. *Différance*, while eventually said by Derrida to be "older" than the transcendental reduction, as well as Heidegger's "ontico-ontological" difference, is, like the latter, uniquely tied to the problem of the transcendental reduction as an origin and Husserl's transcendental standpoint generally, and it thus implies a notion or problem of difference unlike any other—something Fink's treatment of these issues, and my account of it, I hope, make especially plain.

54. Indeed, as I argue further in my next chapters, Derrida may only ever be able to think a more general radical writing (than Husserl's) in 1967 insofar as he approximates or simulates this by showing that both starting points, both Husserl's view of language and its opposite, are held by the same "metaphysical" system, the same teleology. Thus, mounting the "same deconstruction" (of phono-logo-centrism) in each case, Derrida will usher in this new more general notion of inscription, even now perhaps largely negatively.

55. Derrida in 1967 wants to repeat not only the strategy of *Le problème*'s project but its themes; thanks to the "Introduction," however—to put all this in a nutshell—Derrida now substitutes language and writing for the real and genesis, as the primary precursors to Husserl's absolute perspective. These, and what they imply, now "contaminate" this transcendental origin, even as their consideration also firms it up, according to the uniquely "dialectical" schema of Derrida's intervention into phenomenology that has already come forward. Thus in the introduction to *Speech,* offering perhaps the single best expression of Derrida's core views on

language that we have, he will claim that "language preserves the difference that preserves language"—a claim that is only intelligible thanks to the identification of Husserl's transcendental attitude with this difference (insofar as this attitude, in Derrida's eyes, uniquely makes possible, and takes responsibility for, those characteristics of referring to an other, and of bearing a meaning and sense ultimately capable of mapping a world, without which language would not be language) and thanks to which it can be seen that Derrida even now wishes to resolve those issues Fink raised long ago. (See Lawlor's very different gloss on this same statement in Lawlor 2002, 23.)

Chapter 5

1. "Form and Meaning: A Note on the Phenomenology of Language," though first anthologized in the 1972 *Marges de la philosophie,* was also originally published in 1967, and its composition appears to follow that of *Speech.* In a previously published piece (Kates 1998), I have sketched the direction for a possible interpretation of that article, which is further expanded on here in the context of a discussion of *Speech.* In *Le toucher: Jean-Luc Nancy* (2000), Derrida comments extensively on a text by Husserl for the first time in over thirty years

2. This is true of White (1987), Edie (1990), largely of Hopkins (1985, especially 205–7, though he also focuses on time), Lawlor in his earlier works (1996b, 126; but cf. Lawlor 1995, 177), and somewhat less of critics who focus solely on the problem of ideality, such as Willard or Mohanty. Evans, of course, devotes a whole book to *Speech,* yet his reading seems to be decisively influenced by these opening sections (see, e.g., his introduction, Evans 1991, 6–14). Bernet (1995), Marrati-Guénoun (1998), and Caputo (1987), as well as Sallis (1995, 6–18), though his reading is more compressed, and the most recent Lawlor, all comment on *Speech* in a more well-rounded way. Caputo, however, seems to give short shrift to chapter 6, where Derrida actually sets out the phenomenological voice in its specificity and which is the chapter most central to my discussion. In what follows, I make further reference to most of these interpretations—Bernet's, Marrati-Guénoun's, and Lawlor's, especially.

3. For those unfamiliar with the chronology of Husserl's published writings, the actual pages of Husserl upon which Derrida purports to comment in *Speech,* which are the opening pages of the second part of Husserl's *Logical Investigations,* first appeared in print in 1901. They are the first writings of Husserl's explicitly to practice phenomenology, though Husserl's understanding of phenomenology subsequently underwent transformation. Besides *Logical Investigations* II.1, Derrida makes extended reference in *Speech* to *The Phenomenology of Internal Time-Consciousness* (lectures 1907–13, first published 1928), *Ideas I* (1913), and, if the introduction to *Speech* be included, *Phenomenological Psychology* (lectures dating from 1928), and he draws on *Cartesian Meditations* (1929) and *Formal and Transcendental Logic* (1929) at critical moments as well.

4. As noted earlier, Derrida, in line with Gaston Berger's and Fink's interpre-

tation, sees Husserl's first phenomenological writings on logic in *Logical Investigations* as already implying Husserl's more mature explicitly transcendental stance (first set out in *Ideas I*). Husserl's first phenomenological work, concerned largely with the essential truths of logic and ideal meanings, is for Derrida inseparable from his later stance, with its focus on problems of constitution. This interpretation in part accounts for why Derrida sees the totality of Husserl's thought at stake in this initial crossroads of *Logical Investigations* II and his ability to treat it as such (see *LPG* 102, where Derrida makes this view most explicit, and also his 1964 review of Mohanty [Derrida 1964a], which Mohanty has himself commented on [Mohanty 1997, 65]).

5. The French title of *Speech and Phenomena*, as is well known, is in fact *La voix et le phénomène*, or more literally, *Voice and Phenomenon*. The difference in titles is, of course, important to my interpretation here. Significant too, however, is the impulse that led to the English title and the more general problems with understanding Derrida's own intentions that it bespeaks. As we shall see, much of what pertains to the "voice" in the first half of *Speech* has to do most centrally with discourse *(Rede, dire)*, and the distinction between the *use* of linguistic signs and their status as belonging to language *(Sprache, langue)*. The choice to translate "*voix*" as "speech," due to this relation to use or discourse, was indeed understandable, and it clearly attests to an underlying ambiguity or tension pertaining to the totality of Derrida's intentions toward the "voice" in *Speech*, which even today has perhaps not been fully resolved.

6. Though this seems to me a straightforward claim, Lawlor's interpretation, which sees "Violence and Metaphysics" as importantly anticipating *Speech* (Lawlor 2002, 146–50) and in *Speech* often identifies *Levinasian* themes (Lawlor 2002, 174, 179, 189), would appear to imply its denial.

7. Lawlor takes a surprising tack toward this problem, which, in its own way, does not issue all that far from my stance. Early on in his discussion of *Speech* he declares that "of course, there is no concept of the voice in Husserl," and claims "Derrida is importing a certain Hegelian radicalism into Husserl" (Lawlor 2002, 171). While this seems to me a bit overstated, and the reliance on Hegel (and Hyppolite) to be something of a red herring, nevertheless it does give a good idea of the magnitude of the problem that the voice poses to interpretation.

8. Other critics have sensed some difference between the "voice" and the "phenomenological voice" in *Speech* (see Evans 1991, 117; Lawlor 1996b, 127; Marrati-Guénoun 1998, 80), but none to my knowledge has rigorously distinguished them, though Lawlor in his latest work is especially sensitive to this difference, as I document further below.

9. The importance that I have just assigned to chapter 6 depends on my outline of *Speech* as a whole. In chapter 7, however, Derrida does attempt to reintegrate the two developments that I have differentiated, swinging back round to the themes of *Speech and Phenomena*'s opening sections. Not only does chapter 7, along with depending on the results of chapter 6, in its own right, however, focus on a Husserlian account (of occasional expressions) that many Husserlians find partial or inadequate (see Mohanty 1964, 80; Bernet, Kern, and Marbach 1995, 178), but the issues that Derrida ultimately raises on this rather shaky basis, pertaining to

the infinite teleology of Husserl's late history writings—those issues that proved critical in the "Introduction"—are arguably addressed at greater length, in greater radicality, and more perspicuously by Derrida in *Of Grammatology,* where the role Heidegger plays is far more explicit. For all these reasons, then, I propose to postpone my treatment of those issues raised by chapter 7 of *Speech* until my next and final chapter.

10. Steven Crowell, in one of the best short treatments of *Speech* to date, has made a similar point, although ultimately giving it a more negative cast ("the point, then, was never to liberate the sign or give it some work to do, if we understand the sign in the ordinary sense that Husserl excludes" [Crowell 1996, 63, also 64]). Crowell, whose treatment of these matters I discuss further below, also noted the dependence of Derrida's argument on texts other than *Logical Investigations* I, although again rather negatively (Crowell 1996, 63n11). One main difference between Crowell's position and mine is that he, explicitly drawing on Gasché's work (Crowell 1996, 64), sees Derrida's ultimate aim as "a destructive dialectic" of a quasi-Hegelian style (Crowell 1996, 63). I see this dialectical moment as emerging more directly from Derrida's confrontation with Husserl's thought and as thus containing a "restitutive" (as well as a "destructive") moment, as answering a need within phenomenology itself. That there is such a need is something with which Crowell himself, by the way agrees, and to this in part is owed his judicious verdict on the "Husserl-Derrida debate" (which he calls "a stalemate" [Crowell 1996, 61]); Crowell, however, does not apparently believe that such an aim allied to phenomenology falls within the range of Derrida's own intentions.

11. This difference and repetition that Derrida wants associated in some way with signification, yet never to be identified with it as such, being found on the far side of Husserl's transcendental standpoint, is what Derrida later came to call "iterability" (Derrida 1982, 315; cf. Derrida 1988, 46). Thus the same confusion, or absence of clarity, that we already find here concerning the relations of language-related themes to transcendental ones has inhibited the comprehension of what Derrida was after in this discussion, preventing any sort of fruitful outcome of the debate with Searle. With this notion of iterability, Derrida has been thought to be writing a new chapter in the philosophy of language—rather than posing a quasi-transcendental alternative to this undertaking as a whole. For this reason, however, it is best to clear up this movement at the heart of *Speech* before deciding what this latter notion, "iterability," means, and not to rely on it to clarify Derrida's discussions here (cf., however, Lawlor 2002, 181).

12. Lawlor repeatedly emphasizes this point in his latest work—that the voice in *Speech* is finally the product of a *phenomenological* analysis (Lawlor 2002, 188)—a key insight, although we disagree on the specifics, as will become more clear below.

13. Sallis (1995, 6), Marrati-Guénoun (1998, 70), and Lawlor (1996b, 127) all suggest this, though they all go on to complicate this account in important ways as well. (In his most recent account, Lawlor focuses on this same passage [Lawlor 2002, 181]; yet he ties it without further discussion to some of Derrida's remarks in the "Introduction," and concludes on this basis that "the sign in general must be an empirical event." His view thus still conforms to the standard view—that Derrida reduces ideality to empirical signification—though on the next page, this

is perhaps further complicated.) Evans, Hopkins, and Willard take this view (Evans 1991, 30, 53, who believes Derrida identifies *Bedeutungen,* "conceptual meanings," and linguistic expression outright; Hopkins 1985, 203; Willard 1995, 37); and though Mohanty is more cautious, his concerns also finally tend in this direction (cf. Mohanty 1997, 71).

14. The notion of ideality emerges early on in Husserl's thought in that he, like Frege, believed that the *meanings* (*Bedeutungen*—Frege uses this word differently) or contents of speech could be distinguished from what these statements were about (as well as the speech acts that expressed them) by dint of having their own nonspatiotemporally individuated mode of existence (see *Logical Investigations* II.1.§§30–33; cf. Edie 1976, 20–23). What is expressed each time the law of excluded middle is propounded, or even, within bounds, by a phrase such as "Morris's chair is by the door" (whether or not these are true), is not a similar sense, but the *same* sense, whose consistent self-identity across time and space is immediately recognizable, according to Husserl. This notion of meaning thus opens on to the wider area of what Husserl called ideal being, which includes essences and universals, along with these meanings. The final status of ideality is something of a problem in Husserl, it should be noted (cf. Edie [1976, 20], who thinks it does not exist apart from language, with Willard, who insists on Husserl's realism [Willard 1995, 35]). Husserl never seems to have arrived at any sustained account of how ideality comes to be at the disposal of thought, apart from taking for granted that such idealities in some sense were the objects of intentions, and to some extent were also always correlates (or originally accessed within the realm) of culture or *Geist,* though further inquiry into their conditions of existence may well have seemed to Husserl to lead beyond the realm of phenomenological inquiry altogether. Nevertheless, how in particular Husserl's assertion of both real and ideal being at the time of *Logical Investigations,* including the mundane validity of essences, comports with his later transcendental commitments, which seem to derive all the structures of Being from a single source, remains a problem for all comprehensive studies of Husserl. (For example, see Mohanty 1985, 191–212, for a magisterial treatment of this whole problem; see also Landgrebe's "Regions of Being and Regional Ontologies in Husserl's Phenomenology" [Landgrebe 1981c] for an exposition of it with particular reference to the cultural sphere, and Husserl's account of the person in *Ideas II;* also see especially Landgrebe 1981b, 166–71.)

15. Derrida raises this issue of the idea in a Kantian sense right after the last citation, stating that "the concept of ideality [is] . . . at the center of such a problematic" in the discussion that follows at *VP* 58–59, as well as *VP* 91 and 104. As I have already suggested in chapter 2, in all these passages I believe Derrida depends on the work he had already done in the "Introduction" (as he himself indicates, speaking of the "repetition, and therefore *the tradition,* [which] would be assured to infinity" [*VP* 59 / *SP* 53, my emphasis; see also *VP* 58n1 / *SP* 52n2]). Though other commentators have made this connection (in the literature Derrida's talk of ideality in *Speech* and the "Introduction" are often associated), the meaning of this connection is often short-circuited, in the fashion suggested by me above that Lawlor's most recent commentary also exhibits. By contrast, I would stress, that

repetition refers first and foremost to the transcendental-historical institution or inauguration of such idealities, *on which ground alone* their dependence on an Idea in the Kantian sense for their infinite repeatability follows. Though Derrida does in fact allude to this specifically historical dimension, his comments are especially abbreviated in this and other passages in *Speech,* making it seem at times as if ideality and repetition to infinity were connected without further mediation. Though some part, then, of the confusion concerning Derrida's intentions in *Speech* is thus owed to Derrida himself, these claims are indeed sedimented, as I pointed out in chapter 2—and this has opened the way to objections like those of Mohanty and Willard, who both criticize Derrida in *Speech* for taking a "nominalistic" slant on ideality, specifically for seeing it as directly dependent on an extensionally infinite series of repeated acts (Mohanty 1997, 72; Willard 1995, 37). Taking Derrida's claims here as compressed versions of the case he made in the "Introduction," however, as I read Derrida there, the concerns of Mohanty and Willard may be met; since in the "Introduction," in fact, idealities (the essential truths of geometry, etc.) are acknowledged as having first been brought forward in an earlier phase of phenomenology, in very much the way Mohanty, in particular, conceives them—as instantaneously recognizable idealities—and their relation to repeatability and an infinite idea only emerges at a deeper level (see *IOG* 47, 50, and especially 135). Mohanty himself, it is worth noting, is willing to accept Derrida's interpretation of Husserl in the "Introduction," to which I take Derrida's assertions here still to refer. ("These are all perfectly sound readings," Mohanty states, though he quickly stipulates that they are not especially specific to "Derridean deconstruction," something with which I might partially agree, though perhaps on slightly different grounds [Mohanty 1997, 74–75].)

16. Husserl, it is widely recognized, never decided about which was ultimately prior: thought or speech, language or meaning—perhaps in accord with his commitment to phenomenological description and his refusal to frame any "metaphysical" hypotheses, or ultimate causal accounts of any kind. Evans explicitly acknowledges this (Evans 1991, 31), setting out an important citation from Husserl—"whatever the connection of thought with speech may be, whether or not . . . [it] has a necessary grounding in essence" (Evans 1991, 32; Husserl 1970b, 1:250 [1984, 2:13–14])—though this fact has an odd weightlessness in Evans's own evaluation of Derrida's Husserl reading. Nevertheless, Derrida's interest in Husserl's claims about language—in particular his repeated return to *Ideas* §124 and Husserl's insistence on the unproductive character of expression—must be seen as predicated on an awareness of this fact. At the start of the second section of this chapter I establish in more detail the relation in its positivity of ideal meanings *(Bedeutungen)* to language and expression *(Ausdrücke)* as Derrida construes this in *Speech,* and there I also show that Derrida is fully aware that Husserl himself draws a distinction between these terms. Derrida does, however, repeatedly press Husserl's own claim in *Ideas* §124, and elsewhere, that the possibility of ideal meanings is always to be found in tandem with some possibility of linguistic expression—both in his opening chapters, and again in the last, where this culminates in his doctrine of the supplement (*VP* 97, 99), a relation it only makes sense

to invoke, I might add, if no standard philosophical relation (of causality or logical grounding, etc.) is thought to hold among the terms in question.

17. In my first published work on Derrida and Husserl, an extended review essay of J. Claude Evans's *Strategies of Deconstruction,* I argued that the assumption, shared by both critics and defenders of Derrida alike, that the opening phase of "a deconstruction" had some form of traditional philosophical engagement with the author in question (whether the supposedly "dominant" interpretation of the first of a "double reading," or a standard critique) was a misprision of Derrida's own methods that blocked access both to his aims and his true relation to Husserl's thought. My subsequent correspondence and discussion with Evans (who proved in our conversations to be a generous and genial interlocutor) roused me from a certain dogmatic slumber when it came to Derrida's work on Husserl, especially in *Speech.* Thus while I still think this initial objection to the standard approach on both sides holds good, I have come to further complicate my own appraisal, acknowledging that a moment of judgment is inevitable, and I believe a developmental approach is required, among other things, to provide an adequate basis for this, to be fair to both Derrida and Husserl. Lawlor, it should be noted, in his latest work, agrees with me that "nothing in *Speech* is supposed to 'impugn' or 'injure' . . . the apodicticity of phenomenological-transcendental description" (Lawlor 2002, 173); how this claim comports, however, with Lawlor's view of Derrida as a critic of phenomenology, as well as the concrete arguments that Lawlor brings forward glossing what he takes to be Derrida's stance toward Husserl's positions, many of which feature phenomenology's collapse at the hands of a straightforward empiricism, remains unclear, at least to me.

18. A particularly prime example of this is Derrida's rather audacious claim that "the relation to *my death* (to my disappearance in general) . . . conceals itself in this determination of being as presence" (*VP* 60/*SP* 54). The odd thing about this claim, which has caused it to be repeatedly misunderstood, is that it in fact *continues to assert* the certainty of the living present as the ur-form of all experience, and depends on the truth of this assertion for its own. Derrida's point is not that the relation to my death, my finitude, calls into doubt Husserl's result: "the relation to the presence of the present as ultimate form of being and ideality" and as "the movement by which I transgress empirical existence, factuality, contingency, mundaneity, etc." (*VP* 60/*SP* 53–54). Rather, Derrida is arguing that a further condition is needed without which such certainty pertaining to the present could never itself emerge—that the recognition of the present as ur-form could never take hold of itself without an implicit recourse to a death, to a finitude, which is not itself then simply accidental (as Husserl believed). The validity of Husserl's own assertion, then, is not in question as such (though this further condition indeed leads beyond this principle's own avowed content); instead, only the conditions of its self-enactment are here questioned and rethought—and this recasting of transcendental certitude and its unveiling should indeed be seen as a prime instance of Derrida's singularly complex relation to those (Husserlian) doctrines that he "deconstructs" (cf. Lawlor 2002, 182–83, for a treatment of this same claim).

19. Cairns will conclude that "because even the immediately embodying individual moments of a real embodiment may vary while the [verbal] expression embodied [the sign] remains constant, the latter cannot be identical with any complex of real individual determinations of a real object" (Cairns 1941, 457). Cairns, in fact, interestingly ends his essay by asserting that the ideality of "cultural objects in general" and "verbal expressions in particular" is that of "ideal individuals": "ideal entities" which "undergo *historical* change without losing their individual identity" (Cairns 1941, 457; my emphasis). The ultimate status of this description of language, which I take to be Husserl's, as well as Derrida's and Cairns's, is followed up further in chapter 6.

20. Many other ways, it should be stressed, exist of conceiving of the (linguistic) sign that make no appeal to ideality whatsoever. Heidegger's hermeneutic treatment of the sign, the well-known distinction between type/token (though this offers a paralell to it), Wittgenstein's approach to the name in his language game model, Donald Davidson's idiolects—to name but a few—all give accounts of signification, none of which imply ideality of any sort. So too, all these philosophers may be said to have made "the linguistic turn," focusing on language precisely in order to *avoid* notions like ideality (as well as universals and essences). They share a common commitment to avoiding talk of universals and ideal entities of all sorts—whatever their other differences—and in so doing, almost all these thinkers also aim to replace descriptions referring to consciousness with those that take language as more fundamental (as well as the speech act, and/or semiosis). To none of these positions does Derrida subscribe unequivocally.

21. Much good work has been done on chapter 5 of *Speech* by Bernet (1995, 15), Sallis (1995, 13), Marrati-Guénoun (1998, 83 ff.), as well as others, often starting from Derrida's claim near the end of chapter 5 that "doubtless Husserl would refuse to assimilate the necessity of retention and the necessity for signs" (*VP* 74/*SP* 66). Though none of what Derrida goes on to say there seems to me to contradict the claims that I have just made (and in my last chapter I present at some length the notion finally in question here, the "trace," in its relation to Husserl's phenomenology), my assertion is not meant to downplay the importance of this chapter for other possible readings of *Speech*. Thomas Seebohm, too, it should be noted, in his extraordinary article "The Apodicticity of Absence" picks up on this often unnoticed aspect of the proximity of Derrida's claims to Husserl in chapter 5 (Seebohm 1995, 196), and he arguably pushes it quite far in the direction of a rereading of Husserl himself, which both parallels and challenges Derrida's own (Seebohm 1995, 193, 200). Mohanty is also willing to partially credit Derrida's criticism of Husserl's time conception, while refusing what he takes to be a simple rejection of Husserl's account of the subject and object on Derrida's part (Mohanty 1997, 92), and this mapping too conforms to my point here that Derrida at this moment is moving on essentially Husserlian ground.

22. Most recent commentators of *Speech*, including notably Lawlor (see Lawlor 1995, 175; 2002, 187) and Marrati-Guénoun (1998, 173), have at times also stressed the *linkage* between signification, repetition, and ideality, as opposed to simply identifying them all with one another. Lawlor, in his latest work, indeed goes further than previously in recognizing the Husserlian ground on which Derrida

operates in both chapters 4 and 5 of *Speech,* yet he still stresses the break that he sees Derrida as making with Husserl, in line with his overall approach.

23. Lloyd J. Carr in his "Husserl's Philosophy of Language" makes a similar point (Carr 1989, 110); at a number of points in what follows his treatment dovetails with my own, and his is one of the most useful, short, purely explicative studies of these topics in English which I have encountered.

24. John Scanlon's "Pure Presence: A Modest Proposal" is a particularly vivid example of this sort of response (Scanlon 1995).

25. Lawlor in his latest work discusses the arguments upon which I am about to comment; he does this, however, from the perspective of determining "phenomenology's historical destiny," which turns out to mean its relation to metaphysics (Lawlor 2002, 168 ff.), a perspective which seems to me to assume that Derrida's claims are already known to be valid.

26. Among others, White (1987, 53), Edie (1990, 109–10), and Evans (1991, 39–42) have all made criticisms related to the one by Mohanty, upon which I am focusing.

27. Derrida himself eventually seems to takes notice of this fact—that Husserl appears to go out of his way to argue that an essence, a broad genus of any sort, is not in question here. Derrida does so, however, by asking whether a more profound intuition into the status of the sign, the concept of the sign, might not be signaled by Husserl's refusal to recognize a single essence pertaining to it ("by what right presume the unity of essence of *something such as a sign?*" [*VP* 25/*SP* 24, my emphasis]), a question which, though fascinating in its own right, seems to me to presume what is at issue here: namely, that the intent of Husserl's refusal is meant to have any general bearing on the treatment of the sign at all. The title of all of *Logical Investigations* II.1, it should also be noted, is "Essential Distinctions," and perhaps this has influenced Derrida's view that an essence of the sign is in some way at stake in its first paragraph; yet this title covers the entire first investigation, and, for the reasons just given, it is far from clear that Husserl meant it to apply primarily, or at all, to the notion of the sign.

28. This is essentially Crowell's point: that Derrida is right that Husserl never investigated the status of linguistic expression adequately, even if Derrida's own treatment of these matters is also not adequate in itself, at least in Crowell's eyes (Crowell 1996, 64). The concluding portion of Crowell's essay consists of his own investigation into these issues, following questions raised by Derrida in "Form and Meaning," and pertaining, above all, to Husserl's discussion in *Ideas I* §124; a section that I also focus on below.

29. Derrida himself points out at more than one crucial juncture that his commentary takes its cue from his interpretation and not the other way around (*VP* 32/*SP* 31, *VP* 59/*SP* 53).

30. This is not to claim that Husserl pays no attention whatsoever to these matters. I have already spoken of Cairns's amplification of some of Husserl's late remarks, and in my next chapter I will follow up a line of Husserl commentators, to which Derrida himself is quite close, including James Edie, who see Husserl's work on the ideality of meaning overlapping with structural linguistics in important ways (see Edie 1976, xi). Finally, Bernet, drawing on some of Husserl's posthu-

mously published lectures, has done tremendously important work on the status of signification in the speech act, that furnishes the background of my own treatment here (see Bernet 1988, especially 6–7; and also Bernet, Kern, and Marbach 1995, chapters 1 and 6, especially 175–81).

31. Chapter 3 of *Speech* is a peculiarly constructed chapter; Derrida divides it into two sections (A and B), the first of which is divided into three different subsections in turn (numbered 1–3), and in it Derrida comments on three different portions of *Logical Investigations* II.1 (1.5, 1.7, and 1.8), the last of which, where Husserl turns to the functions of expression in soliloquy, becoming the putative topic of the next sixty pages of *Speech*. There are, then, a number of ways of construing the "center" or climax of this chapter, but the discussion at 3.A.3, focusing on *Geist* and making possible the passage from (a) nonlinguistic categories (gestures of *Logical Investigations* II.1.5) to (b) the speech situation (intimation and communication in *Logical Investigations* II.1.7), and thus preparing the way to expression proper (in soliloquy, in *Logical Investigations* II.1.8), is surely one of them. Another important reason exists to give priority to the moment I am about to focus on. Mohanty's objection number four makes evident why Derrida's focus here should be seen, at least initially, as falling on *Geist,* and the spiritual animation of the linguistic sign: namely, that the other obvious candidate, the *bedeuten* and the *Bedeutungen,* as Mohanty points out referring to the latter specifically (and as Derrida well knows), are as much "the correlate of empirical consciousness . . . [as] the transcendentally reduced one" (Mohanty 1997, 70). The *Bedeutungen* are as much supposed to function in the world as within the brackets (which is why, I take it, Mohanty deems the reduction to soliloquy misleading in his 1964 commentary, a point on which White picks up [White 1987, 49; Mohanty 1964, 16, as noted by White]). Only if this role of *Geist* is restored, then, and with it the primacy Husserl gives to *intentionality* in the context of *linguistic signification,* of the semiotics of the *linguistic sign,* does it really become apparent why Derrida eventually sees such a tight connection between *bedeuten, Bedeutungen,* and the possibility of the reductions—a matter I elucidate further at the beginning of the second part of my discussion here.

32. Lawlor, however, does emphasize this in his 1996 article (Lawlor 1996b, 128), as does Sallis (1995, 9).

33. As previous commentators have emphasized, when Husserl turns to soliloquy, Husserl himself, describing the functioning of language, goes out of his way to specify that "a spoken or *written* word floats before us" (Husserl 1970b, 1:279 [1984, 2.1.§8], my emphasis; cf. Husserl 1970b, 1:276 [1984, 2.1.§6]). Husserl does not distinguish between the spoken and written at this decisive moment in his work, and moreover, Derrida is indeed aware of this. Not only does Husserl speak of the written sign, but Derrida cites him doing so, and Derrida's talk of the voice, including his translation of Husserl's *Rede* (talk, or discourse) as "*discours oral*" (e.g., *VP* 32, 39) in these opening chapters (with the exception of an instance I will bring forward at the start of the second half of my discussion), is best understood as anticipating an argument Derrida will later make in the second half of *Speech* where the voice emerges as the phenomenological voice in its specificity.

34. Derrida thus faces a bind in which he himself to some degree is commit-

ted to Husserl being both right and wrong at once (which is another reason to approach this whole vexed area through a developmental perspective). Husserl, after all, must be right, his philosophy must in some respect be true, if this teleology is really what Derrida claims—a teleology commanding *all* that may be thought about these matters, to be brought forward on the basis of Husserl's thought (which cannot then simply be corrigible on any of these points, for they would then simply become errors, rather than symptoms). Husserl's claims must also in some respect be false, however, not simply true—for how otherwise, in the first place, can Derrida motivate the claim that such a predominant or coercive teleology is operative in his work, rather than simply allow that the facts, the things themselves, the truth has dictated Husserl's outcomes?

35. This has been more true of Husserlians than Derrideans, at least when it comes to attention to the introduction per se, if not its relation to the rest of *Speech*. Marrati-Guénoun reviews Derrida's arguments in it in her own fashion, and also gives a good deal of weight to the notion of "ultra-transcendental life" that I am about to bring forward (Marrati-Guénoun 1998, 65). So too, Lawlor pays heed to Derrida's reliance on Husserl's notion of parallelism, in part with the same concern as I, to show Derrida's proximity to Husserl in *Speech* (Lawlor 1995, 176). Lawlor, moreover, in his 1996 essay also assigns great importance to the passage from chapter 1 that I have just cited (Lawlor 1996b, 125). Lawlor uses this as a jumping-off point, however, to profile the rest of *Speech* as aimed at removing the "contamination" of "degenerative metaphysics" from phenomenology (Lawlor 1996b, 128), and while, as I will later note, this aim at times brings Lawlor's reading close to my own (in that Lawlor too believes that Derrida in some sense is furthering Husserl's own goals) with its reversal of the order of dependence between Derrida and Husserl (Husserl, in Lawlor's eyes, condemned to this degenerative metaphysics from which Derrida alone may rescue him), in the end it leaves our readings far apart on some of the most important issues. (Lawlor's earlier account basically jibes with his latest endeavor, though the latter has different emphases. It too discusses the introduction to *Speech* and gives weight to the theme of life in the rest of *Speech* [Lawlor 2002, 173–180].)

36. Derrida initially flags his concern with life as also a concern for language—for the term or concept "life," and this concern thus appears at first to be a specific instance of Fink's notorious question about the language and conceptuality of transcendental inquiry itself.

37. Lawlor is one of a handful of critics to have emphasized this portion of Derrida's account in his 1996 discussion of *Speech* (there following John Protevi, he indicates; Lawlor 1996b, 128n27). In his latest work, he also discusses these themes, which turn out largely to pertain to considerations emerging in *Ideas* §124, with respect to their work in chapter 6 of *Speech* (Lawlor 2002, 190–91). Protevi in his article does focus on just this passage (Protevi 1993, 377–78), placing it at the center of a provocative account of Derrida's thought, which perhaps due to the time when it was written, does not seem particularly interested in clarifying the status of Derrida's Husserl interpretation as such. Finally, Crowell comments extensively on the portion of *Ideas I* at issue here, as well as on relevant parts of Husserl's other writings (Crowell 1996, 65ff.), but I doubt that he would join with me

in seeing Husserl's own mature views on a multilayered expression as playing the axial role in *Speech* and in Derrida's own thought that I assign to them here.

38. Bernet and others have brought forward criticisms suggesting that Derrida presents an overly simplistic (or reductive) view of Husserl's reductions, which sees them as seamlessly sealing out all that pertains to the world and empirical existence (as "cut off from the world and other subjects," as Bernet puts it [Bernet 1995, 9]). Given the circumstances under which Derrida has chosen to present his argument, nominally confining himself to *Logical Investigations* II.1, and thus forced to channel the bulk of his concerns through a discussion of Husserl's turn to soliloquy (circumstances which Bernet himself also brings to the fore [Bernet 1995, 3, 9]), on the face of it Bernet's criticism is not an unreasonable one. For these reasons, as well as others, it seems important to recognize what I have just set out: that the axis of Derrida's argument, when it comes to these notions (of ideal meaning, expression, etc.) as they function in Husserl himself, passes through *Ideas I,* and *Ideas* §124 especially. (Derrida, for better or worse, as previously noted, has always seen the standpoint of *Ideas I* as already implied in *Logical Investigations* II, though this does not mean, of course, that he or anyone may ignore the distinction between the two entirely.) Derrida, indeed, assumes Husserl's transcendental constitutional standpoint in much of his argument, and with that even Husserl's later doctrine of transcendental idealism—which, along with the problem of transcendental solipsism, do not seem to me to be issues so easily settled as Bernet initially suggests (Bernet 1995, 9). Bernet himself, it should be noted, goes on to recognize that "the premises" of Derrida's argument, if not his "conclusions," have value, especially when it comes to the "Cartesian formulation of [Husserl's] project" (Bernet 1995, 10); and if by this Bernet agrees, more broadly, that Derrida's arguments have value once the reductions are presumed to operate on certain terms which were Husserl's own (in *Ideas I*), then he and I are not that far apart—neither on this, nor on another point he seems to indicate at this moment, which I would also phrase differently: namely, that if *language,* at least as an essential possibility, could not be given from the perspective of Husserl's constitution program (through the intentional activities of a transcendental subject), this would prove problematic for Husserl, especially for the project that emerges in his last writings (see Bernet 1995, 9–10).

39. Here another confusion can be cleared up. Alan White, as well as others, have claimed that Derrida folds the object *(Gegenstand)* into the *Bedeutungen* (conceptual meanings), in order to argue that Husserl excludes the referent entirely, and privileges expression over indication ("Derrida . . . claims that he has found a fatal flaw: indication . . . is essential to all language" [White 1987, 51]). While White is importantly right that Husserl does not understand the objective reference of expressions to be a form of indication (though see Bernet, Kern, and Marbach 1995, cited above, for the problems reference does seem to pose for Husserl's account), White's concerns on this point, in respect to Derrida's argument, could be allayed by recognizing that the *Ideas I* model is in the back of Derrida's mind. The "subtext" for Derrida's argument, as White puts it, is not that Derrida believes that Husserl claims that there is no difference between *Sinn* and *Bedeutung* (White 1987, 51), that all senses are already conceptual meanings, but that Derrida, fol-

lowing Husserl in *Ideas* §124, sees individual, *nonlinguistic* referents as already *intentional* objects, as constituted through noemata, and his point is thus that the passage of these into *Bedeutungen* has been secured in advance through their common appurtenance to transcendental intentional consciousness.

40. It should also be amply clear by now—since so many have raised doubts on this score—that Derrida is fully aware of the difference between *Bedeutungen* (conceptual meanings) and both *Sinn* (sense) and *Ausdrücke* (expressions), the linguistic expressions of *Logical Investigations* II.1—since it would be impossible for Derrida to speak of this *double* going forth of this sense in itself, were this not the case. To be sure, some Husserlians make more of a linkage, others less, between these logical meanings and the sphere of expression, and what Derrida is laying out, here in 3.A.1, I am suggesting, is a perhaps novel, yet certainly permissible, extension of Husserl's own views (which in *Ideas* §124 and elsewhere seem to leave this question open), setting out a circuit of expression within the functioning of constituting transcendental subjectivity—something close to Bernet's "pure expressions," though Bernet believes that Derrida ultimately denies these are possible (Bernet 1995, 9). By contrast, I do not think any of this is meant in itself to disqualify Husserl's own distinctions, at least not when Derrida's final deconstruction of the voice in chapter 6 is kept in view. Each layer in this circuit implies the next, without any one being reducible to any of the others, and, emerging within this circuit of expression, the voice in its phenomenological specificity will not in the first instance call into doubt the noematic *Sinn*, or the ideality of the *Bedeutungen*—and never will do so in the fashion which many expect. Indeed, what Derrida has in mind with this talk of the phenomenological voice may only appear in the first place if *Sinn* and *Bedeutung* are granted working validity, and this accords with the fact that the voice's deconstruction passes *through* phenomenology and what Derrida likes to call "phenomenological interiority," as I will eventually show.

41. Of course, Derrida's talk of "inside" and "outside" here should not be taken too literally. The appearance of *real* exclusion that the focus on soliloquy might foster (not yet in place, I should add—Derrida will only come to it in the second half of this chapter) should be dissipated, and this talk must be seen only to go as far as it can be construed along the lines required by Husserl's own reductions, which do indeed imply the bracketing of all worldly facticity, the suspension of the thesis of existence, and a discourse able to conduct itself wholly in a transcendental dimension finally through *eidetic* insights.

42. The whole issue, again (pace Bernet's objections in particular), is to what extent *language* may be introduced as a constitutive condition, a consideration within transcendental phenomenology, as it seems to be at least in Husserl's very last writings, and the stipulations attaching to the reductions still be respected.

43. Lawlor in his 1996 piece on *Speech*, as well as Bernet and Marrati-Guénoun, all recognize the singularity of the phenomenological voice to varying degrees (Lawlor 1996b, 127; Marrati-Guénoun 1998, 80; Bernet 1995, 9). All of these readers, however, even Bernet, seem to think that Derrida's point is that such pure expression is "impossible" (Bernet 1995, 10; Lawlor 1996b, 129). But if this were the sum total of the matter, it would be difficult to see, as I have pointed out more than once, why Husserl's thought should have any exemplary significance,

should not be just a dead end within philosophy (rather than being the site of an unavoidable epochal hold—the exhibition of such a hold, such a *prise* being the stated aim of Derrida's work [*VP* 16]), as well as why Derrida himself continues to maintain the close proximity to Husserl that Lawlor, Marrati-Guénoun, and Bernet, each in his or her own way recognizes, rather than ending up being just another linguistic philosopher. Lawlor in his latest work, in his discussion of chapter 6, goes furthest in emphasizing this singularity of the phenomenological voice in its specificity and the proximity to Husserl's own thought that it implies, on grounds similar to the ones that I have just brought forward (Lawlor 2002, 191). Despite the carefulness of his analysis here, however, Lawlor, still taking his ultimate orientation toward these matters from Hyppolite and Hegel (Lawlor 2002, 190), views the phenomenological voice immediately as an "ultra-transcendental" conception (Lawlor 2002, 191), thus never asking how its phenomenological status and the vector toward language it undoubtedly contains really are to be coordinated. Thus even he finally relies on the standard account, tying ideality unproblematically to repetition of the signifier (as well as the theme of temporality and the notion of the trace from chapter 5) in order to explain the "deconstruction" of the phenomenological voice in chapter 6—hence missing the full specificity of what Derrida accomplishes there.

44. This last claim is intended to be limited to Derrida's treatment of Husserl's core transcendental doctrines. As noted above (see note 9), Derrida in his final chapter of *Speech* does swing back to his opening considerations, bringing forward his own theme of the supplement. These matters, though not this notion itself, are treated in my final chapter, as well as in a forthcoming article of mine, "'A Transcendental Sense of Death'?: Derrida and the Philosophy of Language."

45. In his latest work Lawlor also cites and stresses these remarks of Derrida (Lawlor 2002, 191), yet he takes them in a rather different direction, as shown by the reconciliation between Derrida and Merleau-Ponty that he indicates he intends to propose elsewhere on the basis of his interpretation of this chapter (Lawlor 2002, 191n18).

46. This is a subtle aspect of Derrida's argument that is too often overlooked. From the first moment in chapter 6 that Derrida begins to specify the privilege that he believes accrues to the phoneme over the grapheme, as I have indicated, Derrida's entire analysis is set out "*within* phenomenological interiority" and assumes Husserl's distinctions. The phoneme and the grapheme as *appearance,* within transcendental phenomenological interiority are in question almost from the first, and Derrida repeatedly though subtly insists on this stipulation throughout chapter 6, especially at the crucial moment when the deconstruction of Husserl's thought at the hands of this phenomenological voice emerges. "Considered from a *purely phenomenological point of view, on the interior of the reduction*" (*VP* 88/*SP* 78, my emphasis), Derrida will state, setting out on this final leg of his argument—a passage on which I will comment further below.

47. At this moment Derrida himself, it must be noted, seems to get a little ahead of himself (which doubtless accounts for some of the confusion attending his intentions in these passages), both in the passage just cited, and when he goes on to

state that the voice "produces itself *in the world* as *pure auto-affection*" (*VP* 89/*SP* 79). Not only is it far from clear, however, how this can be thought at all, especially given that all of this has already been said to take place "within the reductions," according to Derrida's own stipulations, but, in any event, the actual deconstruction of Husserl's thought that I am about to sketch and which emerges on the basis of a genuinely pure auto-affection, will not owe anything to this imputed worldliness.

48. This is the interpretation to which both Bernet and Marrati-Guénoun finally come, doubtless partially due to the obscurity in Derrida's own intentions indicated in my preceding note. Despite their other strengths as interpreters (most obviously, Bernet's), both believe that Derrida's deconstruction of the voice and this unique pure auto-affection show them falling prey to an "impurity," which both also ultimately trace back to Derrida's analysis of time in chapter 5 (Bernet 1995, 18; Marrati-Guénoun 1998, 89–90). The deconstruction of Husserl's transcendental program here in chapter 6, however, is not a matter of calling such purity into doubt, but making it manifest as such, and seeing this auto-affection as itself impure thus makes it impossible to follow out Derrida's discussion to the end and gauge precisely his ultimate proximity to, as well as distance from, Husserl. Lawlor also stresses "hearing oneself speak as *absolutely pure auto-affection,*" and maintains that none of Derrida's claims would violate what Husserl in *Cartesian Meditations* designated as the subject's sphere of ownness (Lawlor 2002, 192). At the same time, I find it difficult to put these stipulations together with Lawlor's own account of Derrida's deconstruction in what follows (Lawlor 2002, 192–95), especially 194, where Lawlor brings "writing" and "language" back in and declares them unqualifiedly to be "originary."

Chapter 6

1. A sign, if not of the disarray in Derrida studies, then at least of the remarkably open-ended style of approaching Derrida's corpus, to which the present work intends to be a partial antidote (without, of course, aiming to shut down, but rather further to enable genuinely novel and fruitful lines of future research and argument), is the fact that so few commentators who have approached *Speech* and Derrida's work on Husserl generally have also commented on *Of Grammatology*, the work with which it simultaneously appeared. This remains the case for those more sympathetic to Derrida in discussions of *Speech* (Lawlor and Marrati-Guénoun, apart from a few brief, though important, pages; see note 27 below), as well as those less so, other than White (1995, 103–19). Along with those authors discussed in chapter 1 (Gasché, Rorty, and Bennington, as well as Culler and Norris), whose work on *Of Grammatology* is now more or less canonical, other, more recent readings of *Of Grammatology* which do not give sustained attention to *Speech* are to be found in Beardsworth, Patrick, and Howells.

2. In the second half of *Of Grammatology*, Derrida treats first Lévi-Strauss and then Rousseau—the latter, of course, not to be discounted in his own right as a

philosopher. Nevertheless, the presentation of the "history and system of meta-physics," to which the second half of *Of Grammatology* is dedicated, gives special emphasis to and takes its shape from the moment when "presence" takes on the form of "self-presence," and this version of metaphysics as a totality (what Derrida sometimes calls the "greatest totality"), giving special weight to modernity, and the eighteenth century in particular—seeing this as both continuous with the tradi-tion of philosophy and in some way its culmination (see *G*97–100)—is polemically engaged with Heidegger's rather different construal of this same history and for-mation.

3. Lawlor in his latest work also gives much attention to "Violence and Meta-physics," even claiming "it has an unrivalled privilege in regard to the general development of Derrida's thought" (Lawlor 2002, 146). This privilege, largely, though not wholly, proves to be an anticipatory one, however, based in a rap-prochement between Levinas and Derrida, which really only fully takes hold in the 1980s (see Lawlor 2002, 158–59). His discussion does not, in any case, focus on the theme of history. Peter Fenves has recently turned to this theme, history, in the context of Derrida's first text on Foucault, without discussing his first work on Levinas. These as well as other commentators will be further discussed below.

4. This notion of Heideggerean historicism, or Heidegger as an historicist, is one upon which I will occasionally rely in what follows. Just to be clear, Heidegger is not, after all, a historicist in the sense usually given to this term, which Hus-serl, for example, attacks in "Philosophy as Rigorous Science," imputing it to Dilthey (Dilthey, of course, famously denying this was the case): namely, histori-cism in the form of seeing all knowledge claims, and certainly philosophical ones, as subject to finite *Weltanschauungen,* the movement of the history of societies, cul-tures, or nations, as studied by historians. Behind what may or may not be called Heidegger's historicism finally lies his reinterpretation of Husserl's transcenden-tal standpoint—about which reinterpretation it could be said far more properly than Derrida's that it irremediably fuses the empirical and transcendental. It is radically empirical, factical, perhaps only escaping the charge of empiricism by showing that praxis, the practical, and pragmatics lie at the heart of all claims to truth. Whatever the final validity of this strategy may be philosophically speaking (a question once again beginning to receive the attention it deserves), the out-come of this for Heidegger's own thought is that it does become possible to map the notion to which it is dedicated at least initially, namely Being—the status of the meaning of Being and of the difference between beings and Being—onto a recognizably historical plane (which also happens to intersect recognizable em-pirical languages, I might add: Greek and the Greeks, Latin and the Romans, etc.) far more than is the case with the themes at the core of traditional philosophy, or even perhaps those finally discernible in Derrida's text.

5. As Derrida puts it two sentences later: for *différance* to be "thought in closest proximity to itself," one must "begin by determining it as the ontico-ontological difference" (*G*24).

6. Thus, in the lines just before the sentence I quoted, Derrida, speaking of what in Heidegger may *elude* such phono-logo-centrism (namely Heidegger's *Durchstreichung,* his "crossing through" or "crossing out" of the word *Sein* in his text

Zur Seinsfrage [1956], republished as *On the Question of Being*), had announced that "in as much as it [this crossing out] de-limits ontotheology, the metaphysics of presence and logocentrism, this last writing is also the first writing." Derrida here thus clearly applies his own terms (writing, logocentrism) to Heidegger, while appropriating Heidegger's own (ontotheology, metaphysics of presence) and their temporal parameters (first, last).

7. Derrida, introducing this notion of *Urwort* where I have already begun to quote, goes on to say that this "transcendental word, assuring the possibility of being-word to all other words, as such . . . is precomprehended in all language and—this is the opening of *Being and Time*—only this precomprehension would permit the opening of the question of the sense of Being in general" (*G* 20). Unless I am mistaken, no talk of *Urworts* or universal words of any sort is to be found in Heidegger's text—is to be found at this or at any point in *Being and Time*—though I do not want to say that finally no impetus exists for Derrida making this rather novel suggestion. Ultimately at issue is the question, which I have already raised, of Heidegger's radical empiricism or pragmatism (through which he refashions the transcendental stance of Husserl's phenomenology) and the corresponding authority accruing to Heidegger's own discourse. Derrida is clearly right that at the opening of *Being and Time* Heidegger assigns his discourse priority over all others, over all regional sciences. Nevertheless, the issue of the "sense of Being *in general*" as raised by Heidegger does not imply in the "in general," in the *"overall" (überall)* theoretical universality, as Derrida seems to take it. The force of Heidegger's own claim is not finally found on a purely theoretical plane (see §3 and §4 of *Being and Time* on the ontological and ontical priority of the *Seinsfrage*). In Heidegger's eyes, the rights of his own discourse, in fact, precede all *theorein*, all possibility of universal theoretical claims, including one about what necessarily pertains to all language. The role of praxis (extending across the entire first half of *Being and Time*, including most notably Heidegger's own views on discourse, signification, and reference) is thus ultimately at the root of this difference between Heidegger and Derrida, and not until the prior relation of *Husserl* and Heidegger on these matters is sorted through (in the sort of work now being undertaken by Crowell, for example; see Crowell 2001)—until the status of Husserl's theoretical universalist route to the transcendental attitude (and transcendental difference) and Heidegger's "practical-existential" path are both better clarified—can further progress in this area of Derrida studies be made.

8. Indeed, in "The Way to Language," a companion essay to the ones that Derrida cites for confirmation of his view (*G* 20n11), all of which were written by Heidegger in the late *1950s*, by the way (the only place where I myself have been able to find Heidegger speak of an *Urwort*—though I may well have overlooked something else in "The Nature of Language" or "The Word" in *On the Way to Language*—is where Heidegger speaks of the Tao and its possible translation as Way: "the word 'way' probably is an ancient primary word [*Urwort*]"; [Heidegger 1971, 92]), we also find Heidegger affirming: "There is no natural language of a human nature occurring of itself, without a destiny. All language is historical, even where man does not know history in the modern European sense" (Heidegger 1971, 133).

9. Derrida's "The *Retrait* of Metaphor," along with portions of many of his sub-

sequent writings on Heidegger, provide perhaps the preeminent instances of *actual interpretations* of Heidegger's thorny late thought that we have.

10. Along with this shift of emphasis, alongside this notion of Being as a signifying trace, and this incursion into the sphere of language, Derrida clearly does want to maintain some kind of talk of epochs, some Heidegger-style claim about history. What, however, does Derrida's essentially hybrid attitude finally represent, then; in what does it really consist? Both in *Speech* and *Of Grammatology*, Derrida's own approach displaces the focus of Heidegger's own problematic of Being away from history (as it has always been known, and even as it is identified in Heidegger's discourse) toward a more complex standpoint and referent whose status in its own right, even today, I would suggest, remains unplumbed.

11. Despite the numerous transformations that the science of linguistics undergoes after Saussure, most notably at the hands of Chomsky and beyond, most scholars agree that the working understanding of language as an object of study across these variations, roughly as a synchronic system of some sort, remains indebted to Saussure (Lyons 1969, 38).

12. "Speech," Saussure insists a little later, "is an individual act of the will and the intelligence" (Saussure 1964, 30/Saussure 1966, 14; translation altered).

13. James Edie's brave effort to bring together a range of approaches in both phenomenology and linguistics in his *Speaking and Meaning*, the most extended treatment of these topics in English with which I am familiar, proves instructive as to the vicissitudes that a comparison of Husserl and Saussure may undergo on this point—a comparison of the relation of speech to language in each author. Edie, as I have noted elsewhere, initially aligns Husserl with structural linguistics (in contrast to Merleau-Ponty, whom he initially characterizes as "almost an Oxfordian"; Edie 1976, xi), in that both Husserl and Saussure, as Edie goes on to make clear, give priority to *language*, and to the ideality and objectivity of meaning of which it is capable—Edie even going so far as later to declare that "to consider language in itself is to operate an implicit phenomenological [and eidetic] reduction," referring to Andre de Muralt's work (Edie 1976, 47, 48n9 and n10), which also influenced Derrida (*IOG* 67–68). Edie here thus sees "language in itself" at this moment as being a repository of meaning and structures of ideality, in a way that he believes allows him to assimilate some concerns of linguistics, including structural linguistics, to those of Husserl in *Logical Investigations* II. Nevertheless, later on in his work, when Edie really wants to cash this out, and give *Husserl's* project of a "pure logical grammar" a cogency within linguistics, Edie must turn to Chomsky (and his transformational grammar) now against *both* structuralism and Merleau-Ponty, and give priority to *speech* as the locus of the meaningfulness that Husserl studies—in order to arrive at a *universal* perspective on language, one more consonant with Husserl's logical studies, as opposed to structuralism's empiricism. "The only role of 'system' is to serve creative speech, *langue* is subservient to *parole*, and is absorbed in it," Edie now insists (Edie 1976, 137). Edie's transformation of standpoint, consequently, shows the impossibility of identifying Husserl's "meaning" *(Bedeutung)* with that studied by structural linguistics (which would a fortiori also preclude directly identifying a concern with language and its meanings, as Muralt does, with Husserl's *Sinn* and *Bedeutung*—at least, if Muralt in-

tends language as any linguistics might study it). Edie himself, finally, it should be acknowledged in fairness, is aware that his argument is pushing up against the limits of the empiricism finally at work in both outlooks, of Chomsky and structural linguistics, albeit of different sorts. Edie thus distances himself from both Chomsky's merely anthropological, or species-specific, universalism (Edie 1976, 62–63), as well as structuralism's social or collectivist limitation, its "cultural relativism" (Edie 1976, 30).

14. Due both to Saussure's famous stipulation that signifiers and signifieds were but two sides or faces of a single entity, the sign, as well as his invocation of two axes, paradigmatic and syntagmatic, which he believed to be at work in any actual set of significant signs, the question may be raised as to what extent this founding oppositional distinction between *parole* and *langue* may not find its force eaten away in the face of the actual findings of linguistics as a science. This is part of Roman Jakobson's gesture in "Code and Message," attempting to break down most of Saussure's distinctions, and, in particular, folding *langue* and *parole* into one another in the moment of speech. His conclusion: "All of *parole* as well as all of *langue* simultaneously includes a subjective and an intersubjective aspect, and [each] . . . in its subjective and its intersubjective aspect brings into play simultaneously each of the two forces present" (Jakobson 1990, 108–9). Jakobson makes plain, however, that he is taking a substantially different tack than Saussure. He is commenting on this same opening section of the *Course in General Linguistics,* largely in order to make room for a dialogic theory of thought and communication (one he ultimately allies to Peirce's semiotics), thus indirectly confirming my interpretation here. Jakobson also agrees, it is worth noting, with my claim that Saussure's definition of *langue* and *parole* is oppositional (see his discussion of the role played by "antinomies" in Saussure's thought [Jakobson 1990, 90, 104]).

15. This is not to say that there are no possible construals of philosophy in which the findings of the "human sciences" could not have important implications, though Saussure himself (writing in an earlier period in any case) essentially respected this difference. Part of the issue in France in the debate over structuralism (and the work of the human sciences generally) concerned just this question: the authority of their results for philosophy and philosophical inquiry, in particular with an eye to phenomenology (obviously widespread in France, at the time of structuralism's ascendancy), which claimed ultimate rights of its own. The tension between the two approaches was never as clearly felt in the United States, which is one reason why some of the difficulties I am demarcating here have gone so long unnoticed, due to the prevalence of analytic philosophy (including most forms of pragmatism), which almost everywhere unequivocally allied itself with empirical research in a positivist vein.

16. Especially noteworthy in the American context is Quine's positivism, which takes just the opposite tack. Quine starts from the assumption that philosophy has no subject matter or region of its own; he is indeed dedicated to the withering away of philosophy and its ultimate replacement by the positive disciplines. Thus he starts from linguistics as a working empirical discipline to get an operational hold on these issues in the philosophy of language, precisely to avoid these ultimate philosophical problems, to show that they have no (positivistic) scientific

meaning or status in their own right (e.g., in Quine's famous rejection of the ana-lytic/synthetic distinction, Quine 1953; see Jerrold Katz's introduction to *The Phi-losophy of Linguistics* for a particularly lucid account of the relation of Quine's proj-ect to empirical linguistics [Katz 1985]).

17. Derrida is specifically arguing, as it happens, against both Jakobson's and Hjelmslev's attempts to banish once and for all Saussure's "mentalistic" talk of the psychic image—an aspect of Derrida's comments to which I will return below.

18. Derrida opens his entire discussion of the *Course* with a series of questions, which climax in the following interrogative: "The science of a writing ought then seek its object at the root of scientificity. The history of writing ought to turn back toward the origin of historicity. Science of the possibility of science? . . . History of the possibility of history?" (*DG*43/*G*27). In turn, Derrida begins chapter 3 of part 1 of *Of Grammatology*, "Of Grammatology as a Positive Science," by noting that "graphematics or grammatography ought no longer be presented as sciences, their goals should be exorbitant when compared to grammatological knowledge" (*G*74).

19. Derrida has arrived at two conclusions by the time he closes off section 1 of chapter 2: (a) "the *system* of writing is not exterior to the *system* of language in general," as well as (b) "for the same reason *writing* in general is not 'image' or 'figuration' of *language* in general . . . writing is not a sign of a sign, except if one says it of all signs, which would be more profoundly true"—where the second set of issues clearly refers to language in *use* (*G*43, my emphasis). It should be noted that the whole fracas with Searle to a large extent is owed to Searle's failure to see that the question of writing as posed by Derrida (in respect to its status as regards the logos, as well as the *phone,* to put the same point in other terms) entails that the signs in language as well as in what Searle would call speech acts are being in-terrogated together. Though this is in part understandable, Searle, in fact, quotes a passage from *Positions* nearly identical to the one I have just cited, also concern-ing "texts," "traces," and "systems of traces," in order to argue that Saussure's claim that "language consists of a system of elements whose essential functioning de-pends on the differences between the elements" is not equivalent to Derrida's claim "that nothing, neither among the elements, nor within the system is any-where ever simply absent or simply present"—an objection that would indeed be cleared up, if one saw that it was the constitution of these elements as such, the mode of givenness of the units of speech, and thus signs viewed within language and use at once, that was the real focus of Derrida's concern (Searle 1993, 177; cf. Edie 1990, 113).

20. Edie is again instructive on this point, as well as on the problems faced in moving back and forth from a structuralist to a Husserlian perspective when it comes to these issues. For Edie, following Ricoeur, the status of the "word" sepa-rates Husserl (and the universalist perspective on language Edie takes to unite Husserl to Chomsky) from structural linguistics and its implied empiricism. ("Be-cause . . . [of this] culmination in *words,* it is impossible to limit the discussion of what language *means* to the immanent and intralinguistic structures of phonol-ogy," Edie writes. "With the emergence of words, meaning becomes dependent on syntactic [and semantic] rules and structures, which are not accounted for by

phonology and *morphology*" [Edie 1976, 131; my emphasis].) Edie thus here distinguishes "signs" from "words" as the pairing of signifiers and signified within *langue* from these signs as they are at work *in speech* ("as an element of the semeiotic system, the word is only virtually meaningful; it must be animated by an intention which comes from outside the sound-system as such to take on meaning"; Edie 1976, 134); and only in the latter case, with signs becoming words, do universal questions of semantics and syntax come into play. Edie's own distinctions thus attest to the ultimate importance of the word in Husserl (though he does not address the historical dimension that in particular interests me here). Moreover, as his work goes forward, Derrida's own thought does not finally escape these tensions in a way different than has thus far emerged. Here, in *Of Grammatology,* Derrida seems to want to fuse the two perspectives together, while somehow giving priority to the sign. At crucial junctures throughout his career, however, Derrida may be seen to rely on a model more like Edie's, most notably in *Limited Inc* (in particular, the "Afterword"), where Derrida, to explain his understanding of the rigor of the concept, has recourse to Husserl's notion of a semantic nucleus, a notion drawn from the appendix of *Formal and Transcendental Logic,* and only applicable, as far as I can tell, under conditions much like those Edie describes here—the speaker's intention and a universalist syntax and semantics being granted priority, as well as the word, not the sign.

21. The question of the authentic units of language, the actual identity of the signs that linguistics studies, has long been a vexed one in linguistics. André Martinet, to whose writings Derrida repeatedly refers, though beginning from the other direction in his essay "What to Do about the 'Word'" (asking first if an entity answering to the word can be identified within the field of language as linguistics studies it), ends up largely by stating this problem rather than resolving it. Not only do the ultimate identities of the words themselves remain mysterious, but what he takes to be the smallest significant unit of a language, which he calls the "moneme," turns out not to appear within simple contiguous signs (Martinet 1989, 132). According to Martinet, it is finally itself not identifiable as the same across a number of instances. ("Non seulement la linguistique fonctionelle n'apporte aucune réponse à la question de savoir si deux formes identique sont le même monème ou deux monèmes différents, mais elle enseigne qu'il n'y a, en stricte sychronie, aucune réponse possible" [Martinet 1989, 134].) So too, Jakobson, who arguably sees these difficulties as even more deep-seated than Martinet, flat out claims that Saussure, at least, never solved the problem of the true identity of the sign, "neither Whitney nor Saussure succeeded in solving the problem of the relationship between sound and meaning" (Jakobson 1990, 411). This problem ends up taking him in the direction I indicated above—not only toward the removal of a fixed distinction between *langue* and *parole,* but also toward a Peircean construal of linguistics which brings in iconic and indexical features of the sign, leading him not only to discount (even more radically than Martinet) Saussure's claims about the linearity of signifier (Jakobson 1990, 419), but also to go a long way toward rejecting altogether Saussure's thesis of arbitrariness (Jakobson 1990, 410–11). Derrida himself, it should be noted, will refer to Jakobson's claims here. In a footnote he writes that "a whole system of intra-linguistic critiques can be op-

posed to the thesis of the arbitrariness of the sign" (*DG* 65n8/*G* 44n8). Derrida's disclaimer that follows, however ("these critiques do not breach—and do not claim to do so otherwise—the profound intention of Saussure"), in the case of Jakobson at least seems to me contestable, insofar as it is precisely the distinction Derrida next draws on between the structure and the origin of the sign ("the discontinuity and immotivation proper to the structure, if not the origin, of the sign" as established by Saussure would not here come into question, Derrida declares) that Jakobson indeed brings into doubt in his own resolution to the difficulty of the sign's identity (see, especially, the end of Jakobson's essay where he ends up invoking issues concerning reference, as well as having recourse to the model of the word, both of which, as in Edie above, and in Peirce himself, combine considerations of origin with those of structure; Jakobson 1990, 421).

22. Maurice Lagueux, in an important 1965 article to which Edie draws our attention, in the context of attempting to sort through Merleau-Ponty's talk of Saussure having given birth to "a synchronic linguistics of speech" (Merleau-Ponty's viewpoint differing significantly from Saussure's own, as Lagueux well shows, though in this one case it is strangely close to Derrida's, as I am about to further discuss), sets out most clearly the question which will be Derrida's first and primary focus here: namely, what would be the ultimate ontological status of the sign in structural linguistics, of the unique combination of sign and signifier, of these forms of language as such—in Lagueux's rather rudimentary terminology would this combination, the sign, language at its core, ultimately be a "logical or physical reality" (Lagueux 1965, 358, 360). Though "the system in question," Lagueux acknowledges, "would be that composed of the ensemble of values: differences of ideas and differences of sounds," and "the system (language) [thus] realizes a symbiosis in the most strict sense of this concept" of thought and sound, signifier and signified (the so-called "thought-sound"; Lagueux 1965, 359), Lagueux, insisting "that language is no less real—at the point of elaborating its unities by constituting itself between two amorphous unities," declares, "it is necessary to situate it [language] somehow"; and this question of where language in its reality is to be situated, how it is to be thought, occupies the remainder of Lagueux's essay. Lagueux in fact goes on to suggest that this is what Merleau-Ponty has done: Merleau-Ponty has in effect supplied the answer to this question of the ultimate reality or kind of being pertaining to language in its specificity, perhaps to some degree despite himself, by inserting Saussure's linguistics in the broader context of speech and lived perception (and Lagueux ends more generally, it is worth noting, by arriving at a position close to the one I have already taken here: namely, that "it is necessary to wait upon a philosopher"—that not Saussure's linguistics, but only philosophy, here in the guise of Merleau-Ponty, may reach any ultimate decision about these matters [Lagueux 1965, 364]). This question Lagueux identifies in Saussure, of the ultimate status of these signs, the ultimate ontological dispensation of these linguistic identities, is the question, to a great extent, that Derrida himself aims to answer in the first half of *Of Grammatology*, in the final sections of his chapter 2 in his talk of the archi-trace, archi-writing, and *différance*. Such an aim has been recognized to various degrees (as far back as Gasché's "Deconstruction as Criticism"), even if this problem has not been identified in its

specificity, and lately the possible coincidence of intention in respect to Saussure of Merleau-Ponty and Derrida (although arriving at different outcomes) has come to be more widely recognized (though to my mind Lagueux's treatment allows a greater degree of clarity to be brought to this problem than otherwise has been available). Both Dorothea Olkowski and Len Lawlor in recent publications bring this proximity forward. (Olkowski claims "the question Derrida raises explicitly concerning the architectonic that operates [in Saussure] has been raised implicitly by Merleau-Ponty" [Olkowski 1997, 56; see also 54]; "despite *their undeniable proximity,*" Lawlor starts out, "Derrida is a grammatologist, Merleau-Ponty is an ontologist" [Lawlor 1997, 71; my emphasis], Lawlor thus also stressing their differences in what follows.)

23. Summarizing the initial phase of his discussion, Derrida will declare: "In Saussurean language, what Saussure does not say would have to be said: there is neither sign nor symbol, but a *becoming-sign* of the symbol" (*G* 47, my emphasis). Derrida is about to go on, it is worth noting, to canvas Peirce's semiotics, which "goes very far in the direction" Derrida himself wishes to pursue (*G* 49), and here too Derrida stresses a singular repetition and becoming intrinsic to signs, at once in speech in language, in which "the genetic root system refers from sign to sign" (*G* 48).

24. The criticism made by Vincent Déscombes and others, including Searle, that Derrida simply conflates language and speech, reduces *parole* to *langue,* has its source here, I believe, in Derrida's starting point in Saussure, which indeed tends to obscure Derrida's more complex standpoint. This error is thus understandable, if not inevitable, since as I am about to argue, Derrida himself does not make his own position plain here at the outset of section 2. Alan White, who draws our attention to these criticisms in the course of setting out a distinction much like that of Edie's between words in speech and signs in language (he refers to Ricoeur's "Structure, Word, Event" which Edie cites, and with which he substantially agrees), is aware, it is worth noting, that there is both a structuralist moment, related to *langue,* as well as a moment of "event," often associated with speech and the speech act at work in *Of Grammatology* (White mentions not only Ricoeur but also "John Austin" [White 1995, 112]). I doubt that White would agree with me, however, that both moments hew so closely to Husserl's analysis in the way that I have suggested, because he, like so many others, sees Derrida's work almost solely aimed at breaking with phenomenology, not transforming it, and thus, in my view, underestimates Derrida's proximity to Husserl throughout this discussion in *Of Grammatology.*

25. Only on this condition may the trace be thought as a trace: as something that not only may fail to appear, but whose nonappearance or erasure is essential to its own mode of "being." The trace only appears as a trace by dint of a previous appearance of its erasure; this is intrinsic to its own self-constitution, and consequently even at this early point in Derrida's text the proximity of this notion to Husserl's transcendental perspective must be in view, a certain play of the world be thought, none of which would be possible if what is in question was some anthropological origin, some first moment when language was used, or even the actual employment of any empirical set of signs. Marrati-Guénoun, in the title of

whose book this notion of the trace *(la trace)* appears, also stresses the relation of the trace to its own self-effacement, in the context of a discussion of Heidegger and "Ousia and Gramme": "La trace se produit comme son propre effacement" (Marrati-Guénoun 1998, 159). As I discuss further below, she sees the trace, as do I, as indicating an ongoing proximity to Husserl on the part of Derrida (as opposed to Heidegger), to a degree perhaps unparalleled among commentators. At the same time, she perhaps underestimates the difficulty of establishing the position at which Derrida arrives, in part by skipping over Derrida's development and the question of by what right Derrida has continuing recourse to a transcendental attitude of any sort at all.

26. Obviously the point is a delicate one: while the notion of a trace as such entails repetition for the reasons earlier reviewed (since its own erasure must be intrinsic to it and it can never exist for a first time), not every thought of repetition, or even radical repetition, entails a notion of the trace, especially as Derrida is about to set it out here. This reference, as situated at the heart of language, brings with it a certain kind of transcendental functioning, albeit transformed— the work of something like Husserl's transcendental attitude, or Heidegger's ontico-ontological difference. The trace, then (as archi-trace, or what Derrida also calls archi-writing), by dint of this quasi-constitutive relation to language as such, may never be reduced simply to a moment of repetition, even one inherent in signs for which difference is also primary, and, on this contrast between repetition and the trace, between an absolute past and a certain *enchainement,* largely rests the question of Derrida's relation to Deleuze at this epoch. Derrida himself at the end of this section will refer to stoic logic and denounces its "linearism," now insisting on the impossibility of it and all other talk of the sign ever escaping logocentrism—thus the necessity to be rid of this notion entirely in favor of a thought of a trace (*G* 72–73/*DG* 106). And this, along with Derrida's remarks on Spinoza, which I discuss below (*G* 71/*DG* 104), should make clear the gulf between Derrida and Deleuze at least at this moment. Matters are still further complicated, however, by the development Derrida's own thought undergoes (and here the possible precipitousness of Marrati-Guénoun's conclusions drawn from "Ousia and Gramme," despite their importance, can also be seen). Part of Derrida's condemnation of stoic logic and "its linearism" at this moment rests on it being tributary to what Derrida calls a "vulgar construal of time" (*G* 72/*DG* 105), explicitly following Heidegger. Derrida thus evidently changed his mind concerning the question of time and the line by the time of "Ousia and Gramme," and this reversal raises the question of where in that later essay Derrida in fact comes down in reference to the difference visible here between repetition and the trace: what ends up being the dispensation of a specifically transcendental attitude (which is at stake both in Heidegger's talk of *Anwesenheit* and his privileging of Kant over Aristotle) at this moment in Derrida's own work, and how does it relate to *Of Grammatology* in which Derrida still clearly holds to these reference points?

27. Marrati-Guénoun also refers to this moment in *Of Grammatology,* bringing forward considerations very close to those I set out here (Marrati-Guénoun 1998, 144–46). For her, however, this break with Husserl has already taken place in the "Introduction," and the work it does at this moment is to let Derrida graph a rela-

tion to history and historicity importantly different than Heidegger's. *Of Grammatology*, however, as we have begun to see, granting my reading of the "Introduction" (which takes Derrida to be much nearer to Husserl than hers), is the moment in Derrida's development when he moves *closer* to Heidegger and Heideggerean history. And thus while I agree with Marrati-Guénoun in part, as I make clear below, it is far less transparent to me than it is to her how Derrida can deviate from both Husserl and Heidegger in this way, even while claiming to have extirpated himself more radically than Heidegger from what Derrida joins Heidegger in calling metaphysics.

28. Not only has Derrida already wondered whether "the phenomenological model [is] itself not constituted on as a warp of language, logic, evidence . . . upon a woof not its own," but he has also noted that this woof, and "such is the most difficult problem—is no longer mundane" (*G* 67).

29. Marrati-Guénoun, as well as others, notably Chris Fynsk (cited in Wood 2002, 104), have importantly emphasized this outcome on the part of Derrida: his move away from seeing Being, or something like it, as having fatefully provided an origin of history, and thus making a break with Heideggerean history in this sense (see especially Marrati-Guénoun 1998, 123–25). At the same time—and this is the question to which this chapter is dedicated, especially the final section upon which I am about to embark—how even as Derrida moves away from Heidegger's construal of history and the construction of metaphysics as an epoch, Derrida believes himself warranted to invoke this same talk and apply it to Heidegger—to condemn Heidegger for belonging to such a history and falling prey to such an epochal metaphysics, remains a question. As the discussion of *Of Grammatology*'s opening pages conducted here already showed, while I agree with others, and Marrati-Guénoun in particular, that Derrida in effect moves away from Heidegger's monolithic interpretation of metaphysics (indeed by dint of what Husserl has to offer), and thereby moves toward the discovery of what eludes or exceeds his thought—here the trace (as well as in what Derrida calls inscriptions, chains of signs, texts)—how Derrida can invoke Heidegger's own notion of metaphysics in so doing, and thus claim this is also to move *closer to history* and to Heidegger himself, is what is less clear. That this presents a difficulty for Marrati-Guénoun is evident in her own text in that she first will assert (1998, 125) that Derrida discovers a historicity, which history, including Heidegger's history, would occlude (a claim I will soon discuss), though, in going to cash this out, she ends up with a certain notion of *anachronie* (Marrati-Guénoun 1998, 148). How, however, anachronie and *historicity* relate to one another (which is another version of the question of the relation of the trace to repetition set out above) is again not wholly self-evident.

30. Compare: "It is true that another word ought perhaps be used; the word history no doubt has always been associated with the linear unfolding of the schema of presence" (*G* 85); "One would perhaps say I had just proposed a double grid: historical and systematic. Let us pretend to believe in this opposition" (*G* 97).

31. Suzanne Gearhart, in an important essay, emphasized "the historicity of which Derrida speaks," referring to the implication of Rousseau's discourse in a certain "ensemble," which "can no longer be designated by the term history . . .

because for Derrida this historicity is itself negated when the ensemble in question is reduced to the status of a history" (Gearhart 1983, 78). Gearhart, then, was one of the first to draw a strong distinction between history and historicity in Derrida, in a line of which Hobson is perhaps the most recent important member (Hobson 1998, 47). Gearhart also goes on here to cite Derrida (from "*Différance*") stating that "if the word 'history' did not entail in itself the final suppression of difference, one could say that only differences . . . could be historical," which clearly invites the same questions as his stance in *Of Grammatology*.

32. Interestingly enough, the course of Derrida's reception as a whole may almost be mapped through the shifting focus assigned to these two essays in the literature. Derrida's relation to Foucault was believed an especially pressing topic in the 1970s and 1980s, when Derrida's work was first coming to notice (see, e.g., Felman 1975). More recently, Derrida's work on Levinas has received the bulk of critics' attention. The fact that no one, to my knowledge, has previously examined these essays in relation to one another, despite their importance for all of Derrida's future work, attests to the large lacuna that exists when it comes to Derrida's development and issues related to even the most basic organization of his corpus.

33. Lawlor, rightfully in my view, has seen "Violence," in particular, "as deconstruction in the making" (Lawlor 1996b, 118; a stance he still holds, Lawlor 2002, 146). In my analysis to come, "Violence" occupies a rather complex and delicate position, one worth bringing into view in advance. Initially, "Violence" and "Cogito" are seen together here as part of one whole and as forming a single phase. Good reasons exists for this, which will emerge as I continue. Nevertheless, "Violence" is a far more monumental and volatile work finally than "Cogito"; and in the conclusion of this chapter I take into account those aspects unique to "Violence," most apparent at its end, in which Derrida's mature position, the position to which he will come at deconstruction's advent, are most visibly coming to the fore.

34. Lawlor in his 2002 work, focusing on the section of "Violence" that I am also homing in on, seems aware in his commentary of the rather significant divide that separates Derrida from Levinas at this moment and thus the critical import of Derrida's claims (Lawlor 2002, 151–54). How Lawlor reconciles this with the larger framework of his project, which tends to read back, as I have already noted, Derrida's later, fuller rapprochement with Levinas in the 1980s into these early writings (drawing on the blurring of these differences which Robert Bernasconi was the first to present in his pathbreaking article, upon which I comment below), remains unclear (see Lawlor 2002, 146, among other instances).

35. Near the end of "Violence," in a portion Derrida only added in 1967, we find him making the following assertions, in sentences he himself places in italics: "*Our reference to history, here, is only contextual. The economy of which we are speaking does not any longer accommodate the concept of history such as it has always functioned, and which it is difficult, if not impossible, to lift from its teleological or eschatological horizon*" ("VM" 148/ "VEM" 220). I comment on this later insertion below, along with the context in which it is found. At present, noting this addition should suffice to confirm that Derrida's stance toward history is indeed in flux between the first appearance of "Violence" in 1964 and the version Derrida published in 1967. Though I occasionally refer to the version of "Violence" Derrida originally pub-

lished in *Revue de métaphysique et de morale* in 1964, references to the French are to the version that appeared in 1967 in *L'écriture et la différence* unless otherwise indicated.

36. "Why is it necessary still to use the word exteriority," Derrida asks, introducing this phase of his discussion, "(which, if it has a meaning, if it is not an algebraic X, obstinately beckons toward space and light), in order to signify a nonspatial relationship?" ("VM" 112)

37. In "The Trace of Levinas in Derrida," one of a number of essays that compose what is perhaps the single most important, sustained discussion of "Violence" and Derrida's relation to Levinas generally, Robert Bernasconi seems to want to ward off, or at least hold at a distance, the sort of reading I am offering of these passages which sees Derrida as offering a criticism of some kind of Levinas (Bernasconi 1988b, 16), while offering an account of "Violence" (in some respects parallel to my own) which also sees it as a moment of change, in which Derrida comes to adopt Levinas's trace for his own thinking. Bernasconi, it should noted, handles thoughtfully the projects of both these thinkers (Bernasconi 1988b, 24–25) in this essay, as well as elsewhere, and his discussion is helpful in a number of ways, in particular about Levinas's relation to Heidegger. Nevertheless, his rejection, or amelioration, of the possibility of fundamental disagreement between Derrida and Levinas, at least at this juncture (a tack upon which he will continue to insist; see Bernasconi 1987, 129; 1991, 153), seems to me misplaced. For one thing, to speak to the broadest parameters of his interpretation, Derrida himself seems to have already to come upon the notion of the trace in his first version of *Of Grammatology* and his reading of Saussure's *Course* (in the 1965 version of *Of Grammatology,* Derrida speaks of the trace extensively in passages parallel to those I discussed above, while Levinas is only mentioned in a footnote [Derrida 1965a, 37n13]). And this, along with how I understand the passage from "Violence" that Bernasconi cites at the start of his article, seem to me to cast in doubt the occurrence of a substantial reversal in Derrida's stance toward the trace. That Derrida was already thinking along these lines and did not change his mind about the trace in the way that Bernasconi suggests, goes to the narrower point: namely, that Bernasconi is in the grip of a false opposition when he banishes altogether from Derrida's deconstruction a moment of criticism and critique and thus downplays the differences that I want to emphasize here (though I am, of course, ultimately sympathetic to the claim that deconstruction and criticism do not ultimately coincide). While Bernasconi is doubtless right and Derrida in "Violence" at some point does aim at a result similar to Levinas's (and on these grounds at times even places his project under the heading of Levinas's own, something we shall see him also do, however, with Foucault), and while Levinas, in turn, doubtless has his own justifications for how his own thought may come to speech, this does not entail that Derrida, *at this juncture,* does not also deeply *disagree* with Levinas about *how* this should come about: disagree with him concerning those conditions on which an exteriority exceeding philosophical thought—a trace, a radical alterity, a face—may be discursively articulated, even as Derrida remains deeply sympathetic to Levinas's intentions in other ways. (Much of the difference between me and Bernasconi here rests on our different interpretation of deconstructive

"methodology," to which I have repeatedly alluded [here as well as in other publications: Kates 1993, 2002]; here it leads Bernasconi to affirm the possibility that Derrida may be "producing several texts at once," thus allowing him, if I follow, to admit a radical nonconsequence among Derrida's positions in a single work, which seems to me both doubtful and also to sell Derrida rather short as a thinker [certainly unintentionally], while relieving us of what I believe to be a certain salutary and necessary burden and responsibility as interpreters [Bernasconi 1998b, 16].)

38. Derrida insists on this same "zero-point," which is also an "oriented origin," a little later, distancing himself from Merleau-Ponty's notion of the lived body to which Levinas also has recourse: "body . . . zero point, origin of space, certainly, but origin which has no sense before the *of*, which cannot be separated from the genitivity of space it both orients and engenders" ("VEM" 169/"VM" 115).

39. Derrida's insistence on the rights of a transcendental origin of this sort indeed hearkens back to the privilege that he assigns to Husserl's transcendental-phenomenological reduction, as well as those related themes, such as the phenomenological voice, that I have already repeatedly stressed here (cf. Lawlor, who claims that "Violence" "contains Derrida's longest positive or noncritical interpretation of Husserl" [Lawlor 2002, 161]). In what follows, however, I emphasize instead the forward-looking aspect of Derrida's present discussion: how his outcomes in *Of Grammatology*, in particular, may be thought as bearing a unique relation to history, or historicity, in view of Derrida's argument here.

40. This oriented origin, of speech and space at once, Derrida tells us, is "an *included* origin"; it is "an *inscribed* eastern horizon"; "a *text* of the glance which is also the *text* of speech." "The inscription," Derrida writes on the next page (again material added later), "is the written origin traced and henceforth inscribed in a system, in a figure which it no longer governs" ("VM" 115).

41. As previous citations of Derrida (both my own and Gearhart's) have made clear, there is a standard "account" of why Derrida finally rejects history, an account with which I am of course familiar: namely, that "history" (the concept?) signals "a final reappropriation of presence," a "final suppression of difference," and is "difficult to lift from its teleological horizon" ("VM" 149; see note 35 above). The fact that Derrida himself appealed to the notion of history at a certain stage of his thought, however, requires that his distancing from this notion receive deeper justification. Why did Derrida not believe that his own thought, at least, was able to avoid this outcome, thus reworking the term "history," as others (such as Foucault, Nietzsche, or perhaps even Heidegger) at points had done? The question must consequently be raised of what grounds at this stage led Derrida to move away from this notion and to come to these convictions. Is there some place in his own work at this moment where such a reappropriation of difference by presence at the hands of history is to be found? Derrida's singular trajectory in respect to history—his embrace and subsequent rejection of it as a rubric under which to conduct his own thought—compels us to ask these questions.

42. Bernard Flynn in an earlier article and Peter Fenves more recently both cite the passage that I am about to cite at length (Flynn 1989, 210; Fenves 2001, 278). Flynn's discussion includes Foucault's response, entitled "My Body, This

Paper, This Fire," and focuses on the interpretation of Descartes as such—within these parameters, very helpfully making clear Derrida's points at a number of junctures. Fenves's ambitions are more wide-ranging; like me, he wants to know about Derrida's ultimate stance toward history, and he traverses much of my itinerary here: his essay having bearing on the relation of "Cogito" generally to "Violence," as well as *Of Grammatology* and the "Introduction." Fenves, however, while making a number of insightful points concerning Derrida's work, if I follow him, denies any movement of Derrida in respect to history, denies a phase of the sort that I am arguing for here exists, in which Derrida actively embraces history (Fenves 2001, 286); nor is this at all an issue for Flynn. Not only do I think the internal evidence offered by "Violence" and the changes it underwent amply testify against this, however, but the "Introduction's" place in Derrida's total engagement with Husserl also does so, as well as what transpires in the "Introduction" and in Husserl's late writings themselves. From this perspective, Derrida's views on language (see note 43 below; this is what ultimately interests Flynn) as well as those on history (Fenves's focus) both look quite different.

43. The deep proximity of "Cogito" to "Violence" at this moment is made even clearer by taking note of a sentence immediately following the one that I last cited, part of which, oddly, only appears in the current French edition of *L'écriture et la différence,* but not in the English. Speaking of this rhythmed alternation of speech, of this statement of the excess, whose intrinsic historicity has just come forward (which Derrida here calls the "violent liberation of the word"), Derrida will go on to affirm that this liberation "is not possible and can only follow to the extent to which either it keeps, or it is the trace of this violent originary gesture [confining madness and excess], and to the extent to which it holds itself resolutely, consciously, most closely to the abuse which is the use of speech, just near enough in order to *say* the violence, in order to dialogue with itself as irreducible violence, just enough to *live* and to live as speech [*parole*]" (Derrida 1967a, 94). Thus the same insistence on this more complex role of speech is to be found here as has already been seen in "Violence."

44. Derrida stipulates the impossibility of enclosing the meaning of Descartes's thought within history just before he embarks on his reading of Descartes: "Only when the totality of this [philosophical] content will have become manifest in its meaning for me (but this is impossible) will I be able to rigorously situate it in its total historical form; it is only then that its reinsertion will not do violence" ("CHM" 44). And he will also argue later, on the same terms, clearly invoking Husserl, for the impossibility of finding the significance of the cogito exhausted within a totality of a structuralist style: "structuralist totalitarianism" threatens "an internment of the Cogito" that would embody "violence itself" ("CHM" 57), states Derrida—both of these disqualifications directly stemming from Husserl's arguments, in *Logical Investigations* I and from *Philosophy as Rigorous Science,* as reviewed at the end of chapter 1.

45. At the end of "Violence," Derrida himself broaches this notion of empiricism. Though taking a somewhat sympathetic tack toward empiricism as the "*dream* of a purely *heterological* thought" ("VM" 151), a sympathy which anticipates Derrida's famous talk of his own project as a "radical empiricism" in *Of Gramma-*

tology (*G* 162), as far as I can tell, Derrida believes that the rejection of empiricism as such ("we say the dream because it must vanish at daybreak"; "VM" 151) separates his stance from Levinas (cf. Lawlor 2002, 159), and in regard to such rejection Derrida will never waver (this again being made explicit at the moment above cited in *Of Grammatology*, since this rejection in part separates radical empiricism from empiricism *tout court*). Since Derrida himself always connects empiricism and skepticism (and he does so again at *G* 162) and ties them together as that whose common possibility he rejects (almost always thanks to a lesson learned from Husserl: see *LPG* 16/*IOG* 151n184; "CHM" 57; *P* n32; Derrida 1998, 137), Derrida's rejection of Levinas's empiricism remains one with his rejection of skepticism more generally, an issue that I treated at greater length in my article "Deconstruction and Skepticism."

46. This second formulation is also important insofar as it appears in the original, lecture portion of Derrida's text, while the material I have just cited was added afterward for its publication in the *Revue*. (The square brackets around certain portions of Derrida's printed text mark this difference.)

47. The different stances taken by Derrida and Foucault toward issues of *periodization* (which was and will remain, in my view, along with their different stances toward historicism, the most important difference between Derrida and Foucault) are at stake in Derrida's argument about the logos, though obviously I cannot pursue this here at any length. ("It is in any event certain that classical reason and medieval reason before it, bore a relation to Greek reason," Derrida will state, and thus "it is within the milieu of this more or less perceived heritage, which itself is more or less crossed with other traditional lines, that the adventure or misadventure of classical reason developed"; "CHM" 41–42.) Derrida here affirms a historical reason across all periods (classical, medieval, Greek, and also, it should be added, elsewhere Foucault's own present). By contrast, Foucault's whole point is to map a radical historical discontinuity (a *series* of discontinuities) of thought and knowledge *as such*—within history, across time—first at the moment of modernity, and then going forward. Derrida will always worry that Foucault has precipitously multiplied breaks, while Foucault will worry that Derrida remains too close to reason and indeed to phenomenology—a worry here in part borne out (without denying the validity of Derrida's concerns, especially in respect to Foucault's numerous breaks from the "classical age" going forward) when it is seen that only with Husserl's examples in mind (of sciences such as geometry and logic said to have a history of their own yet exceeding any finite closure), and only by granting the precedence of Husserl's theoretism (for whom the logos, discourse, and signification remain theoretical, not practical achievements), can Derrida object to Foucault's historicism by appealing to a model of reason itself "historical," yet not historicist, itself in history, yet not a finite one.

48. Derrida, where I have last cited him, goes on to speak of this "*historical* reason" *also* as "this *logos* which is in the *beginning*," even as he further claims that it remains the "atmosphere in which Foucault's [own] language moves." At the outset of "Cogito" Derrida thus brings forward a logos at work "in the beginning" and in the "classical age" and at present (at work in Foucault's discourse), one still, however, itself "historical," in part to question on what grounds Foucault will be able

to take full responsibility for his own discourse. And thus here again, as in the case of Levinas, a certain *ur*-situatedness of all logos is highlighted by Derrida and believed to demand being taken into account by the author's own discourse, in this case Foucault's ("CHM" 39).

49. See Bernet's remarks at the end of his essay on the "Introduction" for other important motives for Derrida's decision pertaining to the idea of Europe (Bernet 1989, 152). None of this, as shall become clearer, is meant to deny the importance of these concerns, nor those issues brought forward by Marrati-Guénoun (and Fynsk) when it comes to Derrida's ultimate stance toward history when compared with Heidegger's. My aim here, rather, is to bring forward the *means* by which Derrida arrives at these positions, about whose character I largely agree, means which may, however, highlight an aspect of Derrida's final stance toward history which has been largely unappreciated thus far.

50. After all, Derrida's mature stance toward history entails that the claim that the concept of history implies a reappropriation of difference must be true; and thus that Husserl's late thought, and later, after him, Hegel's stance on history, must in effect be correct. (Accordingly, Derrida in taking leave of Husserl and moving on to a prolonged engagement with Hegel, will assert that Husserl's thought in the end leads one to affirm Hegel's philosophy of history and the advent of "absolute knowledge"; *VP* 115.) This is a problem many of us have long had with Derrida's ultimate treatment of history; Fenves rightfully puts his finger on it as the threat of a lurking idealism, though it seems to me he underestimates the extent of the difficulty (Fenves 2001, 286). Nevertheless, if one must invoke something other than history to avoid sense, to avoid meaning and the logos, history must indeed be subordinate to these; and though the subordination of actual history to the logos and meaning in either a Hegelian or a Husserlian style is a contestable claim, for Derrida's stance to be cogent, Hegel and Husserl must be right that history, at least *as we know it,* remains firmly in the hands of a successful teleology of truth.

51. Internal evidence exists for the closeness of "Violence and Metaphysics'" conclusion to Derrida's mature stance. I have already cited the caveat to "Violence" that Derrida added in 1967 (and which is absent from the version of "Violence" first published in the *Revue de métaphysique et de morale*) in which Derrida declares his "reference to history is only contextual" in light of the difficulty of lifting "the concept of history . . . from its teleological horizon" ("VM" 148). The fact that Derrida was able to insert this stipulation without substantially altering the text surrounding it shows how near to his mature thought he already stands here at the close of "Violence and Metaphysics."

52. Lawlor comments on the continuation of Derrida's argument here (Lawlor 2002, 158–59). His account seems to me, however, to embody a rather literal understanding of Derrida's use of the term "God," something perhaps owed to Lawlor's construal of Derrida's later thought and his assimilation of it to this moment here.

53. Let me stress again, just to be clear, that Derrida's debt to Husserl's late history first of all takes the form of *departing* from it, moving *against it,* in the unique style which is Derrida's. Accordingly, Derrida's ongoing *singular proximity*

and distance to this aspect of Husserl's thought, to his late view of a transcendental-historical logos, is perhaps most evident in the context of Derrida's more recent work in his "Antwort an Apel," where he in fact explicitly defends this phase of Husserl's thinking, and all it implies, against Apel's claim to have superseded Husserl's project through a Peirce-inspired appeal to an infinite transcendental community of interpreters ("AA" 80). In this piece, Derrida also declares, it is worth noting, right after the passage that I cited in chapter 1, that "deconstruction, which I have tried to operate in respect to Husserl's phenomenology, is ever to be pursued with the proviso on my part to have regard for the transcendental dimension of the thought of the trace—this more than any semiotic, and which would also not be a turn back to a pretranscendental empiricism. Thus, expressly and emphatically in *Of Grammatology*" ("AA" 82, my translation).

54. Marrati-Guénoun at the conclusion of her *La genèse et la trace* makes substantially the same point, it should be noted, and she is the only commentator (perhaps with the exception of Bernet) to have also explicitly arrived at this conclusion. "Husserl" and his thought should not be considered as a mere "first stage, indeed as a first 'object' of deconstruction" (Marrati-Guénoun 1998, 208), she writes, but "deconstruction is born . . . in the work of Derrida on Husserl," and thus Derrida's relation to Husserl does not have a parallel "among all those [authors] . . . with whom Derrida is occupied, not even Heidegger" (Marrati-Guénoun 1998, 209).

Bibliography

Beardsworth, Richard. 1996. *Derrida and the Political*. London: Routledge.

Bennington, Geoffrey. 1993. "Derridabase." In *Jacques Derrida*. Chicago: University of Chicago Press.

———. 1994. *Legislations: The Politics of Deconstruction*. London: Verso.

———. 2000. *Interrupting Derrida*. London: Routledge.

Berger, Gaston, ed. 1959. *Husserl: Cahiers de Royaumont*. Paris: Minuit.

———. 1972. *The Cogito in Husserl's Philosophy*. Trans. Kathleen McLaughlin. Evanston, Ill.: Northwestern University Press.

Bernasconi, Robert. 1987. "Deconstruction and the Possibility of Ethics." In Sallis 1987, 122–39.

———. 1988a. "Deconstruction and Scholarship." *Man and World* 21:223–30.

———. 1988b. "The Trace of Levinas in Derrida." In Wood and Bernasconi, 13–29.

———. 1991. "Skepticism in the Face of Philosophy." In *Rereading Levinas*, ed. Robert Bernasconi and Simon Critchley. Bloomington: Indiana University Press, 149–61.

———. 1992. "No More Stories, Good or Bad: De Man's Criticisms of Derrida on Rousseau." In Wood 1992, 127–66.

Bernet, Rudolf. 1988. "Husserl's Theory of Signs Revisited." In *Edmund Husserl and the Phenomenological Tradition*, ed. Robert Sokolowski. Washington, D.C.: Catholic University Press.

———. 1989. "On Derrida's 'Introduction' to Husserl's *Origin of Geometry*." In Silverman, 139–153.

———. 1995. "Derrida and His Master's Voice." In McKenna and Evans, 1–22.

Bernet, Rudolf, Iso Kern, and Eduard Marbach. 1995. *An Introduction to Husserlian Phenomenology*. Evanston, Ill.: Northwestern University Press.

Biemel, Walter. 1959. "Les phases décisives dans le devéloppement de la philosophie de Husserl." In Berger 1959, 32–59.

Cairns, Dorion. 1941. "The Ideality of Verbal Expressions." *Philosophy and Phenomenological Research* 1 (4):453–62.

Caputo, John. 1987. *Radical Hermeneutics: Repetition, Deconstruction, and the Hermeneutic Project*. Bloomington: Indiana University Press.

———. 1993. *Against Ethics: Contributions to a Poetics of Obligation with Constant Reference to Deconstruction*. Bloomington: Indiana University Press.

Caputo, John, and Michael Scanlon, eds. 2002. *God, the Gift and Postmodernism*. Bloomington: Indiana University Press.

Carr, David. 1974. *Phenomenology and the Problem of History.* Evanston, Ill.: Northwestern University Press.

Carr, Lloyd. 1989. "Husserl's Philosophy of Language." In *Husserl's Phenomenology: A Textbook,* ed. J. N. Mohanty and William R. McKenna. Washington, D.C.: University Press of America.

Cascardi, A. J. 1984. "Skepticism and Deconstruction." *Philosophy and Literature* 8 (1):1–14.

Cavaillès, Jean. 1997. *Sur la logique et la théorie de la science.* Paris: Librarie Philosophique J. Vrin, (1946).

Critchley, Simon. 1992. *The Ethics of Deconstruction.* Cambridge, Eng.: Blackwell.

Crowell, Steven Galt. 1996. "Husserl, Derrida, and the Phenomenology of Expression." *Philosophy Today* 40, no. 1 (Spring): 61–70.

———. 2001. *Husserl, Heidegger, and the Space of Meaning: Paths toward Transcendental Phenomenology.* Evanston, Ill.: Northwestern University Press.

Culler, Jonathan. 1982. *On Deconstruction: Theory and Criticism after Structuralism.* Ithaca, N.Y.: Cornell University Press.

Dastur, Françoise. 1994. "Finitude and Repetition in Husserl and Derrida." In Lawlor 1994, 113–30.

De Man, Paul. 1983. "The Rhetoric of Blindness: Jacques Derrida's Reading of Rousseau." In *Blindness and Insight: Essays in the Rhetoric of Contemporary Criticism.* Minneapolis: University of Minnesota Press, 102–41.

Depp, Dane. 1987. "A Husserlian Response to Derrida's Early Criticisms of Phenomenology." *Journal of the British Society for Phenomenology* 18 (3):226–44.

Derrida, Jacques. 1962. Introduction to *L'origine de la géométrie,* by Edmund Husserl, trans. Jacques Derrida. Paris: Presses Universitaires de France.

———. 1964a. Review of *Edmund Husserl's Theory of Meaning,* by J. N. Mohanty. *Les études philosophique* 1 (4):617–18.

———. 1964b. "Violence et métaphysique: Essai sur la pensée d'Emmanuel Levinas." *Revue de métaphysique et de morale* 3–4.

———. 1965a. "De la grammatologie." *Critique* 21, no. 223 (December): 1016–42.

———. 1965b. "'Genèse et structure' et la phénoménologie." In *Entretiens sur les notions de genèse et de structure,* ed. Maurice de Gandillac, Lucien Goldmann, and Jean Piaget. Paris: Mouton.

———. 1966. "De la grammatologie (II)." *Critique* 22, no. 224 (January): 23–53.

———. 1967a. "Cogito et histoire de la folie." In *L'écriture et la différence.* Paris: Éditions du Seuil, 51–97.

———. 1967b. *De la grammatologie.* Paris: Éditions de Minuit.

———. 1967c. "Violence et métaphysique: Essai sur la pensée d'Emmanuel Levinas." In *L'écriture et la différence.* Paris: Éditions du Seuil, 117–228.

———. 1967d. *La voix et le phénomène: Introduction au problème du signe dans la phénoménologie de Husserl.* Paris: Presses Universitaires de France.

———. 1973. *Speech and Phenomena and Other Essays on Husserl's Theory of Signs.* Trans. David B. Allison. Evanston, Ill.: Northwestern University Press.

———. 1974. *Of Grammatology.* Trans. Gayatri Spivak. Baltimore: Johns Hopkins University Press.

———. 1978a. "Cogito and the History of Madness." In *Writing and Difference*, trans. Alan Bass. Chicago: University of Chicago Press, 31–64.

———. 1978b. *Edmund Husserl's "Origin of Geometry": An Introduction*. Trans. John Leavey Jr. Stony Brook, N.Y.: Nicholas Hays.

———. 1978c. "The *Retrait* of Metaphor." *Enclitic* 2 (2):5–34.

———. 1978d. "Violence and Metaphysics: An Essay on the Thought of Emmanuel Levinas." In *Writing and Difference*, trans. Alan Bass. Chicago: University of Chicago Press, 79–154.

———. 1981a. *Dissemination*. Trans. Barbara Johnson. Chicago: University of Chicago Press.

———. 1981b. *Positions*. Trans. Alan Bass. Chicago: University of Chicago Press.

———. 1982. *Margins of Philosophy*. Trans. Alan Bass. Chicago: University of Chicago Press.

———. 1983. "The Time of a Thesis: Punctuations." Trans. Kathleen McLaughlin. In *Philosophy in France Today*, ed. Alan Montefiore. Cambridge: Cambridge University Press.

———. 1984. "My Chances/*Mes Chances:* A Rendez-Vous with Some Epicurean Stereophonies." In *Taking Chances: Derrida, Psychoanalysis, and Literature*, ed. J. Smith and W. Kerrigan. Baltimore: Johns Hopkins University Press.

———. 1986. *Memoires for Paul de Man*. Ed. Avital Ronell and Eduardo Cadava. New York: Columbia University Press.

———. 1987. "Antwort an Apel." *Zeitmitschrift: Journal für Ästhetik* (Summer).

———. 1988. "Afterword: Toward an Ethic of Discussion." In *Limited, Inc.*, trans. Samuel Weber. Evanston, Ill.: Northwestern University Press.

———. 1990a. "Ponctuations: Le temps de la thèse." In *Du droit à la philosophie*. Paris: Galilée.

———. 1990b. *Le problème de la genèse dans la philosophie de Husserl*. Paris: Presses Universitaires de France.

———. 1993. "Circumfession." In *Jacques Derrida*. Chicago: University of Chicago Press.

———. 1995. *Points . . .* Ed. Elisabeth Weber. Stanford, Calif.: Stanford University Press.

———. 1997. *Deconstruction in a Nutshell: A Conversation with Jacques Derrida*. Ed. John Caputo. New York: Fordham University Press.

———. 2000. *Le toucher: Jean-Luc Nancy*. Paris: Galilée.

———. 2002. *Acts of Religion*. Ed. Gil Anidjar. New York: Routledge.

———. 2003. *The Problem of Genesis in Husserl's Philosophy*. Trans. Marian Hobson. Chicago: University of Chicago Press.

Dillon, M. C. 1997. *Écart and Différance: Merleau-Ponty and Derrida on Seeing and Writing*. Atlantic Highland, N. J.: Humanities.

Dummett, Michael A. E. 1994. *Origins of Analytical Philosophy*. Cambridge, Mass.: Harvard University Press.

Edie, James. 1976. *Speaking and Meaning: The Phenomenology of Language*. Bloomington: Indiana University Press.

———. 1990. "Husserl vs. Derrida." *Husserl Studies* 13:103–18.

Elveton, R. O., ed. 1970. *The Phenomenology of Husserl.* Chicago: Quadrangle.

Evans, J. Claude. 1991. *Strategies of Deconstruction.* Minneapolis: University of Minnesota Press.

——. 1996. "Deconstruction: Theory and Practice." *Journal of the British Society for Phenomenology* 27 (3):313–17.

Evans, J. Claude, Joshua Kates, and Leonard Lawlor. 1998. "A Forum on *Strategies of Deconstruction.*" *Philosophy Today* 42 (2):146–230.

Felman, Shoshana. 1975. "Madness and Philosophy, or Literature's Reason." *Yale French Studies* 52:206–28.

Fenves, Peter. 2001. "Derrida and History: Some Questions Derrida Pursues in His Early Writings." In *Jacques Derrida and the Humanities: A Critical Reader,* ed. Tom Cohen. Cambridge: Cambridge University Press.

Fink, Eugen. 1970. "The Phenomenological Philosophy of Edmund Husserl and Contemporary Criticism." Trans. R. O. Elveton. In Elveton, 73–147.

——. 1981. "Operative Concepts in Husserl's Phenomenology." In McKenna, Harlan, and Winters, 56–70.

Flynn, Bernard. 1989. "Derrida and Foucault: Madness and Writing." In Silverman, 201–18.

Foucault, Michel. 1978. Introduction to Georges Canguilhem, *On the Normal and the Pathological,* trans. Carolyn Fawcett. Dordrecht, Neth.: Reidel.

Funke, Gerhard. 1973. "Phenomenology and History." In *Phenomenology and the Social Sciences,* ed. Maurice Natanson. Evanston, Ill.: Northwestern University Press, 1–100.

Gasché, Rodolphe. 1986. *The Tain of the Mirror: Derrida and the Philosophy of Reflection.* Cambridge, Mass.: Harvard University Press.

——. 1994a. "Deconstruction as Criticism." In *Inventions of Difference: On Jacques Derrida.* Cambridge, Mass.: Harvard University Press, 22–57.

——. 1994b. "On Representation, or Zigzagging with Husserl and Derrida." In Lawlor 1994, 1–18.

Gearhart, Suzanne. 1983. "Philosophy *Before* Literature: Deconstruction, Historicity, and the Work of Paul de Man." *Diacritics,* Winter: 63–81.

Greenblatt, Stephen. 1989. "Towards a Poetics of Culture." In *The New Historicism,* ed. H. Aram Veeser. New York: Routledge, 1–14.

Harvey, Irene. 1986. *Derrida and the Economy of* Différance. Bloomington: Indiana University Press.

——. 1987. "Doubling the Space of Existence: Exemplarity in Derrida—The Case of Rousseau." In Sallis 1987, 60–70.

Heidegger, Martin. 1962. *Being and Time.* Trans. John Macquarrie and Edward Robinson. New York: Harper and Row.

——. 1971. *On the Way to Language.* Trans. Peter D. Hertz. San Francisco: Harper and Row.

——. 1993. *Sein und Zeit.* Tübingen, Ger.: Max Neimeyer.

Hobson, Marian. 1998. *Jacques Derrida: Opening Lines.* London: Routledge.

Hopkins, Burt C. 1985. "Derrida's Reading of Husserl in *Speech and Phenomena.*" *Husserl Studies* 2:193–214.

———. 1995. "Husserl and Derrida on the Origin of Geometry." In McKenna and Evans, 61–94.

———. 1996. "Transcendental Ontologism and Derrida's Reading of Husserl." *Philosophy Today* 40, no. 1 (Spring): 71–79.

Howells, Christina. 1998. *Derrida: Deconstruction from Phenomenology to Ethics.* Cambridge, Eng.: Polity.

Husserl, Edmund. 1950. *Ideen zu einer reinen Phänomenologie und phänomenologischen Philosophie,* book 1. Ed. Walter Biemel. Vol. 3 of *Husserliana.* The Hague: Martinus Nijhoff.

———. 1960. *Cartesian Meditations.* Trans. Dorion Cairns. The Hague: Martinus Nijhoff.

———. 1964. *The Phenomenology of Internal Time-Consciousness.* Trans. J. S. Churchill. Bloomington: Indiana University Press.

———. 1965. "Philosophy as Rigorous Science." In *Phenomenology and the Crisis of Philosophy,* ed. Quentin Lauer. New York: Harper and Row.

———. 1969. *Formal and Transcendental Logic.* Trans. Dorion Cairns. The Hague: Martinus Nijhoff.

———. 1970a. *The Crisis of European Sciences and Transcendental Phenomenology.* Trans. David Carr. Evanston, Ill.: Northwestern University Press.

———. 1970b. *Logical Investigations,* 2 vols. Trans. J. N. Findlay. London: Routledge and Kegan Paul.

———. 1973a. *Cartesianische Meditationen und Parisier Vortrage.* Vol 1. of *Husserliana.* The Hague: Martinus Nijhoff.

———. 1973b. *Experience and Judgment.* Trans. James Churchill and Karl Ameriks. Evanston, Ill.: Northwestern University Press.

———. 1974. *Formale und transzendentale Logik.* Ed. Paul Janssen. Vol. 17 of *Husserliana.* The Hague: Martinus Nijhoff.

———. 1975. *Logische Untersuchungen.* Vol. 1. *Prologemena zur reinen Logik.* Ed. Ursula Panzer. Vol. 18 of *Husserliana.* The Hague: Martinus Nijhoff.

———. 1983. *Ideas Pertaining to a Pure Phenomenology and to a Phenomenological Philosophy,* book 1. Trans. F. Kersten. Dordrecht, Neth.: Kluwer.

———. 1984. *Logische Untersuchungen.* Vol. 2. *Untersuchungen zur Phänomenologie und Theorie der Erkenntnis.* Ed. Ursula Panzer. Vol. 19 of *Husserliana.* The Hague: Martinus Nijhoff.

Jakobson, Roman. 1990. *On Language.* Ed. Linda R. Waugh and Monique Monville-Burston. Cambridge, Mass.: Harvard University Press.

Kates, Joshua. 1993. "The Voice That Keeps Reading: Evans' *Strategies of Deconstruction." Philosophy Today* 37:318–35.

———. 1998. "The Problem of *Bedeutung* in Derrida and Husserl." In Evans, Kates, and Lawlor, 194–99.

———. 2002. "Deconstruction and Skepticism: The First Wave." *Journal of the British Society for Phenomenology* 33 (2):188–205.

———. 2003. "Derrida, Husserl, and the Commentators: Introducing a Developmental Approach." *Husserl Studies* 19, no. 2 (Summer): 101–30.

———. 2005. Review of *Husserl and Derrida: The Basic Problem of Phenomenology,* by Leonard Lawlor. *Husserl Studies* 21 (1):55–64.

Katz, Jerrold J. 1985. *The Philosophy of Linguistics.* New York: Oxford University Press.

Kearney, Richard. 1984. "Dialogue with Jacques Derrida." In *Dialogues with Contemporary Continental Thinkers,* ed. Richard Kearney. Manchester: Manchester University Press.

Lagueux, Maurice. 1965. "Merleau-Ponty et la linguistique de Saussure." *Dialogue* 4 (3):351–64.

Landgrebe, Ludwig. 1974. "A Meditation on Husserl's Statement: 'History Is the Grand Fact of Absolute Being.'" *Southwestern Journal of Philosophy* 5 (3): 111–25.

———. 1981a. *The Phenomenology of Edmund Husserl: Six Essays.* Ed. Donn Welton. Ithaca, N.Y.: Cornell University Press.

———. 1981b. "The Problems Posed by the Transcendental Science of the Apriori of the Lifeworld." In McKenna, Harlan, and Winters, 152–71.

———. 1981c. "Regions of Being and Regional Ontologies in Husserl's Phenomenology." In McKenna, Harlan, and Winters, 132–51.

———. 1982. *Fäktizitat und Individuation: Studien zu den Grundfragen der Phänomenologie.* Hamburg: Felix Meiner.

Lawlor, Leonard. 1992. *Imagination and Chance.* Albany: State University of New York Press.

———, ed. 1994. *Derrida's Interpretation of Husserl. Southern Journal of Philosophy* 32, supplement.

———. 1995. "The Relation as the Fundamental Issue in Derrida." In McKenna and Evans, 151–84.

———. 1996a. "The Event of Deconstruction." *Journal of the British Society for Phenomenology* 27 (3):313–19.

———. 1996b. "Phenomenology and Metaphysics: Deconstruction in *La Voix et le Phénomène." Journal of the British Society for Phenomenology* 27 (2):116–36.

———. 1997. "Eliminating Some Confusion: The Relation of Being and Writing in Merleau-Ponty and Derrida." In Dillon, 71–93.

———. 1998. "Distorting Phenomenology." In Evans, Kates, and Lawlor, 185–93.

———. 2002. *Derrida and Husserl: The Basic Problem of Phenomenology.* Bloomington: Indiana University Press.

Llewellyn, John. 1986. *Derrida and the Threshold of Sense.* London: Macmillan.

Lyons, John. 1969. *Introduction to Theoretical Linguistics.* Cambridge: Cambridge University Press.

Marrati-Guénoun, Paola. 1998. *La genèse et la trace.* Dordrecht, Neth.: Kluwer.

Martinet, André. 1989. "Que faire du 'mot'?" In *Fonction et dynamique des langue.* Paris: Armand Colin, 128–35.

McKenna, William R. 1982. *Husserl's "Introductions to Phenomenology": Interpretation and Critique.* The Hague: Martinus Nijhoff.

McKenna, William R., and J. Claude Evans, eds. 1995. *Derrida and Phenomenology.* Dordrecht, Neth.: Kluwer.

McKenna, William R., R. M. Harlan, and L. E. Winters, eds. 1981. *Apriori and World.* The Hague: Martinus Nijhoff.

Merleau-Ponty, Maurice. 1962. *Phenomenology of Perception*. Trans. Colin Smith. London: Routledge.

———. 1964. "On the Phenomenology of Language." In *Signs*, trans. Richard C. McCleary. Evanston, Ill.: Northwestern University Press, 84–97.

———. 1974. "Phenomenology and Sciences of Man." Trans. John Wild. In *Phenomenology, Language and Sociology*, ed. John O'Neill. London: Heinemann.

Michaels, Walter Benn. 1987. *The Gold Standard and the Logic of Naturalism*. Berkeley: University of California Press.

Mohanty, J. N. 1964. *Edmund Husserl's Theory of Meaning*. The Hague: Martinus Nijhoff.

———. 1985. *The Possibility of Transcendental Phenomenology*. The Hague: Martinus Nijhoff.

———. 1989. *Transcendental Phenomenology: An Analytic Account*. Oxford: Basil Blackwell.

———. 1997. *Phenomenology: Between Essentialism and Transcendental Philosophy*. Evanston, Ill.: Northwestern University Press.

Mouffe, Chantal. 1996. *Deconstruction and Pragmatism*. London: Routledge.

Muralt, André de. 1958. *L'idée de la phénoménologie: L'exemplarisme Husserlien*. Paris: Presses Universitaires de France.

Nass, Michael. 2003. *Taking on the Tradition: Jacques Derrida and the Legacies of Deconstruction*. Stanford, Calif.: Stanford University Press.

Nealon, Jeffrey. 1992. "The Discipline of Deconstruction." *PMLA*, October: 1266–79.

Norris, Christopher. 1982. *Deconstruction: Theory and Practice*. London: Methuen.

———. 1987. *Derrida*. Cambridge, Mass.: Harvard University Press.

Norton Anthology of Literary Theory and Criticism. 2001. Gen. ed. Vincent B. Leitch. New York: Norton.

Olkowski, Dorothea. 1997. "Expression and Inscription at the Origins of Language." In Dillon, 45–59.

Patrick, Morag. 1997. *Derrida, Responsibility and Politics*. Hants, Eng.: Ashgate.

Protevi, John. 1993. "The Economy of Exteriority in Derrida's *Speech and Phenomena*." *Man and World* 26:373–88.

Prufer, Thomas. 1993. "Husserlian Distinctions and Strategies in *The Crisis*." In *Recapitulations: Essays in Philosophy*. Washington, D.C.: Catholic University Press, 48–57.

Quine, Willard Van Orman. 1953. *From a Logical Point of View*. Cambridge, Mass.: Harvard University Press.

Ricoeur, Paul. 1967. *Husserl: An Analysis of His Phenomenology*. Evanston, Ill.: Northwestern University Press.

Rorty, Richard. 1977. "Derrida on Language, Being and Abnormal Philosophy." *Journal of Philosophy* 74:673–81.

———. 1982. *Consequences of Pragmatism*. Minneapolis: University of Minnesota Press.

———. 1989. *Contingency, Irony, and Solidarity*. Cambridge: Cambridge University Press.

————. 1991. *Essays on Heidegger and Others: Philosophical Papers II.* Cambridge: Cambridge University Press.

————. 1998. *Truth and Progress: Philosophical Papers III.* Cambridge: Cambridge University Press.

Sallis, John, ed. 1987. *Deconstruction and Philosophy: The Texts of Jacques Derrida.* Chicago: University of Chicago Press.

————. 1992. "Doublings." In Wood 1992, 120–36.

————. 1995. "Doublings." In *Double Truth.* Albany: State University of New York Press.

Saussure, Ferdinand de. 1964. *Cours de linguistique generale.* Ed. Charles Bally, Albert Sechehaye, and Albert Riedlinger. Paris: Payot.

————. 1966. *Course in General Linguistics.* Trans. Wade Baskin. New York: McGraw-Hill.

Scanlon, John. 1995. "Pure Presence: A Modest Proposal." In McKenna and Evans, 95–102.

Schutz, Alfred. 1959. "Le problème de l'intersubjectivité transcendentale chez Husserl." In Berger 1959, 334–65.

Searle, John. 1993. "The World Turned Upside Down." In *Working Through Derrida,* ed. Gary B. Madison. Evanston, Ill.: Northwestern University Press, 170–88.

Seebohm, Thomas. 1989. "Transcendental Phenomenology." In *Husserl's Phenomenology: A Textbook,* ed. J. N. Mohanty and William McKenna. Washington, D.C.: University Press of America, 143–65.

————. 1995. "The Apodicticity of Absence." In McKenna and Evans, 185–200.

Silverman, Hugh, ed. 1989. *Derrida and Deconstruction.* New York: Routledge.

Smith, Barry. 1992. "Letter to the *Times* (London)." Reprinted in Derrida 1995, 419–21.

Sokolowski, Robert. 1964. *Husserl's Concept of Constitution.* The Hague: Martinus Nijhoff.

Ströker, Elisabeth. 1993. *Husserl's Transcendental Phenomenology.* Trans. Lee Hardy. Stanford, Calif.: Stanford University Press.

————. 1997. *The Husserlian Foundations of Science.* Dordrecht, Neth.: Kluwer.

Welton, Donn. 1983. *The Origins of Meaning: A Critical Study of the Thresholds of Husserlian Phenomenology.* The Hague: Martinus Nijhoff.

————. 2001. *The Other Husserl: The Horizons of Transcendental Phenomenology.* Bloomington: Indiana University Press.

Wheeler, Samuel. 2000. *Analytic Philosophy and Deconstruction.* Stanford, Calif.: Stanford University Press.

White, Alan. 1987. "Reconstructing Husserl: A Critical Response to Derrida's *Speech and Phenomena.*" *Husserl Studies* 4:45–62.

————. 1995. "Of Grammatolatry: Deconstruction as Rigorous Phenomenology?" In McKenna and Evans, 103–20.

Willard, Dallas. 1995. "Is Derrida's View of Ideal Being Rationally Defensible?" In McKenna and Evans, 23–42.

Wilmore, S. J. 1987. "Scepticism and Deconstruction." *Man and World* 20:437–55.

Wood, David. 1980. "Derrida and the Paradoxes of Reflection." *Journal of the British Society for Phenomenology* 11 (3):225–38.

———. 1987a. "Following Derrida." In Sallis 1987, 143–60.

———. 1987b. "Heidegger after Derrida." *Research in Phenomenology* 17:103–16.

———. 1989. *The Deconstruction of Time*. Atlantic Highlands, N.J.: Humanities.

———, ed. 1992. *Derrida: A Critical Reader*. Cambridge, Eng.: Blackwell.

———. 2002. *Thinking after Heidegger*. Cambridge, Eng.: Polity.

Wood, David, and Robert Bernasconi, eds. 1988. *Derrida and Difference*. Evanston, Ill.: Northwestern University Press.

Ziarek, Ewa. 1996. *The Rhetoric of Failure: Deconstruction of Skepticism, Reinvention of Modernism*. Albany: State University of New York Press.

INDEX

Absolute, the, 108–9; absolute alterity, xxiv; absolute appearance (voice as), 152; "is passage," 57; and nonabsolute, 108, 111

Absolute Being, Absolute consciousness, Absolute ideality, Absolute past. *See* Being; Consciousness; Ideality(ies); Time

Alterity, 101, 102, 205, 213; absolute, xxiv; infinite (God), 212, 214; radical, 94, 95, 204, 208

Analysen zur passiven Synthesis, 253n10

Apodicticity, Husserl's commitment to, 91, 93

Arche, 225n10

Archi-trace, 167, 175, 176, 178, 181–82, 288n26. *See also* Trace, the

Archive, destruction of the, 72

Archi-writing, xxvii, 10, 155, 156, 286n22; Derrida's focus on, 175–76, 185; as imprint or trace, 192–94, 203; as term in deconstruction, 14, 167, 181, 197, 204, 288n26. *See also* Writing

Aristotle, 216, 288n26; Derrida's passion for, 5–6; *Metaphysics,* 227n14

Ausdruck. See Expression(s); Sign(s), linguistic

"Austin, John," 287n24

Auto-affection, xxvii, 153–54, 155

Bachelard, Gaston, 236n6

Baker, Houston, 222n9

Beardsworth, Richard, 279n1

Bedeuten, Derrida's translation of, 192

Bedeutung. See Meaning (logical)

Behaviorism, 137

Being, 149, 152, 198, 281n7; Absolute, 126, 242n23; vs. beings, 97, 102, 167,

214; Heideggerean, xxviii, 97, 162, 164–67, 193–96, 197, 212–14; history of, 212; mode *(Seinsmodus)* or sense *(Seinsinn)* of, 183–84, 185

Benjamin, Walter, 216

Bennington, Geoffrey, 3, 18, 20, 23–31 passim, 221–22nn7,8, 224n3, 246n35, 279n1; on deconstruction, 26, 259n27; "The Series: (Quasi)Transcendental Questions" (in "Derridabase" in *Jacques Derrida*), 24, 26, 230n4

Berger, Gaston, 242nn22,24, 249n41, 266n4

Bernasconi, Robert, 223n2, 226n13, 229n2, 232n13, 290n34; "The Trace of Levinas in Derrida," 291–92n37

Bernet, Rudolf, 221n7, 230n7, 244–45nn30,31, 248n40, 255n16, 296n54; on "Introduction," 239nn14,17, 240n19, 295n49; quoted, 234n21, 235–36nn1,5, 238n14, 243–44n28, 246n34; on *Speech,* 252n8, 266n2, 272–74nn21,30, 276–79nn38,42,43,48; et al., 240n18, 242nn22,23, 247n38, 253–54nn11,13, 256n19, 263n45, 267n9, 274n30, 276n39

Bhabha, Homi, 222n9

Biemel, Walter, 242n24, 243n26, 261n37

Birain, Maine de, 192

Book, the, 245n32; role of the, 67; transcendental theory of, 239n17

Brentano, Franz, 261n38

Butler, Judith, 222n9

Cairns, Dorion, 124–25, 179–80, 248–49nn38,41

Canguilhem, George: *On the Normal and the Pathological,* 236n6

Sinn. See Meaning

Skepticism, radical, xv, 10, 11, 18; decon-struction and, 5, 17, 20, 23, 223n2, 227n15; Derrida accused of, 128–29, 140; Derrida's views distinguished from, 4–5, 7, 19

Smith, Barry, 232n16

Socratic irony, 28

Sokolowski, Robert, 263n45

Sound: psychic image of, 171–73; "thought-sound," 286n22

Space: appearance of, 153; language in-separable from, 203; primordiality of time over, 262n39; situatedness in, 203–4; "spacing," (pre-eminence of) 156, (as signature term) 155, 197; spatiotemporality, *see* Temporality

Speech, 12, 75, 187–88, 191–93; distinc-tion between writing and, 13, 175; *parole,* 61, 153, 191–94, 203, (vs. *langue*) 168–74 passim; passivity of, 187, 188, 191; Saussure's definition, 282n12; thought and, (Derrida on inseparabil-ity of) 201, (Husserl's disregard of pos-sible connection between) 76. *See also* Language; Voice, the (*la voix*); Writing

Spindel Conference (1993), 252n8

Spinoza, Baruch or Benedict, 195, 288n26

Spirit, spiritual corporeality, 76, 113, 137, 170. *See also Leib*

Spivak, Gayatri, 193, 222n9

Staten, Henry, 230n6

Steinbock, Anthony, 253n10

Ströker, Elisabeth, 236n4, 240n18, 242–43nn23,26, 251nn3,4, 253–54nn10,11,13

Structuralism, 283n13; French debate over, 283n15; structural linguistics, 180, 286n22

Structure, genesis of, 185. *See also* Infra-structures

Subjectivity, 111; vs. empiricism, 14; tran-scendental, xxvii, 64, 117, 182, 185, 257n21; transcendental intersubjectiv-ity, 63

Supplement, logic of, 101, 225n10

Tao, the, 281n8

Teleology: in Derrida's writings, 43, 50, 81, 135–36, 148, 158; Husserl's, xxviii, 83;

illicit, 124, 149; infinite, 81, 122; of truth, 80, 158

Temporality, 189–90, 238n14; absolute, 100, 117, 126–27, 190, 262n39; spatio-temporality, 68, 69, 71, 75, 78, 89, 245n32, 248n41, 249n42; temporaliza-tion of experience, 173. *See also* Time

Thought: responsibility to, 4–6, 18, 19, 23, 30, 31; speech and, (Derrida on insepa-rability of) 201, (Husserl's disregard of possible connection between) 76; "thought-sound," 286n22; Western, 59

Time: absolute past, 187, 190, 193, 196; Derrida's interpretation of, 100, 189–90, 259n31; Husserl's lectures on, 99–100; space and, 262n39. *See also* Tem-porality

Trace, the, 155, 182, 183–86, 187–90, 194–97; writing and, 47, 50–51, 59, 60, 192, 203. *See also* Archi-trace; Imprint

Tradition, 208–9, 214; "traditionality," 97, 102; traditional philosophy, 107

Tran Duc Thao, 91, 92, 93, 94, 100, 214

Transcendental: consciousness, 172–73; difference, 155; discourse, 48, 61; ego, 90, 100, 264n47; experience, 14, 111, 176; genesis, 57, 98; history, 79–80, 103, 239n15; language, 60–61, 120; monad, 91, 94; objectivity, 68; phenomenology, *see* Phenomenology; philosophy (Der-rida and), 234n21; reduction, 60, 155, 172; subjectivity, xxvii, 63, 64, 117, 182, 185, 257n21; voluntarism, 133; writing, 63–64, 70

Transcendental concerns, 14, 16–17, 108; Husserl's transcendentality, 106; vs. transcendence, 228n20. *See also* Quasi-transcendentals

Truth(s): affirmation of, xvi; "disappear-ance" of, 67, 69, 70–73, 78–79, 105, 131; endangered, 72, 75, 239n15; geometri-cal, 57, 73, 245n30; "Here-Now" of, 75; of mathematics, 62; teleology of, 80, 158; validity of, 30, 63; writing/language and, 58–61, 64–69 passim, 73, 75, 77

Univocity, 78, 79, 80

Unthought axiomatics. *See* Husserl, Edmund

About the Author

Joshua Kates, formerly a tutor at St. John's College in Santa Fe, New Mexico, is an associate professor at Indiana University. His work on Derrida and phenomenology has appeared in *Philosophy Today, Husserl Studies,* and the *Journal of the British Society for Phenomenology.*

Consulting Editors